Hither and Yon

Memoirs of a Naval Officer
1937 – 1973

by

Captain C.J.A. Johnson O.B.E., D.S.C. Royal Navy

Paralalia
BRISTOL

First published 2007
Paralalia
1 Elgin Park
Bristol
BS6 6RU

isbn   (10) 0-9548117-4-7
       (13) 978-0-9548117-5-4

© Captain C.J.A. Johnson

Hither and Yon

Memoirs of a Naval Officer
1937 – 1973

Captain C.J.A. Johnson
O.B.E., D.S.C. Royal Navy

All rights reserved. No part of this publication may be reproduced, stored in a retrieval system, or transmitted in any form by any means electronic, mechanical, photocopying, scanning, recording or otherwise, without the prior written permission of the publishers.

Typeset, printed and bound by
Lazarus Press
Caddsdown Business Park
Bideford
Devon
EX39 3DX
WWW.LAZARUSPRESS.COM

With best wishes

Ginny Johnson

Dec 2007

Paralalia
BRISTOL

CONTENTS

Page		
7	Chapter 1	1920-1937 In the Beginning, Cadet Training, *Erebus* and *Vindictive*
15	Chapter 2	1938-1939 Memories of a Midshipman, *Barham* and *Imperial*
38	Chapter 3	1940-1941 *Verity*, Harwich and North Atlantic
52	Chapter 4	1942-1943 *Dauntless*, South Africa, Indian Ocean and Madagascar
61	Chapter 5	1943-1945 *Melbreak*, English Channel, Normandy Landings
74	Chapter 6	1945-1947 *Chaplet*, Southampton, Mediterranean, and Palestine
88	Chapter 7	1947-1949 Boys Training, *Ganges*, Shotley and Little Bealings
71	Chapter 8	1949-1951 *Zodiac*, Weymouth, Home Fleet, Gibraltar
107	Chapter 9	1951-1952 Blue Funnel Line and Naval Staff Course Greenwich
111	Chapter 10	1952-1954 NATO, Fontainebleau and Noisy-sur-Ecole
127	(*Appendix*)	Coronation of Queen Elizabeth II by Joan Churchyard
133	Chapter 11	1954-1956 *Ark Royal*, Camell Lairds, Birkenhead, Channel and Mediterranean
162	Chapter 12	1956-1957 Joint Services Staff Course, Latimer and Chesham Bois
165	Chapter 13	1957-1958 Norway and Norwegian Naval Staff College, Oslo and Snarøya
184	Chapter 14	1958-1961 SHAPE France, Versailles and Andresy

CONTENTS (continued)

Page			
194	Chapter 15	1961-1963	*Hartland Point*, Singapore, Indian Ocean, The Gulf and Hong Kong
209	Chapter 16	1963	...Senior Officers War Course, Greenwich
210	Chapter 17	1963-1965	Admiralty, MOD London
220	Chapter 18	1965-1967	*Phoenix*, Damage Control School, Portsmouth
228	Chapter 19	1967-1969	Flag Officer Scotland and N.Ireland, Rosyth.
241	Chapter 20	1969-1971	*Triumph*, Far East Station and Singapore
262	Chapter 21	1971-1973	*Victory*, RN Barracks Portsmouth.
280	Chapter 22	1973	Sense and Senility. Life in Retirement, Instow.

(Photographic Illustrations)

between pages	
36-37	Family Tree, Cadet Training, *Barham* and *Imperial*.
68-69	Normandy Landings. Omaha Beach.
72-73	*Melbreak*, Marriage, *Chaplet*, and *Ganges*.
132-133	*Zodiac*, Fontainebleau, and *Ark Royal*.
168-169	Norway
192-193	SHAPE (France), *Hartland Point* and Far East.
204-205	*Hartland Point*.
240-241	*Phoenix*, Scotland, *Triumph* and Far East.
264-265	Portsmouth and Retirement at Instow, North Devon.

PREFACE

When my parents died some years ago I came to realise that I really knew very little about what they had done in their younger days and also that I knew virtually nothing about my grandparents. I had plenty of photographs without titles and that was about it. I thought what a pity that they hadn't written something down. True, I remember them well when they were old and frail but there must have been so much more. So that is what I have tried to do and Mary and I hope that in years to come our grandchildren and great-grandchildren may read this and see that once upon a time we too were young and lived and laughed and indeed cried a little, just like them.

In writing all this I am particularly grateful to my wife who, in the 1970s, put up with me shutting myself away and typing endlessly and very badly, on a typewriter which infuriated me by jumping spaces on certain letters, and more recently doing it all over again on a computer which has spells of wilful disobedience. I must also thank the Reverend John Pollock for introducing me to Naval Historian and spare-time publisher, Dr Bruce Taylor, who convinced me that my efforts were worthwhile. In addition, my thanks go to James Saumarez who given me some good ideas, but most particularly I would like to thank Ethne Orton who has spent many hours expertly editing and correcting my amateur effort so that it has some order about it.

Landfall, Instow.
June 2007.

Explanation: When I was born and my birth registered, and also when baptised, I was given as Christian names, Cecil (after my Godfather, Engineer Captain Cecil Johnson DSO) and Agar (after my other Godfather Captain Augustus Agar VC).

From the start my parents never used either of these names. My father called me Jim, my mother called me Jimmy and I have been Jim, Jimmy or James ever since. No one ever knew who C.A. Johnson was. This plagued me through life and while it is possible to change your surname as many times as you like, English law prevents you changing your first names. It was not until I was serving and domiciled in Scotland that, because my birth was registered in Scotland, I could apply through Scottish law to alter my first names. So in 1968, for a fee and a visit to a Commissioner for Oaths, I was able to add James to my first names to become officially Cecil James Agar Johnson; my birth certificate was reissued and the Navy List was amended. So, finally, James became my legitimate name and I heaved a sigh of relief. I was a mystery man no longer.

CHAPTER 1

In the Beginning

1920   I was born on 8th March at Cliff Cottage in North Queensferry. My father, Commander C.C. Johnson, was Assistant King's Harbour Master at Rosyth.

1921   We moved to Pembroke Dock, where we lived in an official house in the Dockyard.

1923   My father, being a navigation specialist, got a job at the Compass Laboratory at Ditton Park and we rented a small house in Datchet near Slough.

1925   We moved again, this time to Lennox Mansions in Southsea, as my father was appointed in command of the battleship *Warspite* in Portsmouth. The ship was in reserve as the fleet was being cut drastically under the 'Geddes Axe'. He was given the rank of Acting Captain while doing this job, a rank he retained on his retirement in 1926.

1926   We had no house of our own, though my father did have a one-seventh share in the old Johnson house, Briarsfield, in Dartmouth. However, my Harding grandparents (at No.2 Bath Terrace) and two Harding great-aunts were living in Instow: Aunt Emily (Mrs. Dering) at Strandfield (now the Commodore Hotel) and Aunt Con (Miss Harding) in Pilton Cottage. Aunt Em had been widowed during World War I and, having plenty of room, offered to take us in until we could find somewhere in Instow for ourselves. Buying a house was not an option as the Tapeley Estate owned most of them, so it was a question of waiting for one to rent. After a brief stay in Westaway, on the back road, we moved to No. 2 Cleveland Terrace in 1927.

1927   Having been to a 'dame school' in Instow in 1926, followed by an unhappy term at the Convent in Bideford, I was sent as a weekly boarder to Ellerslie, a small prep school in Bickington, and became a full-time boarder in 1928.

1933   Having failed to get into Dartmouth, I joined the Nautical College at Pangbourne.

Early in 1937 I sat the exam for the Navy and at the end of April I found myself with fifty other special entry Cadets assembled on the jetty at Whale Island in Portsmouth, ready to join *Erebus*. She and her sister ship *Terror* had been built towards the end of World War I as monitors. Short and beamy they were fitted with one 12-inch turret and were designed specifically for shore-bombardment. *Erebus*, now moored head and stern in the harbour, was used as a turret drill ship and, since 1936, as a training ship for Cadets joining the Navy aged between 17 and 18^1/$_2$. My birthday being in March, I was one of the youngest. With war looming, the Navy was expanding rapidly and the historic training system, based on the 13-year-old entry at the Britannia Naval Training College in Dartmouth, could not supply the numbers. We were to do one term in *Erebus* and then join the Dartmouth leavers (17-year-olds) for two terms in the Training Cruiser *Vindictive* before we all joined the fleet as Midshipmen at the end of the year, having caught up with the 'Darts'.

Erebus was commanded by Commander H.P Currie, who was our mentor, but the whole set-up was under the overall command of the Captain of *Excellent*, Captain Arthur Power. *Excellent* was and is situated on Whale Island and was the Gunnery School with a fearsome reputation for smartness and discipline. It turned out a breed of Chief Gunner's Mates who could hold their own with any Guards Sergeant Major. One, 'Spider' Edwards, was allocated to *Erebus* to put the fear of God into us and did. We were divided into three watches, Red, White and Blue. While one watch would be in school learning navigation or whatever, another would be learning about guns, torpedoes and other technical subjects and the third would be landed for drill, physical training, swimming and boat work. Of course each morning started at six o'clock, scrubbing or holy-stoning the upper deck. Each watch had a Petty Officer in Charge.

Our first task on joining was to stow our gear and deal with our hammocks. We were each issued with a rectangular bit of canvas with about 18 eyelets at each end, two lengths of rope – one for each end – 18 lengths of small line (called nettles) and a long piece for lashing it up like a sausage so that it could be stowed away in daytime, a mattress and two galvanised rings. To each ring we had to splice one of the short lengths of rope, the other end of which had to be 'pointed', and also nine of the short lengths of line doubled so as to make 18 nettles. Each nettle was then tied to an eyelet in the hammock so that when you hung it up or, to use the proper term, slung it, the sides were higher than the middle, otherwise you would of course fall out. All this had to be done to the satisfaction of the Petty Officer in charge of each Watch before you could turn in. There were many who spent a pretty sleepless first night. Actually hammocks properly slung are jolly comfortable once you get used to them; it is also quite a knack to get in and out as they are slung some six feet above the deck, which is rock hard if you fall out!

Forward of the 12-inch turret there was a newly-constructed Gymnasium which was the domain of the rather aptly named Petty Officer Savidge, the PTI, and it contained all the usual instruments of torture but none of these was required for the endless press-ups and bunny hops. One of the main features were the climbing ropes suspended from the high ceiling. Obviously everyone had to be proficient at climbing and coming down a rope. It was one of the essentials for manning boats at sea and I was quite good at it but after the order 'to the top go' for about the twelfth time every muscle in your body ached in protest. However, what I hated most was having to invert myself at the top, grip the rope with my legs and feet and then, with some mysterious twist of the rope round my body, descend to the bottom with arms outstretched. I think it was called 'doing a falling angel'. Well. . . bully for them. Still, no one ever got hurt in the process. I had never been much of a one for gymnastics and, before joining the Navy, touching my toes without bending my legs was a sufficient challenge but on leaving *Erebus*, after 12 weeks or so, I had developed muscles that I didn't know existed.

We were paid the princely sum of one shilling a day, which was actually more money than I had ever had before, and we were allowed to go ashore at weekends. Our rig for going ashore was a sports jacket, grey flannel trousers, a shirt and tie and the obligatory brown trilby hat. The trilby hat was considered essential as you had to doff it to salute anyone senior to yourself, which in effect was everybody that looked like another naval officer. If you failed, the normal punishment was to double round Whale Island. The other thing about the hat was that you had to be wearing it so that you could take it off to salute the quarter deck when going ashore or coming aboard. An ancient custom practised by all navies. Once upon a time all Christian ships had a crucifix at the stern.

I think for the majority of us it all came as a bit of a shock to the system and though I was at an advantage in some ways, having learnt navigation at Pangbourne and been used to wearing naval uniform, nothing had really prepared me for this. Everything was full speed ahead and on reflection it did us all a lot of good; at the end of the summer term I was certainly fitter than I had ever been in my life and as we became more confident we were well able to hold our own against our tormentors. I got used to being heckled by 'Spider' Edwards with cries like, 'Mr Johnson, Sir, it is a rifle you are holding not an um<u>ber</u>ella', and the like.

But one of my lasting memories was of one very hot summer afternoon when I was duty watch. It was Sunday and I was sent for by the Captain to take his 8 year old daughter for a row around the harbour in the skiff and to be back in an hour. I suppose I had been chosen because I was quite good with boats but the skiff belies its name. The naval skiff of that time was a tubby 16-foot clinker-built boat as heavy as lead. However, I went fast and slow, spun the boat this way and that, wove in and out of the ships nearby and did my best to amuse her. Thankful when the hour was up, hot and exhausted, I brought the boat back alongside the gangway and helped her on to the platform at the bottom saying, 'Well that was fun wasn't it', to which she replied in a Violet Elizabeth voice, 'No, I hate boatth'.

At the end of the term a stage was rigged in the 'gym' and the training staff put on a 'Sod's Opera' for our entertainment. They were extremely funny and some of the acts were very clever. It was good, too, to find out that our tormentors were after all human. In actual fact I met 'Spider' Edwards some years later when he was a Commissioned Gunner and you couldn't have a nicer chap. I suppose in reality it was all a big act and they were very good at it. Nevertheless we had made some good friends amongst ourselves and were ready for the next stage.

After a couple of weeks leave we all joined the cruiser *Vindictive* in Chatham. She had been specially converted as a training ship. About 10,000 tons, she had had her main armament of five hand-worked 6-inch guns taken out and replaced by two 4.7-inch guns for training purposes. Abaft the funnel the superstructure had been removed and replaced by a number of well-equipped classrooms. Forward of the bridge was a large boat deck with a mass of boats. Otherwise our accommodation was much the same as before, living in ordinary mess decks, though the Cadet messes were kept apart from the mess decks of the regular Ship's Company. Again we were divided into watches and classes. Already on board were the previous term from *Erebus*, but joining with us were some sixty cadets who had been four years at Dartmouth. There was quite a culture split between the 'Darts' and us lot, known as the 'Pubs', even though a number had come from Grammar Schools. They thought they were superior and we knew that we were! The Darts seemed particularly lacking in character and appeared to us as clones. But of course they had all grown up together and had their own chums. I suppose the total number of Cadets must have been about 180. We were not all seamen cadets; some were engineering and others supply branch but the whole idea of the training cruiser was that we should all get experience of working in each department of the ship. All the work in keeping the ship clean and painted was done by us. The Ship's Company consisted basically of all those required to keep the ship running plus those required for supervision and teaching.

We were split up into 'Parts of Ship' and for this cruise I was a 'Foc'sleman'. That meant keeping the fore part of the ship clean and dealing with the anchors and cables. In fact my first seagoing experience was to find that I had been assigned to work in the cable locker. On leaving Chatham we had anchored off Southend-on-Sea for the night. Weighing anchor in the morning, the cable locker party had to stow the cable. It was a quite large chain and if allowed just to pile up in a heap at the bottom of the locker it would get fouled up, so that the next time it came to let the anchor go it could jam in the cable pipe. Using ropes we had to pull the cable first one way and then the other so that it lay in flakes at the bottom of the locker. We got the hang of it pretty quickly but a couple of hours later, as we were heading down channel against a westerly gale, we were piped to go again to the cable locker. Something had been left open and there was a large quantity of water slopping about. We were given buckets and told to bale it out. The ship was pitching and we were going up and down like a roller coaster ride in a dank and claustrophobic box. I and the rest of the party were as sick as dogs. I suppose it was fortunate that we had the buckets but tough on the people at the far end of the chain who had to empty them! I hadn't felt so ill in my life. As a matter of fact the only friendly face that I knew amongst the officers was the Surgeon Lieutenant, Charlie Pearson from Bideford whose father was our doctor. However I couldn't worry him about being sea-sick and just hoped that it would get better and it did. By the second day out I had found my sea legs and appetite.

Our first port of call was Gibraltar. Like the majority of the cadets, I had never been abroad before so everything was a huge excitement and, with the exception of our next stop off at St Raphael in the south of France, the cruise was designed to be educational. We visited all the tourist spots: Naples for Vesuvius and Pompeii, Greece for Athens and the Parthenon, Delphi and various other spots; Crete to see the ruins of Knossos, where we were shown round by Sir Arthur Evans and his wife, the archaeologists who had first uncovered the site and worked out the purpose of all the different buildings. I remember being most impressed by the lead water pipes which provided running water around the palace several thousand years BC. We also visited a number of other places like Dubrovnik and Argostoli, where we did a massive amount of boat work both in harbour and at sea, always exercising something or other, towing ship, man overboard, collision stations and so forth, while every afternoon we spent in the class room. Returning to Portsmouth for Christmas leave I and, indeed, I am sure everyone else, was looking forward to the spring cruise to the West Indies.

Back on board I found that this term I was in the Quarterdeck Division, our Divisional Officer being a Lieutenant 'Shiner' Wright. He was a very 'press on' character; everything had to be done at full speed and, though naturally fresh-faced, he would go scarlet if things were going wrong. Sometimes in the Navy you meet the same people time and time again during your career and 'Shiner' was to be one of them, whilst others who joined at the same time as yourself you never saw again. I liked him.

Apart from being Quarterdeck I and all the rest of our entry were given a programme for working in other departments, I think I did 3 weeks in the engine room, 1 week with supply or stores and about 2 weeks with the Torpedo-men. When electrical appliances and lighting were first introduced into the Navy they were pretty rudimentary and were made the responsibility of the Torpedo Department. So it had remained, despite being increasingly important and complicated. There were Electrical Artificers who had done five years training and could mend things but the day-to-day maintenance and running of the whole system remained the responsibility of the Torpedo Officer and his men. Thus it was that I was attached to a Leading Torpedo-man for a week to see what he did and another week to work on my own. I remember quietly enjoying this. I was given a little canvas hold-all with some tools, a 'wee mega', a torch and some fuse wire and sent off to look for earths and lights that didn't work. In actual fact everything seemed to be working so I was able to find some quiet corner or caboosh and have a kip until dinner was piped. I quite wished that my week had been longer! Perhaps it was fortunate that none of us was let loose in the galley.

Our first port of call was Funchal in Madeira. Here we anchored in the bay and were allowed ashore to explore the island. I think it was the second morning there, when I was being Cadet of the Watch on the quarterdeck with 'Shiner' Wright as Officer of the Watch, it became clear that a large cruise-liner that had arrived the previous evening had anchored too close to us and, as we swung on the turn of the tide, we could see that our sterns were going to meet. Shiner sent me forward at full speed to find the Chief Bosun's Mate to bring aft the biggest fenders that we had. When we arrived back we saw Shiner standing outside the guardrails, scarlet in the face, pushing with all his might at the stern of this 18,000-ton ship shouting, 'For God's sake somebody bring a b****y fender'. I think we did lose a little paint!

The following day we sailed for the West Indies, with our first port of call Antigua, where you could see the remains of all the buildings used in Nelson's day, then on to the U.S. controlled islands of Puerto Rico where we anchored in the harbour of Mayagüez. We were allowed leave to go into the town and here to our delight we discovered Bacardi rum. There was a big promotion going on and nearly all the bars offered you your first drink free provided it was made with Bacardi. Some of the more hardy chanced their arm in having their free drink and then beating it to the next bar and so on, coming back on board very much the worse for wear. After complaints from the town, our shore patrol quickly put a stop to it. On the last night there the Wardroom gave a party for the local dignitaries and the quarterdeck had to be immaculate. That evening I was in charge of one of the ship's picket boats and at the end of the party took guests back to the town pier. Towards the end I had the Mayor and his party to land. The Mayor had obviously had one too many and on arriving at the jetty I had one of my crew jump on to the jetty to help him ashore. As he was leaving he grasped me by the hand, kissed me on both cheeks and then, turning round, stepped off the wrong side of the boat and we had to fish him out with a boathook.

Next we went to Tortola in the Virgin Islands where quite a few cricket matches were played against a variety of local teams who all seemed very good. It seemed that just about every boy on the island was brought up with a home-made cricket bat. After Tortola we seemed to go island hopping, anchoring off the small almost uninhabited islands,, so that in the evenings parties could be landed for swimming and banyans, or barbecues. Quite often before setting off for the next island, the cutters and whalers would be lowered and we had to sail to the next place. I remember being in charge of a whaler when the wind got up to a strong breeze, with the sea getting up at the same time We spent quite a lot of time bailing and I was very relieved to come up to the ship. I think the passage had taken us about 6 hours and all the other boats had a similar experience but it was all quite an adventure.

I think it was on Beef Island that Rupert Bray and I thought we would explore and, on getting to the far side, we thought that we would walk back to the landing point by going along the shore. All leave expired at 1800 and about an hour before that we found our way blocked by a rocky headland. We hadn't time to retrace our steps so decided to swim for it. At this point we discovered another use for our brown trilby hats. Rupert had an expensive Leica camera which he put in his hat and pulled it down tight while I had our watches and anything else of value in mine. It turned out to be a long swim but we got there just in time to catch the liberty boat back to the ship with our valuables bone-dry, though Rupert had quite a sore place on his head as the Leica was heavy and with few rounded corners! Three cheers for brown trilby hats.

Our final port of call was Hamilton in the Bermudas. This was the Navy's base in the West Indies and there was a small but well-equipped dockyard. There was a large sheltered harbour and it was decided that there would be a rowing regatta between the different divisions on board. All the whalers and cutters were to be used. The start was one end of the harbour and the finish abreast the quarter deck. To do this properly it was necessary to keep the ship parallel to the course and this was done by taking a wire from the stern of the ship and fixing it to the anchor cable so that by pulling on one end or the other the ship could be kept in the right position. The evolution is called 'pointing ship by spring'. At the time my job was to be the Quarterdeck Officer's doggie. As the name implies, you had to follow him around and be at his beck and call all the time to do whatever might be required. At the end of the regatta there was no longer a need to point ship and the next thing was to take in the wire. Our end was quite simple, we just let it go and 'Shiner' Wright told me to go to the Foc'sle and tell his opposite number there that we had let go our end and they could heave it in. As I was doubling forward I met my chum who was the Foc'sle Officer's doggie doubling aft. 'Glad I met you' he said, 'You can tell your Officer that we have let go our end and you can heave in'. After we had stopped laughing I doubled back to tell 'Shiner' that we had 120 fathoms of $3^{1}/_{2}$-inch wire lying on the bottom of the harbour. He was apoplectic and it took several hours with divers to find the wire and get it back on board. The management was not pleased! Neither was anybody else who had had to work late.

It was in Hamilton, too, that I had my first experience of being hauled up before the Captain as a defaulter along with a couple of other cadets. We had been charged with 'behaving in a manner unbecoming to an officer and a gentleman'. It came about like this. One evening we had a very posh dance on the Quarterdeck, all the officers in white mess kit and we had white mess kit too. Apart from lots of guests with their wives, they had somehow managed to bring on board a good number of girls for the Wardroom and for the cadets. I and some friends had met some charming young American girls and, after dancing to the Royal Marine band's rather staid selection of foxtrots and waltzes, we became bored and the American girls taught us how to do a very modern dance called 'The Big Apple' a sort of forerunner to jive. We had found a quiet corner and were getting on fine and singing a song which had the right tempo, It went something like this:

> Morphine Bill and Cocaine Sue
> Went truckin' on down 5th Avenue
> They were truck truck truckin' all the way
>
> Singing honey take a sniff take a sniff on me
>
> And ending
>
> Ashes to ashes and dust to dust
> If the coke don't get you
> Then the morphine must.

Truckin' was a dance step with a sort of heel and toe hip swinging action. All pretty harmless really. But for young officers? No!

We were read the riot act and given 7 days' Number Eleven each. Naval punishments all had numbers, the higher the number the less the punishment. I think

Number One was probably Death! Our punishment put an end to shore leave and we had an hour of extra work and another of extra drill every evening for a week. The extra work was not too bad but the drill was pretty good torture and involved a lot of running around on the upper deck with a rifle bouncing up and down on your shoulder or standing still and holding it in front of you at arm's length until you ached all over, plus a lot else depending on who was taking the punishment session and how sympathetic they were to your plight.

By the time we had finished our punishment the ship was well on her way back to Portsmouth and we were all very much engaged in exams to see if we had reached the required standard for Midshipman. Back in Portsmouth we spent a couple of days squaring off the ship before packing up all our gear and catching the train home to wait for our next appointment. It had been a very good experience; we had worked hard, learnt a lot and at the same time had had a great deal of fun. Now we were ready for the next stage.

CHAPTER 2

Memories of a Midshipman
1938 – 1939

I had just finished my year's training as a Naval Cadet and now received my official letter from Their Lordships to say that I was appointed to serve as a Midshipman in HMS *Barham* and to join on 27th May 1938. I wrote my letter to the Captain as custom required, 'Sir, I have the honour to acknowledge my appointment to His Majesty's Ship *Barham* under your Command. . .', and ended, 'I have the Honour to be, Sir, Your Obedient Servant'. I was told that I had to join in Portsmouth Dockyard. *Barham* was a battleship of the Queen Elizabeth class built in 1915, 31,000 tons, 640 ft long, 140 ft beam, capable of 25 knots. She was armed with eight 15-inch guns in four turrets, twelve 6-inch guns in casements – six either side – and four twin-mounted 4-inch anti-aircraft guns plus two 8-barrelled 2-pounder pompoms. Her complement was 1,100 men but, to avoid overcrowding, only 850 were carried in peacetime.

The ship had been in the dockyard for four months' refitting and now a new Ship's Company was about to join and recommission the ship. There were twelve of us new Midshipmen aged between 18 and 19 – Basil Hearn, Mike Jupp, John Jervelund, Peter Hervey, Teddy Gueritz, Mike Gardner, John Buchanan-Wollaston, Bob Little, Keppel Edge-Partington, Peter Ayling, Rupert Bray and myself – all very smart in our new uniforms with white midshipman's patches on the collar. For best we wore a 'Round Jacket', more commonly called a 'bum freezer', with a row of brass buttons down the front and three buttons on each sleeve. These were by tradition to stop you wiping your nose on your sleeve and gave rise to the term 'Snotty' for a Midshipman. There were other more senior Mids who had been in the ship before.

We humped our gear on board and down to the Midshipmen's Chest Flat, a smallish badly-ventilated compartment below decks with some 30 chests of drawers, one for each person, plus some communal hanging-cupboards. Below again was the Gunroom bathroom. Above and just off the Quarterdeck on the port side, where we lived and studied, was the Gunroom under the charge of the Sub-Lieutenant. He had a cabin and was 'God'. What he said you did, or else. . . However, for our general training and education, because that was why we were there, one of the Lieutenant Commanders had been detailed as 'Snotties' Nurse'. Our nurse was the ship's Torpedo Officer, Terence Maunsell, who was married to the daughter of the White Rajah of Sarawak, Rajah Brooke. Maunsell was a thick set chap with a violent temper, who could be seen to go black in the face with rage, but it was he who saw to what duties we did – second Officer of the Watch, boat running, action stations and so forth. He also arranged instruction every afternoon in navigation, engineering, electrics, seamanship, current affairs and so on. Each Midshipman had to keep a Journal of the ship's activities day by day, together with a fortnightly sketch of some sort to be inspected by the Snotties' Nurse and once a month by the Captain.

But back to our first day... The new Ship's Company was accommodated in the Barracks and on commissioning day was marched down to the ship led by the Royal Marine Band. On board, the task was to find your mess deck, stow your hammock and kit and then it was 'Cooks to the Galley'. I and Rupert Bray were attached to the Boys' Division under the charge of Lieutenant Cobham and Sub-Lieutenant Freddie Copland-Griffiths. A Ship's Company is divided into Divisions under the charge of a Lieutenant Commander or a Lieutenant. Divisional Officers are required to know all about the men in their division, whether they were married, how many children, their ambitions and so forth. Woe betide you if you did not know everyone's name. We had about 100 boys in our Division – seamen, signalmen and telegraphists – all of whom had completed a year's training ashore and now were aged between 17 and 18. A Boy 1st Class earned the princely sum of 1 shilling and 3 pence (6.25p) a day. After a year at sea they would become Ordinary Seamen. They could pick up extra money as 'hammock boys', whose job it was to sling Midshipmen's or senior rates' hammocks at night and stow them away in the morning, for which they received 2 pence a day. Midshipmen's hammocks were slung in the Half-Deck, a largish space just off the Quarterdeck, but it was also a main gangway so you were always getting bumped into or trodden on. There were not enough hammock spaces to sling all the hammocks, so the remainder slept on the deck – fairly hard as the hammock mattress is neither thick nor internally sprung.

Apart from ship's duties there were also Gunroom duties done by the junior Mids such as myself. For example, the duty bathroom Mid's job was to heat the water for the Sub-Lieutenant's bath and indeed for anyone else's ablutions. This was done in a machine not unsurprisingly called a 'calorifier', which was in fact a large open-topped tank full of cold water into which you squirted low-pressure steam direct from the boiler rooms, a sort of giant espresso coffee machine. We had but one bath, which the Sub-Lieutenant deemed inadequate, and we were told to acquire another one by hook or by crook. It was decided to pinch one from *Warspite*, another battleship, refitting in the dockyard. Around midnight we crept on board unnoticed and managed to hump this very heavy cast iron bath up three decks and out on to the jetty. We then carried it about half a mile through the dockyard, like some giant tortoise, without being spotted by the dockyard police. The Sub-Lieutenant had arranged to be the Officer of the Watch so that there was no trouble at the *Barham* end either. We had a luxury bathroom!

The next ten days saw the ship being stored, provisioned and ammunitioned. To ammunition, the ship was moved to a special berth in the middle of the harbour. The lighters came alongside with the shells and cordite. The cordite for the 15-inch and 6-inch guns was supplied in bags stowed in huge cylindrical fibre-board containers. My job was to be in charge of the forward 15-inch shell lighter. Each shell weighed over a ton so you had to be pretty careful to see that they were properly slung. However, all was safely done and we moved to Spithead for gunnery and catapult trials. We had the very latest in aircraft, a Fairy Swordfish fitted with floats, for which a special catapult had been fitted to the after 15-inch turret. It consisted of a launching trolley, on which the aircraft sat, and about fifty feet of rail for it to run on. For the trials a large baulk of timber was used which was the same weight as the Swordfish. The trolley was shot down the rail by a cordite charge but the first firing was a disaster as the trolley disintegrated when it came up against the stops at the end of the rail, and flew into the sea. This meant going back into harbour to get it fixed. However, at last we were off to the Isle of Arran in the Firth of Clyde for our work-up.

We anchored off Lamlash and were to be there for two weeks. No leave was allowed except for recreation for the off-duty watch in the Dog Watches; otherwise while there was daylight we were all taken up with getting to know how everything worked. Because we were basically a floating gun-platform the upper deck had to be kept clear of obstructions so everything was 'handraulic'. There were, of course, plenty of hands; these were required to man the guns, so, except for a capstan forward for the anchors and another aft on the Quarterdeck, there were no winches or windlasses. If you needed to lift a heavy weight you just got a lot of men and heaved. All the boats, with the exception of the two sea boats, were stowed amidships between the funnel and the mainmast and were hoisted in and out by main derrick. The picket boats and launches weighed some 9.5 tons each and required 100 men to control the guys.

My job at evolutions and at sea was to be in charge of the port cutter or sea boat. The cutters – one on each side – were 32 ft long, weighed 2.5 tons and had twelve oars. They hung on davits which, when turned out, stuck out 'miles' so as to clear the huge anti-torpedo blisters on the outside of the hull. Manning the boats at the davits in bad weather was quite a hazardous business. Anyway, we practised hoisting and lowering them, laying out anchors, fire and collision stations, out collision mat and so forth. The men got to know the officers and vice versa. One great drill was to weigh anchor by hand. This involved shipping the capstan bars and rigging the swifter, the rope connecting them. There were 16 long wooden bars to the capstan and with ten men on each bar you got quite a lot of push, especially when the Royal Marine band is playing a double-time march from the top of 'A' turret. Capstan bars had other uses too. . .

Every Sunday after the Captain had inspected the Ship's Company at Divisions everyone went to Church on the quarterdeck. Church was rigged using capstan bars resting on rows of wooden buckets which acted as supports for the pews made from wooden planks, known as church deals, and which could also be used for damage control, hence the sailors' hymn parody – 'The Church is one foundation of capstan bars and buckets'. We had an Australian chaplain, Marson the Parson, who had quite a turn of phrase in his sermons when he got worked up, like 'you sinning lot of bastards'. If we hadn't got a band he would whistle the hymn tunes to give a lead and very well too.

But back to Lamlash. . . On one Sunday afternoon we took the Boys' Division ashore to Holy Island for a picnic and afterwards we raced up to the top. In those days the island was completely deserted except for seabirds and the whole of the top, which is just over 1,000 ft, was a huge nesting area.

Following on from our basic work-up the ship went to Portland for the gunnery work-up. My action station at the time was in 'A' turret, the forward 15-inch turret. A 15-inch gun is quite something when fired and the noise deafening, though not so bad inside as out where there is also a huge shock wave. Inside the turret was by no means a haven of quiet, with men shouting at the tops of their voices to make themselves heard over the bangs and thumps of the machinery. The ammunition came up from the magazine in a huge cage-like lift; the enormous shell came first and then the cordite in two tiers, each having to be rammed home separately by a huge telescopic rammer before the cage descended through the clanging flash-proof metal doors and the great breech block swung home. The layer and trainer for the guns would follow pointers on dials driven from the main gunnery director in the foretop which would be trained on to the target, often invisible from surface level. They shouted 'on' when their indicators lined up with those from the director and the Captain of the Gun would then close the 'interceptor', causing the 'gun ready' lamp in the foretop to light and showing that his gun was ready to be fired and the electric firing circuit activated. I had a special sight to look through to make sure that the gun was pointing in a safe direction.

We were at sea every day and also some nights, so it was good for saving money. A Snottie got paid 5 shillings (25p) a day, out of which he had to pay daily 1s.10d to the messman for food, 6d to the Royal Marine bandsman who looked after his gear and 2d to the hammock boy, plus a monthly mess subscription. Any extras such as fruit or cake were charged, as was laundry and, of course, drinks of any sort. At the end of the month when pay-day came around it was touch and go whether the paymaster paid you or you paid the paymaster, a real Mr Micawber situation. However, to ensure solvency, all midshipmen were required to have £36 a year paid into their account by their parents and, in effect, this was what they lived on. I certainly did.

You may wonder why we paid for food but at that time, and indeed until about 1952, each sailor was allowed a certain sum of money to be credited to him for food. Everyone in a ship was allocated to a mess of between 10 and 20 men where he was victualled. Each mess would appoint a caterer to decide what to eat and each day, by rota, one sailor in each mess was told off to be 'cook of the mess'. His job was to prepare the meal, get the meat, peel the spuds, make the pudding and so forth and when this was done he would take it to the galley for the ship's cooks to cook. If you didn't use up all your victualling money then you would get back what you had saved – mess savings – at the end of the month. The sailor was very badly paid and in messes where there were a number of married men they would buy the mere minimum so as to have extra money to send home. Officers fed at a higher standard and employed a civilian caterer, the Messman, under contract and paid him so much a day to supplement the victualling allowance. Because *Barham* was a Mediterranean Fleet ship we had Maltese cooks and a Maltese messman, who watched us like a hawk at meal times to record the extra bun or orange, or whatever, over the agreed contract allowance and this would be charged to your mess bill. He was also expected to put on a 'full-belly do' once a week for a Mess Dinner. Everyone was expected to dine on board – stiff shirt, white waistcoat (mess dress) – and you could have guests, provided you had enough money to pay for them.

Back to the gunnery work-up... All the guns except the 15-inch were totally handraulic and none more so than the 6-inch batteries. If you have visited *Victory* you can imagine the scene. The guns, six-a-side, stuck out through the armour, twelve men to a gun. The shells weighed 100 pounds each and were manhandled and rammed home into the breech followed by the cloth-covered cordite charge which was rammed in and the breech then slammed shut. After each round fired, the breech and gun barrel had to be swabbed out with a sort of mop called a pizaber to get rid of any burning cordite or cloth which might linger and cause a premature explosion.

When the guns were not in use mess tables were set up between them with all the mess traps, fanny for the rum, brass bound wooden breadbin and so on. At action stations the tables would be triced up to the deck head. The sailors also slung their hammocks in the same space, stowing them in hammock nettings when not in use. The 4-inch guns were a little more modern, shell and cartridge all in one, but still pretty heavy and shoved up the spout by hand. The loading number wore a special glove with a padded fist to shove on the base of the brass cartridge case and also to protect his hand from the breech block which closed automatically.

At the end of the Portland period we were thought to be moderately efficient and returned to Portsmouth to re-ammunition and store ship before sailing for the Mediterranean on 21st July. These old ships and indeed even the more modern ones had problems with fresh water. At sea it had to be made and there was never enough, so ships had large fresh water tanks to be filled when in harbour from a water boat. Portsmouth dockyard had just built a new water boat called *Coronation*, a little ship of about 400 tons. As she had been designed for harbour operation only, her range was pretty limited and *Barham* was ordered to tow her to Malta; this we did with a crew supplied by the ship, who had a mighty uncomfortable passage. Each afternoon the ship stopped and my cutter was lowered to ferry fresh food and to inspect the tow. We were towing her at 12 knots so there was quite a strain. Slipping the cutter at sea is always an exciting business, as is the recovery with one watch of hands on the falls to whip the boat out of the water once it is hooked on.

This towing experience was to stand me in good stead some years later. In 1942 when going from Portsmouth to Capetown in the cruiser *Dauntless* we had in company a Greek destroyer of the Hunt class, Andreas, who hadn't enough fuel for the required speed and I suggested to the Captain that we should take her in tow. This we did, with *Dauntless* making 16 knots and Andreas' engines doing revolutions for just 10 knots and it worked very well.

Barham arrived at Gibraltar on 29th July. However, to allow the Ship's Company to have a bit of a jolly after all the weeks of hard work the Captain got permission to take the ship across to Tangiers for two days so that both watches could have a run ashore. On our way across, a thick fog developed so we approached the anchorage at very slow speed with lookouts high up and low down, while taking constant soundings – we had no radar in those days. Suddenly the Captain, who had been straining out of the bridge windows to listen for fog signals from other ships, said,

'I can smell it – let go the anchor'. Sure enough when the fog lifted we were just about there; Algie Willis had a good nose – it was certainly big enough.

That evening our group of Mids thought we would explore the Kasbah and got lured into a sort of nightclub (no Humphrey Bogart) with a cabaret – all good stuff. When the time came for us to leave, however, we were presented with a most preposterous bill which we could not possibly pay, so when the lights went out for the next exotic dancer we crawled on our hands and knees between the tables until we reached the door and then ran like hell until we got to the quayside where, luckily, a boat was waiting.

On 1st August we were back in Gibraltar, picked up our water boat and sailed for Malta. This time I was one of the two watch-keepers on board *Coronation* and was able to experience the bumpy ride for myself. There was no refrigerator on board and, despite our best efforts, all the butter melted and the eggs that we had brought with us turned out to be bad, so we lived on baked beans, bread and cocoa. It was decided that we should do the last two days under our own steam and were duly cast off. This was much more comfortable and we set off for Malta at 6 knots. However the weather quickly deteriorated and it rained and blew. The bridge of *Coronation* was enclosed and the windows worked on the same principal as those in old-fashioned railway carriages, being raised or lowered by a leather strap. Unfortunately someone opened one of the forward windows to see where we were going, forgetting that the rear ones were already open for ventilation; the Mediterranean in mid summer is hot and in an instant the one and only chart took off and blew out of the window, wrapping itself round the funnel. By the time we had managed to get it back it was soaking wet, badly distorted by the heat of the funnel and just about useless so we were extremely relieved to sight Pantellaria, a small island to the south of Sicily, Cape Bon on the North African side having entirely eluded us. We arrived in Malta on 5th August, having passed a huge floating dock under tow by Dutch tugs on passage to Singapore. 1938 was the year that the Naval Base there was completed.

We handed over *Coronation* to the Dockyard and rejoined *Barham* now secured between her buoys in Grand Harbour. Grand Harbour in those pre-war days was a brave sight when the fleet was in – three or four battleships at their buoys off the Customs House and stretching away up Marsa Creek, were the County Class cruisers of the 1st Cruiser Squadron with their high sides and distinctive three funnels. In Bighi Bay, off the hospital, would be either an aircraft carrier or one of the battle cruisers Hood or Repulse. The Mediterranean was a disturbed place; the Spanish Civil War was in its third year and all the European powers patrolled the seas around Spain to ensure the safe passage of merchant shipping. British, French, German and Italian ships were all involved. The British too had troubles of their own in Palestine, with bombings and terrorism. The Italians were in the process of occupying Abyssinia and the general state affairs in Europe required the fleet to be kept at a high state of readiness; in fact that summer the British Reserve Fleet was mobilised.

On 16th August we sailed, in company with the Tribal class destroyer *Cossack*, for Spanish patrol. As is usual on passage, various exercises were carried out and soon after leaving Malta the 1st Destroyer Flotilla, nine 'G' class destroyers, carried out a mass torpedo attack on us with each of the destroyers firing eight torpedoes, fitted, of course, with cork-filled collision heads. It was an impressive sight. We arrived at Palma in Majorca two days later. Palma was a fleet base for the Nationalist Navy, General Franco's lot. In the harbour, protected by an anti-submarine boom, lay the Nationalist flagship, *Canarias* (a Spanish built County class cruiser), several other cruisers and a minelayer. We anchored outside the boom in company with an Italian fleet oiler and three destroyers of the Turbinia class.

While there we kept our anti-aircraft armament at the ready and kept a close watch and record of the aircraft that flew overhead. During the day several squadrons of Italian bombers would fly over on their missions in support of the Nationalists and also to practise their bombing technique. They were mostly Savoia Marcchetti monoplanes with two engines and retractable undercarriages, very modern. Various British destroyers also came and went, sometimes with a hundred or so refugees on board. The practice was to try and ferry people to the right side of their respective front lines using Marseilles as a swap-over station. This I believe was organised by the Red Cross.

On 29th August *Cossack* returned from Marseilles with a load of medical supplies and mail and the following day *Barham* sailed for Gandia on the Spanish mainland. Gandia had been recently bombed and my picket boat was loaded with stores for the local Red Cross. I was sent in shore only to find that the whole place had been wrecked, five merchant ships including one British sunk alongside and on the quay itself was a wrecked train; the Red Cross store had also been flattened. On my next trip I brought in 500 gallons of petrol for the ambulances and while waiting for the petrol to be unloaded I wandered off to see what I could see and came upon an Italian bomb that had failed to explode but which had broken in half. Thinking that this might be of use to British intelligence I and one of my crew scooped it up and took it back to the ship. I took it down to the Gunnery Office which seemed to me to be an appropriate place. The gunnery officer, a very nice chap called Lloyd-Davies nearly had apoplexy. The whole of the after end of the ship was cleared and everyone including the Admiral mustered on the forecastle. My bomb, which was actually a very small one, was rendered safe by dropping it over the stern and I received nil marks for initiative.

We sailed the following day for Marseilles with three British refugees, two from Madrid and a journalist. We also had about 200 Spaniards mostly women and children. The ship called first at Coldetas to land more stores for the British Consul in Barcelona; it was impossible to enter Barcelona itself because of the bombing so the only way was to land the stores on the beach at Coldetas which had no landing jetty. I towed in two 32-ft cutters laden with stores and slipped them just off the beach for unloading. My picket boat, one of the first of the modern planing boats, 45ft in length, was fitted with four engines capable of about 20 knots and much more fun to drive than the old steam ones.

At Marseilles we anchored some 3 miles from the Vieux Port; during the first night it blew a gale and became too rough to bring off the liberty men that had been landed earlier, so they had to be left on shore overnight. Two days later we were back in Palma. I have only two recollections of going ashore there; the first was going to see a Laurel and Hardy film in Spanish at the local cinema and getting eaten alive by fleas; the second was being arrested by the Spanish police for wearing shorts, in Spain an act of gross indecency. I was baled out by the British Consul and sent back to the ship for a bollocking. I was forbidden to go ashore in Palma again.

On 10th September we were back in Malta and I had my first go at securing the ship between our two buoys with my evolution cutter. The drill was that the ship would come into Grand Harbour and make a 180° turn, ending up stopped between the two buoys. The starboard cutter would take the picking-up rope to the forward buoy and my port one to the stern buoy. The picking-up ropes were in fact 3.5-inch wires with a shackle at the end. I got my buoy jumpers on to the buoy successfully and had just got shackled on when the ship went ahead, towing the buoy under and throwing the two buoy jumpers into the water. In those days I had a very quick temper which went with my red hair and I shouted at the Lieutenant Commander in charge on the quarterdeck to use some ******* common sense and veer the wire. For this I got hauled up for insolence and was mastheaded for the rest of the day, quite rightly so. The masthead in *Barham* was 180 ft, quite a climb. You were required to take an improving book with you and this could be either the Bible or the Seamanship Manual. I think that I was up there for about four hours before being called down.

We spent about ten days in Malta and got to know a bit about the place and where to go. Ashore we played hockey and tennis and swam off the rocks at Sliema, which you could get to by either bus or steam ferry. Then we went to sea for night-action practice; at this time I was searchlight control officer for the port searchlights, great 3-foot diameter drums with a carbon arc light. They were remotely controlled by a binocular sight on either side of the bridge superstructure. As control officer you were expected to sight the target through these special binoculars and report when you were 'ON'. The searchlight was supposed to follow your every movement by means of a rather primitive electrical system known as a step-by-step motor. Such was the state of the art of the system that when the order came to 'Expose the beam' the steps turned frequently into giant leaps and the beam instead of illuminating the target would shoot wildly up into the air or down to the sea – to be followed by cries of, 'Turn the bloody thing off'.

The other thing that was practised at every opportunity was the flying off of the seaplane for reconnaissance. Flying off wasn't much of a problem; the turret would be trained into the relative wind, the engine wound up to full chat and off it went. It always looked as if it was going to hit the sea but never did. Recovery was much more difficult, especially if the sea was rough. What would happen was that the ship would make a sharp turn as the aircraft was coming into land which virtually ironed out a piece of sea and made a lee at the same time. The pilot had to land in this area and then motor up alongside to get under the crane, while the observer climbed up on to the top wing to hook on the sling. It all had to be done very slickly as any delay would mean that the sea would get up and throw the plane about. Up on deck the aircraft handlers had long bamboo poles with padded ends which they used to stop the plane hitting the ship's side and doing itself an injury. Luckily we had a very good Australian pilot called Holbrook so we managed this manoeuvre better than some.

On 22nd September the fleet was diverted to Alexandria because of Germany's invasion of Czechoslovakia and we arrived there on the 23rd, three battleships, five cruisers and two flotillas of destroyers – the 'Gs' and the Tribals. The Tribal class was the very latest thing in destroyers; designed as gunnery ships they were some 600 tons bigger than the other destroyers, carried eight 4.7-inch guns in twin mountings but had only four torpedoes. In the fleet all the ammunition was got up on deck and fused. Fire and damage control precautions were increased and at night we darkened ship. Maidstone, the submarine depot ship, arrived with the 1st Submarine Flotilla and also the aircraft carrier *Glorious*. The new Town class cruiser *Manchester* also joined the fleet from the East Indies station, arriving in East Indies fleet colours of white hull and buff funnels. All the ships were ordered to paint ship with matt grey paint to reduce reflections and some with a mixture of light and dark grey. However, on 1st October we heard with some relief that Germany, France and Britain had signed a treaty and that there would be no war, at least not in 1938. But, as our Admiral was at pains to point out, we could not afford to relax and training went on apace.

Alexandria was a great place in those days, very cosmopolitan, though most of the better shops were Greek or French. We had a treaty with Egypt which gave us pretty much a free run of the port, with its superb harbour protected by a long breakwater running out from the Ras el Tin light – rather like Plymouth but very much warmer. Ashore there was a lot of fun to be had; the Gunroom had a block membership of the Sporting Club which had a jolly good golf course, tennis courts and a swimming pool, all beautifully kept. You could get there by tram for a few piastres or, if there were four of you, it was even cheaper, after a great deal of haggling, to take a gharry with its flyblown horse and tabouched driver.

Money was always a factor in runs ashore but there were some bars which we got to know where, for the price of a bottle of Stella beer, you got a free plate of goulash. We never enquired from what it was made – probably some dead gharry horse – but it tasted good and kept the wolf from the door. If you were feeling really rich there were the most gorgeous sticky cakes to be had at Pastroudi's. Away from the harbour area Alexandria had most elegant buildings and boulevards and along the shore facing the bathing beaches of Sidi Bishe there were rows of grand houses, where all the wealthy people from Cairo would come for the weekends and also where King Farouk had his summer palace. I and some others also joined the Alexandria Rowing Club and were able to take out a scull or a four, much more enjoyable than rowing a service boat.

At this time *Barham* was flagship of the First Battle Squadron, with Rear Admiral Ralph Leatham and his 'Flags', Lieutenant Gordon-Lennox. The C-in-C Mediterranean, Admiral Sir Dudley Pound, flew his flag in *Warspite*. His main headquarters were, of course, in Malta but he also enjoyed the luxury of a yacht in the shape of HMS *Aberdeen*, a small sloop of 900 tons and painted white with a buff funnel. Having an Admiral meant having an Admiral's barge, a picket boat painted blue but of the same type as the two that we already had on board.

At this time in harbour I was running one of them, which I thoroughly enjoyed. Ours were two of the new boats designed by Scott Paine; other ships had similar ones designed by Peter du Cane. Of the two, ours were lighter, faster and easier to manoeuvre. Their principal duties were to ferry officers and mail but they were also used for harbour patrol. In Alexandria, where there was often not a breath of wind, we were used to make waves so that ships' seaplanes and RAF Flying boats could take off. Without something to bounce on, they just could not get unstuck. From time to time we were also required to do the same thing for the Imperial Airways 'Empire' flying boats when their own launch was out of action, so all in all our 20-plus knots came in pretty useful.

Running picket boats was altogether more fun than running a launch. These were very large open boats, 45 ft in length, single screw and used for landing libertymen and ferrying heavy stores. They could carry 120 men and taking them ashore was no problem but coming off late at night with 120 matelots, especially on a pay day, was quite another story and certainly no picnic. You were not allowed to bring your boat alongside until you had achieved order and silence. The usual way of achieving this was to stop the boat and refuse to go any further until everyone was silent. One of our group of Mids got into hot water because late one night he became so fed up with one character, who just would not shut up, that he took off the tiller and bopped the offender on the head with it. This achieved the desired result but also a complaint to the Officer of the Watch that he had been struck over the head by an officer and there were, of course, a lot of witnesses.

The following day the rating in question, a well-known 'skate' and drunk, came before the Captain to state his complaint together with other witnesses (sailors who had been in the boat with him) the Master-at-Arms, the Commander and of course the Snottie in question. Algie Willis, our Captain, had a very dry sense of humour and, turning to the Midshipman, said, 'Right, Mr Gardner, show me what you did'. Gardner took the tiller and tapped the sailor on the head. The Captain said, 'Was that what happened?' 'No Sir', the sailor replied, 'It was much harder than that'. 'Show me again Mr Gardner'; again a modest tap on the top of the head. So the Captain turned to one of the witnesses and said, 'You show me'. This time a fairly hefty blow was given. 'Who else saw this?' asked the Captain'. 'I did', said another sailor who was also in the boat. 'Well take the tiller and show me', said the Captain. Other witnesses were now enjoying the game and an egg of some size appeared on the defendant's head. After the fifth or sixth whack, the Captain said, 'Complaint substantiated and as for you Mr Gardner, a Reprimand will be recorded against you in the Log'. But he never had any more trouble in his boat.

On board, Sunday night cinema on the quarterdeck was always a great thing. Mountbatten had started the RN Cinema Corporation and we used to get quite modern films. Sometimes there were other forms of entertainment and I recall one Sunday night when we had the local 'Gully Gully' man. He was a great success especially when he produced about 20 day-old chicks from every pocket of the

Captain's and the Commander's mess jackets. He also brought a huge Nubian strong man with him, who, after a great deal of grunting, managed to bend a one-inch steel bar into a horseshoe shape round his neck. The 'gully gully' man then passed it to the front row to be examined. The Engineer Commander, who was also pretty strong, calmly bent it straight and passed it back, without a word, to huge applause.

Most week days we went to sea for exercises, sailing at 0800 and returning either that evening or the following morning. A new type of target had just been provided for anti-aircraft gunnery practice. Known as Queen Bees they were radio-controlled model aircraft with a wingspan of 14 ft and a top speed of 120 knots. They were launched from a small catapult and were very much better than a towed target and extremely difficult to hit, perhaps intentionally so, as they were quite expensive and there were very few of them.

One of the features of this time in Alexandria was the Fleet Regatta – big excitement – and training sessions for the crews had been going on for a month with boats away on every possible occasion. On the day of the regatta itself the fleet was buzzing with excitement and a lot of money was to change hands on the Tote. I was bow in the Gunroom gig. The gigs had six oars and were 30 ft long, narrow boats and carvel built. We had scraped about seven layers of paint off ours to try and make it lighter and used a lot of elbow grease in polishing the bottom. Sadly we were beaten into second place by *Warspite*. This was the big ships' regatta and every department in the ship had its crew and sometimes two – Seamen, Stokers, Royal Marines, Cooks, Wardroom and so on, each racing against their opposite numbers from other ships over a distance of a mile. *Malaya* won the Cock of the Fleet Trophy which was then rowed round all the ships amidst great cheers and their chippies made a huge Cock to stand on their 'B' turret.

A couple of days later we had the sailing regatta which *Barham* won. One of the features was the 'obstacle whalers race'. This was started with all the whalers at anchor with awnings spread. At the gun you had to up anchor and down awning, then row for 400 yards, then up masts and sails and sail for 800 yards and so on until you had done everything twice. The finish was under sail. Our gunroom crew were hot favourites having been observed by the tipsters to put up the best times in practices. We had rigged a very cunning system where, by pulling on just one rope, the mast, jib and mainsail all went up together and you were off. The only snag was that the mizzen had to be stepped individually by the helmsman, standing on the stern grating. On the second leg our helm, a Mid called Jones, lost his balance and by the time we had hauled him and the mizzen back on board we could only manage third place.

We would often have sailing races in harbour in the Dog Watches and the Captain allowed me to sail his gig. They were super boats to sail and had two masts with dipping lugs, that is to say the luff of the sail is tacked down well forward of the mast to make a sort of all-in-one jib. The yard had to be on the leeward side of the mast for the sail to set properly and each time you tacked, your crew, which consisted of six men, had to unhook the tack, dip the yard to the other side of the mast, hook the tack back on and get the luff taut. With a well-trained crew all this happened very quickly and easily and the boats were extremely fast, especially on a reach.

In the middle of November the fleet returned to Malta and, as always on passage, carried out a number of exercises. We also did a full-power trial but could only achieve 21 knots because of a dirty bottom. Weed grew very fast in the warm water of a Mediterranean summer. Back in Malta all my group plus 170 ratings were landed at Sliema to do a week's course on the rifle range. We marched out to St Andrew's Barracks to be lodged with the 2nd Devons. Great luxury after our cramped quarters on board to find ourselves two to a room. Unfortunately we all had to move out after the first night because of bed bugs. The range course was fun; I had never fired a service rifle before and wasn't much good at it, though at the end some of the shots were getting close to the bull, which was more than could be said for my pistol shooting. A Colt .45 is extremely heavy and difficult despite what cowboys do in the movies.

Malta in winter is quite a stormy place with gregale warnings coming with monotonous regularity. I remember once being told to take a message ashore to the Captain who had taken a party to the Opera. The Neapolitan Opera used to do a season in Malta and the fashionable thing to do was to give your guests a good dinner and then take them to your box at the opera. On this occasion I found the Captain happily sleeping through the second act of 'The Girl of the Golden West'. I shook him and told him that there was a severe gregale warning. He woke up and said, 'Thank God'; we slipped out and I took him back to the ship. Winter in Malta also saw a lot of sport, football, rugger and other activities. One of our senior Mids, Ken Busbridge, won the fleet marathon by minutes, which was a pretty remarkable feat as, when everyone else would be going ashore to train, he would sit in our locker flat playing the piano. Actually it was his own piano and somehow he had managed to find room for it.

There were dances every Saturday night at the Union Club in Sliema and, provided you could find yourself a partner, you could have a lot of fun. To hire a self-drive car for an evening would cost you 5s.0d. (25p), including a gallon of petrol, or for £2.10s (£2.50) you could have one for a week. As we were on opposite watches and, I think, had different girlfriends, I used to share a car with Keppel Edge-Partington. Finding a girlfriend and not having one wished upon you was hazardous. Many of the senior officers had their wives and families in Malta and there were a number of desperate mothers trying to get their daughters off. Our Captain had two daughters, one of whom was O.K. but excuses were difficult for the other. There were two formidable sisters known in the Gunrooms of the Fleet as the First Battle Cruiser Squadron, but there were also some jolly nice girls and I must say that I was jolly lucky.

On 20th December many of us went to the State Ball at the Governor's Palace in Valletta; Bonham-Carter was the Governor. It was a very posh do with everyone in Ball Dress – white kid gloves, white waistcoat and dirk for us whilst the more senior officers wore tail coats with epaulettes and swords. I believe that there were 1,800 guests. After Christmas we went to a charity fancy-dress ball, also at the Palace and much more fun. I went as a Cossack with a great red beard; this turned out to be a big mistake as I couldn't eat anything without getting a mouthful of hair. The pièce de resistance was our Sub-Lieutenant, Freddie Copland-Griffiths, who had made the most wonderful costume. He was a smallish man and, by building up a sort of frame on his shoulders, he made himself into a very convincing headless Elizabethan courtier with a most realistic and bloody head tucked under his arm. He arranged for a couple of our lot to get him into the long corridor at midnight just as someone else cut the lights, leaving just a few ornamental candles to heighten the effect and let him see, through the lace of his ruff, where he was going. The result was really dramatic with screams echoing through the rooms as he stalked down the corridor.

It was my first Christmas away from home and Christmas in the Navy is quite a thing. On Christmas Eve I went carol-singing round the fleet with a party led by our Chaplain, Marson the Parson, in the ship's launch which broke down and we had to be towed home. On Christmas Day we were woken by someone playing 'Christians awake Salute the Happy Morn' on a cornet broadcast over the ship's loudspeaker system. Roast pork and plum pudding was the traditional naval Christmas dinner and all the officers went round the mess decks led by the youngest seaman in the ship, dressed in the Captain's uniform, to see the decorations and to wish everyone a Happy Christmas. A lot of tots were saved and exchanged and of course there were a lot of thick heads on Boxing Day, which I see in my journal was devoted to Physical Training and clearing up. On New Year's Eve we started our Admiral's inspection which went on both in harbour and at sea for a whole week, ending up with General Drill in harbour when the whole ship was just about turned inside out. When it was all over we de-ammunitioned and docked for a bottom clean.

Malta before WW II was a very popular run ashore for the average matelot. All the ships were secured to buoys and each ship would have a fleet of dghaisas waiting to take you ashore for one penny each if the boat was fairly full – they could carry ten – or whatever you could bargain for if you were on your on your own – no need to hang about for ships' boats and of course you could come off whenever you wanted. A Midshipman coming on board after midnight had, by tradition, to bring the Officer of the Watch a hard-boiled egg. You had to have permission if you were going to be late otherwise leave expired at 2230. The sailor, once ashore, had innumerable bars to go to, all selling the local brew of Farson's beer; there were also many other 'attractions' in the numerous places of entertainment in Strada Stretta and all reasonably cheap. Of course there were the usual risks and those who picked up a 'dose' were moved to a special mess on board, known by the sailors as Rose Cottage, where they stayed until cured.

For the officers there were the Union Clubs in Valetta and Sliema, golf, rugby and polo at the Marsa, and a couple of more expensive nightclubs, Rexford's and Aunties. One of our Paymaster Sub-Lieutenants in the Gunroom, Jack Grist, used to play the violin in the band at Aunties, when the ship was in, to earn a few extra bob. The Street called Straight (Strada Stretta) was strictly out of bounds for officers and you only saw what went on there when on Shore Patrol.

In the new year Rear Admiral Leatham was relieved by Vice-Admiral Geoffrey Layton as Commander of the First Battle Squadron and Second in Command, Mediterranean Fleet. He was quite a ball of fire but very good to us Mids. Later in January our group started our three months' destroyer training; we were sent off in pairs to different ships and Peter Harvey and I joined *Imperial*, an 'I' class destroyer of the 3rd Flotilla. She was typical of the destroyers built between the wars and tiny by today's standards – 1,350 tons, 32 knots with four 4.7-inch guns and two sets of four torpedo tubes, two mountings of 4-barrelled 0.5-inch machine-guns – built in 1937 at a cost of £200,000 with a complement of 120. The Captain, Hilary Worthington Biggs, was a newly-promoted Commander and dead keen. He went on to be an Admiral. The No.1 was Fitzroy Talbot, a grounded Fleet Air Arm pilot; No.2 was John Trechman; the Sub-Lieutenant was Hugh Wake, a direct descendant of Hereward.; the Gunner(T) was Percy Wilcox and the Chief Engineer was Lieutenant John Hoddinott – five officers in all and now two Snotties. A far cry from the 30 or so you would find today.

Imperial had the best polo team and, as I could ride a little, I was told off to be the spare and sent up to the Marsa to learn. However my polo never got further than a wooden horse, on which you sat trying to knock balls up a wooden slope and then trying to hit them again as they ran back at you. I found it extremely difficult and how you did it at full gallop I never found out, as we and all the other destroyers were sent off to sea to practise mass torpedo attacks. There were three flotillas, each of nine ships, and the eight Tribals who, as gunnery ships, were supposed to clear the way for the rest of us – thirty five destroyers in all dashing about at close quarters. Torpedoes were normally launched at under 3,000 yards and a flotilla would advance in line abreast from a given sector all turning at the same time to fire and to make a hasty escape under cover of thick black smoke (no radar then) coming from the funnels and also from smoke floats dropped overboard – jolly exciting stuff requiring cool and accurate ship-handling at high speed and close quarters.

The key figure in all this was the Yeoman of Signals, all the orders in daylight being passed by flag signals and at night by flashing light in Morse code. The Flotilla Leader, Captain(D), would hoist the flag group for the next manoeuvre 'at the dip', to be repeated by all the other ships, then 'close up' when everyone had received it and finally 'hauled down' when the turn or manoeuvre was to be executed. A good Yeoman could read the signals almost as they came out of the flag lockers and have the signalmen on the flag deck bending on the repeating signal in a flash. Longer messages came by light or semaphore and at pretty high speed too.

Quite a number of the destroyer Captains prided themselves on being able to read the signals just about as fast the Yeoman, so as Officer of the Watch you had to have your wits about you. Morse and semaphore practice were daily routines for all midshipmen when ships were in harbour. Our Captain(D) had two special flag signals which he would hoist when the occasion merited – a large chocolate colour flag with a huge strawberry on it, if you had done well, but a large green one with three raspberries if you had made a cock of it. As Midshipmen we had to be 2nd Officer of the watch at sea and also practise our navigation, with all the workings and so forth recorded in a special book to be checked by the Navigator, Hugh Wake, daily and the Captain weekly.

Towards the end of January our Division, four destroyers, was sent on a jolly to Greece escorting the C-in-C, Admiral Sir Dudley Pound, in the sloop *Aberdeen*. The object was a few days' duck-shooting in the Gulf of Arta. The Admiral was to go to Corfu first and *Imperial* was sent on ahead to find the best place to shoot. The Gulf of Arta is on the Dalmatian coast and is a huge landlocked bay with two rivers running into it. There was a lot of marshy land in the vicinity of the two rivers and the whole place was reputed to be teeming with duck. Our first day there it blew a gale, the holding ground was bad and we spent the whole night steaming at slow speed to stop the anchor dragging.

The next day was much better and we all got our guns ready and went ashore in the dog watches for the evening flighting. The marshes were extremely muddy and the grass very tall so we were not very successful, particularly as we had no dogs to retrieve. However, we did get a number of mallard, two coot and an owl which had somehow got mixed up in the affair. The next day we shifted to Koprana Bay, a very beautiful spot surrounded by snow-capped mountains, and the following day the C-in-C arrived in *Aberdeen*. As soon as they sighted *Imperial* they flashed a message to 'report number and type of duck'. Our Captain was ashore and so our No.1, who was a fairly independent character, flashed a signal back to C-in-C which said 'Lots, all Greek'. Ashore there were some magnificent remains of the city of Nikopolis built by Caesar Augustus to mark his victory over Mark Anthony and Cleopatra. I was able to spend a happy afternoon ashore looking round them; the city seemed much on the scale of Pompeii and there were some archaeologists carrying out a dig there at the time.

Unfortunately the weather continued to be poor and on 24th January we sailed for Malta. On the passage back we were detailed to fire some Surface Practice Torpedoes for the rest to shoot at. These were out-of-date torpedoes set to run on the surface at 30 knots and, like the Queen Bee targets, extremely hard to hit. Ours certainly were as, despite the ministrations of Percy Wilcox, the Gunner T, they insisted on running like porpoises, leaping out of the water and plunging down again. Life in a destroyer was very different from that in a battleship. You were no longer just an extra dogsbody, but someone with a job to do and people depending on you to do it properly.

Of course in a destroyer everybody knew everybody and all about them; you were part of a close-knit team of men who were immensely proud of their ship and wanted it to be better than any of the others in the Flotilla, or indeed in any of the other Flotillas. The 3rd Flotilla was tops, the 'G's, 'H's and the Tribals rubbish, so when you were on watch at sea and let the ship get out of its proper station everyone groaned. These little ships were super to handle, the normal distance between ships at sea being one and a half cables (300 yards) or just under three ships' lengths.

Imagine a flotilla or division of destroyers in line ahead or line abreast at 25 knots; there is little room for error. In daylight the distance was checked constantly using a Stuart's Distance Meter, a simple little gadget which, provided you set the height of the next ship's mast correctly, gave an instant answer. At night the best way was to learn by how much the ship you were keeping station on filled your binoculars.

Down below in the engine room the revolutions of the propellers had to be controlled accurately and speed was increased or decreased by ordering the number of revs. When you rang down from the bridge 'up two revs' or 'down two revs', that is what it had to be and if you were ordered to change station on a screen, which required going at high speed, the boiler room teams had to be on the ball to put on extra oil fuel sprayers and adjust the fan speed for the air going into the boiler so that no telltale black smoke was made. In the boiler room the Stoker P.O with his highly polished wheel spanner was king. There is something taut and humming about an efficient ship. She is alive.

We arrived back in Malta on 26th January. Entering harbour was always quite an exciting manoeuvre as all the destroyers were berthed in Sliema Creek and secured to head and stern buoys, two ships to a buoy. Sliema Creek is long and narrow and the practice was to turn in the entrance and make a sternboard all the way up to your buoys, a division of four ships at a time, and hopefully your ship's dghaisa would be waiting, ready to take your lines to the buoys. On our arrival our new Captain joined, Lieutenant Commander C de Winton Kitcat. He was the most junior Captain in our flotilla so we were known as the 'boots' and were given all the odd jobs.

Soon after our arrival, Roy Talbot, our No.1, decided that he would give a party ashore in a friend's house. We were all roped in to help convert it into a passable night club with a flashing sign outside which said 'Le Rat Mort'. There was to be a dance band and also a cabaret. I was told off to collect a Hungarian dancer from a night spot in Valletta and to look after her until it was time for her to do her 'dance exotique'. This I did and got back to the party in good time. She was very beautiful and wore only a fur coat on top of her costume, a fig leaf and a couple of breast dangles and she spoke practically no English except to demand 'orses necks' (brandy and ginger ale) which I provided while we waited for her cue to go on. At last the time came and at the fanfare that announced her act she flung off her fur coat, twirled on to the dance floor amidst riotous applause and fell flat on her face, having passed out cold. Johnson was not popular and I had the utmost difficulty getting her home. One lives and learns.

We were at sea pretty regularly and at this time the fleet did a lot of gunnery and torpedo firing at the old 25,000-ton battleship, *Centurion*. *Centurion* had been fitted with radio control and her armour had been increased especially for the job. She had a steaming crew only and their job was to get everything going and then be taken off by her attendant destroyer, an elderly WW I destroyer, *Shikari*, who could then control the ship by radio, altering course and speed to suit the occasion. After a shoot or bombing, the crew would be put back on board to take her back to harbour. Special shells and bombs were used against her and which fragmented easily. As 'boots' destroyer we spent a lot of time following close behind and photographing the hits and misses for the official records.

At the beginning of March the whole fleet went to Gibraltar to meet up with the Home Fleet for combined manoeuvres; these were an annual event and there was always great rivalry between the two fleets. C-in-C Home Fleet flew his Flag in

Nelson and we were all keen to see *Ark Royal*, our first designed-from-the-keel-up, aircraft carrier. All Home Fleet ships were painted dark grey and looked very sombre when compared with the light grey of the Mediterranean Fleet. The sea exercises were to last ten days and then everyone was back in Gibraltar for the 'wash-up' and for the inter-fleet football, hockey and rugger.

All the destroyers berthed in the 'pens', now a Marina, and it was here that *Imperial* caused a small incident. Suddenly in the middle of the morning there was a burst of machine-gun fire. It was our 4-barrelled 0.5-inch machine gun that had squirted off a short burst in the direction of La Linea in Spain. Great panic, what idiot had done it? Believe it or not it turned out to be a bit of monkey business. The P.O.'s mess had a pet monkey and it had got on to the gun and played with the trigger; it was found in a state of gibbering shock on top of the waist awning and wouldn't come down, Of course the gun should never have been left loaded in harbour but that is another matter.

Going back to the exercises and as a matter of interest. . . one of the Home Fleet cruisers was fitted with R.D.F. (Radar); this in fact was the first radar to go to sea. Another set was fitted in a Sunderland Flying boat; it was a well-kept secret and none of us knew anything about it at the time.

We sailed for Malta on 20th March. During a night exercise on the way the cruiser *Penelope* and the Tribal destroyer *Afridi* were in collision. Both ships were holed and had to be escorted home. On arrival in Malta we careened ship to clean off the weed, not of course by beaching, as in the old sailing ship days, but by transferring oil and water first to one side and then the other to give the ship a good list. On 8th April we were all brought to instant readiness again, this time by Italy's invasion of Albania. Warheads were fitted to the torpedoes and all the shells fused. *Barham* and *Glorious* were in Naples at the time and were ordered back to Malta. The 3rd Flotilla made a high speed passage to meet them and act as an anti-submarine screen. Other destroyers were deployed on patrol at the southern end of the Adriatic. King Zog of Albania escaped to Greece.

Four days later Mr Chamberlain, the PM, made a pacifying statement of Britain's position and some relaxation was allowed. Sadly our destroyer time had come to an end and I and Peter Harvey rejoined *Barham* and met our new Captain, Captain H.T.C. Walker, who had joined us from commanding *Hood*. Nicknamed Hooky, he was a super chap. As a young Lieutenant he had been in the old cruiser *Vindictive* when she entered Zeebrugge in WW I in an endeavour to block the harbour and prevent its use as a U-boat base. During the raid he was badly wounded and lost his left arm and now wore an artificial one with a very smart gold-plated hook. Despite having only one arm he was an excellent tennis player; he could also tie a double-ended bow tie with one hand.

In Malta the defences were being improved and anti-submarine booms put across the entrances to the various harbours. I was sent in charge of an armed guard to the tug *Roysterer*. We had to patrol the entrance to Grand Harbour and our task was to push or tow away any ship which might try to sink itself across the harbour entrance. This was a big tug of 800 tons and fun to handle but after about a week I was recalled to *Barham* and then sent off to *Glorious* for an air course. The idea was to pick out likely candidates for the Fleet Air Arm but after a few hours banging about in the dustbin-shaped rear cockpit of a Hawker Osprey, hanging on to a Lewis gun like grim death and being violently sick, it was decided that I was more of a liability that an asset. So, after a few days of getting acquainted with life and routine aboard an aircraft carrier, I was sent back to *Barham* and happy to be there. At that time *Glorious*, a converted WW I battle cruiser built in 1917, was manned by a mixture of RAF and Navy – 750 RN and 450 RAF – who were referred to by the sailors as 'crabs' because of the colour of their uniform.

At the end of April *Barham* and *Malaya* sailed for Navarin Bay (Navarino) in Greece, at that time a delightful and unspoilt spot. I well remember one day when the Captain lent my group of Snotties his motor boat, well-stocked with food and drink, to take away on a banyan. We found a super, totally deserted sandy beach where we cooked our food and swam, quite idyllic. Also, on another occasion there, Geoffrey Layton, our Admiral, took nine of us on an expedition to explore an old Venetian castle. We had a Greek guide with a donkey to lead the way and carry the grub and when we finally arrived at the top of the mountain on which the castle was perched we had a splendid fry-up.

Apart from being great fun this sort of thing provided a wonderful opportunity for knowing and getting known. Both Captain Willis and Captain Walker made a practice of having the Midshipman of the Morning Watch to breakfast when the ship was at sea. The Morning Watch in the Navy was 0400 to 0730, the Relieve Decks from 0730 to 0830, followed by the Forenoon Watch which ended at 1230. The day following the trip to the castle we had a violent sandstorm, the whole sky turning yellow. Both *Barham* and *Malaya* were painting ship and the result was catastrophic, all hands were put over the side with wads of cotton waste and turpentine to try and wipe the paint off before it dried and turned to sandpaper.

On 5th May we moved to Suda Bay in Crete. This is a huge inlet on the north side of the island with mountains rising steeply from the shore. Here, by treaty with Greece, the Royal Navy had an emergency base. The ships were kept in a state of anti-aircraft readiness and the destroyers were once again ordered to paint their hulls dark grey. The picket boats were armed with machine-guns and depth-charges and we carried out constant patrols. Shore leave was strictly curtailed but the Greek cavalry regiment in the area kindly lent six horses to the ship and David Dunbar-Nasmith and I went for a good ride into the country getting as far as Canea. The roads were dreadful and a horse was much the best way of getting about.

A few days later I had to go with the Admiral, the Flag Lieutenant and a couple of Greek cavalry officers on a tour of neighbouring villages. I soon found out why I had been brought along, for at each village the Admiral was presented with an enormous bouquet of flowers which he would pass to Flags and outside the village Flags would pass them to me to lose, without causing offence, before we arrived at the next village. I would go off at a canter ahead of the party until I found a convenient wall and, with no one in sight, dump the flowers behind it.

While we were still at Suda Bay a special visit was arranged to the Minoan city of Knossos. We went in the destroyer *Inglefield*, Captain D3, to Candia (Heraklion) and had a splendid day being shown round the ruins by Sir Arthur Evans, the archaeologist who opened up the site and now gets blamed for some of the restoration work that he carried out. Once again I was amazed by the ingenuity and the general standards of civilization achieved by these people 3000 years ago.

Shortly after this the fleet moved to Alexandria, leaving behind boom-defence and shore-based anti-aircraft personnel. Back in Alexandria at the end of May it was the turn of my group to do its engineering course and Rupert Bray and I were assigned to the double-bottom party. This consisted of a Chief Stoker, 2 Mechanicians, 2 Leading Stokers and two Stokers. In addition to fuel and water tanks, a battleship of *Barham*'s era was built with an inner and an outer hull divided into watertight compartments and also a blister running along each side below the water line to protect against torpedoes. All these had to be inspected and kept free of rust. The Double-Bottom Chief Stoker is a law unto himself and though ships' companies would change every two years or so, the DB Chief stayed with the ship indefinitely. He was also responsible for all the pipes, pumps and ventilation trunking. Rupert and I spent our first day brushing out and painting No.1 Auxiliary Feed Tank situated underneath B boiler room; there was just three foot of head-room and it was fiendishly hot.

I noticed from my Journal that on 31st May we had a massed march through Alexandria; the Royal Navy, Royal Marines, the Coldstream Guards and units from the Egyptian Army all took part. The whole parade took 45 minutes to pass the saluting base so it must have been a pretty big affair. Of course in those days all the big ships, including cruisers, had their own Royal Marine Band who, at action stations, manned the gunnery control station down in the bowels of the ship and also made up the medical teams in case of casualties in action. The following day we were all shattered by the loss of the submarine *Thetis*. She was on acceptance trials from Cammell Lairds, Birkenhead, with a RN crew and also the trials team from the builders. The bow compartment was accidentally flooded during torpedo loading trials and she dived into the mud where she stuck at an angle of about 35 degrees.

Just four managed to escape despite three earlier attempts which had proved fatal. One of those who did escape was the No. 1, Freddy Woods from Bideford, whom I had known quite well. The stern was visible for three days at low water but apparently there was no suitable equipment available which could get the rest of the crew out without flooding the boat in the process and on 3rd June all hope of rescue was abandoned. Though Freddy escaped he never really recovered from his ordeal and felt guilty that he was alive when his shipmates had perished. He had been chosen to try and escape as he knew the most about the situation in the boat and could advise the rescuers.

Two days later and this time in *Barham*, one of my Boys' division was killed falling from a ladder going down to the Chronometer Room, which was situated low down in the centre of the ship and reached by a number of vertical ladders – a very tragic loss. The three chronometers kept there had to be wound every day at the same time and their rates of gain or loss against each other recorded so that one could work out an accurate Greenwich Mean Time for navigation purposes – no Greenwich time signal in those days.

On 7th June Admiral Sir Dudley Pound was relieved by Admiral Andrew Cunningham. Admiral Pound was to become First Sea Lord and Chief of Naval Staff, a position he held for most of WW II, while Admiral Cunningham became one of the most successful Admirals. By this time everyone knew that war was about to happen; the only question was when. *Barham* was again due for docking and we returned to Malta on 24th June with a destroyer escort. It was very foggy and fog buoys had to be streamed in order to keep the ships together. The idea was to keep station on the ship ahead by keeping close to the buoy which was designed to throw up a spout of water and was being towed at a known distance from the ship ahead. I think the towing wire could be as much as half a mile in length, all now made redundant by radar.

At Malta we de-ammunitioned and entered the floating dock but as it was too hot for the sailors to remain on board; they moved out to Corradina barracks just above the dockyard while the Royal Marines went to Ghajn Tuffieha at the other end of the island. They took with them a cutter and a whaler so that they could continue to practise for the forthcoming Fleet Regatta.

Two weeks later the ship undocked and was ordered to return to Alexandria. Six of us from the Gunroom were sent to bring the cutter and whaler back, the cutter with a Royal Marine crew and the whaler by us. Rupert Bray was put in charge of the cutter as he was wearing a pith helmet and we thought that he wouldn't frighten the Marines! The cutter set off first, followed by the whaler launched by a hefty body of 'bullocks', who so bumped the boat down the beach that the bung came out. It wasn't until the water was lapping round our ankles that we realised the extent of the disaster. After much scrabbling under the bottom boards the bung was found and put back, but we also discovered that we had no bailer. Michael Jupp very gallantly offered to eat his lunch even though it was only 0730 so that we could have the tin to bale with.

Ghajn Tuffieha to Grand Harbour is a little over 20 miles and the intention was to sail. This we did as far as the Comino Channel between Malta and Gozo but there the wind faded completely and we had no alternative but to drop the sails and row the remaining 16 miles or so back to Grand Harbour. We arrived off Sliema at about 1930, weary and sunburnt, and I was put ashore on the rocks there to get a bus back to the ship and organise a tow, which I did. A search party had to be sent to find the cutter which finally got back alongside at about 2230. Next day we were all extremely sore at both ends, top and bottom.

Two days later the ship sailed with *Malaya* for Corfu, it was a peaceful passage and the ships were able to stop for hands to bathe during the dog watches. With us were six Motor Torpedo Boats, MTBs, new out from England; they were 100 ft in length and quite fast. The King of the Hellenes was in his summer palace at Corfu at the time. He came on board several times to be shown round the ship, inspect the Ship's Company and, one evening, to dine in the wardroom, meeting all the officers and afterwards watching cinema on the quarterdeck. He looked very like Prince Philip and spoke perfect English. He also went to sea in one of the MTBs while they carried out mock torpedo attacks on the ship. Corfu was the home of Greek cricket and we played several matches while there.

We were quite sorry when the time came to leave for Cyprus; *Malaya* went to Limasol and *Barham* to Famagusta, arriving on 28th July. I was lucky enough to be lent a horse by the local mounted police and, once I had mastered the controls (they were trained to go backwards if you pressed with your knees), I had a splendid ride through the orange groves. The main reason for our visit was to practise shore bombardment and this we did before sailing for Alexandria where we arrived on 1st August.

Once back in Alexandria we were immediately thrown into a series of exercises and Alexandria itself was subjected to air raid practices and emergency black outs. Two squadrons of Blenheim bombers carried out dummy attacks and also mock gas attacks spraying a coloured liquid which showed up on the paint work if you had been hit. There was a real fear that mustard gas would be used, as the Italians had used it in Abyssinia. On 22nd August Germany signed a non-aggression pact with Russia and this was taken as a warning; the next day all shells were got up and fused and splinter mats rigged round the superstructure and bridge. It looked like the real thing this time but, otherwise, life went on and on the 24th we had a children's party on board for local children with the sailors dressed as pirates, an Aunt Sally, jackstay rides, slides and so on.

However on the 29th we heard that Germany had invaded Poland. The next day the fleet put to sea for exercises, returning at 0900 on 1st September for the Fleet Regatta for which we had all been training whenever time permitted. Unfortunately we did no better than the previous year; the Gunroom team again came second after having broken an oar at the start and having to ship the spare. I was still bow and very disappointed not to have won. *Malaya* won the Cock again by 3 points. Then on the 3rd we were at war. On the 5th Admiral Cunningham came on board to address the Ship's Company and said that having been virtually at war for the past two years we must expect to continue with a rather boring period but on no account must we relax our training. It was to be a time of wait and see and on that same day Italy declared her neutrality. So started the so called Phoney War period but how phoney was it?

In the Mediterranean we proclaimed the right to stop and search all shipping, which indeed we did. *Warspite*, *Malaya* and *Glorious* went to escort the Orient liners Orchades, Orion and Orford, all straight out from England loaded with reservists, to bring our ships' companies up to war strength, and also 1,000 Royal Marines and other soldiers for the defence of Egypt. Some had received so little notice that they had left their London offices only just in time to catch the boat trains, without having time to go home, and arrived in Alexandria complete with bowler hats and umbrellas.

Just off Alexandria the destroyer *Garland* was attacking a submarine contact when one of her depth-charges went off prematurely, blowing her stern off and killing several members of her crew. *Griffen* who was with her carried out a successful attack and the submarine was sunk. *Garland* was towed into harbour on the 18th with a broken back and the same day we heard with great sadness that the Aircraft Carrier *Courageous* had been sunk in the English Channel. The following day, the 19th,

Russia invaded Poland and four D class destroyers, *Duchess, Delight, Decoy* and *Defender* joined the fleet from the China station.

It was about this time, too, that I was sent for by the Commander late in the afternoon, told to put on my best uniform and report immediately to the Chief of Staff in *Warspite*. I had no idea what I had done wrong but clearly something was amiss. On arrival I was wheeled down to the Chief of Staff, Rear Admiral Bruce Fraser, who gave me the most monumental rocket for having taken the Admiral's golf clubs. I tried to protest my innocence but wasn't allowed to get a word in edgeways and it was all too obvious that they were my set of clubs leaning against the Admiral's desk. I went straight back to *Barham* to find out what had gone wrong.

What had actually happened was that I had lent my clubs to one of the newly-arrived reserve officers who, after a glass or two at the Sporting Club had forgotten what my bag looked like and brought back the C-in-Cs. When the Admiral came to pick up his clubs, mine were the only ones left in the locker room and, worst luck, they had my name on them. That was the nearest I ever came to meeting the great Admiral Cunningham but of course Bruce Fraser did pretty well too as C–in-C Home Fleet and later First Sea Lord and a peerage. I was sent to *Barham*'s masthead for four hours for being a bother but was called down after an hour. The RNVR Sub-Lieutenant wrote a letter of apology and no more was heard of the incident. Everyone except Johnson thought it all hugely funny.

On 19th October Lord Haw Haw, the British born purveyor of Nazi propaganda on the German radio, announced that *Barham* had been sunk in the North Atlantic by a U-boat – indeed *Royal Oak* had been sunk in Scapa Flow with the loss of over 800 lives on the same day – but this caused a hotting-up of anti-submarine precautions and our picket boats spent a lot of time patrolling the boom defences.

By the end of the month there were virtually no destroyers left at Alexandria and anti-submarine protection of the harbour was left to some coal-burning anti-submarine trawlers with the romantic names *Jade, Coral* and *Amber*. I was sent to *Jade* as a watch keeper. It was nice to be in a small ship again, even though the coal dust got everywhere, but on 16th November I was back in *Barham* and on our way to Malta for yet another docking. *Barham* was the oldest and least modernised of all the Queen Elizabeth class and I don't think anyone knew what to do with her.

When we arrived in Malta two days later we found the French troopship *Clemanceau* had been brought in with a large hole in her side, having been in collision with another Messagerie Maritime ship, *Marietta Pasha*, off Malta. There had been about 180 casualties amongst the North African troops she had been carrying. On the same day the Cunard ship *Franconia* sailed for England with the MTB flotilla embarked and a number of Polish refugees.

As the Gunroom was being painted we were accommodated in the Royal Mail liner *Alcantara* (22,000 tons) which was being fitted out in the dockyard as an Armed Merchant Cruiser. We lived in the Winter Garden on the top deck abaft the second funnel and ate in the First Class Dining Room, very posh though sadly we had our own cooks and stewards and the ever vigilant messman. I had always had ambition to be able to tap dance like Fred Astaire and got taps fitted to a pair of shoes to prac

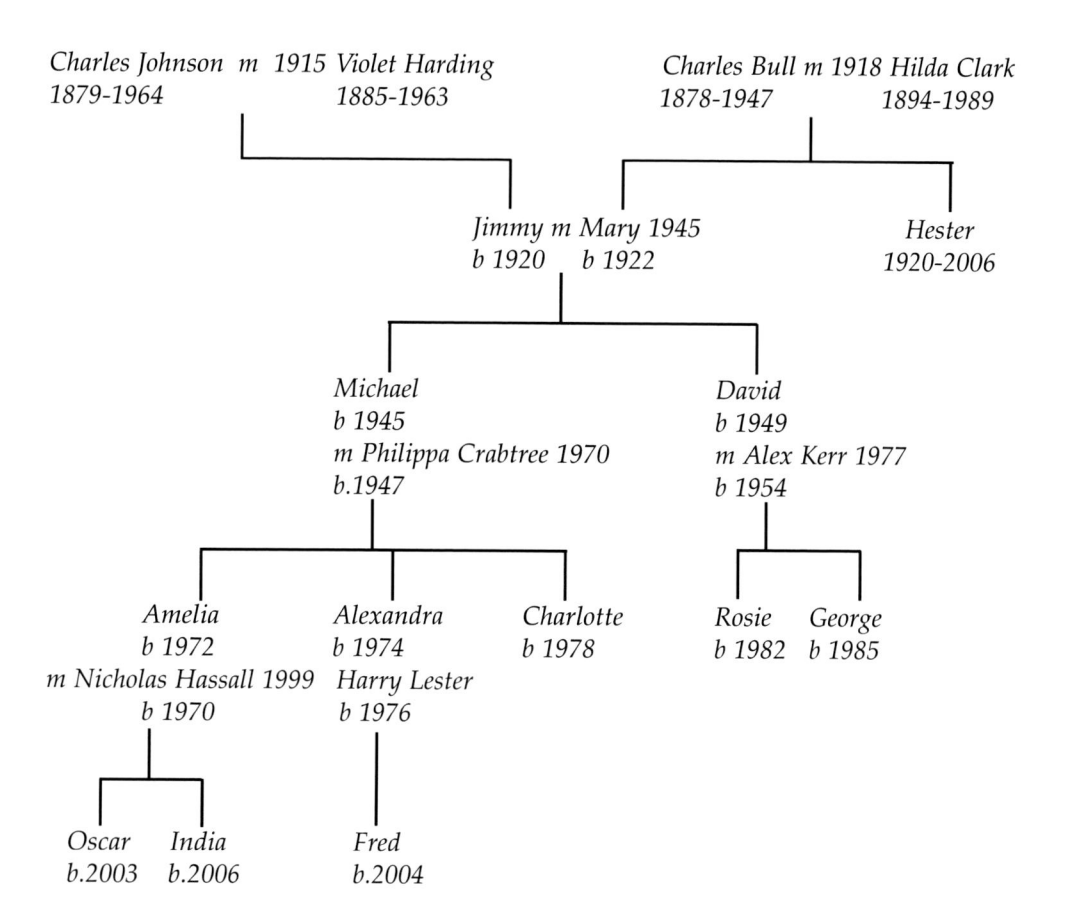

FAMILY TREE

Charles Johnson m 1915 *Violet Harding*　　　　*Charles Bull* m 1918 *Hilda Clark*
1879-1964　　　　　　　*1885-1963*　　　　　　　*1878-1947*　　　　　　　*1894-1989*

Jimmy m *Mary* 1945　　　　　　　　　*Hester*
b 1920　*b 1922*　　　　　　　　　　　*1920-2006*

Michael　　　　　　　　　　*David*
b 1945　　　　　　　　　　　*b 1949*
m *Philippa Crabtree* 1970　　m *Alex Kerr* 1977
b.1947　　　　　　　　　　　*b 1954*

Amelia　　*Alexandra*　*Charlotte*　　*Rosie*　*George*
b 1972　　*b 1974*　　　*b 1978*　　　*b 1982*　*b 1985*
m *Nicholas Hassall* 1999　*Harry Lester*
b 1970　　*b 1976*

Oscar　*India*　　*Fred*
b.2003　*b.2006*　*b.2004*

Left:

The Reverend Charles Bull served in France 1916-1917 and married Hilda Clark of Efford Manor, Plymouth in 1918.

Right:

Hilda Clark, pictured here when a V.A.D. in the Military Hospital, Exeter.

Left:

Captain Charles Cockin Johnson RN, the author's father (taken in 1917).

Below:

My parents were married in Instow, North Devon in 1915. This photograph was taken in front of my maternal grandfather's house at No 2 Bath Terrace. The V.A.Ds (nurses), of whom my mother was one, came from the Convalescent Home for wounded, mostly Devonshire Regiment, soldiers at Nos 4 & 5 Bath Terrace. Note the soldier standing third from the left has a bandage peeping out from beneath his cap. The dog wearing the wedding collar was my mother's Scottie.

Right:
The author - 1938
Ready for Sea!

Below:
My mother and I outside Cleveland.

Above: The 7000 ton Monitor H.M.S. Erebus, Cadet Training Ship (note the gymnasium forward).

Below: H.M.S.Vindictive, 9800 tons, after conversion to Cadet Training Cruiser.

Above: H.M.S Barham passing in front of Fort St Angelo, Malta 1938.

Below: H.M.S. Barham leaving Grand Harbour, 1938.

Above: Spanish Merchant Ship in Gandia, Spain after bombing by Italian Aircraft.

Left: Burnt out Railway Truck   This is where I found my un-exploded bomb.

Above: View from Harbour entrance.

Below: S.S. Dellwyn (British).

Right:

Sunday after lunch in Imperial's Wardroom Mike Rose and Hugh Wake.

Left:

Snotties picnic, Navarino Bay, Admiral Layton is sitting on a biscuit tin cooking the eats.

Below:

Imperial from a sketch in the author's Midshipman's Journal.

Right:
Rupert Bray and myself on the range Malta, 1938. We were both members of the winning rifle team.

Left:
Peter Harvey, Rupert Bray, Basil Hearn, JJ ashore in Crete.

Above: 1940, H.M.S .Verity leaving Harwich, the bow wave and the wave painted on the stern were intended to give the enemy a false idea of speed.

Below: Sub Lieutenant J coming onboard in Harwich.

Verity, looking aft at 'A' and 'B' 4.7 inch guns. The canvas curtain hanging down from 'A' gun was supposed to keep the gun's crew dry! In the centre is the steam capstan. Looking up at the bridge, much of it was painted canvas and the splinter mats hung round gave some protection to the wheel house crew. The glass windscreens were added once we had arrived in the Atlantic and made a huge difference for the bridge crew.

Above: H.M.S. Dauntless (4950 tons). On arrival in Mombassa we repainted the ship in a rather bizarre camouflage pattern designed by Peter Scott consisting of large areas of dusty pink and pale green known by the ship's company as 'elephant's breath'.

Below: Riding Party - Cape 1942: l to r Bardie Douglas-Hamilton, JJ, Kitchie Floyd, Bob Shiers, Eleanor Floyd, Diana Douglas-Hamilton.

tise dancing to the Gunroom gramophone in *Alcantara*'s ballroom. I think I might have succeeded had I had some lessons!

On the 25th we heard that an AMC had been sunk in the Iceland Faeroes gap. This was the P&O ship *Rawlpindi*, whose Captain, the author Ludovic Kennedy's father, had put up a heroic fight against German warships in protection of the convoy she was escorting. She fought to the last and Captain Kennedy was awarded a posthumous VC. All the Ship's Company were lost but the convoy scattered and escaped. We all agreed that we wouldn't fancy *Alcantara's* chances in similar circumstances.

On the 28th we were off to sea again, this time escorted by *Dainty* and *Diana* and bound for Port Said. However on the 30th we were diverted to Alexandria to fuel. That same day Russia invaded Finland. The Ship's Company was granted leave until 2100 and I went ashore for a last look round. That night we sailed for Gibraltar, changing our destroyer escort off Malta, and arrived in Gibraltar on 5th December with *Duchess* and *Duncan*. There were over 60 merchant ships in the bay, French and British destroyers and some French submarines. We landed awnings and awning stanchions and various bits of unnecessary equipment from the upper deck. Leave was granted until 2300 and the following morning, having fuelled, we sailed for the Clyde with *Duncan* and *Duchess* as screen. Everyone was very excited at going home for Christmas. In pre-war days a foreign commission was for two and a half years and no provision was made for families.

We entered the approaches to the Clyde on 9th December. I had the First Watch in the starboard searchlight director and, quite soon after I took over, *Barham* made a turn to starboard and I was suddenly aware of violent vibrations. The ship's engines were going full astern and I heard a lot of shouting. Down our starboard side came what appeared to be a barge or lighter with men running about on the deck. Then the horror of the situation struck. It was *Duchess*. Somehow she had lost her position on the screen and got across our bows. She had been, literally, rolled over. The men who were running about on the upturned ship had been on watch and had run down the side as the ship rolled over. Others were thrown into the bitterly cold water but over three-quarters of the Ship's Company were trapped below, either in mess decks or engine rooms. People were trying desperately to squeeze themselves through scuttles in the ship's side but they were not big enough and all you could see were arms and heads sticking out. We lowered the sea boats and put scrambling nets over the side. Rupert Bray dived in fully dressed and rescued two men, for which he was awarded the Albert Medal for Bravery, equivalent now to the George Medal. Despite all the efforts only 14 men were saved. 130 men drowned as *Duchess* sank.* I suppose the whole event occupied about ten to fifteen minutes but it seemed like a lifetime. What a home coming!

In the Clyde the following day my group of Midshipmen were transferred with all our kit to the Aircraft Carrier *Furious* for our examinations, or Fleet Board as it was called, for the rank of Lieutenant. This took several days and then home on leave as Acting Sub-Lieutenants. Of the twelve of us who left *Barham* after almost two years together, five were killed during the war so I count myself lucky. Of the seven who survived, one, Teddy Gueritz, made Vice-Admiral, Keppel Edge-Partington and I both made Captain and Rupert Bray left the Navy and made himself a millionaire. I have lost touch with the other three, but here ends my Midshipman's story.

*As a result of *Duchess*'s sinking with her people trapped below, all ships were fitted with escape scuttles in the ship's side. *Barham* was sunk in the Mediterranean in 1942 by an Italian submarine with the loss of nearly all hands.

CHAPTER 3

H.M.S. *Verity*
April 1940 – October 1941

Having made the giant step from Midshipman to Acting Sub-Lieutenant all my batch were sent to Portsmouth to complete a shortened form of courses for the rank of Lieutenant in Gunnery, Torpedoes, Asdic (later to become known as Sonar), Communications and Navigation during the first three months of 1940, the so-called phoney war period. The armies were facing each other across the Maginot and Siegfried lines. War in the air consisted largely of scattering leaflets, the Finns were being forced back by the Russians and the war at sea went slowly on until suddenly in February 1940 Germany launched a new weapon, the magnetic mine. This was laid mostly from aircraft in shallow water and was the cause of a number of ships being lost. Luckily for us one of the mines fell on dry land and was defused and analysed. This resulted in a massive programme of degaussing or demagnetisation of ships and in March a large number of electrical boffins were called up and gathered in to HMS *Vernon*, the Navy's underwater warfare school.

I happened to be doing my course in *Vernon* at the time and can well remember being one of the team roped in to show them where to go. About 200 arrived one night from various universities, all but two highly qualified. The two who were not had somehow been wrongly categorized and turned out to be two tram drivers from Glasgow who were duly sent back the following day. Otherwise it was a quiet life, instruction by day and a few duties such as ARP at night.

At the beginning of April the balloon went up. Germany invaded Denmark and Norway, our courses came to an end and I was appointed to HMS *Versatile*, an old destroyer of the V and W class built in 1918, one of the 60 such ships which for the previous 10 years had been the backbone of the Reserve fleet. They were little ships of just over 1,000 tons, armed with four 4-inch guns, six torpedoes and a complement of 130. *Versatile* was in the dockyard at Sheerness. I can remember very little about her except that, as all the modern ships were with the Home Fleet fighting in North Norway, we were rushed across to Holland with the rest of our Flotilla, when the Germans invaded Holland at the beginning of May, to evacuate the Dutch Queen Wilhelmina. Our activities were quickly cut short after being strafed by a Heinkel 111 which resulted in a lot of bullet holes down the starboard side of the ship but by some miracle no one was killed. However, the damage to the ship meant that we had to return to Sheerness for repairs.

The blitzkrieg was in full swing, with the German Army going on through Belgium and round the end of the Maginot line and the British Expeditionary Force falling back towards the north coast of France. Having been in *Versatile* for about three weeks I was ordered to join *Verity*, another V and W but with 4.7-inch guns. She was at Portsmouth and my job was to be the Gunnery Control Officer at sea and to run the Ship's Office in harbour. The Sub-Lieutenant that I was relieving showed me the office and said that there was no typewriter in the ship so, if I didn't wish to copy everything out in longhand five times, I had better go and buy one as he was taking his with him. I immediately rushed ashore to Messrs Geives on the Hard at Portsmouth and bought an Imperial portable on the never-never. It was to serve me loyally for the next 40 years though it never learnt to spell.

Things were happening with frightening rapidity and *Verity*, with others, was sent to evacuate the Guards Brigade from Calais, going alongside the mole to embark as many troops as possible. The Germans were in the outskirts of Calais and we were firing our guns at what we thought were the enemy in this very confused situation. We were again lucky not to suffer any real casualties, though after disembarking our load of soldiers at Dover it was discovered that we had an unexploded shell lodged in the boiler tubes of B boiler – we had three boilers A, B and C in two boiler rooms. Both boilers in that boiler room were immediately shut down and we were sent back to Portsmouth to have it removed. In doing so we missed the evacuation of Dunkirk, which I for one didn't regret. The shell turned out to be an 88-mm armour-piercing shell which had been decelerated by the nest of boiler tubes, without going off, but the bent tubes had to be removed and replaced.

This gave us time to take stock. *Verity*, like many of the ships taking part in the evacuation, had acquired a considerable amount of booty. I should explain that these old ships had no anti-aircraft protection save for a Lewis gun either side of the bridge, the 4.7 inch guns elevated to about 30 degrees and that was it. So it was with glee that we amassed the Bren guns left behind by the soldiery and, despite orders to return them, we hung on to about ten which we mounted round the ship. I also acquired an adding machine. The Pay Corps Sergeant who had brought it on board said that he had carried the thing for sixty miles and that now it was safe he didn't want to see the f***ing thing again. Our Yeoman of Signals, Leading Signalman Durie, had acquired a very smart Major General's greatcoat, complete with insignia, which had been left behind and which he always wore on the bridge, so much so that he was known by everyone, from the Captain down, as the General.

What we really wanted was a proper anti-aircraft gun. The policy for our sort of ship was to remove one of the sets of torpedo tubes and in its place mount a 12-pounder (about 3-inch) gun. There were several in Portsmouth Dockyard sitting on railway trucks waiting to be fitted, each gun with the name of its intended ship painted on but none with *Verity*. The Captain told me to get a gun, so, armed with some pots of paint, we crept out at night and painted out the name of *Wren* and painted on *Verity*. The next morning the Captain went to see the Manager of the Dockyard to complain that *Verity*'s gun had been lying about in the dockyard and why wasn't anyone fitting it. The very next day work started and it was put on board. I think that we all felt some slight sense of guilt when six weeks later *Wren* was sunk by dive bombers off Harwich, but then again it might have been us. All is fair in Love and War!

Another significant happening during our brief stay in the dockyard was the fitting of Radar or RDF (Radio Direction Finding) as it was then known. Being the latest out of school I was told that Radar Officer would be added to my list of jobs. The set, called a Type 86, had been fitted experimentally in Sunderland Flying Boats and it had been decided to try it out in a destroyer. One of the Navy's top radio boffins, a Commander Cecil, brought it on board and, with the aid of a couple of helpers, put it up. The aerial consisted of a wooden cage with some dipoles on it which was, literally, tied to the top of the mast with spunyarn. The set itself, about the size of a small suitcase, was installed in the Captain's sea cabin over the foot of his bunk. I should explain that in harbour the Captain had a relatively palatial cabin aft but at sea he was not expected to leave the bridge, hence the sea cabin which was a slot of a compartment immediately below the bridge measuring about eight feet by four, so it was pretty bad luck on the Captain, trying to get some rest, to have one or sometimes two radar operators peering into a cathode ray tube over the end of his bunk.

Meanwhile I had to learn about the set and how to keep it running. To do this Commander Cecil took me up to the laboratories situated in the Signal School in Portsmouth Royal Naval Barracks. The set worked on the principle of two fixed beams being transmitted at about 20 degrees either side of the bow. Alternative transmissions were achieved by a beam-switch motor which made a great noise and frequently had to be replaced. To search for a target it was necessary to steer a zigzag course; a contact would show as a blip on either the starboard or port side of a vertical line down the centre of the tube, depending on which side of the bow it was on. To find the exact bearing it was necessary to point the ship until you achieved a blip of equal size on either side of the median line on the tube, but after a bit of practice one could give a fair estimate of the bearing by interpolation without turning the ship. *Verity* was the first destroyer in the war to be fitted with radar and to operate it we had six undergraduates from Oxford who had been reading physics.

While we were in the Solent testing out the new equipment, we received a signal from C-in-C Portsmouth to go immediately out into the English Channel, find the French Channel Fleet and, having found them, tell them to come to Portsmouth. It was a dull drizzly day with very poor visibility. We set off in the general direction of Cherbourg when, after about an hour, we obtained a radar contact which, on closing, turned out to be the French battleship *Courbet*, a couple of cruisers and some destroyers.

The Captain mustered his best French and we signalled to them by light, 'Suivez moi a Portsmouth'. The reply was negative. We signalled to C-in-C that they wouldn't come and were ordered to return to the vicinity of the Nab Tower, pick up the French Naval Attaché and try again. Having found the squadron again the French NA seized the 10-inch signal lamp and flashed, 'Suivez moi au Portsmouth', and without any more ado they turned and followed us in.

What followed is perhaps worth recording, for, having secured alongside, it must have been judged by intelligence that the loyalty of the French ships' companies was in question and the Commodore of the Barracks, H T C Walker, my Captain in *Barham*, was ordered to board all the ships and take them over. Armed parties boarded the ships at about two in the morning, much to the indignation of the French, but perhaps it was a wise precaution as a great many of the crews did not wish to fight on and were shipped back to France. The *Courbet* was too ancient to play an active part in the war and was finally sunk off Arromanches in 1944 to form part of the outer breakwater for the Mulberry harbour.

The next thing was to put us to work and we were sent round to Harwich to join the rest of our Flotilla (9 ships) of V and W's known as the Harwich Striking Force. The Germans' next step was to be the invasion of England; our task, in common with many others, was to stop such a thing happening. Unlike today, when most goods are transported by lorry, all heavy loads went by sea and the power stations situated around our coast depended entirely upon the arrival of the colliers. Daily coastal convoys were of vital importance and the Germans did their best to disrupt them by air and E-boat (Motor Torpedo Boat) attack. The major danger area was from Yarmouth down to the Thames estuary, further north being out of normal operating range; south of the Thames estuary was somebody else's problem. The air attacks came from airfields in Holland and Belgium and the E-boats mainly from Ijmuiden in Holland.

Initially the convoys sailed through our area by day but this soon proved too costly. *Wren* was sunk by dive bombers while trying to defend her charges and a number of ships were sunk or damaged. Even with our 12-pounder and Bren guns we could scarcely defend ourselves, let alone offer any protection to ships in the convoy, whose best protection was from the barrage balloons flown from specially fitted trawlers. One of the destroyers in our flotilla, *Whitshead*, developed a fairly novel and effective defence against air attack known as the *Whitshead* whirling spray. What to do if attacked was to elevate the guns to their maximum of 30 degrees, train them on the starboard beam, ring on full-speed and put the wheel hard over to starboard. This meant that you went round in a circle with the ship listing about 15 degrees to port, so increasing the effective elevation of the guns to about 45 degrees. You banged off the guns as fast as you could with shells fused to go off at about 1,500 feet. It could never shoot down an aircraft but it confused the enemy, boosted morale and no one got hit.

However, after a short time the convoys were re-scheduled so as to pass through the danger area at night but, remember, from Yarmouth to the mouth of the Thames is about 100 miles and the speed of the convoys only six knots. It was a testing time for everyone; the task of our flotilla was to sail at dusk every evening, either to reinforce the convoy escort or to carry out offensive sweeps towards the Dutch coast. On a good day our radar could pick up an aircraft at about 12 miles and a ship at about six, though E-boats, being pretty small targets, could only be detected at about 3 miles if it was calm and not at all if it was rough.

As we were the only ship at Harwich to have radar we always had to go in front. The drill was to go to action stations on clearing the harbour and remain at a relaxed state of action stations, called 2nd degree of readiness, until the ship returned to harbour the following morning. We then cleaned ship, stored and fuelled before noon, after which everyone tried to get some sleep before sailing again the following evening. We had several encounters with the enemy but without result, our gunnery system being far too primitive to have a chance at night. We were the first ship in the Royal Navy to open fire on the enemy on a radar range and bearing but sadly not the first to hit anything.

With the Battle of Britain going on in the air, the massing of German troops and barges in the Channel ports, the surrender of France, the invasion of Lithuania, Latvia and Estonia by the Russians, and air raids on London, we were faced with the grim realization that Britain, though still supported by its Empire, was entirely alone and in the front line. There was a lot of discussion in the wardrooms of the Fleet, and I don't doubt elsewhere, on what should be done if the Germans were successful in invading Britain. Should the ships sail for Canada to continue the war, would the ships' companies be ready and willing to go, to abandon their families and loved ones? In *Verity*, the married men were for staying behind, while the others thought that they would probably go and continue the war from Canada.

Morale was low and loyalties were in question and I suppose that it was for this reason that, towards the end of September, as many of the ships' companies as possible were gathered together on the quayside at Parkstone to hear Winston Churchill make one of his great 'fight on' speeches. He stood on a flat goods truck with everyone gathered around. I remember being rather disappointed on seeing the great man in the flesh. He was such a hunched little man, fat and heavy jowled and his navy blue pea jacket covered either with scurf or cigar ash. Nevertheless it was a great shot in the arm.

But life was not all doom and gloom. These old ships had to have their boilers cleaned after every so many hours of steaming otherwise they got clogged up. Cleaning boilers took about three days and so boiler cleaning leave to the non-duty watch was looked forward to eagerly. From Harwich it was possible to get up to London and do a few nightclubs. On one occasion I remember making a very extraordinary trip to North Devon in crowded trains running to no fixed timetable and with no ticket except my identity card, which seemed to be good enough. Perhaps it was to be the last chance before an invasion, or so we feared.

Another little luxury one was able to indulge in from time to time was a hot bath, though not on board the ship. On board any hot water that was available had to be collected in cans from the galley. For the Ship's Company living forward, the water came from the Ship's Company forward galley, and for the officers, who lived aft, it came from the wardroom galley. Both galleys were on the upper deck and coal-fired. In theory officers could have a bath as, from the deckhead of each cabin, a circular tin basin, about 3 foot diameter and 6 inches deep, was suspended by three hooks.. The theory was that having got your water from the galley you filled your bath and squatted in it but invariably while you were doing this another ship or launch would come past, making a wash and causing the ship to roll. Your precious water then slopped out of the bath all over the cabin floor. The answer to this was to take your gas mask out of its haversack, replace it with towel, soap and razor and go to the railway hotel on Parkstone Quay where, for two shillings and six pence, you could have as much hot water as you liked.

Our Flotilla Leader was *Malcolm*, a ship of the same vintage but slightly larger to accommodate Captain (D) and his staff. In September a new Captain (D) joined in the shape of my Godfather, Captain Augustus Agar VC, his VC won in Motor Torpedo Boats in the Baltic in 1919 during the Russian revolution. He was quite a fire-eater and we were bidden to draw up plans for blocking Zeebrugge and bombarding Dunkirk. The object was to destroy landing barges or if possible block them in but, I think with hindsight, luckily for us none of these came to fruition and we pursued our routine of nightly patrols.

Quite clearly we were not the right ships for the job. New ships were being built, in particular the Hunt Class destroyer designed especially for short sea escort work, fitted with a proper anti-aircraft armament and modern gunnery control equipment. As they came on the scene so the V and Ws were released for other duties and about mid-October we were relieved by a Type I Hunt. Saying goodbye to the few V and Ws remaining, the 'Smokie Joe' minesweepers who daily cleared the channel (coal burning ships from World War I, hence the nickname) and the variety of the other craft from motor yachts to paddle steamers (all of which had been pressed into service), we sailed north about to Londonderry where we joined the Sixth Escort Group to play our part in escorting Atlantic Convoys.

Our Escort Group consisted of six ships: *Veteran* the group leader and ourselves; two S class destroyers, *Scimitar* and *Skate*, both smaller and more primitive than ourselves, being only 900 tons and armed with three 4-inch guns, one forward and two aft; and two of the new Flower class Corvettes, simple seaworthy ships especially designed to be built in merchant-ship-building yards for Atlantic convoy duties. Londonderry was a delightful place and a great change from Harwich. Almost 20 miles from the sea up the River Foyle and remote from the German Air Force, it was a real haven. In those early days it played host to about three escort groups and a number of armed trawlers, including a Canadian Navy one, *Man of War*, which seemed to have a bottomless supply of Canadian Club whisky and ginger ale. The Naval Officer in Charge was a colourful character called Jacky Slaughter. He ran the place with the aid of two glamorous Wrens, Pam and Prue.

Atlantic Convoys were another story. There were two sorts, fast and slow. Fast convoys were 8-knot convoys, slow were 6-knot. Merchant ships making up a convoy would sail in groups or feeder convoys from such ports as Cardiff, Liverpool, Belfast and Glasgow so as to come together just North of Ratlin Island to form a convoy of between forty and sixty ships in the case of the slow convoys and about twenty for the fast ones. The actual formation was that of a number of ships in line abreast each leading a column of about eight ships. The ships in the slow convoys were usually vessels of between 6,000 and 8,000 tons, while the ships in the fast ones were vessels of up to 12,000 tons and included tankers. The really fast ships such as liners were sailed and routed independently. Each convoy had a Convoy Commodore, either a retired naval or Merchant Navy officer, who sailed in one of the better-equipped ships with a small team of signalmen. His job was to manoeuvre the convoy while the escorting warships tried to protect it from attacks by submarine or aircraft and acted like sheepdogs to try and keep the convoy together.

Turning a convoy to a new course was a slow and cumbersome business taking several hours.

Far the biggest worry to us was not the Germans but the weather. Winter in the North Atlantic seemed to be a long succession of gales and outward-bound convoys, especially the slow ones heading into a westerly gale, sometimes made no forward progress at all. Generally speaking these were in ballast, that is to say empty, and as they rolled and pitched the propellers would come out of the water and thrash like a paddle steamer. None of the ships had radar so that keeping in station was entirely visual and sometimes just by ear. You knew that when you heard the propeller of the ship ahead you were getting too darned close. It was usual after a dark night for the escorts to spend the forenoon trying to get the convoy back into some sort of order.

Life aboard *Verity* and her sister ships was pretty rugged; as the ship rolled and pitched, the riveted seams of the deck would work and water dripped into the forward messdecks. Some warmth was achieved forward through a steam pipe which ran along the deckhead, while aft in the Wardroom we had a coal burning bogie stove with a 'Charlie Noble' sticking up on X gun deck. The stove was situated immediately above the hatch to the after magazine and this led to some argument between the magazine crew and the wardroom as to how and whether it should be put out at action stations. In the event it seldom was!

These little ships had a very limited radius of action, just about enough to escort a convoy out to about 15 degrees West – about 400 miles – pick up an incoming convoy and escort it home. From our point of view this was a blessing as these ships had no refrigerators and very limited storage. Fresh provisions lasted about three or four days, depending on how many people felt sea-sick and after that it was corned beef and biscuits for the staple diet. There were four watchkeeping officers: Adams the First Lieutenant, Clive-Powell the Navigator, myself and the Gunner. We also had one RNVR Sub-Lieutenant West for training. The Engineer Officer, Mr. Boddie, and the Surgeon Lieutenant called Byrne, who also acted as Cypher Officer, made up our team.

On watch the bridge was a fairly small affair, about 23 foot square, with a chart table stuck in one corner. We were protected from the elements by a canvas screen attached to railings which came up to about waist height, outside which were hung splinter mats. At the back of the bridge was a small 6-foot range finder and a Director Sight for the four guns. The idea was that two senior Gunnery Ratings, the Director Layer and Director Trainer, would aim at the target and if the electrics were working correctly the layers and trainers at each gun position would merely have to follow pointers on a dial and all the guns would point in the same direction.

My job at Action Stations was to control this lot by means of a voice pipe and in this I was assisted by a Rate Officer, a Leading Seaman, whose job it was to pass estimated courses and speeds of the enemy, together with the range or distance, down another voice pipe to the Transmitting Station (TS) situated on the foc's'le deck level of the bridge structure. Here a couple more ratings, with the aid of a clockwork gadget called a Vickers clock and another gadget called a Dumresq which, if worked correctly, would tell the guns what predicted range and deflection to set in order to hit a moving target. That is to say that it would predict where the target might be, allowing for the time it takes for the shell to reach the target, perhaps as much as 45 seconds depending on the range.

Immediately below the bridge were the wheelhouse, Captain's sea cabin and the Charthouse, and on wings either side was the flag deck. In daylight all orders between ships were passed by flag hoists. In the centre of the bridge itself were the gyro and magnetic compasses, with 10-inch signal lamps and Aldis lamps on either side. At the back of the bridge were a bucket to be sick into and a small brass urinal to pee into, known as a pig's ear. All communications to and from the bridge were by voice pipe. About the only other electrical gadget on the bridge was the loudspeaker from the sonar so that you could monitor the pings and hear and assess the echoes.

Our Captain, Commander Ronnie Mills, had had his previous ship, the anti-aircraft sloop *Bittern*, sunk under him by German aircraft at Narvik, with considerable loss of life. In consequence he suffered from terrible nightmares and from time to time would shoot up on to the bridge shouting 'Action Stations, why aren't we at Action Stations? They are bombing us,' and so on – really very alarming – and it took quite a lot to calm him down but in all other respects he was a very able and experienced chap.

It was a cold, wet life. We looked in envy at the Corvettes and trawlers whose sturdy and seakindly hull shape took them over the waves, while we and, more especially, Skate and Scimitar went underneath them. When coming from the wardroom to the bridge along the upper deck you had to pick your moment and cling firmly to the lifelines which ran down each side of the upper deck. Perhaps the two most important things that kept people going was the daily tot of rum to the Ship's Company and pusser's cocoa or 'Ki'. Not the insipid stuff out of a packet but great big bars of chocolate with all the natural oils which would be brewed up in a huge pan in the galley. This with tinned milk and brown demerara sugar was nectar. Your spoon could stand upright in a good brew.

Christmas 1940 was spent in Derry with plenty of Christmas spirit at the Northern Counties hotel, reputedly a hotbed of German espionage. Anything remotely confidential said in the Northern Counties was across the border and radioed back to Germany within two hours, or so it was reckoned. The Wardroom was invited to lunch in the local Army garrison mess and afterwards we were given rides in Bren gun carriers. The one that I was in set off at a great pace across country and it wasn't until we noticed that the policemen were wearing funny uniforms that we realized that we had crossed the border and hastily beat a retreat for home before causing an international incident.

Over Christmas, *Verity* was lying alongside *Broke*, the leader of another escort group, and in which a friend of mine, the ornithologist Peter Scott, was serving as a RNVR Lieutenant. I had met him first at Instow where he had a girlfriend, Jane Howard, whom he later married. He invited me to have a look at his cabin. It was quite something as he had whiled away the time off watch by painting duck and wildfowl all over the deckhead, or ceiling, and anywhere else that there was room.

Many convoys had been attacked by submarine during the winter of 1940 but none of ours, though there were a good many alarms and excursions which all proved spurious. We continued to battle with wind and weather and everyone would heave a sigh of relief when, on the homeward leg, Inishtrahull Light was sighted and we turned into the sheltered waters of Lough Foyle to fuel from the tanker at Moville before making the long winding trip up to Derry, with green fields on either side and cows grazing just a stone's throw away. No one was more pleased than our Chief Engineer. Poor old Chief was chronically seasick the whole time that we were at sea but doggedly refused to be invalided ashore.

However, our fortunes were to change but not for the better. One night in February *Broke* and *Verity* were sent to escort an inward-bound 8-knot convoy of some 20 ships. *Broke* was stationed ahead and zigzagging across the front of the convoy, while *Verity* was doing the same thing across the rear. The practice was to patrol at about 12 knots going back and forth, so with an 8-knot speed of advance you could do a pretty broad zigzag. I had been on watch during the middle watch (midnight to 0400) and had been turned in for only a short while when I was woken by a loud bang and the ship taking a great lurch. Looking dozily through the entrance to my cabin I saw Chief leaping up the ladder and was just thinking 'poor chap going to be sick again' when No.1, whose cabin was next to mine, shouted 'Get up on deck. We're sinking!'

One never fully undressed at sea so, leaping into my sea boots and duffel coat, I too dashed up on deck. The ship had a list to port and the cabin flat already had a foot of water. On deck I could see the bows of another ship off our port side; the sea was lapping the upper deck and a depth charge in the port thrower was burning with a brilliant flame. We kept well clear in case it exploded. What had happened was that Peter Scott, who was officer of the watch in *Broke*, had failed to notice a gyro failure or had dozed off and his ship had come right through the convoy, striking us amidships and then grinding on down the port side, where the friction between *Broke* and the depth charge had set it alight.

The engine room, engineers' store and gearing room were flooded, together with the Captain's cabin. We still had both boiler rooms and one generator. Luckily there had been no loss of life and the night was calm. All watertight doors were closed and we took stock of the situation. The ship was lolling to port and the sea covered the port side of the upper deck to amidships. It looked as if we could float, only just, but of course we couldn't move. What we had to do next was to stop the situation from getting any worse.

The first big thing was to lighten the ship and everything on the upper deck that could go over the side, went. That included the depth charges, torpedoes and ready-use ammunition. This brought the ship up to a point where the water was just about lapping the port gunwhale and enabled us to rig collision mats – huge canvas mats with one side covered in hemp thrums – and anything else that could be used, such as lashed up hammocks. Having done this we were able to pump out enough water to give us about 6 inches of freeboard while we waited for a tow.

Meanwhile *Broke*, with badly damaged bow, was making her way stern-first towards home. We were a sitting duck for about thirty-six hours before one of the rescue tugs came to take us in tow for Belfast and repairs, which were to take about a month. While we were in Harland and Wolf's yard, the opportunity was taken to give leave to the Ship's Company and also to fit a much improved Radar, Type 286. No longer would the operators be crouched over the foot of the Captain's bunk. The set was fitted in the TS and had a sort of motor-car steering-wheel and Bowden drive to the aerial at the top of the mast which allowed it to be rotated through 360 degrees instead of just looking ahead. It also had a much better ability to detect ships and aircraft.

I was glad of my week's leave and took home with me four tyres for my father's car, unobtainable in the UK but which I had been able to get from the Irish republic. I defy anyone to think of anything more awkward than four tyres to take on a wartime train to Devon but we made it. We enjoyed our time in Belfast and the local hospitality. While there I celebrated my 21st birthday and the arrival of my second stripe. I was now a Lieutenant and my pay shot up from 7s.6d to 12s.6d a day and I felt rich.

Having completed our repairs and mini refit – which included fitting glass panels around the top of the canvas dodger round the front of the bridge so that we were now protected from the elements – we stored, ammunitioned and rejoined our escort group. We were in for a rude shock. When we were about 12 degrees West with a convoy, the destroyers on the screen were detached and ordered to carry out a search for the German battle cruisers, *Gneisenau* and *Scharnhorst*, which had broken out into the Atlantic. We all wondered how long we should last if we found them. Estimates varied from 30 seconds to a minute. The visibility was poor with a lot of fog about and they both arrived at Brest undetected on 22nd March, having achieved their aim of creating a diversion so that the raider, *Admiral Scheer*, could slip through the Denmark Straits and return to Germany after several months in the Atlantic.

Since we had been away, our escort group had increased in size by the addition of one of the fifty 4-stack destroyers supplied by the Americans under 'Lease-Lend' and several more Corvettes. Also, we were no longer based at Derry but in the Gladstone Dock at Liverpool, quite a different kettle of fish. Better in some ways, especially for leave, but very much more business-like. The war in the Atlantic was hotting up. The German U-boat building programme, which in 1941 was for 230, was in full swing. From their bases at St Nazaire, Brest and La Rochelle, submarines were sailing in groups or wolf-packs to attack our convoys at night on the surface, the positions of convoys being detected by either patrolling submarines or long range aircraft. Focke Wulf Condors made daily flights from bases near Bordeaux to North Norway.

To counter this, ships needed to be practised in operating together. There was no time to do this at sea, neither could the ships be spared. Instead the Western Approaches Tactical School was set up under Captain EBK Stevens, in the Liver Buildings which housed the Naval Headquarters known as *HMS Eaglet*. Margot Hamilton, a friend of mine from Bideford, was one of the Wrens attached to the tactical school, all specially picked.

Each ship of an escort group would send its Command team – Captain, OOW, sonar team, signalmen and so forth – to play out real life situations on the tactical floor. Each ship manned its own cubicle into which was fed all the pertinent information – convoy formation, your station on the screen, general situation, what you would be able to see or hear, signals received and sent, in fact all the things that would happen in a real situation. RAF Coastal Command Sunderland and Hudson pilots were also there as was the Convoy Commodore and his team. You were required to react and make whatever moves were necessary. At the end the lights would go up revealing the tracks of all the ships drawn out on the floor, plus those of the enemy submarines operated by the staff, and all would gather round for the critique to see what sort of a mess you had made of it and what should have been done; it was a quick and excellent way of learning and where new tactics could be developed. On the dockside were mobile Sonar Attack Teachers, where the Captain, with his sonar team, could practise handling his ship and carry out attacks on U-boats, all in real time and in realistic simulated conditions.

Another leap ahead was in the matter of communications. Until now it had been flags, semaphore or flashing lights. You could not use radio, which was either long- or medium-wave, because enemy direction finders would quickly plot your position, the only exception being when making an enemy contact report.

Captain Walter Couchman, whose parents lived in Loventor at Instow, was one of the Escort Group Commanders in *Veteran*. He was so fed up with the situation that he personally went out and, for each of his ships, bought VHF radio telephone sets of a type similar to those used in our fighters. This transformed their operational efficiency and Admiral Max Horton, who was C-in-C Western Approaches, was quick to insist that all his ships were so fitted, including our group. The seven miles of Liverpool docks was a busy sight with ships loading and unloading vital cargoes. Some of the liners and bigger merchant ships would also dock in the Gladstone dry dock, one of the biggest in the world. I remember once having a slap-up lunch aboard one of the Blue Funnel ships there, *Ixion*, Commanded by Captain Dark, whose father had taken me several times from Instow to Lundy Island in Lerina when I was a boy. (Ixion was sunk in May 1941 by U-94; Dark and most of his crew were rescued).

My job of running the ship's office included paying the Ship's Company once a fortnight. To collect the money, I used to take the Overhead Railway which ran along the length of the docks to the Liver Building. There I would go to the Pay Office, collect the cash, stuff it into my pocket and go back to the ship with no thought of being robbed. How different from today when every sort of security measure has to be taken. Admittedly it was only in the region of £500 but then you could buy quite a good house for that.

Back at sea the U-boats were making their attacks further out into the Atlantic and at the same time the United States, though not yet at war, were safeguarding convoys from North America and patrolling their side of the Atlantic out to about 40 degrees West. To close the gap from where the British escorts left off and the Americans and, of course, Canadians began, it was necessary to extend our operational range by putting into Iceland to fuel. A base with boom defence and fuelling facilities was set up in Hvalfjord whilst, ashore, Coastal Command Hudsons were based on the airfield near Reykjavik.

The British had occupied Iceland much to the anger of the Icelanders and, though the situation was to improve later in the war, in 1941 any Icelandic girl seen fraternizing with a British serviceman was liable to have her hair shaved off. On the couple of occasions that I had to go ashore in Reykjavik, the capital, people on the street would stop and turn their backs to me as I walked by. Not a nice feeling. However, by refuelling in Iceland we could extend our radius of action to about 35 degrees west, a big improvement.

In early April our group, having taken over a convoy out of Halifax, Nova Scotia, were attacked by about 4 U-boats who had closed the convoy under the cover of fog and darkness to attack us around midnight. Some six merchant ships were hit by torpedoes and several were burning fiercely. We got a contact on radar and on firing a star shell saw a U-boat about 2,000 yards away in the process of diving. We opened fire but, as luck would have it, the shock from the guns going off tripped the breaker on the main switchboard so, without electrical power, we were unable to make sonar contact. All we could do was to drop depth charges in the vicinity of where she dived.

The Captain was justifiably furious at having missed our big chance. However, one submarine was sunk by the destroyer *Harvester*, who picked up the survivors. We were ordered to stand by one of the merchant ships that was sinking and later picked up her crew and put them on board another ship. Later the U-boat crew were transferred to *Verity* to take back to Liverpool and POW Camp. The officers were bunked down in the Wardroom and were quite an amusing bunch. One was an artist by profession and made sketches of all of us during the passage.

It was on another one of these convoys some weeks later in May that I had the morning watch. It was a beautiful morning, calm with the sun just risen and all seeming at peace with the world, when the duty signalman thrust a signal into my hand which said simply '*Hood* sunk position so-and-so', a position in the Denmark Strait. It was 24th May. I immediately called the Captain who was quite grey with shock. It seemed impossible.

An amplifying signal from *Prince of Wales* told us that *Bismarck* and *Prinz Eugen* were heading South into the Atlantic shadowed by *Norfolk* and *Suffolk*. HMS *Hood*, the largest warship in the world, had gone down with almost all her 1,500 hands. Only one Midshipman and two Ratings survived, having somehow been thrown clear from the spotting top as the ship rolled over. *Bismarck* was about 100 miles to the North and coming our way. What price death or glory now?

To say that we were scared would be an understatement. We wondered if we would be ordered to go and search for her as had been the case with *Gneisenau* and *Scharnhorst* a few months earlier. However, we were ordered to remain with our convoy and in the event *Bismarck* turned westward. She was sunk three days later by ships of the Home Fleet. *Prinz Eugen* escaped the net.

Later in the summer our group was frequently put on escorting convoys southbound to Sierra Leone, not that we were able to go that far. This made a pleasant change weather-wise but one was much more in range of enemy aircraft and the Focke Wulf Condors were quite impudent in making bombing attacks, though not with any great success. They would come out of the sun and at low level so were not detected by radar until quite close. Every ship in the convoy had a gun of sorts and this was an excuse for everyone to have a go and very difficult to stop, with the result that many an unsuspecting Sunderland, Hudson or Catalina approaching a convoy after a Condor attack would invariably be fired at by the merchant ships, who cared little for aircraft recognition. Luckily they were all rotten shots.

But 'Jerry' didn't always get away with it. One morning just after breakfast the alarm bells went for Action Stations. I was in the heads so, pulling up my trousers, I rushed out on the upper deck to see a Condor coming straight for us on the port beam. I dashed forward and up the vertical ladder to the bridge, holding my trousers with one hand as they kept on coming down. When I got to the top the Captain was hopping up and down shouting, 'Why aren't the guns firing?!'

My leading seaman rate officer was already there but had been trained by me to take no notice of what the Captain shouted because he always did shout. He reported guns ready. By this time the Condor was pretty close and firing her cannons. I grabbed the voice pipe and yelled 'SHOOT!' All four 4.7s went bang and, to our surprise and delight, the port wing and engines of the Condor burst into flames and she came down in the sea. We picked up the crew, who were most indignant at their bad luck, but I am sure that it would have been a different story if I had not been in the heads when the alarm bells went. But on a question of luck, no one was luckier than the trainer of X gun, one of the after 4.7s. A cannon shell from the Condor hit the object lens of his telescope and penetrated every lens except the eyepiece itself. Back in Liverpool no one would believe our story, but we had the aircrew to prove it.

In the Gladstone dock we were often berthed alongside the ex-American 4-stacker destroyer now manned by Norwegians. She belonged to our group and we got to know their wardroom quite well. Often we would notice that one of the officers was missing and when you enquired where Bjorn or Per was, you were told that he was away on a course. It was not until after the war when I was in Norway that I learnt that these chaps had been going home to Norway on leave via what was known as the Shetland bus. I don't believe that any were caught by the Germans though there were many close calls.

The 4-stackers were even more primitive than the V and Ws and were prone to a variety of breakdowns. One of the commonest was suddenly to start going round in circles with the steering jammed. This was because the cables, which ran from a huge 5-foot diameter steering wheel on the bridge to the rudder head down aft, went along the upper deck through a series of tubes and pulleys. It only required somebody to drop a piece of rag for it to get caught up in the wire and jam the whole works. But of course every additional warship on a convoy screen added to the U-boat Captain's problems, so on balance they were a help.

Wartime Liverpool was not the jolliest of places, subject to bombing attacks and little for the sailor to do except get into trouble. For the Wardrooms the general meeting place was the Adelphi Hotel next to the station. I counted myself lucky as I had family friends at Rowsham near Chester and several times I was able to get out there and spend a day in the country, being met at the station by Mrs Heap in her pony and trap to save petrol.

There were new factors coming into the war at sea as U-boats increased their operational range and also their invisibility by the use of snorkels, which allowed them to run their diesels while under water. It became increasingly necessary to improve the operational range of our escorts and one of the solutions was to do away with the V and W's forward boiler and use the space gained for fuel tanks and better facilities. So it was that in September 1941 *Verity* was once more back in Harland and Wolf's yard in Belfast for major surgery.

Verity was not the only one requiring major surgery; I had developed a septic sinus due to a tooth being knocked out playing a rather stupid game, called Human Torpedoes, in the wardroom after a guest night. Part of the tooth had broken off in the sinus itself and I went to Belfast hospital for treatment and from there I was sent on leave to await my next appointment. Unfortunately the treatment at Belfast hadn't cured the problem, only alleviated it, and I had to go to Roehampton for further treatment.

I was there for about three weeks and the treatment, though painful, was a success. I had, as my next door neighbour in the ward, Duncan Sandys, who had been badly wounded in the foot in North Africa. Whether it was because he was Churchill's son-in-law or just his nature, he complained about everything and everybody, which annoyed me intensely as the nurses and doctors were excellent. However Diana, his wife was a sweetie and used to bring me bunches of grapes from Chartwell.

I was discharged fit and returned to Instow to wait for my next appointment. I had been hoping to go to a Hunt class destroyer as First Lieutenant and looked forward to being in a modern ship, but this was not to be.

CHAPTER 4

H.M.S. *Dauntless*
January 1942 – February 1943

After being sent on another Radar and Gunnery course I was ordered to join *Dauntless* in Portsmouth in January 1942 as Assistant Gunnery Officer and Radar Officer. The very elderly D class Cruiser, *Dauntless*, was preparing to sail to join the Far East Fleet. Commanded by Captain JG Hewitt, she was a light cruiser built in 1919 and fitted with six hand-worked 6-inch guns in single mountings. Originally she had had 12 torpedo tubes, six either side, but these had been removed to make way for three single-mounted 4-inch guns and two multiple pom poms. She was a ship of just under 5,000 tons, 473 feet overall and capable of 29 knots. Her complement was about 500 including a detachment of Royal Marines, who manned the two after 6-inch mountings, and a Royal Marine Band, who manned the very antiquated gunnery TS (Transmitting Station). There was a Heath Robinson device known as the Dreyer Table, invented by a soldier, Major General Dreyer, who used to live in Limers Lane, Northam when I was a boy and later in Instow.

The radar for which I was responsible consisted of an improved type 286 (10cm) for aircraft detection and an entirely new and much shorter-waved set, a 5-cm Radar Type 273, for surface work. This was mounted on top of a structure that looked like a lighthouse amidships and could give very accurate ranges and bearings. It was capable of picking up small objects such as buoys and, hopefully, on a calm day, a periscope. With large ships and land its range was over the horizon.

In bigger ships it was customary to have specialist seaman officers for Gunnery, Navigation and so forth, but in these ships the job was done by officers, who took a short course where necessary and for which they were paid an extra shilling a day. Our 'bob-a-day' Gunnery Officer was a RNR Lieutenant, James Hamilton, and the Navigator (another RNR) George Towell. Our Commander, Nathaniel G Leeper, had left the Navy in about 1930 as a Lieutenant Commander to go into the gin-marketing business. He had been brought back at the beginning of the war with the rank of Commander but retained a keen taste for gin! Mike Woolcombe from South Devon, a fanatical fly fisherman, was First Lieutenant, and the Captain of Marines was Bob Griffiths who now lives in Northam. Besides our technical duties we also had divisional duties. I had the Maintop and a friend of mine, Charles Alington, whose father was Headmaster of Eton, the Foretop. In all there were about 30 officers including six Midshipmen.

We sailed from Portsmouth at the end of January in company with a Greek-manned Hunt Class destroyer, *Andreas*, destined for Alexandria. We called into Gibraltar, Freetown and Pointe Noire in the Congo for fuel. During our passage we heard that Singapore, our destination, had surrendered to the Japanese. We were required to make good speed from Pointe Noire to the Cape. Neither ship had very long legs as *Dauntless* had run aground off Nova Scotia in 1928 and some of her fuel tanks, which had ruptured, were filled with concrete. But, while we had fuel to cruise at 16 knots, *Andreas* had not; her economical speed was 12 knots and if she went any faster it would be necessary to put into Walvis Bay. Remembering my Midshipman's experience of being towed from Portsmouth to Gibraltar in the water-boat *Coronation* by HMS *Barham*, I suggested to the Captain that we should have a similar ploy with Andreas. The weather was favourable and we took her in tow. She steamed at her economical speed and the tow made up the difference.

The first sight of Table Mountain was a great excitement, as was our arrival in Simonstown, the naval dockyard. Everyone looked forward to a good run ashore. The train from Simonstown to Cape Town was packed with matelots eager to sample the various delights that were on offer. No blackout, no food rationing, cheap booze and the ultimate stomach tester, Cape Brandy. James Hamilton had a cousin living in Rondebosch, so I was soon 'up homers' and enjoying the fabulous Cape hospitality. 'Bardie' Douglas-Hamilton threw her home open to us and also lent us her car and found some very nice girls just the right age; one of them was Katherine Floyd, 'Kitchie', whose mother had a riding stable; it was fun to ride out into the country.

It had been the intention to go to Ceylon to join the Eastern Fleet at Trincomalee but the Japanese carrier force under Admiral Nagumo was operating in that part of the Indian Ocean with four carriers and three hundred aircraft. We were ordered to stay in Simonstown to await the next military convoy which we were to escort up the East Coast. The cruisers *Dorsetshire* (commanded by my godfather Gus Agar) and *Cornwall* and one of our smaller carriers, *Hermes*, were sunk just to the South of Ceylon by Japanese carrier aircraft on 10th April. At that time the Mediterranean was virtually closed to allied shipping. The Germans under Rommel were driving towards Cairo and in India troops were being reinforced and deployed to hold the Japanese invasion of India from Burma. The convoys of troopships had to be escorted up as far as Aden and then, either up the Red Sea or across to Karachi or Bombay.

One of the things I remember having to do while in Simonstown was to help the navigator 'swing the ship' and I can clearly recall climbing from a boat on to a rock outside the entrance to the harbour clutching a dip instrument to get the 'angle of dip', as everything had to be recalibrated because we were now in the Southern Hemisphere.

The troopships to be escorted were mostly liners from such well-known shipping companies as Union Castle, Orient, P & O and their like, mostly between 12,000 and 20,000 tons. Our role was to keep away any surface raiders, but none came our way. Cape Town to Mombasa was fine, but Mombasa to Aden was a real killer because *Dauntless*, having been designed for service in the North Sea, had only the minimum of ventilation and it was virtually impossible to sleep down below. Heat exhaustion in the engine and boiler rooms was a common occurrence and many of the Ship's Company went down with malaria as at that time there were no preventative pills to take. At one time about 20% of the Ship's Company was out of action and our two doctors, John Cave and Bob Shiers, were kept hard at it. By the middle of April we were in Mombasa with the remainder of the Far East Fleet under the command of Admiral Sir James Somerville, a super chap with a great sense of fun. Soon after arrival he came on board to talk to the Ship's Company during which he told them that many a good tune was played on an old fiddle. However *Dauntless* was certainly no Stradivarius.

Kilindini, the fleet anchorage, was a huge natural harbour and was filled with ships, including the aircraft carriers *Indomitable* and *Illustrious*, the battleship *Ramilles* and ships from many navies, e.g. Australian, Dutch and Indian, as well as our own. Leave was normally granted until 2200 and there was great difficulty in getting all the returning liberty men into the right boats for their ships from the rather inadequate landing stage. The Naval Provost Marshall hit on the idea of putting up a series of wooden railings to guide sailors to their boats from fenced areas that looked very much like sheep pens. The experiment lasted one night only as, led by the Aussies, several thousand penned-in liberty men started baaing like sheep. The noise was deafening and could be heard for miles.

Admiral Somerville was keen to find a task for the fleet in order to restore morale after the Singapore debacle. It was feared that the Japanese might take and use Madagascar as an advanced base. Diego Suarez, the French naval base, had the largest dry dock in the area and so it was necessary for the Allies to get it first. Madagascar is a very large island, nearly 1,000 miles in length, and at the time was under the control of the French loyal to Vichy. De Gaulle's offer to help in its capture was refused by Churchill who feared another disaster on the lines of Dakar. It had, therefore, been decided to use British troops on their way to India, with the understanding that once they had secured their objective they would be free to continue on their voyage. The operation was code named 'Ironclad'.

Diego Suarez – at the north end of the island – with its huge natural harbour, naval dockyard and dry docks was the principal objective. The approaches had been mined and the entrance, which is on the eastern side of the tip of the island, was defended by shore batteries mounted in casements at the top of a tall headland. The plan, therefore, was to land our troops on the West Coast so that they could force their way across a fairly narrow isthmus, to take the naval base and its defences from the rear. Aircraft from *Illustrious* and *Indomitable* were to deal with any French naval forces and the airfield. There was a large German merchant ship, *Wartenfels*, in the big dry dock. *Dauntless* marines were to be transferred to the fast minelayer *Manxman* for the landing and we also had to embark a battalion of the King's African Rifles. This was a difficult process; none had ever seen a ship or climbed a ladder and each terrified soldier had to be helped on board by two sailors. Though we had cleared space below decks, none would leave the upper deck and slept by just pulling a blanket over their heads. I think that this particular lot were Masais, very tall and slim. Being warriors they could not be persuaded to clean or clear up their mess or empty their latrine buckets, all of which had to be done by very mutinous sailors.

On the way from Kilindini to Madagascar, *Dauntless* was given the task of capturing the French island of Mayotte, close to the Comoros Islands in the Mozambique Channel. There was a small airfield on the island which was required as an emergency landing strip by the RAF. *Dauntless* marines and a company of the KARs landed at dawn and soon had the situation under control and the airfield cleared of the obstructions left by the French to prevent its use. The PMO and his first-aid team were the only casualties. They landed after the main party, wearing their tropical white uniform. They ran into a platoon of the KARs who spoke no English and they, no Swahili. The KARs thought that they were French and tied them up and left them by the side of the road, to be discovered and released about three hours later when a search was mounted to find them.

The main force included three Assault ships and nine troop transports – thirty-four ships in all under the overall command of Major General Sturgess, Royal Marines. The landing on 5th May met with fierce resistance from French and French Colonial (Malgache) troops. To bring the fighting to a speedy end it was decided to try and capture the French Commander and his Command Post. The Marines from *Ramilles*, under the command of Captain Martin Price and Lieutenant Jimmy Powell, were embarked in the destroyer *Anthony* and so, led by minesweepers, who swept and cleared an 8-mile channel, entered harbour under cover of darkness undetected by the French coastal batteries who were being bombarded by *Ramilles*'s 15-inch guns. *Anthony* landed her marines on the quayside.

Jimmy Powell, who was eventually to replace Bob Griffiths in *Dauntless* and who later came to live at Instow, told me that what followed was a comedy of errors. They had been briefed to follow a railway line for about a mile inland which should lead them to the French Headquarters. They started out well but soon came to some points where the rail divided. Not knowing which line to take in the dark, they tossed up and set off again, only to find nothing. The company sat down under a wall for a breather and to think. To their surprise they heard French voices on the other side of the wall so, leaping over it, they found the French General and his staff who had evacuated their headquarters for fear of attack and were busily setting up a mobile Command Post. They were quickly taken prisoner and fighting in the Diego Suarez area came to a halt. It had taken three days.

Our African troops had been landed in assault boats from the assault ships and were used to capture the French Coastal Batteries. There had been a number of casualties and the Corvette *Auricula* sank after striking a mine. However, once the fighting was over the clearing up began. Part of the fleet entered harbour while the remainder returned to Mombasa. *Dauntless* was ordered to be the headquarters ship and our Captain to be Naval Officer in Charge of the port.

Soon after the French had surrendered I was invited by the Officer commanding the KARs to go and watch their victory celebrations called an N'gomo. For this they were allowed to brew their own form of native beer and revert to all their old tribal customs. All uniform had disappeared and out came shields, spears, drums, monkey skins, gourds and rattles and full war-paint, mostly red and white. It was quite a sight. Huge bonfires were lit and the dancing went on for about 24 hours non-stop. While I was there each tribe would dance up in front of the CO with each group trying to outdo the other in the ferocity of their appearance and the height of their jumping. It was really quite frightening as you felt as if you might be the next one for the pot.

It had been reported that one of our ships had gone aground in the harbour and that the chart was inaccurate. As a consequence I was told off to do a survey of quite a large section of the harbour. I had never done such a thing before so got out all the books. My start was an astronomical fix and a chain-measured base line from which we set up triangulation points. The land around Diego Suarez is most remarkable, being flattish but dotted with small extinct volcanoes and curious bottle-like trees called baobabs. Every afternoon the wind would blow at about force six and cover everything with a layer of red dust, so one used to come back on board quite red. Sitting in the top of a tree trying to take horizontal sextant angles and getting them to add up to 360 degrees was no joke either. However, we plotted the shore line and our Midshipmen were kept hard at it running lines of soundings, using the motor cutter and a hand lead and line. We eventually made a chart which was sent to the Hydrographer but in fact our chart coincided pretty well with the local French one, so I was rather pleased.

On 29th May a small seaplane overflew the anchorage and everyone was brought to a higher degree of readiness. The following evening *Ramilles* and a tanker were torpedoed by a Japanese midget submarine. The seaplane had come from the parent submarine I-10. The tanker settled upright on the bottom but *Ramilles* was able to sail for Durban on 3rd June for repairs. The midget submarine was found wrecked on the shore a little way south of the harbour entrance but there was no sign of its crew.

During our time there, we were allowed recreational leave during daylight hours and it was possible to explore the countryside a little as I was able to borrow a horse from what had been the French cavalry stables but the saddles were impossibly uncomfortable. We spent nearly six weeks in Diego Suarez during which time nearly every mess had acquired a pet lemur, friendly little monkey-like animals native to the island. Towards the end of our time there I was told to take a small armed boarding party which was to embark in a Corvette and, with an armed trawler, to go to the island of Comoro in the Mozambique Channel about 400 miles west of Diego Suarez. There I was to capture a Vichy-held Greek merchant ship of about 8,000 tons and bring her back. She had been moored out of sight in a very narrow creek close to one shore.

We took with us a Raiding Boat, or R-boat. The plan was to rendezvous at dawn off the island, embark the boarding party in the R-boat, go in and take the ship. Unfortunately the force became separated during a severe gale on the second night out and it was assumed, after a long search, that the R-boat had sunk. The Captain of the Corvette, a Lieutenant RNR, decided to take his ship through the gap in the coral reef that surrounded the island and use the ship's two boats to land the boarding party. Unfortunately when half way through the gap, the mast head lookout shouted 'reef ahead'. This was in fact incorrect but the Captain very rightly went full astern. Once stopped, however, the ship was set on to the main reef by a strong cross-wind and current and she stuck fast. There was quite a swell running and the grinding of the ship's bottom on the coral was a horrifying sound. We laid out a kedge anchor to try and pull her off but without success. Finally to our surprise the trawler and R-boat turned up and at the same time an Australian Coastal Command Hudson (a twin-engined aircraft), scheduled to support us, flew overhead, signalled 'good morning' by light and flew off. With the R-boat we were able to capture the ship and sail for Madagascar leaving the unfortunate Corvette still stuck fast with the trawler standing by. She made a useful channel mark as we steamed out past her at our maximum speed of 5 knots.

All was not plain sailing. As our boarding party clambered aboard the merchant ship on the starboard side, the French escaped down the port side and made their way ashore taking with them all the charts and the ship's compass. There they sat with machine guns trained on the ship, while on board we had ours trained on them. Neither side wanted to fire the first shot, so we left unhindered having hoisted the R-boat on board. Luckily we had a diary with a map of the world and the compass from the R-Boat. With these we made the 400 miles back to Diego Suarez. On board we had a crew of twelve Malagash seamen, ten Arab firemen and greasers with their own dragoman, two pigs, a goat, six guinea fowl and about thirty hens plus a well-stocked wine cellar, so we lived well for the next five days that it took for the passage. The ship had been built in Newcastle upon Tyne in 1912 and had not seen a lot of care. However, everyone seemed pleased to see us arrive safely. Our Corvette was towed off the reef three days later and suffered no damage other than a highly-polished bottom and a leaking Asdic dome.

At the end of our six weeks *Dauntless* went back to Kilindini where we were ordered to join another lot of troop ships and their escorts for the landing and capture of Majunga (now Mahajanga), a port some way down the west coast of Madagascar. The French had by no means surrendered the whole island, which is vast and at that time had very poor communications. At Majunga everything was over in a day. My job there was to take an armed party and secure any French shipping in the harbour but, in the event, there were only a few tugs and harbour craft and though my lot were all armed to the teeth there was no resistance. *Dauntless* was soon released to go to Durban for a few days' rest and recreation.

There was great excitement as we came into Durban past the whaling station on the port side and we also passed gangs of convicts chained together. Then we approached the port itself where, standing on the end of the breakwater on our starboard side, was a large lady with a large megaphone and an equally large voice. Perla Seedly-Gibson sang to all the warships and troop ships entering and leaving harbour and Land of Hope and Glory boomed out in a strong contralto. Once alongside, my job was to visit the local hospitality centre to see what they could offer. The organization was truly amazing. Arriving at the centre I was asked simply, 'How many men do you have?' I replied, 'six hundred'. 'Easy', said the lady in charge, 'Go back on board and find out what sort of things people would prefer, like town or country, sporty or relaxing, swimming, walking, whether you like to be by yourself or with a chum and so on. Come back in two hours' time and we will have everyone who wants fixed up and allocated to a family by this evening'. So it was; fleets of cars came down to the ship and everyone who wanted to go was whisked off and given a fabulous three days away from it all.

I went with Charles Alington to stay on a farm near Howick Falls belonging to a Miss Lila Morton, whom his father had known when he had visited Natal to study farming there before the First World War. She was a wiry little woman in her 70s and ran this large farm in the foothills of the Drakensberg mountains. Except for the paranormal we had a splendid time, fishing and riding, but meal times were a distinct strain. The table was always laid and food served to her brother and his wife, both of whom had been dead some years but who were talked to and waited on by Miss Morton and the house boy just as if they were there and alive. It was all really quite spooky. But we were sorry to leave and Miss Morton sent my parents super food parcels of sugar and tinned ham and other luxuries each Christmas during the rest of the war and for some years afterwards.

Back on board everyone agreed that they had had the time of their lives but sadly we had to say goodbye to our wonderful hosts and get back to work, while they got ready to welcome the next lot. No one who was in South Africa during the war had enough words to praise their generosity and kindness.

Then we were off to sea again with a northbound convoy which took us as far as Aden, calling in at Zanzibar for fuel. Zanzibar is a fascinating place full of scents and mysteries and one longed to know what went on behind the huge heavily-decorated wooden doors. On the way back to Kilindini we were ordered to search for and take in tow a British merchant ship, *Herisle*, that had lost her propeller. That gave us a good exercise in seamanship. Back in harbour, James Hamilton left for home and I took over the job of Gunnery Officer and duly received my shilling a day extra.

Entering and leaving harbour was always a bit of a palaver as paravanes, our protection against mines, had to be either streamed or recovered. *Dauntless*, being an old fashioned lady, was without winches on the upper deck and so this was an evolution requiring one watch of seamen, about a hundred and fifty men, to pull and haul on the guys and recovery wires. There was no room for error, for if your team was not pretty slippy the paravane would trip and run under the ship. If that happened you were in real trouble. There was great rivalry between Charles Alington's Foretopmen who had the starboard paravane and my Maintopmen who had the port one, as to which would get theirs in and stowed first and many a tot or sippers was won or lost in bets.

Another great sport was rat-hunting. The ship had a great number which lived mostly in the ventilation trunkings and made a great noise as they ran about overhead. We ran National Rat-Hunt days with prizes for whoever could produce the most corpses. But rats weren't our only problem; we had cockroaches by the score. In the wardroom we kept chameleons which ate a fair number but I found that the answer in my cabin was to keep a really big 'cocker' which ate all the little ones. If there weren't enough little ones for it to eat you could feed it on toothpaste which it seemed to love. I suppose it was the minty flavour.

It was at about this time in Kilindini that I began to notice that some of my shoes would disappear and then later reappear. The mystery was solved when I discovered that Molloy, my Royal Marine servant, had the same size feet as myself, and when he went ashore, my shoes went too. After a little bollocking we came to an amicable arrangement as, in all other respects, he was jolly good.

The whole of Madagascar had still not been secured and in September we were back again with another landing force to capture the port of Tamatave (now Toamasina), about one third of the way down the east coast. The force arrived off the port at dawn; our Captain and Brigadier Frankie Festing went ashore in our motor boat flying a huge white flag to seek a meeting with the French and arrange a surrender. As they closed the shore the French opened fire on them and they beat a hasty retreat. The ships of the force, including *Dauntless*, opened fire on the French positions and by 1100 it was all over and the port surrendered. However, fighting went on inland as our troops advanced towards Tananarive (now Antananarivo), the capital of the island and situated high in the mountains. The capital was not taken until 23rd October and all resistance finally ceased on 5th November. However, we had left long before that, taking back to Durban £7 million in gold bars.

We arrived back in Durban about the middle of October where our new Captain, Williams-Powlett joined on the 18th. We spent a fairly short time in Durban, just long enough to savour the delights of this attractive city and do a few circuits on the crowded floor of the Stardust, a highly popular nightclub before sailing for Simonstown with a convoy. On the way the ship developed condenseritis, which meant that the salt water was getting into the feed water for the boilers. This and other defects kept us in the dockyard there for about six weeks as it was decided to give us a docking and short refit. No one complained and I renewed my acquaintance with the Douglas-Hamiltons and the Floyds. Later it was decided to fumigate the ship to get rid of all our rodents and cockroaches. Everyone moved ashore and I was lucky enough to be invited to spend a few days on a fruit farm near Elgin, owned by some charming people called Deniston, who also had the attraction of having two daughters. However, all good things have to end some time and once more we were on our way with another convoy up the East coast, carrying with us memories of riding out to Seige Flei, dancing at the Candlelight and the Country Club, tennis and super teas, eating fresh peaches in the Deniston's swimming pool and Able Seaman Albert, a bulldog with a self appointed task of looking after liberty men on the train from Simonstown to Cape Town. He was a well-known character who never failed to be on the last train back to the ship.

My relief arrived from England on 24th February 1943 and I was put ashore in Mombasa to wait in the transit camp there for a ship home. As there was nothing in the offing I was asked if I would like to go on leave up-country. Naturally I was delighted and was soon on the train on my way to stay with the Masterton-Smiths who farmed near Thompson Falls (now Nyahururu), about 100 miles NNW of Nairobi. Three of us went and we had a fascinating time. Our hosts had quite a big farm and one of their problems was to stop huge herds of zebra breaking down the fences and getting into the crops. We were sent out with rifles every morning to try and drive them away.

Another task was to shoot gazelle for the pot but at the high altitude, about 7,000 feet, I found it quite impossible to hold the rifle steady enough to shoot anything.

Besides, by the time you had got close enough by crawling from behind one anthill to another so as to keep out of sight, they looked so attractive that you didn't want to shoot them anyway. Many of the farms had Italian prisoners of war and many others were employed on improving Kenya's dirt roads, a much-needed task which they did exceptionally well. Just when I was getting used to the life, a telegram arrived ordering me back to Mombasa. The town class cruiser *Sheffield* was in Kilindini on her way home and I was to join her for what turned out to be an uneventful passage back to Portsmouth.

Back in England I was told to go on leave and wait for an appointment. Instow at that time was in full swing as an amphibious training base and the estuary was full of landing-craft. To my surprise I was rung up and told to join a Flotilla of Mark 4 tank-landing-craft and to navigate them to North Africa. The Allies were preparing for the invasion of Sicily and Italy and the landing-craft were required for this. I joined on Instow beach after first reporting for my instructions to Odstock, the house on Instow front between Bath Terrace and The Commodore Hotel but in those days the Naval Headquarters. There was little room on board so I slept at home which was very convenient.

The first thing that we had to do was to go up alongside Fremington Quay, where we were loaded with lengths of railway line to act as ballast. With all this extra iron on board the compasses were all affected and I spent a couple of days swinging the ships of our Flotilla and making out new deviation tables. There were three Flotillas of landing craft due to go, each with a regular naval officer on board as navigator. The RNVRs who commanded these craft had done only a pretty basic course in coastal navigation.

The day came for us to sail and we all set off in fine style but, as we approached Outer Pulley, the landing craft in which I was embarked developed trouble in one of the engines and we stopped. The captain reported the situation and we were told to go back and pick up a head and stern mooring off Tapeley. In doing this the remaining engine failed to respond to the orders given from the bridge and we ran over the mooring, fouling a propeller and ending up against the embankment. The CO of the landing craft was furious, as was Rear Admiral Gordon Franklin, the Naval Officer in Charge. It transpired that the Petty Officer Motor Mechanic in the engine room had deliberately sabotaged the engines so that we would be unable to sail. He was later Court-Martialled and sent to jail. With that my short experience in Combined Operations and Landing craft came to an end.

I reported by phone to The Admiralty appointers that I had not gone to North Africa after all and was told that my next job would probably be First Lieutenant of a Destroyer and therefore I should go and do a Damage-Control Course. This was in London at St Paul's School, now evacuated to the country and the building taken over by the Navy. After this one-week course I came back to Instow to wait for a phone call or letter to tell me what to do next. It came on 12th July 1943. I was told to be in Plymouth by noon the following day to join *Melbreak*, a Type III Hunt class destroyer.

CHAPTER 5

H.M.S. *Melbreak*
July 1943 – January 1945

Melbreak was lying alongside the wall in Devonport Dockyard and looking a bit of a mess. Two nights previously she had been in action with some German destroyers off the French coast. The Captain had been killed, the First Lieutenant had lost both his legs and there had been a number of other casualties. The ship had been brought out of the action and back to Plymouth by a RNVR Sub-Lieutenant, Martin Jenkins, using the emergency conning position amidships. I was shown down to the wardroom where I saw another RN Lieutenant, Geoffrey Kirkby, who had been a Midshipman in *Malaya* when I was in *Barham*. We looked at each other in surprise and then Geoffrey asked 'What is your seniority?' I told him. 'Right' he said 'I'm a year senior to you so I reckon that I'm the new Captain and you are the new First Lieutenant.' And that was how it was.

The bridge structure having been hit, *Melbreak* was in no shape to go to war and the first job was to effect temporary repairs so that she could be sent for a proper refit. About a week later we were ready for sea and ordered to make our way round to the Thames and to Green and Siley Wear's Yard in the West India Docks. This pleased the Ship's Company as *Melbreak* was a Chatham ship. This of course was in the days when ships were manned from the three main Naval ports, Chatham, Portsmouth and Devonport. I had never been in a Chatham ship before. 'Chatty and Happy' was the common description implying that the Chatham ships were scruffy and ill-disciplined compared with the Pompey ships, which prided themselves on being the best and most 'pusser'. Guz ships had the reputation of being very correct but slow. Well, Chatty and Happy they may have been but a cockney Ship's Company was quite something to get used to, though of course there was a smattering of Scots and Northerners as well. Things did not happen in the ways that I had been accustomed but, my goodness, they happened all the same and with great speed. The average Londoner is a pretty quick-witted chap and, provided he understood what was wanted and why, you couldn't ask for better.

Our refit in the East End of London was a great success despite the bombing and devastation round about. The shipyard worked with a will and gave us just about everything we asked for plus a little more on the side. It was fun being in London with its theatres and nightspots like Quaglino's and the Saturday dances at the

Dorchester. The Captain knew Robert Donat, the actor, who came to lunch on board several times and was most interested in all we did.

By mid-September we were back in one piece, ready to fuel and ammunition and return to Plymouth for a quick work-up and to rejoin the 16th Destroyer Flotilla, a mixture of Fleet Destroyers and Hunts. The Flotilla had two main tasks: one was to carry out offensive sweeps against German convoys sailing between Cherbourg and Brest and cover mine-laying operations off the French coast; the other was to escort our own convoys. In this we would take over from other escorts off the Isle of Wight and escort them to the mouth of the Bristol Channel, fuel at Milford Haven, pick up another convoy and come back. There were normally just two escorts to these coastal convoys.

There were two main threats to the convoys passing through our area: attack by submarine or by E-boat. There was some threat from the air at the eastern end of our beat but fighter-cover normally was enough to keep them away. The convoys themselves consisted mainly of colliers and small coasters in two long lines and there was a constant battle to prevent stragglers. There was a school of thought among some masters that it was safer to be well behind the convoy, which of course was the prime target. We kept a black list of known offenders to whom everyone was particularly beastly. From the point of view of defence it was impossible to give any protection to a group of ships strung out over several miles of sea. Once we were chasing up a Dutch coaster that had fallen well behind when the Master shouted at us through his megaphone 'Captain, I would like to keep up but my wife, she won't let me', and from the wheelhouse came this enormous Dutch Huisvrouw (pronounced house-frow), presumably armed with a rolling pin.

While the submarine threat was there all the time, it was the calm nights that suited the E-boats. One seldom got much warning of attack, despite the various aids to detection. The long-range surface warning radar on Portland Bill was pretty good but better still were our 'Y' operators. Very hush-hush, these were specially trained radio operators who spoke German and were able to tune into the E-boat operating frequencies and could pick up careless chatter and operating signals and, in action, what damage they had suffered. So, on a dark calm night we had to be instantly alert. The Captain slept on the bridge in a sort of dog kennel he had made underneath the chart table. Our Flotilla was split into two divisions, one camouflaged for bright moonlight nights and the other for dark or moonless nights. *Melbreak* was one of the latter, being painted a matt white broken up with pale blue and green patches. Designed by Peter Scott, it really did work and on a black night we were virtually invisible. We had a number of encounters with E-boats, one of the most successful being off the Scillies on 6th January 1944 when we sank one and seriously damaged two others.

The Type III Hunts were quite small ships, just over 1,000 tons, and were armed with two twin-mounted 4-inch guns (one forward and one aft), a four-barrelled multiple Pom-Pom, two twin-power-driven 20mm Oerlikons either side of the bridge and a state-of-the-art TS both for anti-aircraft and surface fire, with its Director Tower and own radar (Type 285) on the bridge. Amidships were two 21-inch Mark 9 torpedoes in a mounting which could be trained on either side. Their main weakness was a lack of speed; even with Chief sitting on the safety valve we could do little better than 26 knots.

Being in a modern ship, the Ship's Company of about 140 were split, with half living forward and half aft, while the officers' cabins and wardroom were amidships under the bridge structure. They were dry and seaworthy little ships. Geoffrey Kirkby, our Captain, insisted on only the best and made sure that he got it. We were a very close-knit team and a very efficient one in all respects. In the wardroom we had eight officers: myself as No.1 and Principal Control Officer (for all the armament), Paul O'Connor a RNVR Lieutenant and Gun Control Officer in the Director, Sub-Lieutenant Mike Shirley-Beavan as Navigator and Action Officer of the Watch, and Sub-Lieutenant Jenkins 'Jenks' as Plot Officer.

We had a plotting table where our position was kept up to date by a mechanism driven by the gyro compass and the ship's log and on which all the information from the various sources was plotted. The Captain could gain a picture of what was going on by looking through an eye-piece on the bridge situated directly over the plot. He could see the tracks of ships, friendly and enemy, and assess what to do and where to go. One of the captain's strongest points was that he could instantly take in and assess a situation.

In peace time 'Jenks' had been the pianist in Jack Payne's dance band. 'Guns', our Commissioned Gunner was a huge man, about 6'2' and weighing about 18 stone. He would get very argumentative when he'd had a skinful and would put his face about six inches from yours while prodding you hard in the chest with an enormous forefinger to make his point, often with tears streaming down his cheeks. Our Chief, an Engineer Lieutenant, our Doctor, Surgeon Lieutenant Thompson and a RNVR Midshipman Peter Eyres, who after the war went on to become Chairman of Imperial Tobacco, made up my team.

Mine-laying and anti-shipping sweeps off the Brittany coast were fairly nail-biting affairs. The main German escorts were small fast destroyers of the Elbing Class. They could do 34 knots, carried ten 21-inch torpedoes in quintuple mountings and three 100-mm guns, one forward and two aft. Because of our mine-laying efforts the Germans were pretty much constrained to keep to their swept channels and we to areas where we had not sown mines.

Our first encounter with the enemy was in early October. With two other Hunts, the Canadian Tribal Class *Athabaskan* and the Fleet Destroyer *Jervis*, we encountered 5 enemy warships off the Brittany coast. After a brief exchange of gunfire the enemy turned away, firing torpedoes. We also turned away to comb the tracks and no one was hit. We claimed one 4-inch shell hit on an Elbing that we were engaging, but it was all a pretty inconclusive affair. Nevertheless we were relieved to be back in Plymouth in one piece.

Because of our lack of success, C-in-C Plymouth planned that the next sweep should be led by the cruiser *Charybdis* with two fleet destroyers and four Hunts. *Charybdis* was new and not fully worked up and had certainly had no experience of this sort of operation; neither had the force any practice in working together. Intelligence reported that the Germans were trying to pass a large merchant ship, the *Munsterland*, up the Channel.

Our force sailed on 21st October and encountered the German force in the early hours of the 22nd. The Elbing escorts employed the same tactics, turning away and firing torpedoes, as they had done a fortnight previously. But *Charybdis*, the senior officer of the group, seemingly did not appreciate what was happening and gave chase. Both she and a Hunt, *Limbourne*, were hit by torpedoes and sank with considerable loss of life. The Germans subsequently picked up a number of survivors. The whole affair was ill-conceived and badly executed and the unfortunate *Charybdis*, being solely an anti-aircraft cruiser and armed with 4.5-inch AA guns, was a sitting duck. It was always well to remember that the Elbings were armed with ten torpedoes and had a much superior speed, 34 knots, neither of which they were hesitant in using.

Plymouth had been badly blitzed and because of this I met my wife to be, Mary Bull. It must have been in November 1943 that I had arranged to meet a girl at the Officers' Club, the Astor's house just behind the Hoe. I arrived for my date but the girl that I was meeting never turned up. I was stomping up and down the Hall fuming when I saw a very pretty girl that I had not met before, also clearly in a fury. It turned out that both she and I had been 'stood up' by our respective partners. The girl turned out to be Mary Bull, a Petty Officer Wren. Fate was on our side and we never looked back.

The Hunts, like the V & Ws, had to have periods off for boiler cleaning, though new techniques made these less frequent and at the same time all the more welcome when they did come along. At other times even when leave was given it was necessary to stay in the port area and be prepared for recall. It was a common occurrence for notices to be flashed on to the screens of Plymouth cinemas saying 'all personnel from HMS so-and-so are to return on board immediately'. Officers had to say where they would be and how they could be contacted. Recalls depended on intelligence of enemy convoys sailing or of E-boat sorties and it was a matter of pride to be ready for sea just as soon as possible. If, before sailing, you found yourself short of any key personnel, these would be made up from other ships in harbour and off you went. There was also always an emergency destroyer at 30 minutes' notice for sea either anchored in the Sound or at a buoy near Drake's Island.

This was generally the occasion for what might broadly be termed a musical evening in the wardroom. 'Jenks' could play any type of musical instrument and had on board a clarinet and a piano accordion; the rest of us all tried to play something, even if only lavatory paper on a comb. I was the drummer with a pair of drumsticks and the back of a wardroom chair and Chief was hot stuff with a mouth organ. We also had a good radiogram with a good stock of records as backing.

We had been at anchor in the Sound on Christmas Eve and had a very good Ship's Company Concert with a lot of cockney humour. On Christmas Day we went to 2 hours' notice and were allowed to give leave until 1800. Having done messdeck rounds in the morning and having been required to accept the hospitality of various messes, all of whom had saved their rum ration for this special day, I can just remember weaving a very high-stepping zigzag course to the Wrens' Quarters in Seymour Road, where I was let in through a ground floor window and plied with tea or coffee until the ground stayed still again.

The New Year saw an increase in mine-laying activity and every moonless or overcast night we would set out with a team of MGBs (Motor Gun Boats), especially equipped for minelaying, and sometimes we would go further afield to cover the fast Mine-layer *Apollo*. We were never so keen on the latter task as, although she was restricted for speed while laying mines and stayed behind us during the approach, as soon as her mine-lay was finished she would signal,' Thank you very much', increase speed to 40 knots and head for home, leaving us, with dawn coming up and uncomfortably near the French coast and German aircraft, to come back at our very best speed of 26 knots. But though we did this a number of times, we never got caught.

At about this time two new inventions came into our lives. One was GEE, later to become known as Decca navigation, which made life very simple in enabling you to know exactly where you were at any time, though in the beginning there was nothing remotely automatic about getting a fix. The other was a German invention, the BX or radio-guided bomb. In January 1944 *Athabaskan*, the Canadian Tribal class destroyer, was hit by one of these just at the base of the bridge superstructure, where it did considerable damage. Jammers were eventually brought out, but in the meantime the instructions were to keep some electric razors on the bridge to be switched on if you thought a BX attack was being made. The spark from the make-and-break circuit in the razor was enough to interfere with the bomb's guidance system and put the bomb off course.

Also, in the Spring of 1944, we saw the arrival of the Americans; invasion was in the air and we began to rehearse for our role. We had the reputation of being a pretty efficient gunnery ship and, as a welcome change from convoy escort, we were put on to being the bombardment training ship for U.S. and British Army gunners based around Plymouth. Not that the soldiers fired the guns themselves; the object was to train Artillery Officers in spotting and directing the fall of shot from ships at sea. Obviously any invasion force would be accompanied by a large number of warships whose guns would be used to support the Army. To get accurate results it was necessary to have someone on the ground near the target reporting back to his opposite number on board. Our job was to train these 'Forward Bombardment Officers'.

A huge practice area had been cleared of people and livestock to the west of Dartmouth, at Slapton Ley between Strete and Torcross and running inland to a depth of about ten miles. My cousin Jack Bartlett, who farmed at Little Dartmouth and who owned the hotel at Torcross, was both amused and surprised to hear that our first shoot at Slapton involved the destruction of a rival and rather better hotel than his, situated in the middle of Slapton beach. It actually belonged to the uncle of a prep school friend of mine, Norman Heard. We demolished it very efficiently, never to be rebuilt though, hopefully, Mr Heard was well-compensated after the war.

In addition to the bombardment practices we also took part in full-scale landing exercises there, using live ammunition and all the supporting wizardry such as the Landing Craft, which had been converted to fire a carpet of 500 mortar shells each on to the beach and the area immediately behind it to neutralise the German land mines and defensive positions. To watch these things being fired off was better than any firework display. The force put ashore was normally of Brigade size with all its supporting arms and armour and was sometimes British and sometimes American.

In addition to these practice landings the mine-laying off the French coast was stepped up and it was while we were off on one of the expeditions that, on 28th April, an American force waiting to carry out a landing was attacked by E-boats and a Landing Ship was sunk with the loss of about 600 American soldiers. It was most unfortunate to say the least, that we and other destroyers had been called away on operations leaving only the very elderly and practically toothless World War I destroyer, Skate, as the sole escort.

May came and the South Coast was sealed off from all comings and goings to preserve secrecy. Towards the middle of the month we received our copy of the orders for Operation Neptune, the naval part of Overlord, the landings on the Normandy coast. Marked Top Secret and about four inches thick, it took a lot of reading. Only the Captain and I were privy to what was going on and attended various briefings. As D-Day approached so the information and orders were passed on to all who needed to know.

Melbreak was attached to the American force destined for 'Omaha' beach. The force under an American Admiral Kirk included the battleships *Arkansas* and *Texas*, two French cruisers *Montcalm* and *Georges Legues*, British and American destroyers and also, of course, the huge number of Troop and Landing Ships. We were assigned special targets for the pre-landing bombardment and at a special briefing our targets were explained to us. For 40 minutes, before the actual landing by the first wave of troops, our target was to be a gun battery near St Honorine des Pertes. After the landing, which would be at 0630 or H hour, we would be available to give support as called for by the troops ashore for a further hour.

The landings were scheduled for 5th June and the 4th saw our part of the enterprise, several hundred ships, anchored in Weymouth Bay. However on the 4th the weather forecast was so bad that General Eisenhower postponed the operation. This meant that the second and third wave of ships, coming from as far a field as Scotland and already at sea, had to be turned back while others remained nervously at anchor. Somehow secrecy was maintained and twenty-four hours later the operation was on. The huge force got under way, undetected by the Germans, and formed into its various columns, all in the right order for arrival at the beach-head.

When your Captain is the most junior of the Group, you tend to get given the jobs that no one else is particularly keen to do. The minesweepers were to sweep a channel to within about 4,000 yards of the beach, then come round in a half circle and come out again, leaving a sort of banjo shaped area with the round piece of the banjo nearest the beach. The job given to us was to lead our Task Group and Landing Force down the swept channel and to anchor in the centre of the round bit at about 0300 and act as a marker for the arrival of the rest of the force. The long slow approach seemed to take an age and to say that we were shit-scared would be an understatement.

On our way into the beach we realized from our GEE, or Decca Navigator, that the Dan buoys that the minesweepers were laying to mark the channel were being swept out of place by the cross tide. There was of course strict radio silence and so, using our very smallest light so as not to be seen, we signalled this information to *Arkansas*, the flagship. To our horror, back came a signal flashed on a 10-inch searchlight that we thought could be seen in Bayeux, 'Lead right on sonny we will follow you', and as we lowered our anchor as silently as possible to the bottom we could see the beach and the coast line all too clearly and could not understand how it was that the Germans could not see us. It seemed an interminable time to wait and it was with great relief that we heard the bombing start at 0500. Then wave after wave of aircraft came in to drop their loads, followed by scores of planes carrying airborne forces and towing gliders for the landings of the American Airborne force in the region of Saint Lô.

At about 0530 we weighed anchor and took up our position, along with *Arkansas*, the two French cruisers *Montcalm* and *Georges Legues*, the U.S. destroyers *Doyle* and *Endicott* and two other Hunts from our Flotilla, *Tanatside* and *Talybont*, for the bombardment that was due to start at 0600. For half an hour all hell was let loose on the areas behind Omaha beach situated to the west of Port-en-Bessin. At 0630 the gunfire lifted and the Americans started their landings. Despite the massive aerial and naval bombardment, the Germans stuck to their gun emplacements and a new German Division on night exercises was already there. Omaha beach with its marshy area beyond the actual beach, the low sand dunes and the wickedly steep slopes behind was a death trap. The Americans suffered terrible casualties as they stormed ashore. Of course we in *Melbreak* had no way of knowing what was happening ashore and were relieved to have survived so far.

Our next task was to support 47 Commando Royal Marines, who were going to land on Gold beach just to the east of Port-en-Bessin and take the port. Moving back in company with *Tanatside* and *Talybont* to meet the 47 Commando LCAs (Landing Craft Assault), we passed close to the French cruiser *Georges Legues* (commanded by Philippe Jaujard, later to become my boss at Fontainebleau) and as we did so we heard the sound of many voices coming across the water. It was their Ship's Company singing the Marseillaise. It was a most moving moment and forcibly reminded us that, while we were fighting to get rid of the Germans, they were fighting to come home.

Covering the Marines' landing we came under fire from the batteries at Port-en-Bessin. There were concrete gun emplacements on the higher ground to the west and also concrete pill-boxes on the breakwater. *Tanatside* was hit and had to retire and, though we could land shells on the gun emplacements without difficulty, the thickness of the concrete prevented us from doing any damage and they continued to fire. Clearly something had to be done about it and I suggested to the Captain that if we could bring the ship in close enough, the Chief Bosun's Mate, who was also the Director Layer, and myself would take over the laying and training of the forward 4-inch gun mounting and, just as if we were shooting some enormous gun on a rifle range, we would try and post the shells in through the slits in the concrete from which the German guns poked out. We closed in to under 3,000 yards, where the trajectory of our shells would be just about flat, and, keeping bows on, we started target practice. We had almost instant success and to this day, if I close my eyes, I can still see those grey-clad soldiers running from their bunkers up the green hillside and being speeded on their way by bursts from our oerlikons. After that the commandos made good progress in taking the port.

Behind us great activity was going on everywhere and old merchant ships and warships, including my old friend from 1940, the French battleship *Courbet*, were being towed in towards the beach and sunk in lines, head to stern, to form the outer breakwater of the Mulberry harbours. In the first 24 hours over 130,000 soldiers were landed, with the Americans suffering by far the worse casualties. However, well before evening we had expended all our ammunition and, in company with Talybont, we were sent back to Plymouth to fuel and re-ammunition. This was to be a quick turn-round and no one was allowed ashore but I did have the opportunity to ring Mary from the Oiler to say that we were still in one piece and that all was O.K.

Just as soon as everything was completed we sailed again for the beach-head area and were put on a patrol line to the east of the anchorage. The fear was that the Germans might mount some sort of operation from Le Havre and in particular there was a threat from German human torpedoes. The Germans had developed a torpedo-like vehicle with a sort of Perspex bubble on top and manned by a couple of frogmen. They were designed to run on the surface with just the bubble showing but, though several were sighted and destroyed, the threat never amounted to much. The important thing was that we enjoyed almost complete air superiority, otherwise life would have been very different indeed. It was fascinating to watch all the huge components of the Mulberry harbours, towed by an army of tugs, arriving at the beach-head, all to be fitted together like some giant's Meccano set. The whole thing was awe-inspiring in its size and concept.

About two weeks after the landings we were sent to join a mixed bag of British and American warships – battleships and cruisers – to act as escorts while they bombarded the big gun emplacements around Cherbourg. The Allies badly wanted a proper port, especially as the Americans had had their Mulberry Harbour broken up by a gale. The Germans were holding out on the Cherbourg peninsula with determination. The 16-inch guns at Cap de la Hogue were among the main targets. Fortunately they were not particularly accurate but the huge spouts of water landing in the sea round about us were most impressive. Cherbourg fell to the Allies on 27th June and we went back to escorting convoys between Portsmouth and the beaches.

Early in July we thought that we had detected a submarine so carried out an attack with depth charges. As we ran over the target there was an enormous explosion and *Melbreak* leapt out of the water. A couple of the gun crew on the after gun deck were shot into the air and landed on the quarter deck, one injuring his back and another suffering a broken ankle. We came to the conclusion that we must have attacked a sunken ammunition barge – it was certainly no submarine. Unfortunately, though all things in the engine room were mounted on shock-proof mountings, this was much more than the average shock and the feet of one of the turbines were fractured. We were sent back to Plymouth for repairs, which took ten days.

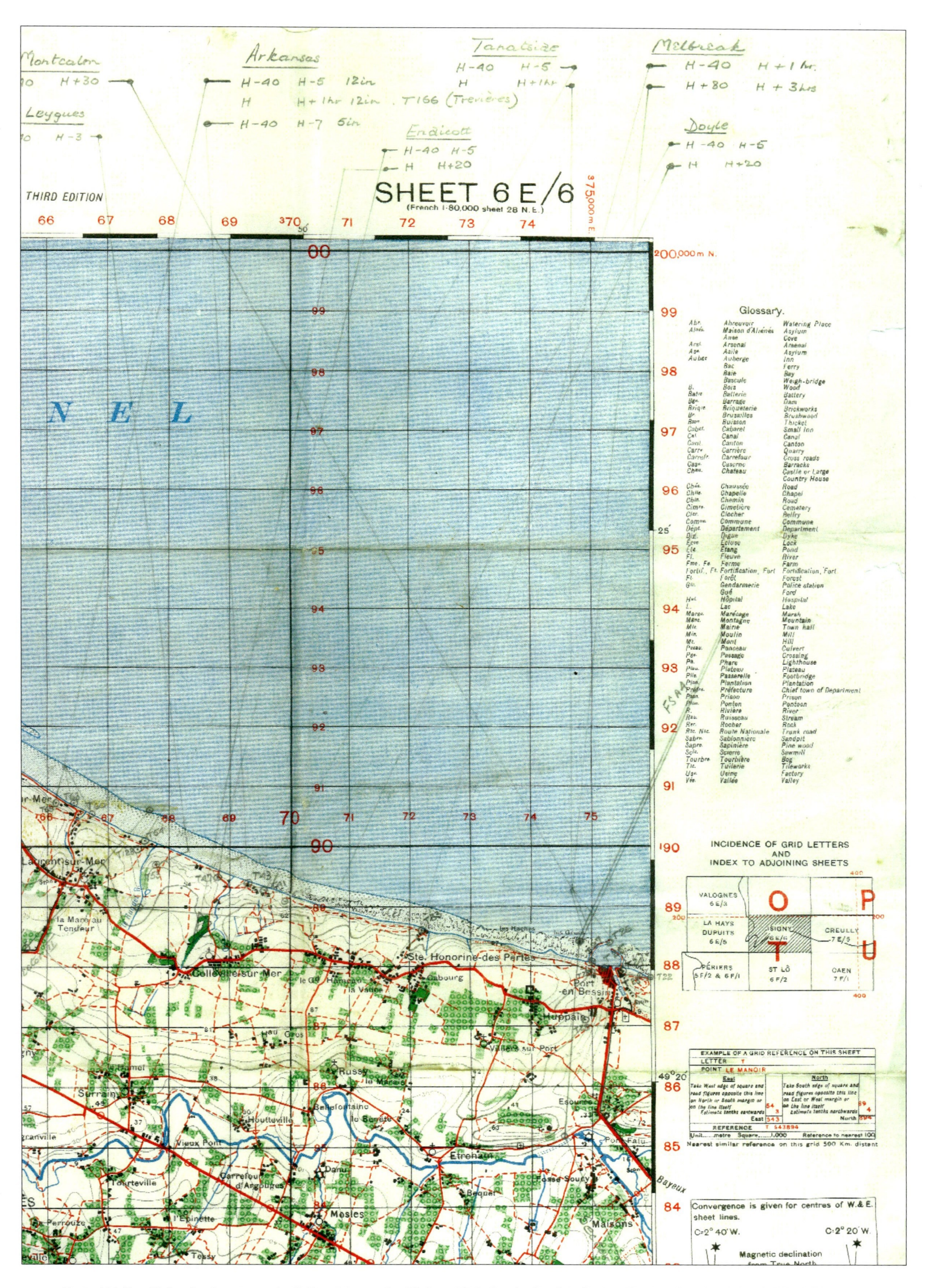

Part of Melbreak's bombardment map for D Day, Normandy, 6th June 1944. Omaha Beach to Port-en-Bassin. Showing (at top) ships taking part

It was during this time that Mary and I got engaged and we had a big expedition to Launceston on the bus so that I could introduce Mary to my parents. They too had come on the bus, from Bideford, and we all had lunch together in the White Hart Hotel. They approved, but it would not have made any difference to us had they not!

Back in Portsmouth in August, we were given a new role which Geoffrey Kirkby was very excited about. The Germans were supplying their garrisons in the channel ports by sea and at night. This had to be disrupted or stopped. The idea was to use MTBs, backed up by a Hunt class destroyer, to attack these convoys with both the Hunt and the MTBs being vectored in, like fighter aircraft, by another ship fitted with a very powerful surface radar. The ships chosen to do the directing were the American-built Captain class frigates *Stayner* and *Retalick* with high resolution radar fitted at the top of very tall masts.

The German convoys were very heavily protected by E-boats, minesweepers and special flak ships armed with a large number of 88 mm and 37 mm guns. The idea behind the attacks was that the MTBs would attack first and try and break up the enemy and then the Hunt would go in and shoot up the merchant ships in the convoy. We had special flares to fire to light up the scene. It worked very well and we met with considerable success.

The important thing to remember was to keep more than 2,500 yards from the flak ships, as, being flak ships, they fired anti-aircraft shells from their 37 mm guns which were set to self-destruct at that range. So, though you saw streams of tracer coming straight at you in a most alarming way, it never actually arrived. Our Captain was a past master at getting the ship in the right position and we all had the greatest confidence in him, as did the COs of the MTBs working with us.

I remember very well explaining to John Keddie – a friend of mine and the Captain of *Cattistock* – who was about to go out on one of these special operations for the first time, how vital it was to keep outside the magic range of 2,500 yards just before they sailed. They had been berthed alongside us. Unhappily he must have got carried away in the excitement of the moment and got his ship much too close. He and a number of his crew were killed and many more wounded before they were able to break off. The Commanding Officer of our Flotilla of MTBs was a very much decorated RNVR Lieutenant called Arnold-Foster, who later in life became editor of the Guardian newspaper. Of course, not all the attacks on German convoys were carried out by the Navy; the RAF was hard at it too and, to avoid confusion, we had clearly defined bombing and no-bombing areas. We, of course, operated in the no-bombing areas.

At this time too the Germans were still going strong with their V1 flying bombs, the 'doodlebugs', launched from the Pas de Calais area of France. We could often see them setting off for England and on one occasion actually managed to shoot one down as it passed overhead. The gunner on this occasion was our Canteen Manager, who, we had discovered sometime back, was ace shot with our 20-mm oerlikon guns and used to man one at action stations despite the fact that he was a civilian belonging to the NAAFI and a non-combatant.

We had carried out a number of these anti-convoy sorties and were becoming quite confident about them when, early in September while in the process of being vectored in to attack a convoy and just about to open fire, an aircraft dived on us and dropped a stick of high fragmentation bombs. These caused a massive amount of damage; we later counted more than 600 holes in the starboard side and over 200 in the port side. The Chief Bosun's Mate called me on my head-set to say that Paddy O'Connor, the Control Officer in the Director, had been hit and asked for permission to train the Director fore and aft so that he could be got out. I told him to remain trained on the aircraft in case it came in for another attack, an order that I have regretted ever since. Had we got him out straight away it might have been possible to save his life. In the event the aircraft did come back but didn't attack and we saw that it was a biplane.

Seventeen men were killed in the attack including the Coxswain in the wheelhouse directly beneath my feet, about thirty more were very badly wounded and others not so bad. We broke off the action and I left the bridge to try and assess the damage. Water was pouring in through the many splinter holes and we appeared to be sinking despite the fact that the damage control parties and all spare hands were trying to stuff up the splinter holes with soft wood plugs and anything else that came to hand. But it was a losing battle as the further we sank in the water the more holes there were to let the water in. In addition the ship was developing a list and was becoming unstable. I reported to the Captain that we were sinking; it certainly looked as if we had had it this time.

Suddenly the Chief appeared on the bridge with an inspirational idea. He asked for permission to open the hatches to all the magazines and store rooms and so let the water on the decks above run down. On the basis that we had nothing to lose, the Captain gave his permission. The effect was immediate, the ship was brought upright and in consequence scores of holes were back above the water again so that the plugging of them could start again. By this inspirational action the ship was saved and in fact the action we had taken became a classic demonstration and lesson taught in the Damage Control Schools in England and America for many years and for all I know, it still is.

Meanwhile the Doctor and First-Aid parties were dealing with the wounded, the forward messdeck being turned into an emergency sick-bay. Doc Thompson quickly ran out of blood plasma for transfusions as many of those badly hit were losing a lot of blood. As a substitute he ordered saline drips to be used, making up the solution with distilled water and salt from the galley. This action too was the first of its kind and saved a number of lives and for this Surgeon Lieutenant Thompson was awarded the Distinguished Service Cross.

I spent most of the morning watch in the forward messdeck doing what I could. It was heartbreaking to see men, whom you had known so well and with whom you had shared so many adventures, dying before your eyes. The best that I could do was to go round trying to reassure people that they would be all right and trying to write down whispered messages to wives and girl friends. That morning the Chief Bosun's Mate and I committed twelve men to the deep; all had been terribly mutilated and one, a little cockney called Meek, had been cut clean in half. Each was lashed in a hammock with a 4-inch shell for weight and dropped overboard.

We made our way very slowly back to Portsmouth under our own steam and with emergency cables supplying power to essential places as nearly all the main supply cables had been severed. Off Haslar we were met by one of the big hospital launches, which took off the worst of the wounded, and then went on to a berth in the dockyard. Subsequently only the Captain and I were told that our attacker had been a RAF Albacore out of its allotted area.

In Portsmouth we cleared up the mess as best we could and patches were welded on to make the ship seaworthy. There was damage everywhere and about the only thing that we could do was to steam so we were sent back to Plymouth to wait for news as to where we would go for repairs. Mary was in hospital at the time, having her appendix out, and remembers seeing *Melbreak* coming up harbour, her hull a mass of red splodges from the red lead covering all the patches. Mike Shirley-Beavan's father was Managing Director of the Barry Dock Company in South Wales and he persuaded the Captain to lobby hard for the ship to go there for her refit knowing full well that we should be given 'red carpet' treatment. The graving (dry) dock at Barry was empty, our argument prevailed and off we set for Barry, arriving there at the beginning of October. We and the Navy could not have made a better choice, everything that we asked for was done with a will and by the end of November we were back in Plymouth and looking really 'tiddly' (Navy slang for smart) within and without. All the messdecks had been painted by a cheerful and efficient gang of lady dockyard maties in a new scheme using pastel colours chosen by a psychiatrist.

Life in Plymouth was much more orderly than before, the end of the war was in sight, no longer was there a danger from air or E-boat attacks. Only the U-boat remained a threat, coming round the North of Scotland to operate in the approaches to the English Channel or in the Channel itself. Our sole task now was convoy escort.

One of the favourite things that the Captain and I used to like to do was, whenever possible, to go to the Saturday night dances at the Moorland Links hotel at Yelverton. The drill was to have supper on board and then set off by taxi. Geoffrey's girlfriend was a Wren Officer and was allowed to wear civilian clothes; Mary as a rating, was not. However, this did not stop her, despite the dire warnings, and it was fun setting off with two girls in evening dresses to enjoy an evening away from it all. The Moorland Links had a fabulous dance band and it was always a super evening right down to the squash in the taxi coming home.

We had not planned on getting married until the war had ended but, come December, we couldn't see much point in waiting and rang our respective families from the call-box in Thornhill Gardens to say that *Melbreak* was due for a boiler clean and docking on 27th December and that we would like to be married on the 28th. Geoffrey agreed to be my best man and Rosemary Hickling, now married to Tony Griffin the No.1 of Talybont, would be Matron of Honour and also lend Mary her wedding dress. Of course the wedding would be at Milton Abbott with Mary's father, the Vicar, taking the service. Mary's mother at once got busy planning the reception and invited various relations to stay in their large Vicarage, while others were to make their way there as best they could, my parents coming on the bus from Bideford.

Melbreak was duty destroyer over the Christmas period which we spent at a buoy in the Sound. On Boxing Day we organised a Ship's Company Concert. Mike Shirley-Beavan, I and Peter Eyres* did Leslie Henson's version of 'The Green Eye of the Little Yellow God' and later Peter and I performed a song and dance act. At the end of the show the Ship's Company presented me with a set of silver soup spoons as a wedding present and the Wardroom a pair of Sheffield Plate entrée dishes. All was set for going in to dock the following day.

The morning of the 27th dawned with the news that the Polish destroyer *Blyskawica* had been in collision with another ship during the night and would have to dock in the dry dock allocated to *Melbreak*. We were required to sail as soon as possible and take over the Polish ship's convoy. I was just able to get a message to Mary to say that the wedding was off; meanwhile Geoffrey rushed off to see the Chief of Staff to get a date for being back in Plymouth again. It is not difficult to imagine the scene of dismay at Milton Abbott with a house full of guests and all the hard-won food for the wedding already prepared. We were promised that we would be back on 1st January and the wedding was fixed for 1400.

Melbreak was to be brought in from the convoy and remain at short notice in the Sound. This meant that the Captain had to stay on board and I was without a best man. The only person to be spared was the RNVR Midshipman, Peter Eyres. On 1st January he and I were put ashore with strict instructions to be back in Plymouth by 1830. We caught the train to Tavistock where a taxi was waiting to take us on to Milton Abbott. It was a bitterly cold day with a good covering of snow and the taxi driver went very slowly. Thinking that we would be late I urged him to hurry up, to which he replied, 'Us'as been waitin' for you for two days and us isn't goin' to 'urry now'.

Everything went well and we had a lovely wedding and reception. At 1700 we all set off for Plymouth, Peter to go back on board and Mary and I to the Duke of Cornwall Hotel. Everything would have been fine if our 'Honeymoon suite' had not had rats running up and down inside the walls all night and making a terrible noise. Still, we had made it, even though I had to be back on board by 0800 the following morning and off to sea. It was ten long days before we were back again and this time, with the ship safely in dry dock, Mary and I had a week's honeymoon at Budleigh Salterton, the furthest afield that we could go in her parent's Morris 10 which had been given to us as a wedding present, a magnificent gift indeed. Arriving back we had planned to move into a flat just vacated by Tony and Rosemary Griffin. However this again was not going to be.

*Peter Eyres, my emergency Best Man, and I remained good friends until his death in the 1980s. After the war he married Surgeon Lieutenant Thompson's sister, whose father just happened to be a Director of a large but now defunct tobacco company and Peter, at his father-in-law's instigation, entered the industry. He did pretty well and ended up as Chairman of Imperial Tobacco. He used to say that he owed his success entirely to what he had learnt in *Melbreak* about leading, organising and taking good care of the people working for you.

Above: On the Bridge, the Captain is 4th from left wearing an open sheepskin jacket, I am sitting back to the camera, the Yeoman of Signals on my right.

Below: H.M.S. Melbreak at about 25 knots.

Above. Left to Right:
Jackson (Gunner), Peter Eyres
(Snottie), Jenkins (Jenks),
Mike Shirley-Beavan (Pilot).

Left:
'A' Gun, Twin 4 inch
Mounting.

NAZI SHIP SUNK IN CHANNEL

ANOTHER ON FIRE

Light forces of the Royal Navy sank an enemy auxiliary vessel, damaged a minesweeper by gunfire, and set an R.-boat on fire, in two short engagements, north of Cap d'Antifer, near Le Havre, early on Saturday.

The action, announced in an Admiralty communiqué yesterday, began when the destroyer Melbreak (Lt. G. J. Kirkly, D.S.C., R.N.), attacked a minesweeper, escorted by R.-boats, about two miles north of Cap d'Antifer. Several hits with gunfire were obtained on the minesweeper, and one of the R-boats was set on fire, before the enemy turned inshore and escaped.

Later forces under Lt. M. Arnold-Foster D.S.C., R.N.V.R., intercepted an auxiliary vessel in the same area. The enemy was hit at close range with torpedoes and sank.

A number of survivors were picked up and made prisoner. All H.M. ships returned safely to harbour, having suffered neither casualties nor damage.

Cherbourg June 25th 1944

The British cruiser Glasgow emerging from a smoke screen to take part in Sunday's heavy naval bombardment of Cherbourg.

The first salvo was fired by the 14-inch guns of the United States battleship Nevada, one of the warships raised from the mud of Pearl Harbour after the Japanese attack on Dec. 7, 1941.

She was flying the flag of Rear-Adml. Deyo, U.S.N., who, at the conclusion of the scheduled 90 minutes' shelling against strong fire from the shore batteries, extended the bombardment to about three hours so as to remove further obstacles to the land troops' advance.

The battleships and cruisers which took part were:
AMERICAN. — TUSCALOOSA, Capt. J. B. W. Waller; TEXAS, Capt. C. A. Baker, flying the flag of Rear-Adml. Carleton Franton Bryant; NEVADA, Capt. P. Rhea; ARKANSAS, Capt. F. G. Richards; QUINCY, Capt. Elliot Senn.
BRITISH.—GLASGOW, Capt. C. P. Clarke, R.N., and ENTERPRISE, Capt. H. T. W. Grant, R.C.N.

Destroyers engaged included:
BRITISH.—ONSLOW, Capt. J. A. McCoy, R.N.; OFFA, Lt.-Cmdr. R. F. Leonard, R.N.; and MELBREAK, Lt. G. J. Kirkby, R.N.
AMERICAN. — O'BRIEN, Cmdr. W. W. Outerbridge; MURPHY, Cmdr. R. A. Wolverton; RODMAN, Cmdr. J. F. Foley; and EMMONS,

---

DESTROYERS IN "BATTLE OF THE SCILLIES"

Early Morning Drama

WEST PORT INTERVIEWS

By H. P. TWYFORD,
"The Western Morning News" War Correspondent.

"WE caught them well and truly, and all they could do was to bolt full speed with us plastering them with everything we had got, until they were completely hidden by smoke."

That was the characteristically Navy way in which the first lieutenant in a destroyer described to me at a Westcountry port yesterday the early morning' battle between British destroyers and E-boats which had ventured across the Channel within a few miles of the Isles of Scilly.

In fact, it might almost be called the Battle of the Scillies. The engagement was the outcome of a fine piece of co-operation between Coastal Command aircraft and the Royal Navy.

It was in the comfort of the wardroom that the commanding officer of one destroyer told the story of the lively engagement which was fought out in the half-light of a misty morning. It was due to fine appreciation of the position and judgment that the interception of the E-boats was made so successfully.

The destroyers were out when they got the signal that E-boats were being shadowed by aircraft, and that they were to proceed at top speed to intercept and engage with them.

The E-boats were reported to have crossed the Channel and were "just around the corner" from The Land's End, as the Navy described it. Aircraft had shadowed and harassed them all the way over. They had apparently fulfilled their mission, so that it had to be on the return that the destroyers' chance of interception would arise. The interception called for fine judgment, and it was completely successful. But let me tell you the story as it was given me.

TAKEN BY SURPRISE.

"We—that is, the two destroyers —were sent at full speed. We crowded on everything we had. We knew it had to be an interception on their return journey. The captain was just right in his calculations and we had the good fortune to run slap into them. There were a number of them in the force. They seemed to be cruising home quite comfortably. What a shock they got. They were taken completely by surprise when we illuminated them with star shells and opened fire. They did not appear to have the faintest idea

They crowded on all the power they had and were driving for home, smothering themselves in a smoke screen. We gave them everything we got. One was hit badly and was set on fire. The others quickly made dense smoke and bolted at full speed under that protection.

"The destroyers continued the search and finally came across one E-boat lying low in the water and stopped. This was obviously the one that had been badly hit earlier, set on fire, and abandoned. We crowded up to this boat and sank her with deliberate fire. Throughout the engagement the E-boats replied with gunfire, but they had been caught completely by surprise and the shooting was so wild that neither destroyer was hit and not a single casualty was sustained."

"A GOOD SHOW."

"Quite a good show," was the laconic summing-up of one destroyer captain, who praised warmly the way in which the ship's company had stood up to a lively engagement. He added that the entire success was due to the fine interception calculations made by the senior officer. The aircraft-reporting was brilliant, too. From our point of view it was an ideal night —a misty moon and a flat sea."

Another officer specially praised some of the young seamen in action for the first time. Among these were two ordinary seamen, still in their 'teens, who joined the ship only a fortnight ago and were in their first action. They had a responsible job, exposed just outside the gun turret, and were responsible for certain of the apparatus. They played a vital part, and did it well, especially as they had had very little opportunity of practice.

SAILORS' IMPRESSIONS.

Earlier everyone had been at action stations, so that when they had the order to proceed to engage the E-boats they were quite on their toes. "The general performance of every one was most satisfactory," said the skipper.

One of the two lads he mentioned was Ord. Smn. George Kelly, of Glasgow, who seven months ago was a student at Abbey School, Fort Augustus, Inverness. He was very thrilled with the experience "I was too busy to be scared, and I didn't even know that they were firing back at us. All I knew was that I had to get on with my own job, and that it was important."

Ord. Smn. W. H. Jackson, of Wallasey, who was 18 last Saturday, a former butcher and van driver, who has been in the Navy since last October, explained that it was his first action.

"It was all right while it lasted. I was glad to be in the action and to sink some of the enemy's ships," he said. "We had the gun depressed almost straight level, and the job was to get the shells in and avoid hitting our own deck," he confided.

"It was rather frightening at

Extracts from newspapers 1944.

Top Left : 21st August, action in the Channel.

Left: Naval bombardment of Cherbourg.

*Above Right: Saturday March 18th
The destroyers were Tanatside & Melbreak. The author gave the interview and had an expensive time giving drinks to chums who had come to see 'the comfort of the wardroom'.*

In Port En Bessin, first Normandy port in Allied hands, waterfront buildings are scarred by battle and a German flak ship has been sunk by naval bombardment. Royal Marine Commandos fought a bitter engagement here before they triumphed over the stubborn resistance of German defenders.

Devon Wedding

Younger daughter of Rev. C. R. and Mrs. Bull, of The Vicarage, Milton Abbot, Tavistock, Miss Mary Ravenscroft Bull was married at St. Constantine Church, Milton Abbot, yesterday to Lieut. Cecil Agar Johnson, D.S.C., R.N., only son of Capt. C. C. Johnson, R.N. (retired), and Mrs. Johnson, of Instow, North Devon. The bride's father, assisted by Rev. E. W. Moore (vicar of Kelly), officiated.

The bride was given away by Maj. J. C. Bull and Lieut. P. Eyres, R.N., was best man. A reception was held at the vicarage.

Jan 1st 1945

NAZI SHIPS HIT NEAR LE HAVRE

Light naval forces, in two actions off Cap d'Antifer, north of Le Havre, early on Saturday, sank an enemy auxiliary vessel, damaged a minesweeper and set an R-boat on fire, the Admiralty announced last night.

The minesweeper and one of its escorting R-boats were hit by the destroyer Melbreak (Lieut. F. J. Kirkly, D.S.C.).

Later, light forces led by Lieut. M. Arnold-Forster, D.S.C., torpedoed the auxiliary vessel from short range. Our ships suffered neither damage nor casualties.

21 Aug 1944

> Admiralty,
> Whitehall,
>
> 26th December, 1944.
>
> The KING has been graciously pleased to give orders for the following appointment to the Distinguished Service Order and to approve the following awards:-
>
> For gallantry, skill, determination and undaunted devotion to duty during the landing of Allied Forces on the coast of Normandy:-
>
> THE DISTINGUISHED SERVICE CROSS.
>
> Lieutenant Cecil Agar Johnson, R.N. (Instow).

Above:
A very nice Christmas present from the King!

Left:
Wedding Bells at Milton Abbott 1st January 1945.

Top: H.M.S. Chaplet, 1946.

Left: While in Bone, Chaplet and Chevron were invited to shoot boar by the local sheik who also gave us a magnificent lunch. I had a hungry dog to eat my leftovers!

Below left: The Sheik and his son.

Below right: Our Captain, Lieutenant Commander Austin at the boar hunt, Algeria.

Above: The Minesweeper Moon prepares to board as Chaplet's turning circle was too large.

Left: MV Alma with 600 illegal immigrants.

Above: Close up of Alma. Boats are turned out to make boarding difficult.

Above: Martin Fortescue and I (with axe) trying to chop away the rigging of capsized caique.

Below: I have just fallen in (but I hang onto the axe!)

The Manor House, Little Bealings. Our sitting room was the one with the open French window and our bedrooms were on the right starting from the window with the bars across. On the left of the front door was the dining room which we shared. The pig sties were off to the right.

Above:
Drake Division. Centre front row is the author; on his left is Mr Cooke his Assistant DivisionalOfficer.

Below: Left to Right: The author, Geoff Robson, Admiral Cunningham The King's Birthday Parade and Inspection (I think he had forgotten about the golf clubs!)

Top: Shotley Ball-The Lambeth Walk. Matron; the author, Mary; Ken Allan-Williams, Geoff Robson, & the Farnfields.

Above left: Michael.

Above right: Joan Churchyard; Mike; David, Caroline & Andrew Bray.

Left: Mike 1948. We had snow for several weeks.

Annual Athletic Sports

commencing at 9.30 a.m.

ON

Wednesday, 8th June, 1949

followed by

PRESENTATION OF PRIZES

by LADY EDELSTEN

at approximately 6.40 p.m.

OFFICIALS.

President	Captain W. G. A. Robson, D.S.O., D.S.C., R.N.
Referees	Commander G. L. Farnfield, D.S.O., D.S.C., R.N.
	Lieutenant L. R. Hollis, R.N., P. T. & W. Officer.
Chief Steward and Clerk of Course	Mr. B. J. Reid, Snr. Cd. P. T. & W. Bos'n., R.N.
Assistant Clerks of Course	C.P.O. J. H. Rogers, P.T.I.
	Ldg. Sea. Carnelley, P.T.I.
Chief Track Judge	Instr. Lieut. W. Micklethwaite, M.A., R.N.
Track Judges	Lieut. Cdr. L. R. P. Lawford, D.S.C., R.N.
	Rev. C. Prior, M.A., Chaplain R.N.
	Instr. Lieut. P. H. Mellors, B.A., R.N.
	,, ,, R. J. Keyworth, B.SC., R.N.
	,, ,, D. W. Houghton, B.SC., R.N.
Corner and Take-Over Judges	Rev. J. F. Dougherty, Chaplain, R.N.
	Instr. Lieut. D. G. F. Munson, R.N.
	,, ,, J. S. Nix, B.SC., R.N.
	Mr. W. E. Allen, Cd. Stores Officer, R.N.
Chief Field Judge	Instructor Lieutenant S. Bentley, R.N.
Field Judges (Jumping Events)	Instr. Lieut. A. E. Kinsey, R.N.
	,, ,, C. E. T. Gray, R.N.
	,, ,, R. Dane, B.SC., R.N.
Field Judges (Throwing Events)	,, ,, K. Oliver, R.N.
	3rd Officer M. Howie, W.R.N.S.
	Instr. Lieut. D. J. Lennon, R.N.
	,, ,, G. J. Holt, R.N.
	,, ,, M. S. Adams, R.N.
Chief Gymkhana Judge	Rev. A. A. Orrock, M.A., Chaplain, R.N.
Gymkhana Judges	Instructor Captain F. C. Sobey, B.A., R.N.
	Surgeon Captain D. M. Beaton, O.B.E., L.R.C.P., L.R.C.S., R.N.
	Rev. D. A. R. Keen, M.A., Chaplain, R.N.
	Surgeon Lt. Cdr. (D) E. B. Mackenzie, L.D.S., R.N.
Starter	Mr. J. Chamberlain, Cd. Gnr., R.N.
Assistant Starter	Ldg. Seaman J. Meadows, P.T.I.
Lap Scorer	Instructor Lieut. S. F. Richards, R.N.
Chief Timekeeper	Captain (S) E. S. Satterthwaite, R.N.
Timekeepers	Captain H. G. Bruce, R.M.
	Mr. W. H. Sleep, Cd. M.A.A., R.N.
Announcer and Commentator	Lieutenant Cdr. A. Cameron, D.S.C., R.N.
Broadcast System	Mr. T. R. Brooks, Snr. Cd. C.O., R.N.
Chief Recorders	Instructor Lieut. R. B. Hollis, R.N.
	Mr. D. W. Martin, Snr. Cd. Wtr. Officer, R.N.
Assistant Recorders	Mr. F. V. Naylor, Snr. Cd. Bos'n., R.N.
(Boys)	Mr. A. H. Kitley, Snr. Cd. Eng., R.N.
(Ship's Co.)	Instructor Lieut. H. Chester, R.N.
(Prize List)	Second Officer K. A. Hatton, W.R.N.S.
Score Board	Instructor Lieut. M. W. Burnham, R.N.
	Instructor Lieut. R. Mayland, R.N.
Press and Prize Steward	Sgt. H. R. Smith, R.M., P.T.I.
Chief Competitors Std.	C.P.O. F. W. Parrick, P.T.I.

Competitors Stewards ...

Anson	C.P.O. Knowles.	Blake	C.P.O. O'Clarey.
Benbow	C.P.O. Tel. Riddell.	Collingwood	P.O. Hancey.
Drake	C.P.O. Williams.	Duncan	C.P.O. Pearce.
Exmouth	C.P.O. Tippett.	Grenville	C.P.O. Heyhoe.
Hawke	C.P.O. Fryers.	Rodney	C.P.O. Carmichael.
W.R.N.S.	R.P.O. Deakin, W.R.N.S.	Establishment	C.P.O. Ridley.

When I arrived back on board I was told that my relief had been appointed and would join before the end of the month. I was to go to Yarrow's Yard in Glasgow to stand by, as First Lieutenant, a new fleet destroyer, *Crozier*, being built there. This dashed our hopes of starting our married life in a flat in Plymouth. Wrens were allowed one compassionate draft to be near their husbands and as I was likely to be in Glasgow for 4 to 5 months, Mary applied for a draft to Greenock.

I left *Melbreak* on 29th January 1945 and said goodbye to the Ship's Company and, in particular, Geoffrey Kirkby. We had been through a lot together and had been a very close team. Altogether we had fired over 4,000 rounds of 4-inch ammunition at the enemy that we could see. We had been credited with five E-boats sunk and twelve badly damaged. We had sunk six German merchant ships and one Flak ship and damaged an Elbing class destroyer and several minesweepers. In a ship recognition and awards go rightly to the Captain who, at this time, had gained a DSC and two Bars (i.e. the DSC three times), a Mention in Dispatches and a year's seniority. The Doctor, Surgeon Lieutenant Thompson, and I were proud to have been awarded the Distinguished Service Cross, whilst six ratings including the Chief Bosun's Mate and the Canteen Manager, the Distinguished Service Medal. I left the ship, which was anchored in the Sound at the time, by boat and I was very moved and proud that the Lower Deck was cleared and that I was cheered ashore.

Up in Scotland we hunted frantically for somewhere to live, eventually finding a room in a bungalow near the golf course at Kilmacolm. As luck would have it, after 10 days at Yarrow's, I was told that my ship had been sold to the Canadian Navy and that I was to proceed to Southampton forthwith to stand by a similar ship, *Chaplet*, fitting out in Thornycroft's yard at Woolston. This was a cruel turn of fortune and VE Day, 8th May 1945, found Mary still at Greenock while I was stuck in Southampton.

Shortly after this, Mary, being pregnant, was able to get a compassionate discharge from the Wrens and joined me at last. I had found a bed-sit in a house in Bitterne, where we lived until *Chaplet* sailed for the Far East. Luckily, by the time we reached Malta the war with Japan had come to an end (VJ Day was 15th August) and we stayed in the Mediterranean, the newly built CH class forming the 14th Destroyer Flotilla. I was not to see Mary again for another 18 months. The peace-time adventures which followed make another story.

CHAPTER 6

H.M.S. *Chaplet*
1st March 1945 – 17th May 1947

Chaplet, the ship to which I had been appointed, was fitting out at Thornycroft's Yard at Woolston in Southampton. Thornycroft's like Yarrow's had a great reputation for building the Navy's destroyers and there was a great family atmosphere about the whole concern. People are appointed to ships building at various stages in the construction program, the technical officers first so that they are familiar with the installation and layout of the various systems, then the First Lieutenant about three months before completion, so that he too could know the ship thoroughly, write the ship's orders and make out the Watch and Quarter Bills which allocate the Ship's Company to their various stations and duties. In addition he has to arrange for the training of the various weapon teams and ensure that the ship is fitted out according to the specifications, while, at the same time, scrounging any extras that would make shipboard life better along the way. The last person to arrive is the Captain, who would expect to find everything ready for the sea trials and final acceptance from the builders.

Chaplet was the last of a batch of Fleet destroyers which had evolved during the war starting with a fairly basic and simple design, the 'O' and 'P' classes. These were each of eight ships, making up a Flotilla They were followed down through the alphabet to the 'Z' class during which the design was stretched and the armament and equipment improved. After that the process began again with four Flotillas of the 'C' class. The 'Ca's were the same as the 'Z's, but the 'Ch's 'Co's and 'Cr's all had the very latest in gunfire control and radar, typified by the Mark 6 Director and Type 275 Radar. This was a quantum leap forward. The director, situated at the rear and above the bridge, was a large greenhouse of an object with what appeared to be enormous motorcar headlights on either side. This was a type of radar which transmitted a very narrow and powerful beam and which enabled it to give really accurate bearing, range and elevation of a target. It allowed, for the first time, a ship or an aircraft to be fired at 'blind'. No longer did you have to be able to see your target.

The only snag was that we still had the single-mounted 4.5-inch hand-loaded guns with a maximum elevation of about 50 degrees. Besides these four guns the ship had eight 21-inch Mark 9 torpedoes in two mountings, a twin 40-mm Bofors anti-aircraft mounting with its own radar, several twin 20-mm Oerlikons and of course Sonar and depth charges. These destroyers were designed to screen the large ships of a battle fleet and to be able to attack surface ships with guns and torpedoes. The war with Japan was still very much 'on' in the Pacific, as were fleet actions, and this was our destination.

The 'Ch's were just over 1,700 tons, 362 ft in length with a 36ft beam. Their 40,000 horsepower engines gave them a speed of 34 knots. They had a Ship's Company of 24 officers and 200 men, quite a tight squash, and, apart from the Captain, myself and the Chief who had the luxury of a single cabin, all the other officers had to share and were mostly four to a cabin. There were over twice as many officers as we had had in *Melbreak* but they were judged to be necessary for the very much more sophisticated and untried equipment. We had two electrical officers and a long course RNVR gunnery officer, Herbert Walkinshaw, a pint-size Glaswegian, very keen and with a chest full of medals.

Arriving some months before completion it was not possible to live on board so we had our office in a small terrace house outside, just opposite the dockyard gates and lived in a small guest house near to the floating bridge. Once I had got myself organised my main priority was to find somewhere for Mary and me to live, no easy task. The whole Southampton area had been badly bombed and flats, houses and even rooms were at a premium. It wasn't long before I found out that the only way to have a chance was to sit on the wall outside the Southampton Evening News office along with many others and as soon as the paper came off the press, you bought your copy, scanned the adverts and then, leaping on to your 'pusser's' issue bike, you pedalled off as fast as you as you could to get to your chosen place before anyone else.

I had been doing this for about two weeks without any luck, when I heard of a bed-sitter in Bitterne at the far end of an unadopted road off Glenfield Avenue in Rossington Road. The house was called Homefels and I got there just as fast as I could. It was a typical 1938 semi-detached house owned by a lady whose husband was a Squadron Leader in the RAF and out in the Far East. For a rent of rather more than I had hoped, we could have the back bedroom which was quite a decent size, big enough to have a double bed and a small table and chairs, and the shared use of the kitchen and bathroom at stipulated times.

I was delighted to have somewhere at last and moved in immediately. Mary, now pregnant, was able to get herself discharged from the Wrens and was able to join me towards the end of May. We also collected the Morris 10 that her parents had given us as a wedding present. Known to the Bulls as Oh Be Joyful (the number plate was OBJ), it was a tremendous asset despite the petrol rationing. At long last we were to have a chance of living together, made all the better by the knowledge that the war in Europe was over – no more blackout, no more air raids, no V2 missiles.

Early in June we were summoned to the Palace where I received my DSC from King George VI, while Mary and my Godmother, Hazel McGoverne, sat in the Ballroom to watch. We were all lined up according to our worth by a lot of efficient Gentlemen Ushers; VCs and GCs in a special room where they sat in comfort, DSOs in a queue to the left, DSCs, MCs and DFCs in queues on the right, all in the Long Portrait Gallery. I believe that the King did one of these each week while the Queen did another. However it was no rushed-through event; everyone was spoken to and questioned about themselves and what they had done. The King clearly took a great interest in the whole thing and had obviously been very well-briefed.

While the fitting out went ahead as planned, the country prepared for a General Election. The Coalition which had served the country so well could not go on. Party politics came out into the open and the country had to make a choice of Clement Attlee and the Labour party or Winston Churchill and the Conservatives. There were a number of mass meetings outside the gates of the shipyard during the dinner hour which we could watch from our office window on the first floor and listen to all the speeches, the promises and the heckling. It seemed to us almost inconceivable that Winston, who had had the country in the palm of his hand for the war years, would not win. But the country was fed up with war and privation. All those who had been called up wanted to get back to civvystreet and their families, yet Churchill in his election speeches continued to press the war with Japan but, more importantly, raised the bogey of Soviet ambition. This was not what the man in the street wanted to hear. Labour stressed that the Soviets were our friends and allies and that their brand of socialism was something to emulate.

In England the election took place on 5th July but, because the Forces were to vote and were scattered all over the globe, the votes were not counted until 24th July and the results showed a massive vote for Labour. Clement Attlee was called to form a government and Churchill, who had returned on the 23rd from meeting Stalin and Truman in Potsdam, where the Allies had agreed the new boundaries for Germany, couldn't believe that he had been spurned by the country that he had fought so hard to save. He was never the same man again.

On 30th July President Truman, on his way home from Potsdam, was received by King George VI on board *Renown* in Plymouth Sound, just three days before Hiroshima was destroyed by the first Atomic bomb. Events followed swiftly. On 5th August the Soviets declared war on Japan and advanced into Manchuria. Nagasaki was destroyed by Atomic bomb No.2 on the 8th and by 10th August Japan had surrendered. How thankful we were; perhaps *Chaplet* would be able to stay in home waters; but this was not to be.

While all these events had been taking place, the Ship's Company had been building up to full strength and the ship was commissioned on 26th July under the Command of Lieutenant Commander D.W. Austin. He was a big man and older than most officers of his seniority as he had transferred to the Royal Navy in 1937 from the Merchant Navy, where he was a member of the Royal Naval Reserve. Married before the war with two children, he had spent most of the war in Corvettes and Frigates; he was a solid and reliable seaman but with none of the dash of a Destroyer captain. Amongst the other officers who joined I was delighted to find that Mike Shirley-Beavan, our navigator in *Melbreak*, had been appointed to carry out the same task in *Chaplet*.

Our sea trials went very well, with the exception of the Mark 6 Director which refused to behave and kept us back several weeks while it was put right. By the end of August we had said our sad farewells and set off for Malta, where the 14th

Destroyer Flotilla was to form. We were the second of the Flotilla to arrive; *Chevron*, having completed several months before us, was already there and worked up.

Malta had suffered an enormous amount of damage and in 1945, just two years after the bombing had stopped, work was going on everywhere to restore buildings and facilities. In 1939, when in *Imperial*, I had been based in Sliema Creek and now six years later I was back there again. From that point of view little had changed and we soon had our ship's dghaisa organised. But our job now was the transition from war to peace. Most of the Mediterranean countries had unstable governments, countries ravaged by war, large occupation forces of different nationalities, worthless currencies, racketeers, profiteers and opportunists. We had British forces in North Africa, Palestine, the Lebanon, Greece, Crete, Yugoslavia, Italy, Cyprus, Rhodes and Egypt. There were many minefields to be cleared by the Minesweepers under the control of the Allied Mine Clearance Commission and, if this wasn't enough, everyone wanted to be demobbed. This of course was just not possible. The country and its battered industry could not accept large numbers of men returning en masse and, in any case, law and order in the liberated countries had to be maintained. British or Allied Control Commissions needed time to hand over government and, as always in these situations, there was always a danger of civil war.

Admiral 'Algy' Willis, my Captain in *Barham*, was appointed Commander in Chief Mediterranean Fleet and it was his difficult task to maintain morale and keep everyone busy – no easy task – and he had to be extremely, some thought excessively, firm in trying to get the Navy back to pre-war standards of cleanliness, discipline and efficiency. He was particularly rigorous over drink and drunkenness and officers' wine bills were carefully scrutinized. Gone were the eccentricities of rig tolerated in wartime and back came the Captain's inspections between decks every Saturday and the inspection of Ships Companies followed by rounds of the upper deck on Sunday mornings. There was a lot of moaning at the time but I am sure that he was right and we worked hard to make *Chaplet* shine above the rest.

After a work-up at Malta we were sent off with *Chevron* (Lieutenant Commander John Bush, who later became C-in-C Fleet) and *Javelin* (Lieutenant Commander Marjoriebanks) on a visit to Algeria to show the flag and meet the French. We went first to Ferryville near Algiers and then to Bône. For reasons that I cannot remember there were large quantities of pre-war British Naval stores at Ferryville and we loaded ourselves with all sorts of hitherto unobtainable things, including hundredweights of real grey enamel with which to paint the ship.

Wartime paint was matt and had no lasting qualities. Our Chief, George Yorke, who was a real wheeler-dealer, swopped a crate of whisky for a Jeep at the U.S. Army Transport Depot. The Jeep stowed neatly on the Quarterdeck and we hung on to it for about three months before we were ordered to land it. He also sold another crate of whisky to a French Army mess for a huge amount of French francs. It wasn't until we were at sea a couple of weeks later that we learned that the French notes were no longer legal tender but luck was on George's side. We met up with a French cruiser on her way back to France from Indo-China (Vietnam) and thinking correctly that she would have these notes anyway, George was sent across by boat and managed to swop them for two boxes of very good champagne.

After Ferryville we sailed for Bône where the French frigate *Tunisien* was our host and most hospitable they were too. Dances, parties and sporting fixtures were laid on for both officers and ratings. Several of the French officers had their wives there and I was invited home to supper on several occasions. We were also invited to take part in a boar hunt in an oak forest belonging to the Bey of Algiers. We had to have our shotgun cartridges reloaded with ball and had to be ready to leave at six in the morning.

The Captain, myself, Chief and Mike Shirley-Beavan, plus four from each of the other ships including *Tunisien*, set off in trucks. After a drive of about 40 kilometres, we arrived at the farm of the local Sheik, where we had coffee, and then set off on foot into the forest. We were each posted about 25 yards apart in little clearings while about twenty or thirty Arab beaters with dogs, drums and trumpets drove the wild boar towards us. The boars made a terrific noise as they crashed through the undergrowth but none came into my clearing for which I was quite relieved. However one was shot by *Chevron*'s Gunner. After the drive we all assembled for a huge open-air lunch given by the Sheik. There were about ten courses, including a sheep roasted whole, and everything was eaten with our fingers. Luckily I was able to pass on some of mine to a huge dog sitting expectantly behind me. After we had finished the beaters were allowed to have a go at the food, followed by a host of small boys and then finally the dogs. No washing up!

After everyone had fed we went back to our stations in the forest for another drive but I was overcome by the lunch and sat under a tree and went to sleep. I was indeed fortunate as nothing came my way. However, another boar was shot by our hosts and we were presented with both to take back. We gave the smaller one to *Tunisien*'s wardroom and humped the bigger one back on board *Chaplet*. The ship's butcher flatly refused to have anything to do with it, so Mike S-B, Chief and myself set about skinning and cleaning it. It weighed about 250 pounds and was no easy job. When we had finished we all needed a bath. Once it was looking like a carcass the ship's butcher condescended to take over, but it was never properly hung and was as tough as old boots.

The following day, 14th December, we were invited to dinner at the Prefecture – a very splendid affair – and it was just at the beginning of this that a messenger came from the ship with a telegram to say that 'Baby had arrived' and that 'Mary and it were both well'. No sex was given! I passed the telegram along the table to the Captain who immediately leapt to his feet and hammered the table for silence and then, in his best schoolboy French, he announced 'Ce soir Monsieur le Deuxième (French for First Lieutenant) est un père; il a sonné la cloche le premier fois; Bravo Monsieur le Deuxième'. Then everyone stood and we drank the baby's health, then Mary's health and finally my health. Michael was borne on 14th December at the Woodhayes Nursing Home in Exeter and I was intensely pleased and proud. In those days mothers were kept in bed for a week or more after the baby was borne and Mary and Michael got back to Gertrude Terrace just in time for Christmas. It was extremely frustrating to be so far apart and with pretty poor communications. However, it was a wonderful end to an eventful year.

Leaving Bône we went to Palermo in Sicily for a few days before arriving back in Malta for Christmas. Palermo was run by the Americans and, as soon as we had secured alongside, their Military Police came on board to warn us about the danger to sailors going ashore singly or even in pairs. Apparently between the dock area and the town were gangs of small boys aged about ten who operated from the sewers. If a lone sailor approached, he would be set upon by about twenty of these ten year olds, dragged to the ground and stripped naked by these kids, who would then disappear back into the sewers with all his belongings including his clothes. On a couple of occasions I saw American patrols chasing these children with stock whips, really pretty awful and we were glad to leave.

The harbours of Malta were always pretty full, as, besides the small Mediterranean fleet, there were other ships passing through either on their way to or returning from the Far East, so you had a great chance of meeting your chums. By Christmas most of the 14th Flotilla had arrived including the Flotilla Leader, *Chequers*, with our Captain (D), a fire-eater by reputation, one J.H. Ruck-Keene. He came on board to introduce himself to the Ship's Company who were mustered on the Foc's'le. A fierce-looking man with a jutting beard, he said something to the effect that, 'You've all heard that I am a shit; I know I'm a shit, so you'll have to watch out'. But in actual fact his bark was a lot worse than his bite and I always got on with him very well.

He set out to try and weld the flotilla into an efficient unit and we spent much of the month of January practising flotilla torpedo attacks, both by day and by night. A manoeuvre called a Star attack was the most popular but also the most difficult to achieve. It involved surrounding the enemy ship and attacking simultaneously from four different quarters. Our Captain was not much good at driving the ship 'blind' and we frequently ended up in the doghouse. But at gunnery we were excellent; Walkinshaw was as keen as mustard and we had a very good gunnery team.

In February I received the very sad news that my father-in-law had died. Charles Bull had died at Exmouth; he was 68 and they had been at Exmouth for less than a year since retiring from Milton Abbott. Both Mary, with baby Michael, and my sister-in-law Hester were there. My mother-in-law was just 52 at the time and was left with the responsibility of a largish house in a strange town and with very little means of support. In those days clergy widows were not entitled to a pension. For me, what was particularly sad was that I never really came to know him; I had met him on only two occasions other than our wedding day. Again I was frustrated at being miles away and unable to be of any support.

Soon after I received the news the ship sailed for Thessalonica to act as guard ship for the local elections. Macedonia had, and I believe still has, a large Turkish element and troubles were expected. We were there for about a week but it was cold and pretty dismal. The Captain and I were shown round by the British Consul and briefed on what we might have to do but in the event the elections went off quietly and we sailed for Haifa. There, the Palestine situation was far from quiet. Palestine was a British Mandate. The persecuted Jews from Russia and the rest of Europe wanted it as Israel, their national home and, with the aid of American money, were determined to make it so. The Palestinian Muslims and indeed the Palestinian Jews, whose country it was, wanted just the opposite and, of course, no one wanted the

British. Terrorism was rife and the very tough Palestinian Police, supported by the British Army stationed there, were unable to control it. Many terrible atrocities were being committed by the Irgun Zvi Liumi, the Jewish terrorist organisation.

Against this background the Navy had to patrol the coast to prevent illegal immigration. The British, I believe, had agreed to allow 10,000 Jews a year to enter the country but the numbers coming from Europe were far in excess of this. Their goal was to make their way to Trieste, Marseille or Genoa where they would be stripped of all their possessions of any value, especially any gold and even gold fillings from teeth, to pay for their voyage and then crammed into tiny coasters to sail clandestinely to Palestine. It was by no means unusual for six or seven hundred men, women and children to be crammed into the holds of ships of only about 600 tons, with very little food or water, for a voyage lasting up to ten days. If caught (the intelligence was pretty good), they were shipped to holding camps in Cyprus. From there the luckier ones were allowed into Palestine in accordance with the agreed number.

There were generally a couple of destroyers in Haifa to prevent illegal landings and, if not actually on patrol, the ship was required to be at short notice for sea. Haifa was quite a pleasant spot and the countryside behind most attractive, especially at that time of year before the hot weather set in. No one was allowed ashore after dark as it was not safe, so life was pretty restricted, though within the port area there was a NAAFI club, officially known as a Wet Canteen, where the sailor could get a beer. Because of these restrictions the ships rotated fairly frequently and went either to Beirut for rest and recreation or to Port Said for any repairs that were required.

Beirut in those days was a delightful spot – elegant houses, shops and restaurants, fertile countryside with the hills and mountains behind and ,of course, the pervading scent of the cedars of Lebanon. In February and March it was possible to send parties up to the Elephant Ski Club, which was run by the Army, with skis and snow aplenty. Walkinshaw and I made an expedition to Damascus and, on the way back, to Baalbek (Heliopolis of ancient times). Some of the individual stones for the enormous temple there weighed over a thousand tons and had been brought down the Nile from Aswan, across the Eastern Mediterranean and then hauled through the mountains to this magnificent site. During our first visit there, the Captain and I made various official calls and were invited to take coffee at the houses of the local leaders. These were always pretty sticky affairs. The language used was French (it was a French Mandate) and you had to sit perched on gilt chairs placed around the sides of a large room with a beautiful carpet in the middle and across which you were supposed to make polite conversation. I soon realized that the carpets were for looking at and not for walking on. There were, of course, never any women to leaven the gathering.

Patrols at sea were carried out fairly close inshore between Gaza and Sidon, I suppose really to show the locals that we were there and watching. Towards the end of March we went to Port Said for boiler cleaning and maintenance and there I was lucky enough to get leave to go on one of the Army's educational trips up the Nile to Luxor to see the temples and the tombs of the Pharaohs. Travelling by train overnight from Cairo in the excellent sleepers of the Wagons Lits, we were put up in the Savoy Hotel at Luxor on the banks of the Nile – not quite of the same standing as the Savoy in London, where Mary and I had stayed, but it was bug-free and fairly adequate. The Temples at Karnak and Luxor were truly wonderful in size and sheer magnificence. Looking out across the Nile at the barges with their huge lateen sails and at the fields, where irrigation was by donkey power and the hand-worked Archimedes screw, you had the impression that time had stood still for the past two thousand years.

The day after our arrival we all, about thirty of us, set off on donkeys to visit the Valley of the Kings. It was about a 9 mile ride to the tombs and the donkey boys ran behind all the way. The tombs are situated at the ends of long tunnels, some about 300 feet long, hewn out of the sandstone rock and sloping steeply downwards. They were very hot and dry inside which accounts for why the decorations covering the walls are as fresh and bright as if they had been done only yesterday. We had time to see only three tombs, Seti I, Tutankhamun and Timotheus I, of which the last was the best.

The following day was market day in Luxor, with everyone coming in from the surrounding villages to sell their wares. Heavily-laden donkeys and camels, small boys carrying lambs, women with live chickens and pigeons, water-sellers with their bulging and slimy water bags made from goatskins and behind them all, small girls with baskets picking up the camel and donkey droppings to carry them along too, a truly biblical sight. That night, after visiting the temples again, we caught the train back to Cairo and the following morning I was able to visit the Museum to see all the wonderful artefacts that had at one time been in the tombs and to marvel at their sophistication and craftsmanship.

I arrived back in Port Said totally broke; the whole trip had cost me nearly £10 and I had gone on the understanding that it was only going to cost £4.10s! (£10 in 1946 would be about £200 in 1990). What is more, there had been an immigration ship reported as being on its way and *Chaplet* had sailed early for Haifa. I reported to the local headquarters and was fixed up with a sleeper to Haifa and, at the same time, I was issued with a service revolver. It was considered dangerous to travel on this route unarmed as various shootings had taken place. Imagine my apprehension when I discovered that the other person in my sleeping compartment was a Jewish gentleman. He was also armed and very ostentatiously checked that the magazine of his revolver was fully loaded before putting it under his pillow. I did likewise with mine and I think we both spent a very uneasy night. I was very glad when we arrived at Tel Aviv.

By May we were back in Malta and allowed to give Station Leave. There was a Rest Camp in Sicily, at Taormina for officers and near Catania for ratings, and a large party from *Chaplet* set off on a week's leave. As a part of war reparations the Italian Navy ran a ferry service between Malta and Catania using destroyers, so it was a quick trip, about six hours at 20 knots. Taormina is a beautiful place and had previously been chosen by the Germans for the same purpose. We were put up in a 5-star hotel. My room seemed the ultimate in luxury, with a balcony looking down over the hillside to the deep blue Mediterranean below and, to the south, Mount Etna. It also had its own huge bathroom with a marble bath and lashings of hot water. I had never seen anything like it and couldn't believe my luck. We had a carefree week, walking, swimming, eating and drinking. Such are the spoils of war.

After our leave period we were sent up to Genoa calling at Elba on the way. The Captain thought that it would be a splendid idea to get everyone ashore for a great cross-country expedition and this we did. We landed the entire Ship's Company bar six. They were to walk from one side of the island to the other while the Captain, myself, the Chief Stoker, the Chief ERA, the Cox'n and Chief Bosun's Mate steamed the ship round to the other side to await their arrival. It was a footsore and weary lot that arrived after about a 12-hour hike, including, of course, stops for refreshment. What the inhabitants thought of it all heaven only knows. We certainly never warned anybody or asked for permission. It was just that it was a fine day and so we did it. It was Italian, we had won the war and that was good enough!

The same attitude went for Genoa. There were a large number of British soldiers there, mostly 1st Army who had fought in North Africa and then up through Italy and were now the occupying force. They had taken over some fine Palazzos as messes but basically they were bored stiff and wanting to be home. A regiment was told off to look after us and we repaid their hospitality by taking them on trips to sea. The only thing that sticks in my mind is that a rather drunken Major Hamlyn, at a party in our Wardroom, was going round slapping people on the back saying,'If you ever want a job after this f-----g war, come and see me in London'. Two years later Mike Shirley-Beavan, who had decided that the peacetime Navy was not for him, knocked on the door of Binder Hamlyn, one of the City's biggest firms of accountants and said he had come for the job. He got it and eventually ended up as Senior Partner.

Back in Malta things were settling down and we were told that it was now permitted for wives to come out to join their husbands. I immediately applied for a passage for Mary and the baby. I was told that I was 19th on the list so we were full of hope and I set about finding somewhere to live. However it turned out that people with shore appointments were to have priority over sea-goers so, by the time I was relieved about 10 months later and despite numbers of wives arriving, I had sunk to number 36. On the other hand, people were being demobbed and the size of our Ship's Company was reduced both in officers and ratings which made life on board far more comfortable for everyone, though it didn't help my particular problem.

One Sunday morning an officer from C-in-C's staff arrived on board in great haste to say that the crew of *Javelin* had mutinied. *Chaplet* was to sort it out and, if necessary, was to go alongside *Javelin* and arrest the ring leaders. It was all to be done as quickly and quietly as possible as it was feared that the mutiny might spread. Peter Baines, who was First Lieutenant of *Javelin*, was the same term as me and so I was sent over to *Javelin* by boat to assess the situation.

I was allowed on board by the crew and found that the Captain, Lieutenant Commander Marjoriebanks (pronounced Marshbanks), was being held under arrest in his cabin and that all the officers were kept to the wardroom. Everyone was very friendly, not knowing what to do next. I was allowed to meet Peter Baines who explained to me that the Captain had been behaving in a tyrannical and totally unreasonable manner and that all anyone wanted, including those in the wardroom, was to have him relieved of his command. Anyone who has read the book 'The Caine Mutiny' will understand the situation. I went back to explain the position to my Captain, who immediately went to see the Commander-in-Chief. Marjoriebanks was taken from his ship and a very cheerful Lieutenant Commander called Hutchinson appointed in his place. A couple of weeks later Peter Baines was also relieved, as it was judged by the powers that be that he had condoned the mutiny, which I think was probably correct.

After that *Javelin* returned to normal and had no more troubles. Peter Haines was sent to join the staff of the GOC Palestine where he had a lucky escape from death when the King David Hotel was blown up by terrorists on 22nd July and a number of the staff, whose headquarters it was, were killed.

At just about the same time as the *Javelin* incident, the fleet had a nasty shock when *Venus*, another destroyer, struck a mine off the Albanian coast with the loss of about 30 men. Her bows had been blown of and James Munn, her Captain, had been lucky to get her back to Malta without sinking. This caused a serious international row as the Albanians had laid these mines after the end of the war and had not told anyone about them.

In July the flags were out in Malta for the arrival of the new Governor, Mr Douglas. I was chosen to be in charge of the naval contingent of the tri-service Guard of Honour, each service providing 100 men, and quite a bit of rehearsing went on, luckily in the early mornings before it got too hot. On the day itself everything went very well and I had just one member of my team pass out so I was both pleased and relieved. This was the first time that Malta had had a civilian as Governor but the appointment was paving the way to Independence.

That summer my friend, Herbert Walkinshaw the Gunnery Officer, was relieved by Martin Fortescue and Bruce Macbeth took over from George Yorke as Chief Engineer. Martin and I were to become close friends and shared many escapades together. On the other hand Bruce Macbeth was a most difficult character. He wanted to leave the Navy and took every opportunity to make a nuisance of himself in the hope that it would speed him on his way, including writing letters to say that he had joined the Communist Party and could no longer give his loyalty to the Crown. Not that he had actually done anything of the sort. His one redeeming feature was his dog, a very characterful bull terrier called Dumbo, who became a firm favourite throughout the ship.

Back in Haifa the situation had got worse. Alongside in harbour there was the threat of 'limpet' mines and searches of the ship's bottom were frequently ordered. Sentries had to be posted on the upper deck day and night, armed with hand grenades, in case any terrorist frogmen were seen. In addition, small charges were dropped into the water at irregular intervals to make a bang which, while supposed to scare off attackers, spoilt everyone's beauty sleep. If teams went ashore to play football it was necessary to provide, in addition to a referee and linesmen, a sentry to be stationed at each corner of the pitch armed with a light machine gun.

The Naval Bomb Disposal Officer was a Lieutenant Commander RNVR called Crabbe, later to become famous when in 1955 and no longer in the Navy, he disappeared after carrying out an underwater inspection of a Soviet Cruiser visiting Portsmouth. His headless body, dressed in a frogman's suit, was found floating in the English Channel several days after the cruiser had sailed. By sheer coincidence, Mary and I had had an amusing chat with him about old times while we were all standing on the slipway of the Gosport Ferry landing place, just two days before he disappeared but had no inkling of what he was planning to do. He was a most extraordinary character. In civilian life he had been an antiques dealer in Chelsea and had joined the RNVR just before the war. He had volunteered for Special Duties and was trained as a frogman for beach reconnaissance and mine clearance. A small man with a marked cast in one eye, he seemed to relish danger. On one occasion when we were in harbour and there was a scare on, he found a limpet mine stuck to our bottom, which he brought on board and up to the Captain's cabin. The Captain was horrified and said, 'Take the thing away, I don't want it here', to which Crabbe calmly replied, ' Oh it's perfectly safe Sir; it's got about half an hour left to run and if you would like to put it to your ear you can hear it ticking'.

The number of illegal immigrant ships was on the increase and they were also making themselves more difficult to board. The men and women who came from Russia and Germany and who had lost everything were desperate to reach the Promised Land. A common tactic was for the immigrant ship to put the helm hard over and go round in tight circles making it impossible for a destroyer to get alongside to board. As a consequence minesweepers, with their much tighter turning circle, were brought in to do the job of boarding. Once on board it wasn't easy as there was generally a fair bit of organized resistance, chiefly by the women, who formed the front row, armed with sharpened knitting needles to stick into vulnerable parts! Boarding parties soon became well-padded-up before trying to take a ship.

In addition we were issued with Tear, or CS, gas grenades fired from a large-bore gun which looked a bit like a blunderbuss. When we were first given these grenades I thought that it would be a good idea to have a demonstration. The idea was to fire the grenades from the bridge and try and land them on 'X' gun deck about 100 feet away. Having gathered the key people from our boarding parties on to the bridge and having ordered all the ventilation fans shut down so that the gas didn't get sucked in to the mess decks, I fired off three grenades and managed to get one to land on the gun deck.

Shortly after this an infuriated Leading Torpedoman arrived on the bridge with a very dead-looking canary lying on its back in its cage with its legs in the air. 'If you've killed my f******g canary I'm going to f******g-well do you', he shouted in my face with tears running down his cheeks. But happily, with the canary held up facing the wind, it quickly recovered and so I escaped! What had happened was that in those days the torpedo-men were responsible for the distribution of electricity in a ship and they had made a private arrangement with the main switchboard that if at any time the ventilation to the mess decks had to be turned off – a thing that often happened in harbour when the load on the ship's diesel generator too great – the air supply to their mess would remain on. They had been caught out at last, much to the amusement of everyone else in the ship. In the event we never had to use tear gas in anger.

The ship was due back in Malta in December and just before we sailed a couple of Officers from the Palestine Police arrived on board at night with a prisoner for questioning. We anchored clear of the harbour and the questioning went on relentlessly for about 24 hours. The prisoner was believed to be the second-in-command of the Jewish terrorist group, the Irgun Zvi Liumi, and in return for information given, he was to be removed to a place of safety. Two nights later we put him quietly ashore in the middle of the night on a small beach in Rhodes with a suitcase containing £10,000 of used notes, a very considerable sum of money in those days. As a result of information given to the police they were able to make a number of arrests but, when Israel finally became independent, he was able to return and became a very senior member of the Israeli Government and finally Prime Minister. I can't help wondering whether his information was of real importance and to what use he put the money – most probably for the purchase of weapons.

Back in Malta I found that I was able to buy a new car, a Morris 10 export model. It was virtually impossible to buy a new car in England but by some quirk of the regulations, which I didn't query, it was possible to buy a new car in Malta and have it delivered in England and indeed to Exmouth where Mary was living. Even better, because of the shortage of cars, she was able to sell our old 1939 Morris for £350, which was more than the cost of the new car!

But in Exmouth Mary was having much more to contend with than a new car. January 1947 was the coldest since 1894. Coal was strictly rationed and it was constant hard work to prevent No. 4 Gertrude Terrace from freezing up and suffering burst pipes, as did most other houses. Some even had their mains water supply frozen and were completely without water. The freeze went on for some time and I was able to send Mary some locally-made fur boots. The freeze was also exacerbated by coal and electricity strikes which went on through February.

A friend of mine Roddie MacDonald, who had married Algy Willis's younger daughter, had taken over from Mark Tennyson as Flag Lieutenant and I was invited to a couple of very good Scottish Country Dance evenings at Admiralty House in Valletta, which certainly kept my feet warm. But despite the cold weather in Britain, all of us who had come out in *Chaplet* eighteen months earlier were looking forward to going home. In preparation, I thought that I should equip myself with good tweed overcoat and would beat the clothes rationing by having one made by a good Maltese tailor in Sliema. I chose a very good cloth and looked forward to the day that it would be finished. Imagine my horror when I went to collect and tried it on, to find that one sleeve was three inches shorter than the other. I was furious with the tailor, who said that he was very sorry but when he came to make it he found that he had not quite enough cloth and could not get any more. As we were just about to sail, I had to take the coat with its one short sleeve and this plagued me every winter for about ten years, before I could afford to buy a new one.

Towards the end of January, in company with the minesweeper *Moon*, we captured the immigrant ship *Alma* to the south of Tel Aviv. She had some six hundred refugees on board who were taken to Cyprus and who, I suppose, eventually got to

Israel. After this we spent several days in Famagusta where Martin Fortescue and I were lent a couple of horses by the local police and so were able to see something of the countryside, very pretty at that time of year. Then it was on to Port Vathi in the island of Samos where the famous wine is made. However it turned out to be much overrated as far as I was concerned as it was horribly sweet and sticky. From Samos we went to Piraeus so that the Ship's Company could have a run ashore in Athens, which was popular. There was galloping inflation in Greece at the time and I recall being paid 200,000 drachma which was worth less than £20.

We were moored Mediterranean fashion, stern to the quay, and for the four days that we were there the Chief Bosun's Mate refused to leave the foc's'le as there was a formidable Greek lady with two children camped out on the quayside who proclaimed loudly to all and sundry that he was the father of her children! The truth never outed but he was a very relieved man when we eventually sailed for Malta.

Derek Austin, our Captain, was relieved in March by another Lieutenant Commander, EG (Izzie) Forsberg. I had got on quite well with Austin and we had had a good report from Captain (D). He was a very fair man and the Ship's Company were sorry to see him go. He left with a mountain of packing cases. His hobby was joinery and he had spent most of his spare time making furniture, really very good tables, bookcases and the like. I often wondered if the Naval Stores ever considered why our damage-control timber was always having to be replaced.

Forsberg was a totally different kettle of fish. A rotund little man with a florid complexion and fussy beyond belief, his main claim to fame – and quite a claim it was – being that he had swum the channel from Dover to Calais in 1939. We were lying alongside in the dockyard at Corradino wharf when he joined and on the first day I was sent for, to be told that there were cockroaches in his bed and that the whole thing was to be taken out on to the dockside and burnt. At the same time the Chief was sent off to organize a new bed from Naval Stores. The bed having been burnt, the Chief gleefully reported that there were no new beds in Naval Stores and it took our Shipwright about ten days to build him a new one.

Chief's dog 'Dumbo' also took an instant dislike to the poor chap and started to use the Captain's cabin for his 'morning georges' which, not unnaturally, caused paroxysms of rage. The dog was ordered to be shot but this caused a near-mutiny and eventually a *modus vivendi* was arrived at and everyone simmered down. But it was certainly a very shaky start. He was really quite a proficient chap but I needed all my tact to keep the Wardroom calm against a stream of petulant notes to all and sundry which emanated from the Captain's cabin.

During this time in Malta, Mike Shirley-Beavan had got engaged and married to Mary, who was a Queen Alexandra's Nursing Sister at Bighi. Though they were both very nice people, they were an ill-assorted couple, but we all wished them every happiness and threw a big party for them on board. By April we were back off Haifa for another stint of patrol duties. This time we were seldom allowed to enter harbour and spent many days anchored outside.

Here our new Captain was able to demonstrate his swimming talents. Between six and ten in the morning the sea was usually calm and windless and he used to send for me at six to say that he was just going for a swim and, if he was not back by ten,

I was to weigh anchor and look for him. I would tell the duty signalman to keep a telescope trained on him but after about half an hour he would disappear from sight and I would wonder what I should do and where I should look if he really was missing. But I needn't have worried as, to some people's disappointment, he always turned up as fresh as a daisy having had his four hours' worth.

We rotated between Haifa and Beirut which kept everyone more or less happy. On one of the visits to Beirut I engaged a conjuror, at great expense to the ship's Welfare Fund, to give a show on board in the forward messdeck. He had very good credentials but what I did not know was that he had the DTs. When he came to give the show his hands shook so much that hardly a trick came off. I thought that I would be lynched by the members of the Welfare Committee for wasting so much money but the sailors thought it the funniest show they had seen for a long time and I had to organise a repeat 'non-performance' the next time we were in.

Thankfully we were back in Sliema Creek at the beginning of May and I was able to get everything ready to turnover to my relief, John Miller. Having packed my bags and said farewell, I embarked in the old Cunard liner, *Ausonia*, which was trooping from India. Mary and Mike Shirley-Beavan were also on board, as were a number of *Chaplets*, and I found myself in charge of the naval contingent. This involved doing rounds of the ship and inspecting the cells, where there were several soldiers being sent home for imprisonment. I was horrified one day to find the cells empty and, on asking the sentry where the prisoners were, I was told that they had been given brooms and told to sweep the upper deck. I took exception to this as one of the prisoners was a convicted rapist and murderer. I sent for the Sergeant of the Military Police, who told me that it was quite all right as they couldn't go anywhere. However, nothing happened and we arrived back in Liverpool on about 26th May and then it was on to London by train.

Mary met me at the station and after a night in London it was off to Devon and leave. Michael had been left with Granny Bull and Mrs Barnes, so in the morning we caught the train to Exmouth, I with a great feeling of excitement and pride to see my son, now eighteen months old, for the first time. How exciting and marvellous to be a real family at last.

CHAPTER 7

H.M.S. *Ganges*

September 1947 – September 1949

At the beginning of June Mary, Michael and I moved up to Instow to stay at Croft with my parents. Michael was just 18 months old and fully mobile and I was quickly initiated into the rigours of fatherhood. Instow was returning to normal after having been taken over for amphibious training during the war, although the School of Combined Operations was still at Fremington Manor with its ancillary training camp at Instow, so that there were still a lot of military personnel about. The Yacht Club, then in the Round House by the Quay, was going strong with its full complement of 16 Taw and Torridge One Designs. Five of the boats belonged to the Club and it was possible, if your name came out of the weekly draw for boats, to race most days during July and August and Mary was indoctrinated into the mystique of racing these rather heavy, but fun to sail, boats.

However, I had been on leave only a short while before receiving my appointment to the Boys' Training Establishment, HMS *Ganges*, at Shotley near Ipswich as Divisional Officer for Drake Division. I was to go to Portsmouth for a week's Divisional Course at the RN Barracks on 21st July and then to Shotley so as to join two weeks before the end of the Summer Term. The idea was that I should have a good turnover so as to be able to start the job proper after the three week summer leave period. The prospect of having two years ashore was terrific and Boys' Training was considered to be a good job to get, though I hadn't an inkling as to what was involved.

Just as we were wondering how we should go about finding somewhere to live, we got a letter from Rupert Bray to say that he was already at *Ganges* as Signals Officer and that he had found a house which was too big and expensive for them alone and wondered if we would like to share. Sharing was the last thing that we had in mind but houses were like gold dust so we wrote and asked him to hold on to it until I arrived.

I joined at the end of July, arriving at Ipswich Station with all my gear, and was duly transported to Shotley. That same evening Rupert drove me over to Little Bealings, a distance of some 16 miles, to see the Manor House because the owner, another naval officer called Mike Chapell, was just about to sail for Malta and needed an immediate answer. It was a lovely summer's evening and having seen the Manor House I was easily persuaded that it could be divided up and that it was the place for us, despite the distance and lack of petrol which was, with all other fuels, strictly rationed.

Rupert and I each rang home that evening to say that we had taken the house and shortly after that Mary drove up to Lovington in Somerset, where the Brays were living, to meet Rosemary. Up until then it was only Rupert and I who had known each other and were enthusiastic about sharing and I was relieved at having found such a nice house. I hadn't realised that Rosemary, being Rosemary, made the rules.

The following day, having met the Captain, Eric Bush – a formidable tough character with two bars to his DSO and a famous Cruiser Captain during the war who had written a best selling book about it – I set about taking over Drake Division. *Ganges* was an enormous place, mostly single-storey buildings, which housed some two thousand boys. There was a school block, a huge gymnasium, indoor swimming pool, a signals school, a vast parade ground, a huge expanse of playing fields, a jetty and river frontage for innumerable boats and, towering above everything else, the Mast, reputed to be the highest in the United Kingdom, being about 200 feet.

The establishment was organised into ten Divisions each of about 180 boys. There was also a new-entry Division which took in the school leavers aged between 15 and $15^1/_2$, taught them how to wear their uniforms and to look after themselves and at the same time assessed their educational abilities. The boys stayed at *Ganges* for between a year and eighteen months, with the Communications boys staying the longest. Rupert was responsible for their training. The Seamen boys were divided into bright and not-so-bright classes and the brighter ones, along with the Communications boys, were expected to sit School Certificate (now GCSE) in a number of subjects. Drake, and indeed all the Divisions, had a mix of abilities and I found that I had two Communications and three Seamen classes.

Each class consisted of about thirty-five boys with two schoolmasters (Instructor Lieutenants) and 2 Chief Petty Officers or Petty Officers per class, I also had an Assistant Divisional Officer in the shape of a very nice Commissioned Gunner, Ken Chanter. Time was divided fifty-fifty between school and technical training. In the afternoons during the winter and in the evenings in summer everyone had to take part in some sort of sport. After supper the brighter boys did 'prep'.

The day started with a parade at 8 o'clock in the morning and ended around 7 o'clock at night. On Saturdays you were free after games at about 4 o'clock and on Sundays by lunch time, unless you were 'duty', in which case you slept on board. To make up for all this we had two weeks' leave at Christmas and Easter and three weeks' in the summer plus 'Half Terms' from Fridays to Monday. You were expected to be able to referee or umpire every sort of sport. There was no doubt that if a boy was willing and able *Ganges* gave him a splendid start in life but, inevitably, there were a number of slow learners to whom everything was pain and grief.

By the time summer leave came along I was only too aware of what I had been let in for, i.e. to be dead keen and hyper active! But, led by a very nice but dedicated bachelor Commander, John Hicks, and a jolly and enthusiastic Training Officer, Wally McKendrick, there was a great spirit about the place and everyone went about their business with a will. I thought that I should probably survive.

Drake Division itself consisted of four long single-storey buildings down one side of the 'Short Covered Way' which led down to the Main Galley. On the other side were offices, including mine, and store rooms. Beyond the Galley was the Long Covered Way either side of which were another four Divisions. Each building or 'Mess' had an area with tables and chairs called the Mess Square where the boys ate and beyond this, two rows of beds. Everyone had to collect his food from the Main Galley so the Drakes were lucky being next door and got their food reasonably hot but other Divisions were not so lucky, the 'Cooks of the Mess' (the boys sent to collect the food) having up to a quarter of a mile to walk.

While the turnover was going on Rupert and I, helped by the long summer evenings, managed to get over to the house, get things sorted out and deal with a massive plum harvest. There was an orchard of plum trees and we bottled pounds of plums using some curious plastic stuff called Porosan to seal the jars. I have never seen it since but it worked well and both families were to eat plums endlessly throughout the year that followed.

Back on leave in Instow, we organised the remainder of our belongings and eventually set off for Little Bealings with our car loaded to bursting point. Devon to Suffolk in those days was a major journey and it took us two days. The Brays had already got there by the time we arrived and had moved into their part of her house. The Manor House was part of an estate of three houses and had been a sort of Dower House for the Grange, a rather grand house owned by a local industrialist called Hervey. The main drive ran from the village past the Grange to our house but this route we seldom used. Our usual entrance was up a lane past the Manor Farm, where the farmer was also called Johnson. The house itself had started life as a half-timbered cottage dating back to the 16th century but had been extensively built on to in the 1920s so that the back of the house was ancient and the front modern.

Upstairs the Brays had a double bedroom over the dining room, a single bedroom for Caroline who was not quite three and Andrew aged about three months. They also had a bathroom and WC over the front hall. At the opposite end of the landing Mary and I had our bedroom with a bathroom and WC and also a dressing room which was used as a bedroom for Michael. Our bedroom and the room under it were even more modern, having been added in the 1930s. Downstairs we shared the large dining room, with its cosy stove, for main meals and also the large stone flagged kitchen. Off the front hall and opposite to the dining room we had our living room with a large open fireplace and French windows, which gave on to the garden beyond, and through our room was the Brays' smaller sitting room with a side entrance and WC.

Beyond the kitchen was the boiler room housing a coke-fired boiler, which heated the hot water and did a little intermediate central heating. There was also a back kitchen and passageway which led to a rather delightful back yard in which was the well – fitted with an electric pump – for our water, a prolific peach tree and, on the far side, a row of pigsties and outhouses. The whole place was surrounded by fine trees and to the north of the house were fields and a small stream.

Rosemary Bray, being a mixture of farmer's daughter, blue stocking, domestic science practitioner and economist, was quick to have everyone and everything organised. Food, fuel and clothes were still rationed and in the house everything was recorded to the last halfpenny. Rupert and I were responsible for stoking the boiler and we kept a record of the number of shovelfuls we put in on each day so as to eke out our allowance but I have to confess that I did a little cheating when the weather was really cold. I wonder if Rupert cheated too... Over and above the ration books, both families were limited by a general lack of cash. However we had great schemes to supplement the rationing.

We kept a couple of dozen hens and some pigs. The rule then was that if you raised and fattened your own pig you could, when you took it to be slaughtered, keep half of it for your own use. This in turn led to a great pig-swill industry. We dug and planted a huge area for potatoes and fetched waste food by the dustbinful in a trailer towed behind the Brays' car. All this had to be boiled up in the back kitchen on an ancient Valor paraffin cooker and fed to the pigs, who were all given names like William and Bertha. There was always a great to-do with the children when one of the pigs was taken off to the abattoir and it was very difficult, in fact impossible, to get a pig silently into the trailer. Even more tear-jerking was when, just before her date to go, Bertha broke out of her sty on Christmas day and was seen looking hungrily through the dining room window at our lunch. What do you give a pig for Christmas when you are looking forward to eating it in the New Year?

Whenever possible Rupert and I used to share a car, setting off each morning just after 7 o'clock, and often we picked up Mike Pawsey, another Divisional Officer, in Ipswich on our way through. At 8 o'clock all the boys 'fell in' on the Parade Ground by Divisions for muster and drill. The Gunnery Officer, Dennis Barton, or one of the Divisional Officers would take the parade. I had a fairly loud voice and rather enjoyed doing it. It gave great satisfaction to get some 1,800 people to perform in unison at your command and it needed a fair old shout to reach the back of the parade.

Shotley was naturally a cold place and the parade ground in winter was freezing. The Captain, Eric Bush, was a great believer in mind over matter and, never wearing gloves or an overcoat himself, forbade anyone to wear such sissy things. Consequently it often took about ten minutes after entering their class rooms for the boys to be able to bend their frozen fingers and hold a pen. On one occasion when I was driving Rupert into work on a very icy day, huddled in rugs and greatcoats (there were no heaters in cars in 1947), we saw the Captain standing at the roadside at the top of the road leading down to his house. Presumably the road was too icy for his car so we stopped to give him a lift. Getting into the car he immediately demanded that I should open the windscreen (you could do it in those days by winding a small handle over the middle of the dashboard) as he couldn't understand how we could stand the fug. Things changed in the spring when he was relieved by Geoff Robson, a charming chap who had a much more relaxed approach to life.

One of the main hazards when driving to or from Shotley was fog. Somehow the area was very prone to real pea-soupers and quite often it was necessary for your passenger to get out and walk in front of the car to show the way.

The Captain of Shotley lived about a mile from the place itself in a very attractive Elizabethan manor house, Ewarton Hall, once owned by the Boleyn family. In fact Anne was born there. Daily supplies were sent each morning down to the house in a coffin-like box slung on two poles so that it could be carried on the shoulders of four boys like the Ark of the Lord. These four had to help in the house and also in the enormous garden before carrying their cargo back in the evening.

Sport rated very highly indeed and competition between Divisions was keen, wins at each particular sport gaining points on a league table, with the Division coming out on top at the end of the Summer Term being awarded the Divisional Cup. Drake had won it the term that I joined and we struggled successfully to keep it at the end of the following Summer Term, despite a disastrous final in the cricket when my team was bowled out for 15 runs. What I always considered as my masterstroke was how we won the rugger final by putting our very good and highly trained basketball team into the three quarter line, where their speed and style of play baffled both the opposition and the referee and we scored about 20 tries. No other Divisional Officer would speak to me for weeks!

The big competition of the Summer Term was one run on the lines of the Field Gun competition, nowadays held at Olympia, and called 'Seamanship Rivers'. The Petty Officer Instructors used to make a book on this event and a lot of money would change hands. I had always been keen on devising new ways of getting a number of people to coordinate their different actions so as to make something happen quickly and for this competition we had a new way of getting two sets of sheerlegs, rigged with loads, whistling across the 'chasm' in minimum time. We won the trophy in both years.

Ganges was lucky to have one of the yachts taken from the Germans as a part of 'reparations'. She was the 60ft yawl *Helgoland*, built in 1938 for the German Navy and designed for ocean racing; Wally McKendrick had the job of running her and I wasted little time in getting myself qualified as a 'skipper'. She was used for boys' training and also for pleasure and racing. But, of course, most of the training afloat was carried out in service whalers and cutters and went on throughout the year and never mind the weather.

Not all the boys at Shotley were taken with the system. They had been entered into an engagement by their parents that committed them to service in the Navy for twelve years and so from time to time a boy would take off. The most common way to 'escape' was to go for a cross-country run and just keep on running. However, the local police were well-versed in what to do and, with Shotley being at the head of a narrow ten-mile long peninsular, it was not difficult to bring them back. If a boy was really unsuitable he would be discharged but otherwise it was not possible for a boy to leave the Navy once he had completed his first six weeks' initial training and 'deserters', when caught, were harshly punished. Looking back, this seems pretty inhuman and beastly but it was normal at that time.

I had one boy missing for eight weeks and his parents were extremely worried that he hadn't come home and no one had heard from him. He was eventually found hiding in the roof space of the Sickbay, where he had made himself a sort of nest, and had come out at night through a trap door to steal food from the galley. He was in an appalling state of filthiness when found. After he had been cleaned up and properly fed he was judged to be unsuitable and sent home for good.

Of course this was only one side of the coin. On the other side, one has to remember that with the school leaving age at 15, particularly for the brighter ones who joined the advanced classes and were able to continue their education, joining the Navy as a boy was quite an attractive option and many of the parents took an active interest in their son's progress, either visiting *Ganges* or writing to the Divisional Officer. Shotley was only part-one in a boy's training; after their year or 15 months they would be drafted to a Boys' Division in one of the larger ships – Cruisers or Carriers – where, as Boys 1st Class, they would continue with a mixture of practical and school work until they were 17 to 17$^{1}/_{2}$.

The brighter boys would be fast-tracked and many would eventually qualify as Warrant Officers or, through the 'Upper yardmen' scheme, as Commissioned Officers, Sub-Lieutenants or Lieutenants, according to their age. One other type of entrant is perhaps worth a mention: all three services were obliged to take a proportion of young offenders ex-Borstal (the predecessor of the present Young Offenders' Detention Centre). The only person privy to this, as far as name and previous record were concerned, was the officer in charge of the New Entrants' Division and this information was never disclosed even if the boy subsequently misbehaved. However, I had it on good information that the vast majority of these problem youngsters came good and the rigorous training with the prospect of a new life was just what was needed.

The highlight of the Summer Term was always the King's Birthday Parade followed by Sports Day. In the summer of 1948 the Guest of Honour was Admiral Cunningham, the famous ABC of World War II and now Viscount Cunningham of Hyndhope. A great deal of practice went on before the great day, just like the Trooping the Colour on Horseguards Parade except that, in addition to the parade, the Mast was manned for the Royal Salute. This took over a hundred specially selected boys. The greatest honour was to be chosen as the 'Button Boy', the boy selected to stand on the truck or button at the top of this 200-ft mast. This required a great deal of courage as the truck was about 3 ft across and certainly not a place to have vertigo. The only aid, an important one, was that it was possible to hold on to the lightning conducter when climbing on to the button and on standing up you could grip it between the knees.

Many of the boys had their parents for the occasion and all of us our families, my mother and father having come up from Instow. Two year old Andrew Bray was there with a black eye, having fallen out of a chair on to the stone floor of our kitchen when Mary, who was in charge at the time, wasn't looking, thus incurring the full blast of Rosemary's fury. Nevertheless the sun shone and everything went well and the following day Lady Cunningham presented the prizes for the Sports. One of the biggest events of the day was the 10-mile relay in which 800 boys, 80 from each Division, each ran 200 yards. This was a Shotley special and the excitement was terrific with leaders constantly changing. Eventually Drake finished second to Mike Pawsey's Hawke Division.

At Little Bealings we were very lucky to have found Joan Churchyard to help with the children. Aged 27 and unmarried, she loved the children and they her. Joan was to stay with us until 1954. We certainly needed someone, as Caroline Bray was a real little mischief and, under her leadership, she and Michael got up to all sorts of things like overflowing the bath to make a waterfall and pulling up all the flowers, carefully planted by Mr Wright our taciturn gardener, quite apart from wandering off to the stream and into Farmer Johnson's muck yard. Pulling up Mr Wright's flowers wasn't altogether bad as he was a very boring gardener who came with the house and who had a maddening habit of planting everything in the same colour and in straight lines. The summer of 1948 was a very dry one and we were worried that our well would dry up but, despite never having more than eighteen inches in the bottom, we had no problems.

On the social side of life there were occasional dances at Shotley and various other sorts of entertainment, while at the Manor House we had various people to stay – my parents, Mary's mother, Hester and others. We were lucky in having the sort of house to which you could have people to lunch or supper and give children's parties and everyone seemed to like coming to our 'country mansion'.

Our spare bedroom was quite interesting, to say the least, as it was in the 16th century part of the house and the floor, though absolutely solid, tilted at an appreciable angle. We had to prop up the legs of beds and furniture to get them level otherwise a night in the double bed could have been interesting. During the leave periods we were able to see a little of Suffolk and make an occasional trip to London. We had the excitement of seeing Mary Martin in 'South Pacific' at the Theatre Royal, Drury Lane, the first of the new breed of American musicals that we had seen, and we were thrilled by it. On one occasion we humped back a pedal car from Hamleys for Michael which, to my great annoyance, he could make go only backwards.

The Autumn Term of 1948 saw some changes. John Hicks was promoted to Captain and a new and rather portly Commander Farnsworth joined to replace him. Everyone likes to make his mark and his way was to try and cut down on the amount of foul language used, a laudable aim but not easy to achieve. His punishment for anyone caught swearing was to muster outside the Commander's office four times a day when each boy was made to gargle with an especially filthy tasting concoction, specially brewed in the sickbay, while chanting, 'Ahoy Ahoy this will make me a clean-mouthed boy' gluggle gluggle gluggle! It all took a lot of effort and didn't have much lasting effect.

Ken Chanter, my Assistant Divisional Officer, was also relieved by a very keen character, a Gunner (Warrant Officer) called John Cooke. He was a great swimmer and Water Polo Coach, quite an asset especially as every boy had to learn to swim and reach an acceptable standard. William Loftie of Rodney Division was also relieved by a remarkably keen and serious character called Norman Carrington. He had been a barrister before the war and had managed to transfer from the RNVR to the regular Navy after the war. He was a Lieutenant Commander and had a great many theories about training, so much so that he was able to convince the powers-that-be that competition was a bad thing because the less endowed got left out, a theory that has sadly become the norm in our school system today. The Divisional Cup was abandoned and the heat taken off inter-divisional matches.

This made life more relaxed but also led to a marked increase in petty crime as, rightly or wrongly, life had lost its focus. Healthy rivalry is a great incentive and was certainly needed in a place like Shotley. The real world is all about being competitive or sinking without trace.

Both Rupert and I were beginning to think about what we would do for our next jobs. We were due for our half stripes in the New Year (Lieutenant Commander) and it seemed a good idea to pass the Destroyer Command exam. This entailed going down to Chatham for a week in April 1949 to be examined in a variety of subjects, so we spent the entire winter swotting up. Mary used to sit up in bed questioning me from the various books while kicking me frequently to keep me awake. After our all-go day we liked to be in bed by nine thirty! Happily we both passed.

Another arrival was Tom Baird to take over Duncan Division. Tom got off to a bad start when at a Wardroom Guest Night, which tended to be rather rowdy affairs. He decided to demonstrate his fire-eating act which involved taking a mouthful of lighter fuel and blowing out a jet of fire. Unfortunately, having had rather too much to drink and swallowing instead of blowing out, he burnt his throat badly and was out of action for several weeks. One of the most popular after dinner 'sports' was for everyone to follow the Mess President over the mast. Luckily this didn't mean going right to the top but climbing up the lower shrouds to a sort of platform reached either by the futtock shrouds or, if you were not feeling brave, the lubber's hole, and then down the other side (the futtock shrouds leaned outwards at about 30 degrees so you had to hang on tight) and of course all this in mess kit with stiff shirt and winged collar.

Another good friend of ours was Hugh Wake, a direct descendant of Hereward! A Suffolk lad, he and his wife had a very nice old house in the country. He had been the Sub-Lieutenant in Imperial when I was there and now, as Exmouth Divisional Officer, he had been the greatest help to me when I first joined. Now he was to be relieved by Donald Cameron who had won the Victoria Cross when, on 19th September 1943, he had managed to get his midget submarine under the German Battleship Tirpitz, berthed in a Norwegian fjord. After releasing his massive explosive charges which were to cause Tirpitz considerable damage, his submarine surfaced and was sunk by the Germans; he and his two crew were taken prisoner. Arriving at *Ganges* in November with his wife Eve and their two children, they had been unable to find a house and we offered to put them up. They had the spare room, with their two children sleeping in two drawers from a chest of drawers. They were a difficult lot and we were glad when they found a place of their own and moved out.

Little Bealings was clearly a fertile place. Geraldine Bray was born in February 1949, Nurse Maude, a very nice elderly midwife, taking up residence for about a fortnight. Mary was also pregnant when, in April, Rosemary, stepping down from a chair while trying to close the bathroom window, put her foot through the floor and, in trying to save herself, her arm through the window. Hearing the screams Mary came to the rescue to find Rosemary streaming blood. Wrapping her arm in a bath towel and making her hold it above her head, Mary drove her as fast as possible to the casualty department of the Ipswich Hospital where they put in thirty stitches. Tradition has it that the signalman at Little Bealings station held up the train and kept the level crossing gates open for the emergency dash. Joan was left to try and feed the 8-week old Geraldine with a teaspoon. We discovered that there was dry rot in the beams and the floor over the hall and the whole lot had to be ripped out and renewed.

The Summer Term passed with all its usual activities and as Mary grew steadily bigger we experimented with needles suspended on a length of thread over her stomach, while she lay on her back on the floor, to see whether we were going to have a boy or a girl. Rosemary had a theory that if the needle swung back and forth it would be a boy and if round and round, a girl. In the event Mary woke me early in the morning of 3rd July to say that she had started and I shot off as fast as I could for Ipswich to fetch Nurse Maude. Having installed her with all her bits and pieces, I kissed Mary goodbye and set off to work. That afternoon a phone call told me that David had been born around three o'clock and, returning in the evening, I found everything in very good order and marvelled at our new son. This was the first time that I had ever seen a newborn baby. I don't doubt that Nurse Maude shooed me off after a few minutes. She kept us all in order and we were all rather in awe of her.

Just as soon as Mary was fit it was time to start getting ourselves packed up and ready to leave. My relief had been appointed and I was due to depart after the summer leave period. Towards the end of July I had been delighted to get my next appointment to command the Fleet Destroyer *Zodiac*. I think that Geoff Robson must have put in a good word for me as I was only 29.

We left the Manor House at the beginning of August, making the long drive down to Instow with David just 5 weeks old and Michael 3½; Joan stayed behind at Little Bealings. At the end of my leave I returned to *Ganges* to turn over to my relief, returning to Instow on 16th September to sort out my gear and get ready to join *Zodiac*. The ship was at Portland so, abandoning Mary and the children, I set off on 23rd September by train from the Great Western Station in Barnstaple to take up my first command. The train went via Taunton, Langport, Yeovil and Dorchester to Weymouth and I remember that the entire Guard's Van seemed to be filled with my bits and pieces. And so another chapter in our life opened.

CHAPTER 8

H.M.S. *Zodiac*
23rd September 1949 – 2nd April 1951

Taking over the command of a ship is quickly done. Once you have signed for the various bits and pieces and have been introduced to your officers, your predecessor departs and suddenly you are 'it', the Captain of one His Majesty's Ships and the two hundred or so souls in her. In one instant you find yourself set apart; whatever rank you may hold from Lieutenant to Captain, all captains of ships are treated in a sense as equals. You are the Captain and that is it. If you attend a meeting with other captains you are addressed as *Zodiac* or whatever the name of the ship is that you happen to be commanding. I found it a great feeling and something to which I had always aspired and had at last achieved.

My first task was to call on my Captain (D) – Destroyers – in *Zephyr*, the Flotilla Leader. Terence Maunsell had been the Torpedo Officer in *Barham* and our Snotties' Nurse; there had not been much empathy between us to say the least. However, he welcomed me warmly and explained that he himself was to be relieved shortly and that, in any case, *Zodiac* was to be lent to the 6th Destroyer Flotilla which consisted of the newly-built and building Weapon Class. They were one ship short of their eight and *Zodiac* was to make up the missing ship required for Fleet exercises. I was to sail for Portsmouth the next day to go into dry dock and have the experimental bow sonar dome removed; it was a device which stuck out on a short protrusion and was suppose to cut down ship noise. Our normal sonar dome was to be put back to work.

Zodiac was properly one of the ships of the 2nd Training Flotilla whose function was to train Command Teams in anti-submarine tactics and, along with several submarines, was based at Portland where HMS Osprey, the Anti-Submarine Training School was located. However, new devices were also tried out and *Zodiac* was to some extent earmarked as a trial horse. Except for a slightly less sophisticated gunnery director, she was identical to *Chaplet* and had been completed in 1944.

The First Lieutenant was Derek Hallifax, a Lieutenant and one year younger than I; he had been First Lieutenant of a number of ships and knew it all. My predecessor had been seriously ill and Hallifax had commanded the ship for about six weeks before my arrival and saw no reason why he should not have been allowed to continue to do so. We were to have a rather sticky relationship because his ideas as to how to do things were frequently different from mine. Nevertheless, we had a good team; Gordon Whale, the Chief, had been at Pangbourne with me; Francis Eddy was a good Operations Room Officer and No.2; John St Aubyn-Sayer the Navigation Officer and Harold Burns a cheerful and energetic Gunner TAS made up the team.

Arriving at Portsmouth I was relieved at being able to put the ship alongside without any disasters and with only a couple of engine movements. I have always believed that a Ship's Company will judge a 'new boy' by how he handles his ship, so I set a lot of store in getting it right. We were in dock for about a week while the work was carried out and then back to Portland to meet my new Captain (D) 6 – 6th Destroyer Flotilla – Kay Edden in *Battleaxe*.

It was customary to have a big exercise in the North Atlantic each autumn. Though I had been around a fair bit during night exercises I had absolutely no experience in the driving seat, neither did I know how my operations team would perform. I was pleased to find Geoffrey Kirkby in command of *Crossbow* and nipped over to him for some advice. Happily for me my Yeoman of Signals was excellent, as was Francis Eddy in charge of the Ops Room, and we survived some four weeks of dashing around on Carrier screens without anything too dreadful happening. It was a baptism of fire and I certainly learned a great deal about Fleet work very quickly but at the end of it all I think everyone in the ship felt justifiably pleased with themselves. We had a very nice signal from D 6 when we were relieved by *Scorpion*, the missing member of his Flotilla. During the exercises we had to put into Londonderry a couple of times to fuel, which brought back memories of going up the Foyle in *Verity* during the war.

While *Zodiac* was dashing around the North Atlantic, Mary was trying to find us somewhere to live near Weymouth and was writing to and ringing up various friends in the neighbourhood. Eventually someone came up with a guesthouse on the road to Preston called Streamside which she took thankfully. As a guest house it was closed during the winter and it was agreed that we could have the use of one end with our own kitchen and bathroom, while the owner Mrs Jordan, a lady in her forties, retained her bit at the other end. This would take us up to Easter, when it was due to reopen. Once Mary had cleaned the kitchen, which was filthy, it really did us quite well though we never knew whether the owner was there or not. The exception was when her boy friend called. He was a traveller in milking machines and on nights when we saw a pile of Alfa Laval machines in the hall, we knew that they were in residence and tried to keep quiet! Mary and the children moved in during October while *Zodiac* was away and Joan Churchyard came to help and look after the children.

Zodiac arrived back in November and, after a few days in Portland, set off again for Portsmouth for a six-week refit. This meant that I should be able to get home quite a lot. During the refit we were to have two important alterations. The first was to take out the circulating pumps from the main condensers, whose function is to turn the steam quickly back into water after it had been through the main turbines which drive the ship and then, of course, back into the boilers to be once more turned into steam. The theory was that the ship's passage through the water would, with the aid of venturi-shaped intakes, drive sufficient seawater through the cooling pipes of the condenser to turn the steam back into water without the use of pumps which, in themselves, used quite a lot of steam and energy to drive them.

The second alteration was to install an advanced type of torpedo-control-sight on the bridge. The Japanese had been very much better than we were during World War II and this new sight was supposed to be an advance on the Japanese system. It would calculate when to fire and give the right intervals between the launch of individual torpedoes, of which we had ten in two quintuple mountings. Once the order had been given to fire torpedoes the new system would off all ten automatically. Hitherto it had all been done by hand, using a good right eye and a prayer.

Our time in Portsmouth Dockyard was not without its troubles. While on Christmas leave I was rung up by Derek Hallifax to say that *Zodiac*'s Coxswain had been arrested along with two other Chief Petty Officers for smuggling. These three had been stopped in their car while leaving the Dockyard and the Police had found a quantity of cigarettes and meat wrapped in brown paper parcels in the boot. Each of the three said that they thought that the parcels belonged to someone else. However the Police claimed that the cigarettes came from *Zodiac* because of the Customs numbers on the packets, which, according to the Customs, were different for every ship. I was sent for by the Commander-in-Chief, Admiral Sir Arthur Power, who was furious.

At the subsequent Court-Martial held in the Great Cabin in *Victory* all three men were found guilty, despite the fact that the defending counsel produced cigarettes from no less than ten other ships then in the Dockyard all bearing the same Customs Numbers. My Coxswain, his brother from HMS *Maidstone*, and the other Chief Petty Officer were all dismissed the service, which I thought to be grossly unfair at the time and still do, as absolutely nothing had been proved. However, what was clear was that *Zodiac*'s victualling system and records were shown to be pretty sloppy and I received a certain amount of displeasure. I also caught a streaming cold from the freezing conditions aboard *Victory* during the Court Martial. I can only think that Nelson must have worn much warmer clothes.

Nevertheless life went on and we were soon back in Portland to carry out trials of the new equipment. The trials of the new condenser system required a lot of steaming at full power and we achieved 35 knots over the measured mile but, what was more remarkable, 24 knots astern. To do a measured-mile-run going astern required fairly calm water to avoid water slopping up over the stern and doing damage. The interesting thing was that, once the ship had been wound up to full speed on the astern turbines and provided you had steadied the ship on the right course, no helm movements were required and the ship went as straight as an arrow.

We also had to test our torpedo-firing arrangement which worked so well that it was decided to make an instructional film to show how it should be done. This involved firing ten torpedoes in the direction of Portland Harbour breakwater where the Torpedo Recovery Launches from the Experimental Establishment there could easily recover and service them and then get them back to us ready for the next shot. The torpedoes were each fitted with blowing heads, that is to say that when the torpedoes had run their distance, a compressed air charge in the warhead would blow the water ballast out and the torpedo would rise to the surface. In the operations room we had drawn a limiting line on the plotting table past which torpedoes must not be fired. We had to be further than 5 miles from the breakwater otherwise the torpedoes might hit it and be severely damaged.

All this worked well in practice, but was much more difficult to achieve once the film-shooting had started because the producer wanted the sun shining from the right direction and the helicopter doing the filming had to be in the exact position to see the torpedoes enter the water, track their run and so forth. Francis Eddy had strict instructions to warn the bridge if we were in danger of crossing the limit line. After about the fifth attempt the sun popped out from behind the clouds and we squirted off our ten torpedoes. As the last one went on its way Eddy shot up from the Ops Room to say, 'We were just a little over the line that time Sir'. I was horrified and we followed our torpedoes as they ran at 40 knots towards the breakwater. As they got closer not one had blown its warhead and I wondered how I was going to report the destruction of ten torpedoes on Portland Breakwater and who would relieve me in Command. In the event two had gone through the harbour entrance and the other eight had surfaced about 100 yards short. It was my lucky day after all.

Back working with the 2nd Training Flotilla, we got to know the rest of the ships. The new Captain (D), John Whitfeld, was a super chap with a great sense of fun. His Flotilla consisted of a mixture of ships which included four destroyers, *Zephyr*, *Myngs*, *Zest* and *Zodiac* and four Castle Class Corvettes. George Kitchen, a friend of mine from *Barham* days, drove *Leeds Castle* whilst *Zest* was commanded by an extremely wealthy Lieutenant Commander called Marten. He ran a very efficient ship 'in absentia'. He had large estates nearby and seldom came aboard more than two days a week when the ship was in harbour. When he did he was brought down to the ship in a chauffeur-driven Bentley followed by another car bringing his valet and chef. He left the Navy in the summer to manage his affairs and was relieved by a very nice chap, Bobby Ramsay whose wife was a ballet-dancer. Bobby always kept a pair of her ballet-shoes fixed to the top of the mast.

At Streamside our tenancy was up at Easter and we were lucky to find a jolly nice house further up the road towards Preston. The house belonged to Captain Dalrymple-Smith who was out in Bahrein. It was a great advance on Streamside and had a nice garden with the same stream running through it. We took on the Dalrymple-Smiths' Khaki Campbell ducks: Eenie, Meenie, Minie and Mo, their cat and also their rather decrepit gardener who gave advice while Mary dug! Across the road lived Dr and Mrs Sloane; their son David was just about the same age as Michael and they became very good friends, while their daughter Penny, who was a bit older, liked to come and help with our David. It was indeed a very friendly place with lots of children about the same age as ours.

Captain Caspar Swinley, who was the Naval Officer in Charge at Portland, was very concerned about the lack of security-consciousness in the base. There had been a spy scare and bomb threats and he decreed that ships should tighten their security arrangements. To test out the organisation, he introduced something called Operation Cuckoo. A ship would be detailed secretly to test out the security organisation of other ships in harbour by any means fair or foul that they thought fit. As

Zodiac had been away a lot and not well-known by the other ships, we were detailed off to be Cuckoo of the month.

We had a field day! We sent our Gunner TAS and a Chief Electrical Artificer, suitably disguised as dockyard maties, aboard *Myngs* where they successfully dismantled and came away with some vital bits of her sonar. In *Zephyr* we connected into her internal broadcast system with a microphone on the end of a very long lead which we took up to the cabin of a dockyard crane. From this vantage point and armed with a Bosun's call, we were able to create minor havoc for a whole day by giving a series of bogus orders and alarms. Derek Hallifax, dressed as a very sloppy Able Seaman, went aboard *Zest* in the Dog Watches and painted their forward 4.5-inch gun bright red. When asked what he was doing he replied that the effing First Lieutenant had told him to do it as part of his No. 11 punishment.

Another day we sent two Chief Petty Officers ashore, dressed as three-badge Able Seamen with forged joining instructions, to join *Myngs*. Armed with smoke bombs in their kit bags, they were deposited at Weymouth station where they were told to ring up for transport to their new ship. They were eventually picked up and taken off to their ship. Arriving on board they were allocated messes and jobs. That evening they fell in with the libertymen to go ashore, having first set the timers on their smoke bombs. They had the satisfaction of seeing smoke pouring from the forward mess decks of *Myngs* just as their boat arrived alongside the jetty. I forget who, but one of the Electrical Artificers had made the timers on board which was pretty clever.

Finally on a very calm night we unshackled *Zephyr* from her buoy and, using our motor boat, we towed her to another one but, in trying to shackle her on, we made too much noise and woke the Quartermaster 'on watch', who raised the alarm. We slipped everything and left her adrift. Having no power for the engines she had to drop anchor. After our last escapade the Cuckoo idea was dropped. However, *Zodiac*'s guilt was never discovered and I was able to remain friends.

Our daily task now was to take various classes out to the submarine practice area where they could have a go at finding and attacking a submarine. The most hairy were the Commanding Officers' courses as you were supposed to turn over the bridge to them and let them get on with it. I used to sit in my cabin below the bridge listening to every sound and trying not to worry. Every Thursday we used to do a night exercise with each CO in the Flotilla taking it in turns to produce the orders. This was good because it avoided repetition and stereotyping.

In June all the destroyers left Portland for the Western Approaches to take part in an annual pro-submarine exercise known as FOSM's (Flag Officer Submarines) Summer War. The exercise area was to the North and West of Ireland and based on World War II Fast Convoys. The weather was *glorious* and we had a very good ten days being attacked by and chasing submarines in the wide ocean, a nice change from Portland. At the end the ships went off to visit various ports and *Zodiac* was lucky enough to go to Douglas in the Isle of Man.

The Manx hospitality was quite something – free cinemas and dances for the Ship's Company, while I was taken round the famous T.T. course, to herring smokeries, for rides in a horse-drawn tram and to a splendid function in a sort of Casino, after which Captain George Eyston and I had to choose the winner of a Beauty Contest. Not an easy task when it comes to it and I think we failed to pick the favourite.

George Eyston turned out to be a really nice chap and not at all seeking the limelight. A famous racing driver, he had set up several records in the years before the war, culminating in setting a new World Land Speed record in 1938 of 357.5 miles an hour in his twin Rolls Royce engined car 'Thunderbolt'. This was taken from him by John Cobb in 1939 and because of the war the record stood until 1947. He and Cobb had been tremendous rivals in the quest for speed, but Eyston reckoned that now he was too old to have another go.

I had him to Sunday lunch and after he had gone ashore I thought that I would have a nap in my armchair. I woke to find people queuing to have a look at me through one of the scuttles of my cabin. The ship was open to visitors and I had become a major attraction so I had to feign sleep to avoid disappointing the populace. I heard one lady say, 'Ooooh look, I expect he's tired poor dear'.

Back in Portland we were detailed to act as Guardship for the Weymouth Regatta. This involved floodlighting the ship and, as we had the kit for doing only one side at a time, we had quite a game trying to keep the 'lit-up' side facing the shore. I thought that Mary and I should sail the ship's 14-ft RNSA dinghy in the regatta. Finding all the gear caused quite a bit of drama but eventually it was ready. We started in fine style but the wind got up and as the boat heeled, the water came pouring through the seams that had not taken up (they were traditional clinker built boats). Despite energetic bailing we sank lower and lower in the water until it was up to the gunwhales and we had to be rescued. I am sure that there were lots of people in the ship who were delighted that the skipper had been paid out for kicking up such a fuss about the state of the dinghy. We also had a Flotilla regatta in Portland harbour and I stroked the Wardroom whaler. We came a creditable second but I wasn't as fit as I should have been and thought that I was going to die in the attempt.

During the summer leave Mary and I took delivery of a new car from Heard's garage in Bideford. It was one of the first post-war-designed cars, a Morris Oxford with steering column gear shift and a bench front seat, both copied from the Americans. It had torsion bar suspension and, for the very first time, a heater. We made an unfortunate choice in colour – maroon – which faded very quickly.

Derek Hallifax had for some time wanted to be relieved and saw in Admiralty Fleet Orders that the Duke of Edinburgh was looking for a Sailing Master for his Dragon class yacht *Bluebottle* which had been given to him and Princess Elizabeth as a wedding present. I knew that he had been keen but had no idea of his sailing ability. We managed to arrange an interview with the Duke at St James's Palace and, much to the surprise of both of us, he got the job. We were both well-pleased. Derek's relief was a keen, fresh faced young Lieutenant, Dick Clayton, later to become Admiral Sir Richard Clayton. Francis Eddy was also relieved by another Admiral-to-be, Sub-Lieutenant Paul Greening, who much later became Comptroller of the Royal Household. I was well-pleased with the changes.

In October we were told that we were to be the headquarters ship for trials of a new Sonobuoy, an acoustic device dropped by maritime aircraft to detect submarines. The trials were to take place initially in the Channel and, eventually, off

Gibraltar in the New Year. The code name for this was Operation Candid. We went round to Portsmouth to have extra communications fitted and also a new US Navy invention, an underwater telephone. This would allow us to talk to a submerged submarine and tell it what to do. The 'A' class submarine *Aurochs* commanded by Toby Weston, an old friend of mine, was also allocated to the trials and we spent some time testing the underwater telephone and finding out its capabilities and limitations. Our Transducer had to be lowered over the side on a derrick which meant that the ship had to be stopped for it to work. However, when it was at the optimum depth, we found that we could get a range of about ten miles.

The Sonobuoy that we were to try was a British improvement on the American omni-directional buoy. The British one had a built in compass so that it was able to transmit a bearing of any underwater noise detected. In theory, if two or three of these directional sonobuoys were dropped near the position of a submarine, the aircraft could fix its position from the compass bearings transmitted and carry out a fairly accurate attack. At the same time as receiving the bearings the operators in the aircraft would also be able to hear the noise made by the object detected and decide whether the noise was being made by a submarine, fish or whatever. If the trials were successful this would be a very big advance in anti-submarine warfare and put us ahead of the field. After initial trials in the Channel we were to sail for Gibraltar in January 1951.

We had a good Christmas at Preston with lots of activity and parties for the children. We gave a largish party on a pouring wet day and everyone arrived in 'wellies'. In those days they were uniformly black and we managed to get about twenty pairs inextricably mixed; parents were swapping odd boots for days afterwards.

Before sailing for Gibraltar our 'Cuckoo' talents were once more called into play. The destroyer *Scorpion*, Commander Mallinson, was due to sail in company with us. Caspar Swinley, the NOIC, thought that Mallinson took life far too seriously and sent for me to see if we would be party to a little deception. The idea was that *Scorpion* should be asked to take some apes out to Gibraltar to replenish the stock of apes on the Rock, which was extremely low. This is of great importance, as the saying is that when there are no longer apes in Gibraltar, the British will be forced to leave. I said that we would do our best and everyone was sworn to secrecy.

I telephoned Derek Hallifax in London and asked him if he would get hold of some Royal Zoological Society headed paper – which he did without difficulty – on which I wrote a letter to the Captain of *Scorpion* saying that, with Their Lordship's blessing, the London Zoo had been asked to prepare four Barbary apes for passage to Gibraltar in *Scorpion*. An official from the Zoo would visit Weymouth at a convenient time and date to discuss arrangements. We also sent a signal to *Scorpion* purporting to come from The Admiralty which told them to give the Royal Zoological Society and the London Zoo every facility. I had arranged a suitable London address for the correspondence which was of course all sent on to us in *Zodiac*.

Our Gunner TAS, Harold Burns, was a Londoner and his wife had a London phone number on which to take calls. We enlisted him to be a Keeper of Apes at the

London Zoo and to phone the Captain of *Scorpion* to arrange a visit. This went off well and the Chief Shipwright in *Scorpion* was soon to be observed building a cage on the Quarterdeck as a sort of annex to the deckhouse for their anti-submarine mortar, Limbo, which was to be the apes' sleeping quarters. He also arranged for *Scorpion* to get on board several bales of straw and a large quantity of bananas. *Scorpion* wasn't too happy about the mess being made in his ship and I was asked over to lunch to discuss the problem. I listened sympathetically to his worries and tendered suitable advice.

The day came for us to sail and *Scorpion* was ready with cage, straw and bananas but no apes. The Captain made a signal to NOIC Portland, copied to *Zodiac*, asking for permission to delay sailing until the apes arrived. The reply came back from Caspar Swinley personally saying, 'Sail forthwith: guess who's been making a monkey out of *Scorpion*'. So off we went, keeping very quiet about the whole affair, but we all had a jolly good chuckle. However, I think the gods wanted to get their own back on me as, on the second day out, I missed my footing on the ladder coming down from the bridge and sprained my ankle very badly indeed and was in agony for days.

On arrival in Gibraltar we berthed in the pens – now a Yacht Marina – and *Magpie*, commanded by Prince Phillip, berthed outside us. He was the only Commanding Officer in the Fleet who was junior to me and so came to call. Meanwhile our trials team gathered. In *Zodiac* we had a very eminent scientist Professor Jones and another Chief Scientist called Norton with their various technicians; an anti-submarine specialist, Commander Ponsonby; and Wing Commander Hodgkinson, the RAF Trials officer, who was a tremendous help to me. He eventually became C-in-C Coastal Command. Under my operational control I had the submarine *Aurochs*, the RAF ship *Bridport* (ex coastal minesweeper) commanded by Squadron Leader Laughlan, two RAF Air/Sea Rescue Launches, a RAF Sunderland flying boat commanded by Squadron Leader Burgess and a RAF Anson, quite a little circus.

We were given two areas in which to operate, both on the southern side of the Straits, one to the East of Ceuta and the other in the Atlantic. This meant crossing the shipping lanes twice a day with my team, which became extremely worrying during the February fogs which are common in the Gibraltar area. We went to sea without fail every weekday for twelve weeks so were very glad of our weekends alongside.

We had not been in Gibraltar long before *Vanguard* arrived flying the Flag of C-in-C Home Fleet, Admiral Sir Philip Vian, as both the Home and the Mediterranean Fleets were gathering for the annual combined exercises. The C-in-C wanted to know what our motley collection of craft were doing, so I and *Bridport* went to call on him. Laughlan was a small red-haired man with a huge moustache. Vian took one look at him and said rudely, 'And by what right do you command one of His Majesty's ships?' Laughlan drew himself up to his full 5ft 2ins and said, 'An Extra Master's Certificate, which is more than any bloody Naval Officer, SIR'. After this all went well until I was told that my areas were interfering with the Fleet exercises and that I would have to go elsewhere. However, when I went to see Hilary Worthington Bigge, who had been my Captain in *Imperial* and was now a Rear

Admiral and the Chief of Staff, he was much more sympathetic and, after having explained our requirements, he arranged for both fleets to keep clear of our areas.

I have very disconnected memories of our stay in Gibraltar such as going off to play hockey or tennis on the pillion of Dick Clayton's motor bike; being taken on Sunday picnics into Spain by the General Officer Commanding (GOC), a fanatical bird watcher called Stayner; taking the AOC's 9 and 11 year-old sons to sea and getting them covered in paint and sent home stinking of white spirit (the Buffer, to my fury, had let them have a go at painting ship with disastrous results); of the great hospitality shown by the Garrison Battalion, The Duke of Wellington's LI; of watching the real apes and getting my cap pinched by one of then; of flying in the Anson and being in charge of the undercarriage which took 150 winds of a handle to get it up or put it down; and of nearly getting written off in the Sunderland. Hodgkinson had offered to take me up but there was little or no wind and despite starting our take-off runs from near Algeciras, we totally failed to unstick on the first two attempts. On the third attempt we just managed to clear the dockyard breakwater at Gibraltar and flew within a few feet of the Rock Hotel.

Another panic was when *Aurochs* suddenly came through on the underwater telephone to say that she was sinking. She had been snorkelling during this phase of the trial when her snorkel mast fractured allowing water to pour into the boat and, before they had been able to shut the intake valve, she had gone into an uncontrollable dive. At about 300 feet they managed to halt the descent and did an emergency surface by blowing every tank. She surfaced at an angle of about 45 degrees and the whole of her hull forward of the conning tower was clear of the water, quite a remarkable sight.

Later back in harbour I went to see Toby Weston, the Captain, to see if they were all right. On walking past the ship I noticed two stubby axle-like things sticking out on either side of the hull. I asked Toby what they were. He said, 'Good God the after hydroplanes have fallen off', and they had but no one had noticed. They were a very shaken bunch of submariners; our trial areas had been selected for the depth of water and if they had gone down much further they could have been crushed. As it was we had to wait several days before we could resume the trials.

But the trials had gone very well; the Sonobuoys had fulfilled their expectations and we had developed excellent techniques for their use. By the end of April we had completed our task and, after saying goodbye to all the friends we had made, we set off back to England arriving in Portland on about 30th April to find the hills behind Weymouth covered in snow from a freak snow storm. We had changed out of white uniform only the day before and didn't think it a very kind welcome.

I was due to be relieved and had sent a signal to my Captain (D), John Whitfeld, inviting him to lunch on arrival. With great forethought I had bought several pounds of delicious Spanish strawberries for the occasion. However, my steward in a fit of zeal had put them in the deep freeze to keep them fresh, so you can imagine my horror when (D) helped himself to strawberries and they clunked on to his plate like marbles. After the disappointment we were able to have a good laugh about it. He asked me what I wanted to do next and I said, 'The Naval Staff Course please'. He advised me against it saying that if I wanted to get on in the Navy I should stay at sea.. But, as always, I thought I knew best and stuck to wanting the Staff Course, for which he reluctantly recommended me.

We went on round to Portsmouth to give leave and I was relieved on 3rd May by Lieutenant Commander Geoffrey Wardle. He was quite a bit older than I and had been a prisoner of war in Germany, where he had achieved great notoriety as a locksmith. On one occasion in his Stalag, when all the British prisoners had been handcuffed by the guards, he had the whole lot unlocked and freed within about 20 minutes. For this he was sent to Colditz where his skills were put to good use by the escape committee. I was sad to leave *Zodiac*; I had had a good run, but it was nice to be home again.

Two years later *Zodiac* was sold to the Israeli Navy and renamed *Eilat*. After taking part in several actions she was sunk by a Soviet-made missile (like Exocet) fired from an Egyptian Navy Missile Boat on 21st October 1967.

CHAPTER 9

Staff College, Greenwich
1951 – 1952

As I had hoped, I was duly appointed to the Naval Staff College at Greenwich, a six month course starting in September 1951. As I had time to spare Their Lordships thought of ways of occupying it. One of the criticisms levelled against the Royal Navy by the Merchant Navy during World War II was that it didn't understand about merchant ships and how they ran. Had the RN been better informed things might have gone better. It was decided therefore that some officers would do a Merchant Navy liaison course which would last 2 – 3 months and this is what I was sent off to do.

My instructions were to report to the Blue Funnel Line head office in Liverpool complete with both blue and white uniform and they would arrange the rest. Blue Funnel was the nick-name for Alfred Holt Ltd, one of our most prestigious shipping companies whose ships were distinguished by an outsize blue funnel and all were named after characters in Greek mythology. As luck would have it one of the Directors of Alfred Holt was a Thornton cousin of Granny Bull and he took me under his wing.

The first ten days were spent in learning how ships were routed, loaded and unloaded and I was appalled by the amount of cargo stolen from the dockside and regarded as stevedores' perks. Holts was one of the largest shipping companies and traded with Europe, Australia and the Far East plus all ports in between. Many of the ships were general cargo carriers and each morning there was a meeting in the 'Ops Room' of Alfred Holt when ships positions and capacities were reported. From this, ships were re-routed or sailed to pick up cargoes reported and negotiated by their agents all over the world – a truly impressive set up and most efficiently run. Being a very large company of about 100 ships, Holts never insured any of their ships against loss but took immense care to see that they didn't lose any. Twenty miles off a headland was the closest permitted and at the end of a voyage the Master had to bring all his charts to Head Office where they would be examined minutely by the Marine Superintendent to see if the instructions had been adhered to; nothing was allowed to be rubbed out.

After my ten days I was instructed to join *Jason*, bound from Liverpool to Australia via the Suez Canal. She was one of their latest ships, 15,000 tons, with accommodation for 35 passengers in a fair degree of luxury. I was signed on as an Extra Fourth Mate. Captain Cooper, the Master, was a real martinet. The ship was spotless and ran like clockwork. The officers ate with the passengers and the food was out of this world! The idea was that I should go as far as Aden and then transfer to a ship homeward bound. We had an interesting lot of passengers with whom we were expected to be friendly at our respective tables and to help entertain when not on watch, but woebetide anyone observed by the Captain getting too chatty with the ladies.

I was attached to different officers in turn to see what they had to do in running the ship and also kept watch at sea but was not allowed to do so on my own as I had not the necessary 'Ticket'. Each day I accompanied the Captain on his rounds. Nothing eluded his eye and nothing but the best was accepted. Another daily ritual was the noon sight when all the deck officers were required on the Bridge with their sextants. The Second Mate who was the Navigator would give the cry 'Noon Sir!' when everyone from the Captain down would 'shoot the sun' and then, starting with the Midshipmen, each would report his reading of the sun's altitude. This was averaged out by the Second Mate and the Captain would declare the 'official altitude' to be used in calculating our Latitude and this in turn was written in the ship's log and used by the Midshipmen who were also keeping their own navigation logs as part of their instruction.

I didn't have a sextant of my own so, after the first day, the Chief Officer offered to lend me his. Arriving on the Bridge with it, I found that I couldn't see a thing through the telescope. 'How do I make this work?', I asked. 'You don't', said he, 'You just hold it up to your eye and when it's your turn to give your reading just choose a figure close to that of one of the Midshipmen'! The Chief Officer was quite a character; he had been in the Glen line before the war and had won a DSO for his part in Operation Pedestal, a convoy to re-supply Malta in1942 when the Germans did everything in their power to stop it getting through. His ship, the *Deucalion* was sunk the day before the convoy was due to arrive at Malta, having been attacked repeatedly by Stukas, JU99s and MTBs. Rescued from his ship he was transferred to the stricken Oil Tanker *Ohio* which was eventually towed into Grand Harbour.

Of the 14 merchant ships that sailed from Gibraltar escorted by 3 Aircraft Carriers, 2 Battleships, 7 Cruisers and 25 Destroyers and with the route covered by 8 submarines, only 5 ships got through. However this was enough to ensure that Malta based aircraft could attack Rommel's supply routes to North Africa and force a postponement of the enemy's offensive to drive the Allied troops out of Egypt. It also meant that, with 32,000 tons of supplies unloaded, Malta's meagre rations could be extended to keep the island going for another 3 months.

Jason made a short stop to bunker at Port Said before passing through the Canal. Though I had been to both ends of the canal a number of times, this was the first time that I had made the passage through. At this time the Canal was run by the Suez Canal Company who provided the Pilots. These were mostly British or French and they lived in some style at Port Fouad or Port Suez. Each Pilot came aboard with his own team of Egyptian Quartermasters who, as far as I could see, were left on the bridge to steer the ship through the Canal while the Pilot went below with the Captain to drink gin. I thoroughly enjoyed the experience; it was one of those ancient and modern experiences. Here was I gliding through in great luxury, whilst ashore the scene was timeless, of camel trains and donkeys.

Once through the Canal the ship went up to its usual cruising speed of 18 knots for Aden. Here I transferred to *Menelaus*, a much smaller ship of 8,500 tons on her way back to Europe with a cargo of Latex (liquid rubber) and Copra. She also carried 12 passengers in First Class accommodation but, while Jason was a passenger/cargo ship on a fixed schedule, *Menelaus* was a general cargo ship with the ability to take some passengers. Goods were picked up or unloaded along the route as directed by Liverpool.

My new Captain was a very relaxed individual and, as a consequence, the whole ship was reflected in his attitude but not necessarily for the better. However for me, it was all very enjoyable. The Chief Officer had two main worries: one was to keep the Latex at the right temperature to keep it liquid and the other was to deal with the swarms of copra beetles which got into everything.

Back at Port Said we had 48 hours to embark more cargo, mainly cotton, so I took the opportunity to visit James Hamilton, an old chum from *Dauntless* days and now a Canal Pilot. The Canal Company had a cantonment of very super houses at Ismaelia on the Bitter Lakes, each with its swimming pool, land and tennis courts. It was nice to meet up with James again and to meet his wife and family but I reckoned that, with all the luxury and huge pay, it was a really idle life. But this suited James down to the ground as he had always been a pretty relaxed character.

On the way home I again did a mixture of watchkeeping and being attached to different officers but here I was allowed to keep watch on my own as we steamed homewards at 12 knots. Once out of the Mediterranean the copra beetles began to succumb to the colder weather and things were more peaceful, though none ever penetrated the passengers accommodation. It was in this ship that I was introduced to a new wonder of modern living – Instant Coffee; this had come to the ship from America via Hong Kong and we all wondered if it would ever catch on!!

It had been planned that we should go to Hamburg to discharge some of our cargo but at the last minute our destination was changed to Dublin, where we spent about three days before returning to Liverpool. How very different it was coming up the Mersey from what it was coming back in 1941 in *Verity* after the rigours of an Atlantic convoy. Back in port the crew were paid off immediately and a special harbour crew took over to see to the unloading and any repairs and maintenance that were required. So, within two hours of our final docking, I was once more back at the Head Office where I was grilled about my experience and what I thought of the two very different ships. I had nothing but praise for both of them.

After a couple more days during which I was shown what happened to ships once they were home, it was off to Exmouth to Mary and the boys. Exmouth was to be our base while I was at the Staff College and Michael was starting school at Magnolia House with Miss Kemyss-Jenkins, where also, of course, was Philippa Crabtree. (Mike and she were to be married in 1971).

I joined Greenwich on 24th September 1951 along with about thirty other Lieutenant Commanders and Commanders. It was very much 'back to school' for all of us, with lectures in the mornings and 'prep' in the evenings. A Captain Crawford was in charge and we were split up into syndicates of about eight, with a member of the Directing Staff in charge of each. My mentor was a very nice Paymaster Commander called Peter Gick, a very different 'cup of tea' from his aviator brother Percy, who was real exhibitionist and 'fire-eater'. The course was designed so as to let you get home at weekends, so there was plenty of time to catch a train to Exeter on Fridays. However, while at Greenwich you were expected to work and the various schemes and tasks that we were given to do ensured that the corridors echoed with the clack of typewriters well after midnight on at least three nights of the week. Quite apart from finding the right solution, all work had to be presented properly in accordance with a strict format of paragraphs and sub-paragraphs, neatly typed and ready to be handed in the following morning. With one exception, we all found this a bit of a bind but the underlying idea was to teach you to work quickly and neatly under pressure.

The one exception was an Engineer, Kenneth Douglas-Morris, a term-mate of mine. He had taken the precaution of marrying an heiress, a Miss Pink, and they owned amongst other things, a chain of garages around London which Kenneth ran in his spare time. Ken would be picked up each day by his chauffeur in a very beautiful Lagonda, complete with his Secretary. On the way home to his house in Wimbledon he would dictate the solution to the set scheme to his secretary, who would type it up in the approved Staff College format ready for him to hand in the following morning. I believe that his solutions weren't always that good but they were immaculate. In later years it was the same Kenneth Douglas-Morris who put up much of the money for the Naval Museum in Portsmouth Dockyard, which also includes some of his own collection.

Despite all the scribing, I enjoyed the course and many of the lectures were extremely interesting as well-known figures in Government, the Trades Unions and Industry came to give us their views on post-war Britain and a variety of other subjects. One of the lecturers was Ian Fleming of James Bond fame, talking to us about intelligence-gathering during World War II, his job during the war. He arrived in a simply splendid black Aston Martin and in every way was the Bond role model.

During the course we had a number of talks about Europe and The North Atlantic Treaty Organization (NATO). I was impressed by the premise that a unified Europe backed up by the USA was the answer to peace for the future, so, when asked if we had any preferences for a job at the end of our course, I plumped for NATO. Thus, soon after Christmas I had a phone-call from my 'appointer' to say that I was to go to a NATO job in Germany and that I had better start learning German. Shortly after this the whole course went off to a final three weeks at the Joint Anti-Submarine School at Londonderry in Northern Ireland, I armed with Hugo's 'Teach Yourself German'. I suppose that we had been there for about a week when I received another call from the Directorate of Officers' Appointments to say that they had just found out that the NATO Headquarters to which I was being sent was actually in France. He also added as a by-the-way that it was a requirement to be able to speak French and that he had assured them that this was so. I told him that though I had done French at school I was far from being a French speaker. 'Not to worry', he said. 'You won't be going to Fontainebleau for a month so you will have plenty of time'. I threw Hugo's German into the River Foyle and went out to buy Hugo's 'Teach Yourself French' instead. That night I rang Mary to tell her the news. Neither of us had really liked the idea of going to Germany and, despite our lack of French, we were very excited at the prospect of living in France for two years.

CHAPTER 10

Flag Officer Central Europe
Fontainebleau
April 1952 – May 1954

So it was that I came to be appointed to Fontainebleau on the Staff of the Flag Officer Central Europe (NAVCENT) as the Staff Officer (Plans). I was to relieve Loftus Peyton-Jones and, along with all the instructions for joining, we had a letter telling us that accommodation was very difficult to find and that we would be put up in a hotel in Fontainebleau until something turned up. Loftus himself was a bachelor and consequently there was no house to hand on. It was clear that we would have to leave the boys with Joan at my parent's home in Instow until such time that we had found a place to live, when Granny Bull and Joan would bring them across to France. Mary and I would take as much as we could in the car, while the rest of our belongings – about seven trunks and packing cases – would come via the British Embassy in Paris aboard the small collier that made a monthly run across the Channel and up the Seine to keep the Embassy in coal!

It was very exciting but at the same time quite an anxiety. What would it be like to live in a foreign country? France was very expensive; how would we manage? Would my parents be able to cope with the children in our absence? Michael, who was now six, was certainly very apprehensive at being left behind. To take his mind off it I bought him a Gauge OO electric train set which turned out to be very fiddly, so no one was able to work it. The large piece of plasterboard that I had bought to screw the track to was already a source of annoyance to my parents as it was heavy and unwieldy. The only useful piece of the kit which turned out to be of any use was the transformer, which went on for years in a variety of roles.

At the end of March we set off for France on our great adventure; my appointment was to take effect from 4th April. The maroon-coloured Morris Oxford was loaded to capacity and so, with several boxes on the roof rack, we set off for Newhaven to catch the ferry for Dieppe. This was before the days of drive-on ferries and each car had to be slung on board by crane and stowed in the hold. On being hoisted out in Dieppe, one of the legs of the sling caught in the roof rack, lifting the two front feet and driving the two back ones into the roof. This caused two large dents and much Gallic shoulder-shrugging and, as if that was not enough, we found that we could not tighten the holding-down straps sufficiently to stop the whole rack and its precious cargo shifting every time we went over potholes or cobbles. This meant that whichever of us was not driving had to put their arm out of the window and hold it on. Not an auspicious start!

Driving south via the outskirts of Paris we found potholes aplenty and cobbles were the normal paving when driving through small towns and villages. It was well after dark by the time we arrived and we wondered if there was some sort of strike or power cut as there was not a sign of life anywhere. What we had not realised was that, in the first place, because it was Monday everywhere was shut and, second, that the French closed every shutter at sundown so that no lights were visible and that, at that time, street lights were few and far between. However we eventually arrived safe and sound at our small hotel near the Chateau and Loftus was there to give us a warm welcome.

Loftus had the rest of the week to show me the ropes and to introduce me to all the people with whom I would be working. Loftus was a Channel Islander, his mother was French and he himself bilingual. I think I was a grave disappointment as I stumbled along in my best schoolboy French! While this was going on Mary was trying to find somewhere for us to live. We were allowed two weeks in the hotel on the Navy, but after that we were on our own. Fontainebleau was the Headquarters for the Central European Command of NATO. The Northern Command was in Oslo and the Southern in Naples. The Centre consisted of the Allied Occupation Forces in Germany to the frontier with the Soviet Occupation Force in Germany. Within our Command were France, Belgium, the Netherlands and Luxembourg. The Supreme Allied Commander (SACEUR) had his headquarters near Versailles. The Centre's front line in Germany consisted of the British, US and French sectors running from North to South.

The Allied Forces Central Europe was commanded by a very tough Frenchman, le Marechal Juin. Juin had commanded French native cavalry, the Spahis, in North Africa. He had landed in Sicily in command of the French troops and Foreign Legionnaires and had led them in heavy fighting up through Italy. He had an American Colonel, ex Foreign Legion, as his Interpreter and Aide. Together they made a very impressive team.

Because of the Atomic Bomb the Americans played a pretty key role in Central Europe and the Central European Air Forces were commanded by an American Four-Star Air Force General, Laurie Norstad, very Scandinavian in appearance with piercing blue eyes. His Second-in-Command and in charge of the Allied Tactical Airforce was Air Vice Marshall the Earl of Bandon, a very cheerful Irishman known as the Abandoned Earl.

On the naval side was the Commander Allied Naval Forces Central Europe (COMNAVCENT), Monsieur le Vice Amiral Philippe Jaujard, a wiry little man with a small moustache, full of energy. It was he who, during the Normandy landings, was commanding the French cruisers, Montcalm and Georges Legues that had made such an impression on us by singing the Marseillaise while waiting off the beaches to give gunfire support. As a sort of counterbalance, the Chief of Staff was Rear Admiral Peter Cazalet, a very comfortable officer, whose brother trained the Royal race horses. He had a nice sense of humour and never seemed to lose his cool approach to life.

Our Command had responsibility for a variety of wartime tasks and took in the squadrons of Patrol and Landing Craft on the Rhine, the Kiel Canal, German ports, minesweeping along the North Sea coast and the logistic support of our forces by sea. The Americans, French and British each had squadrons on the Rhine and, in addition, the British had the Naval Base at Cuxhaven with the Flag Officer Germany, Rear Admiral Sherbrook VC in command. On the wider front we dealt with the Commanders of the two French maritime regions, PREMAR I at Cherbourg and PREMAR II at Brest. In the UK we worked with the Commander-in-Chief Channel at Portsmouth and, in Belgium and Holland, with those sections of their navies assigned to NATO in war or in peacetime for exercises.

Our offices were in the old part of the Chateau, le Cour Henri IV, built in the 17th century and which, apart from some very dicey electric light, had changed very little. I found that I was to share an office with a very nice Dutch naval aviator, Lieutenant Commander Ted Wils. My immediate boss was a rather serious Dutch naval Captain Ter Poorten, though it seemed that in most cases I had to deal directly with the Chief of Staff. On my first day I was taken to call on Admiral Jaujard who launched a flow of quick-fire French at me. When he saw that I was totally lost, he smiled and said in rather broken English, 'In England I speak English, in France you speak French', and that was it. Following that I went to see Admiral Cazalet who said, 'My boy, never write or say anything official in French: you are bound to get it wrong. Just stick to English and shake hands with everyone and you'll be all right'! Then he added, 'I believe the French even shake hands with their wives before getting into bed'!

Apart from the purely naval side I was also the naval member of the Joint Planning Committee headed by a charming and very erudite Brigadier called Spence, whose assistant was Colonel John Hunt, who later led the first successful Everest expedition, for which he was Knighted. My opposite numbers were a Major Somerville, who had been with French Resistance during the war, a very nice Frenchman, Lt Colonel du Hay, who was killed in Indo-China in 1954 at Dien Pen Phu, and a RAF Wing Commander who had escaped after being shot down over Germany and had made his way back to England via France, Spain and Portugal. It was becoming no surprise to me that all these Joint Planners were fluent in French!

On the housing front, Mary was in the hands of the Allied Housing Agency whose job it was to find places for all the different families and nationalities. France was woefully short of housing and the owners of the houses that were available were out to make as much money as possible. They therefore tried to let them first to the Americans as they had the most money, then to the Belgians who were not far behind; next came the Dutch and after them the British, whose allowances were niggardly, and finally to the French who had no allowances whatsoever and very little pay. What was left for the British usually was very grotty or a long way away. We had hoped to find something near to Fontainebleau, as that was where Michael would go to school, but nothing she was shown was anywhere near habitable.

At last, in desperation, we were put in touch with a Monsieur Barker, a house agent in Milly le Forêt some 20 kilometres west of Fontainebleau, who took us to see a house at Noisy sur Ecole, a little village nearby. Monsieur Barker's father had been an English 'Tommy' in the First World War but he spoke no English. However he was very keen to please. The house belonged to a doctor, Count Serge Tolstoï, a grandson of the author, and he had lived there during the war and afterwards used it as a weekend escape from Paris until his marriage broke up in 1951. Despite the distance from my place of work, the exorbitant rent, rising damp and lack of mains water, it was by far the best thing that we had seen. So, after much haggling over the price, we agreed to take it. It had charm, it had a garden and a bathroom and also a small cottage housing Madame le Loup, the guardienne and daily help, and her husband who was a gardener. It was a condition of the let that we took both of them on. Everyone thought that we were mad to live so far away and so did we. But there seemed no choice.

The house, which was long but only one room wide, appeared to have been originally two cottages which had been knocked into one. On the ground floor it consisted of a long living-cum-dining room with a log-fire at one end, then a small alcove that housed the central heating boiler and, beyond that again, another small room. On the other side of the entrance hall and down some steps was a largish kitchen with a smart newish wood-burning kitchen range and a two-burner cooker running on bottled gas. Up the stairs and on the side nearest the road was a large double bedroom which Mary and I chose and on the other side was a bathroom and lavatory complete with a musical toilet roll. On through the bathroom were two other bedrooms, the furthest of which had a huge and very ornate Napoleon-style bed and a door at the end, opening on to a raised bit of the garden and an enormous pile of rocks which typified Fontainebleau Forest and the surrounding area.

We decided to move in straight away and set to work to get ourselves organized. Though it was the beginning of April, it was still jolly cold and everything in the house was cold and damp. For the first two nights we went to bed in our clothes in an attempt to keep warm. We also bought a large supply of logs and some distemper (water based paint) and set about trying to smarten the place up. We were, of course, of great interest in the village – *les anglaises*; we might have come from another planet and people used to walk up and down the street outside the house trying to catch a glimpse of us. This was actually quite difficult to achieve because of the high wall that separated the garden from the road.

However, our immediate neighbours were most hospitable – Monsieur and Madame Marrotte at the farm where we got our milk and eggs, Madame Bioult across the road, Monsieur Mason the garagiste, and of course Monsieur and Madame le Loup who thought that we were quite mad but did their best to understand our rotten French and see that our needs were met. The le Loups' spaniel, Diane, was equally welcoming. On either side of us there were weekend houses; one belonged to André and Généviève Déroulède with their two daughters, Brigitte and Kathrine aged about 12 and 10. On the other side was an elderly doctor, Monsieur Dior, the older brother of the famous fashion designer Christien Dior.

Life at Noisy sur Ecole in 1952 was pretty simple. The several farms were quite small in acreage and grew mostly vegetables for the markets in Paris. Mechanical aids were few and far between and the ploughing of the fields in and around the village was accomplished by women using a sort of two-woman yoke to pull a small plough while the farmer steered. The milking of cows was solely for local needs and hygiene was unheard of. Mary would go with a can each day to collect our milk and took great care to strain out all the foreign bodies and then boil it. Each house had its own well and cess-pit, though we had the luxury of an electric pump for our well which was fine but temperamental.

Laundry was taken down to the village wash-place, a little stone building beside the river Ecole, little more than a wideish stream, and sheets and so forth were pounded on the stone slabs with a liberal dosing of Javel (a popular bleach), before rinsing off in the river, which of course carried all the waste on to the next lot of villagers about two kilometres downstream, who would be doing the same and so on. Butchers and bakers and the necessities of life came almost daily to the village in their vans and would stop outside the house with great hooting of horns. For a greater choice, however, Milly was only a couple of kilometres away with a very splendid covered market, while nearer at hand was le Vaudoué with a few small shops. Noisy boasted a Bar/Tabac and a very primitive hotel and restaurant, l'Hôtel des Roches, where the cuisine was presided over by an enormously wide lady who produced very good meals.

We quickly discovered that we had the only telephone in the village and anybody wanting the doctor, midwife or some other emergency would turn up on our door step. To telephone you had to lift the handset and then crank vigorously on the small handle in the base of the set. This generated a current and caused someone in an exchange to answer. You then demanded the number and hoped for the best.

As none of the villagers had the courage to do it themselves, Mary found herself passing on the messages and trying to understand the answers. Payment was always generous and in kind – a chicken, half a dozen eggs and so forth.

France was still showing the evidence of war and round about us on country railway lines were the remains of burnt-out trains, which had been strafed by Allied Air Forces, as well as war-damaged buildings. The country was very unstable and Governments seemed to change every few months. However, in contrast with Britain, there was no rationing except by price. We were delighted to have left our ration books behind but life in France was extremely costly; indeed we had to watch every centime. Because of galloping inflation in the years immediately following the war, the rate of exchange was about 1000 francs to the pound and a simple ice-cream in Fontainebleau cost 1000 francs. Petrol too was at a huge price but happily NATO forces had a ration of special coupons which, if you went to the right petrol station (Caltex), you could fill up at about half-price. Nevertheless, to drive into Paris was a very expensive adventure.

By the end of April we reckoned that we were sufficiently organised for Joan and the boys to join us. Granny Bull was in charge of the party and they were to come across on the night ferry from Southampton to le Havre and then on to Paris, where we would meet them at the Gare St Lazarre. Just how we got everyone, plus Joan's and Michael's bicycles, back to Noisy in our car I cannot imagine, but we did and in those days there were no rules about how many people you could cram on to the front bench seat. David's first words to his mother after not having seen her for six weeks were, 'Why have you got your best coat on?'

Back at Noisy everyone was delighted with the house and the boys thought it great fun to run through Michael's bedroom, out of the house, to where there were masses of bluebells amongst the rocks and trees, slide down the bank on to the front lawn and then back in and up through the house to do it again. They were also intrigued by the le Loups' little house at the far end of the garden, their dog Diane and the rabbits in their cages (kept by the le Loups for the pot but, of course, this was a closely guarded secret!). The other bit of livestock in the garden were the bees. Dr Tolstoï had left several hives for which we were responsible. The hives were tended by the village drunk, Monsieur Jules, a very tough customer indeed, but perhaps because of the general aura of alcohol which surrounded him, he never got stung.

Mary's mother stayed for about a week and we tried to show her as much as possible in the short time before putting her on the train for home. Meanwhile school had started for Michael. There was a school for the children of the British element in Fontainebleau, so he had to set off at eight o'clock each morning and was brought back by school bus in the evening. As Noisy was the last place on the route and the journey home took anything from an hour to an hour and a half, he was seldom back before five thirty, a very long day for a six year old. Additionally Mary was totally stranded unless she took me to work in the morning and then came back to Fontainebleau at around six in the evening to bring me home.

It was obvious that we needed a second car. The problem was to find one that we could afford to buy and, almost more important, afford to run. Geoffrey Kirkby was at SHAPE, near Versailles, and he and Daphne together with their two daughters, Auriole and Emma, were also living out in the country. Geoffrey, being the clever chap that he was, had already solved the problem with a Bond Minicar. This was a small three-wheeler shaped like a flat iron with the pointed end in front, where the single wheel, which also steered the machine, was driven by a 187cc Villiers two-stroke engine. Not designed to have any great speed, it did about a hundred miles to the gallon. We resolved to get one during the two weeks' summer leave back in Instow. As the Morris Oxford didn't seem very well-suited to the bumpy French roads, we had already planned to change that for a Vauxhall Velox, a 1500cc saloon which we thought was the ultimate in modernity.

Back in England we soon discovered that second-hand Bond Minicars were few and far between but, just when I was giving up all hope, one turned up actually in Bideford and I bought it immediately for £80. This was about two days before the end of our leave, so, with scarcely time to find out how to drive it, we set off back to France, Mary in our very smart dark green Vauxhall Velox and I going ahead in the pale blue Minicar. All went well to Southampton and in loading but shortly after leaving le Havre I hit a large pothole; the driving chain flew off and I came to a grinding halt. Getting it back on again was a difficult and messy business but by the time we arrived at Noisy I had become quite good at it. However we did go the whole way from Instow to Noisy on two and a half gallons of petrol, though Mary had a worrying time waiting at various rendezvous for Michael and me to turn up.

I was depressed about the Minicar's driving chain; it seemed that the chain was continuously stretching and becoming loose but a motor-bike garage in Fontainebleau fitted a new French chain, which totally solved the problem. Travelling in the Mini one had a great feeling of enormous speed as the bench seat was only about four inches off the ground but, in point of fact, the maximum speed was only about 40 mph and a good thing too, as braking was not one of its strongest points. Neither, for that matter, was starting which was achieved by jerking a lever – situated by the side of the driver – which was connected to the kick-start of the motor bike engine under the bonnet. When this failed, as it frequently did, pushing was the only answer! Happily the car was such a novelty in a place like Fontainebleau that a crowd quickly gathered to see what manner of beast it was and once three or four were gathered round it was a simple matter to lean out of the window and ask for a shove.

Getting in and out was also a crowd-puller. The car had no doors and so, when the roof was up, the only way to get in was head first through the small slot between the side of the car and the roof. Getting out was even less elegant as it was necessary to get your feet out first while lying on your back across the seat. Once you had emerged as far as your middle it was possible to roll over on your front, extricate the rest of you and stand up. This invariably got a round of applause from any curious onlookers who had gathered to watch.

During our first months at Noisy, Mary was able to find some good friends both for herself and for the boys. The Gowlands, Pusinellis and Stenhouses were all frequent visitors and Jessica Gowland was a fine friend for David. However David quickly endeared himself to Madame le Loup and others in the village, such as young Claudette Marrotte and the Déroulède girls, and quickly picked up enough French to be our official interpreter which Joan, who had not learnt French at school, found particularly useful when she went off exploring, with David strapped to the child's seat on the back of her bike. Mike also went on some of these outings and on one occasion she and Mike pedalled their way to Fontainebleau and back, some 20 km each way.

At the AFCENT headquarters we were kept pretty busy. I made several visits to Germany to find out what went on and watched various exercises on the Rhine near Heidelberg and Mulhouse. One of the first things that I had to plan was the blocking of the Kiel Canal should the Soviets attack. Originally it had been thought that blowing up the lock gates at either end would be sufficient but I was able to prove that once the gates had been cleared away the canal would still be navigable for shallower draft vessel even though it would be tidal. To prevent this, large concrete towers would have to be – and subsequently were – built that could be toppled into the canal and effectually block it for several days at the very least. Whether it would have worked in practice is another thing but everyone thought it was a splendid idea.

Both the French and the Americans, but particularly the French, were very keen on finding ways of launching floating mines into the Rhine to disrupt any attempted Soviet river crossing. The Royal Navy at Krefeldt were not so keen on this at all and I wrote endless letters about 'Mines Fluviales'. The British rightly thought that being at the downstream end they would receive the lot. Finally after many trials, when all the dummy mines launched ended up tangled in the banks of the Rhine after a relatively short distance, the idea was dropped.

Soon after I arrived Vice Amiral Jaujard was promoted to Vice Amiral d'Escadre, which was only one from the top in the hierarchy of French Admirals, and I accompanied him in this rank to Portsmouth to call on Admiral Sir Arthur Power, the Commander-in-Chief Channel Command. As was – and still is – the custom, Admiral Power received my Admiral aboard HMS *Victory*, an act which Jaujard considered as a studied insult to the French Navy and it took a lot of talking to unruffle his feathers but in the end sense prevailed and we had a very successful visit.

The Cour Henri IV had no facilities for feeding and the long French lunch hour, more like two in reality, was designed so that people could go home for lunch. In my case distance made this impracticable and so I would go to the French Army Club on the edge of the town. Here you could get lunch at a very reasonable price with a ration of French Army wine, pretty rough stuff but all right provided you drank it half-and-half with water, which everyone did. I normally had lunch with Major Mike Carver (now Field Marshall Lord Carver), who was on Field Marshall Montgomery's staff. Monty lived in the Chateau of Courances which had been lent to him for life by a grateful French nation. Each day Mike and I would put the world to rights; he was an exceptionally nice chap who had been an Acting Brigadier at the age of 28 at the end of the war but, in the funny way that the Army do things, he reverted to his substantive rank when the war was over.

General Eisenhower was the Supreme Allied Commander Europe (SACEUR) and Monty was his deputy. In this capacity he was the prime mover in a sort of military Think Tank in which Mike Carver was one of the principal thinkers. Each year Monty would give a presentation to a large and illustrious audience of Allied Commanders and their staffs with the object of stretching their minds into the future and, in particular, to think about the problems brought about by the proliferation of nuclear weapons, very much a new concept and about which people knew extremely little.

I went to two of these while at Fontainebleau and Monty, being a showman and guru rolled into one, made a considerable impression. Quite apart from the concept, which was excellent, Monty had certain rules that had to be obeyed even by four-star Generals. One was no smoking and the other was no coughing. Before each session orderlies would come into the small theatre in Paris, in which these presentations were held, bearing tray-loads of cough-sweets. If, despite your cough-sweet, you coughed you were politely shown the door and had to wait outside until the next interval. All these presentations were either in French or English with simultaneous translation and everyone attending had to be able to understand one or other of the two official languages. Half way through the first morning that I was there an Italian General rose to his feet and suggested that it should also be translated into Italian. Monty, who clearly had no high opinion of the Italian military said, 'Very well General, you know the rules and if you can understand neither French nor English you are wasting your time and mine too. I suggest you go home'. He did!

During the autumn there was a big NATO exercise, part of which was to move to our war headquarters. These were situated near Soisson in part of the old Maginot line and had been used by the German High Command under General Von Runstedt for the defence of France. Consequently many of the signs and notices designed to tell you how to get round in this vast concrete rabbit warren were still in German. The communications as far as we were concerned were hopelessly inadequate in controlling anything, let alone a dummy war. The Army and Airforce fared little better and the Marechal Juin was furious about the whole thing. However, more modern underground headquarters were in the process of being built near Fontainebleau. During the winter too we had to organise and umpire coastal exercises along the Netherlands coast from Den Helder, the Dutch naval base. The weather was freezing cold with fog for most of the time, so here again we had quite a little difficulty.

The winter of 1952 was indeed a cold one and at Christmas we had a good covering of snow. The river at Noisy was frozen, so we could skate on it, and we also built a huge snowman in the garden. We had been going each Sunday to the Protestant Church in Fontainebleau and this Christmas Michael was a King in the Nativity play put on by the children of the British School and very well-done too. The French did not go in for Christmas trees and I had been asking around the village about how to get one. There were plenty of suitable trees around but they all belonged to someone and were not for sale so we were very disappointed. However, shortly before Christmas day, there was a loud knocking on our door just before midnight and on opening the door I was confronted by Monsieur Bioult with an enormous tree which he insisted that we accepted as a present. This we did gladly though it was quite clear that he had hijacked it from someone's estate in the middle of the night. Ask no questions seemed to be the best line to take. It was a splendid tree, reaching from floor to ceiling, and we had to make a dash to Paris to buy more decorations from the Gallerie Lafayette, which we still have. Of course we had real candles and when lit it looked a real picture. Many from the village came to see it and there were oohs and aahs when the candles were lit. I was always hugely relieved when they were blown out and we had not set the house on fire. It was a wonderful Christmas.

In the middle of January Peter Cazalet was relieved by Rear Admiral Howard-Johnston, a very different sort of chap from his predecessor. He was an all-go person and expected everyone else to conform. Each morning he went riding by arrangement with the French local cavalry regiment and would arrive in the office at about 1030, when he expected a briefing from the British contingent about what was or was not happening. He would then work until about 7 o'clock in the evening and none of us was supposed to leave before he did. He had the reputation of being a workaholic in his younger days and, when Captain (D) in Portsmouth, is said not to have noticed that his wife was getting off with his First Lieutenant. His marriage finally broke up after a tragic event. His son was a Sub-Lieutenant in the submarine *Affray* when she sank in the English Channel with all hands. H-J had been in charge of the force searching for her and was unable to locate the submarine until it was too late. It might have been too late in any case as she must have sunk instantly when her snorkel mast broke off and she fell into a sort of crevasse in the sea bottom near the Channel Islands.

H-J had married again, this time to the daughter of Earl Haig, the Commander of the British forces in France in World War I. She was very nice and they had small children about the same age as ours. Mary and I were enlisted into trying to find them somewhere to live and we put him on to a small chateau near Milly le Forêt, which they took. His mother was French and lived in some style in a large apartment off the rue Faubourg St Honoré, quite close to the British Embassy, where at one time he'd been Naval Attaché. He spoke uninhibited but not particularly good French. In fact Rear Admiral C.D. Howard-Johnston CB, DSO, DSC and Bar was a pretty uninhibited chap altogether. When travelling by train to London, which was the usual way in the '50s, he would have his Secretary ring up the Station Master at Victoria Station to notify him of the time of his arrival and departure and expected to be – and indeed always was – met and escorted to and from his carriage by the Station Master dressed in Top Hat and Frock Coat. I liked him.

Early in the Spring we moved from our rather quaint office in the Cour Henri IV to purpose-built Headquarters at Camp Guynemer, about $1^1/_2$ kms away on the edge of the Forest and next door to the Airforce HQ (AIRCENT). Only the Army remained in the old Palace. The new offices were a great improvement, being light and airy, though not particularly well-built, as we were to find out when one day the Chief Writer, who was in charge of the Confidential and Secret Material so carefully kept in the Strong Room, slammed the door and the wall fell down.

Spring was a beautiful time in the forest and great areas were carpeted with little wild daffodils, les jonquils – really delightful. When the weather was nice, Mary would meet me with David and a picnic lunch, either in the forest or by one of the large lakes in the grounds of the Chateau. Feeding the swans was always a great excitement and one old swan, whom we called Alphonse, was always there ready and waiting. It was on one of these occasions that David caused a great stir by falling in. Mary quickly jumped in to fish him out and I was told off for not doing anything because I was in my best uniform!

Towards the end of March we packed everyone into the car and set off for the Costa Brava in Spain, where we had booked in for a week at a small hotel on the coast about 20km north of Barcelona, the Fonda Levante near Palafrugel. Having heard terrible stories about the drinking water we took with us a vast stock of Evian, 90% of which we brought back undrunk. We spent a couple of nights on the way, one at Cahors in the Railway Hotel and the other near Carcassonne, a wonderful medieval walled city. The French roads were not much to write about but the Spanish ones were infinitely worse, with no metalled surface in the villages and small towns, but the Vauxhall behaved impeccably.

The Fonda Levante was primitive but clean and right on the beach and we ate all sorts of things like squid and octopus that we had never had before. For most of the week it was pretty warm and everyone bathed, the boys wearing cork lifejackets. Michael had just about learnt to swim when the weather changed and a bitterly cold wind came down from the Pyrenees for our last two days before we made the long journey home. It was the greatest help to have Joan in the back to keep the children amused.

Our second spring at Noisy was delightful and we tried to get as many people to the house as possible. Apart from friends and relatives we made a big effort to get to know the other nationalities. Anke Wils was a frequent visitor and we would look after their spaniel when she and Ted went on leave to Holland. We also got on well with the Baudouins (he was a French naval Captain in charge of the Logistics division) and André Beau and his very glamorous wife. Beau was a Capitaine de

Frégate and Jaujard's Chef de Cabinet and, like H-J, was a very keen horseman and hunted with the local staghounds in Fontainebleau Forest. The members of the hunt were always beautifully turned out in dark green jackets and the ladies wore tricorne hats. However the local soldiery – mostly cavalry – who took part, turned out in uniform and consequently Beau wore naval uniform, cap with chin-stay down and very smart white riding breeches and riding boots.

The Fontainebleau hunt was a very famous affair and many rich Belgians would come from Brussels for the weekend's hunting. We used to go and watch the meets which were a great spectacle and run to a strict format. What amused us most was the team of hunt servants, splendidly dressed, who would play the appropriate tune on great curly hunting horns and then pile into a 15 CV Citroën Traction Avant which followed the hunt at great speed down the forest track to the next point or stage in the hunt, when they would leap out and play the tune for the 'kill', 'gone away' or whatever. These curly hunting horns were also carried by all the mounted members as a part of the uniform but I never saw anyone trying to play one. They were carried with the loop over the right shoulder and the horn under the left arm facing to the rear. Great on looks but not good news if you fell off and most of them were well-dented.

As a senior member of the French Navy, Admiral Jaujard would get special tickets for the theatre in Paris which he very kindly passed on. Mary and I accepted them gladly and made several visits to the Comédie Francaise and also once to the Opera, so we became well-indoctrinated with French classical theatre seeing such plays as Phèdre, La Porte soit Ouverte ou Fermée and Carmen.

It was not long after our return from Spain that Madame le Loup had a stroke and Mary had to summon the doctor and persuade him to do something about saving her life, a thing he was most unwilling to do, saying that it was pointless trying to save the lives of elderly working class people. I suppose she was about 60 and had worked hard all her life. However Mary prevailed and she was taken to the General Hospital in Fontainebleau. She was there for several months and we used to take le Loup in to see her. Run by a nursing order of nuns it was a very basic place indeed with an all-pervading lavatorial smell. Nevertheless they got her back on her feet and, though paralysed down her right side, she was able to go back home and made a very good fist of running their little house where everything was polished to the nth degree. Of course she was no longer able to help Mary but she and her husband lived on together for another twenty years, so we always felt that our trouble had been worthwhile.

In 1952 as a result of the Bonn agreement, West Germany became an independent state and a member of NATO. Now, in 1953, moves were afoot to re-arm the country and bring Germany into the NATO Command organization. Consequently there were a number of secret meetings in Paris to try and determine what form the re-arming should take and how the public could be brought round to accept the new situation. Only seven years after the end of the war the memories of all the things perpetrated by the Nazis were all too fresh in peoples minds. Indeed, in the Forest close to Noisy there was a monument bearing the names of people tortured and killed by the Germans and plaques could be found in churches and public places throughout France telling the same story. Inevitably, talk of re-arming the Germans was an emotive subject and not only in the occupied countries but in Britain too.

The new West German forces were to come within the Central European Command and as a consequence NAVCENT was made responsible for the shape and size of the new German Navy. As Staff Officer (Plans) I was set the task of working out the number of ships and men and what their function should be. This involved a lot of preparation work, meetings under the Chairmanship of H-J with World War II German naval officers in little used offices in Paris (the Germans of course as civilians) and then a series of briefings for French, British and Benelux naval authorities as well as the US naval forces. This went on right through the summer.

At the same time as all this the British were getting very excited over the Coronation of Queen Elizabeth II in Westminster Abbey on 2nd June. There was an allocation of seats to watch the procession and being lucky enough to get two we decided that Joan and Michael should go. Finding somewhere for them to stay was the next problem but we got on to a friend of mine, Dr Michael Pallot, who had a practice in the suburbs and who agreed to put them up for a couple of nights. It was not the greatest success as I think Michael and Joan had to get up at 4.30, be given breakfast and then catch the Underground to Trafalgar Square to be in their seats by 7 o'clock along with millions of others doing the same thing. Their seats were near The Admiralty Arch and they had a very good view, quite an experience for a seven year old, but it was a very very long day! The next morning the Pallots put Michael on a plane back to Paris and Joan went off to Suffolk for a few days to see her family.

Meanwhile at Fontainebleau, Mary and I decided that we would have a Garden Party at Noisy to celebrate the Coronation and invited 50 or 60 people to come and eat strawberries and cream and drink champagne. The day we had chosen turned out to be a super one, but fate was not kind. That morning Mary discovered that she had German measles and though not feeling ill, had to remain in purdah in her bedroom and have strawberries and champagne brought up by anyone not scared of getting the bug. Really rotten bad luck after so much hard work and preparation but, thanks to just that, the party was voted a great success.

About four weeks after that we took the whole family into Fontainebleau to see a special screening of the Coronation film, which thrilled us all, but on the way home disaster struck. As we were driving along a straight but narrowish road through the forest, a tractor towing a load of logs suddenly came out of a forest track immediately in front of us. I tried to miss it but couldn't and the car spun round and rolled over several times before coming to rest the right way up in a ditch. Of course no one had seat belts in those days; David was on the bench seat in the front with Mary and me, while Joan and Michael were in the back. We all tumbled about like peas in a drum. I was bleeding from a cut on my forehead and Joan had taken a hard knock on one side but otherwise we all seemed to be in one piece.

The first thing any of us can remember was a Frenchman peering in through the side window and saying, 'Heureusement, personne est mort'. (Luckily, nobody's dead.) Somehow we were all taken to Fontainebleau to see the duty Army doctor who took a cursory look at us, put some stitches in my head and sent us home with instructions to rest up a couple of days. The car was a write-off and I went to the police to try and get some satisfaction from the other party but it turned out that the tractor driver was self-employed, had no licence to be on the road, had no insurance and had a wife and six children. We were on our own.

We had all been terribly shaken up but everyone was most helpful. H-J lent me his official car until such time as I could get myself organised and we still had the Bond Mini. But life had to go on and I can remember having to go to a meeting in Portsmouth the following week with my head feeling like a football. Getting a new car was a problem, for, though we could order one easily enough, it had to be paid for in France. The insurance could only pay us in England. At the time there were strict exchange controls limiting the amount of sterling that could be taken out of England and I regret to say that we had to break the law by enlisting the aid of a number of people to bring us enough money out of England. It was a great relief when we took delivery of another Vauxhall Velox, this time pale metallic blue.

Almost more difficult was getting rid of the old car. The authorities said that it had to be either shipped back to England, where it would be liable for 33% Purchase Tax, or imported into France at a similar expense before it could be officially scrapped. (It was a perk for the job that we had been able to purchase it in the first place free of tax). In the end the garage in Fontainebleau managed to 'lose it' for a modest sum and nothing more was said.

Work on the new German Navy was going apace and in September there was a meeting in Paris to reach a final agreement. The head of the German delegation was General Spiedel who had been Chief of Staff to Rommel's Afrika Corps in 1942 when they almost drove the Allies out of Egypt. Later he was second in command to Kesselring in Italy and was quite a German war hero. He had, however, supported Rommel in his plot to overthrow Hitler and had not been considered by the Allies as a 'War Criminal'. As a consequence he was permitted to represent the new German forces.

Everyone having agreed to the proposed shape and size of the German Navy and Spiedel having signed on the dotted line, H-J announced that we should celebrate but first we should all go back to his mother's flat and change into civilian clothes. I had no civilian clothes with me and neither did Admiral Sherbrook, who was the British Representative, but H-J insisted that he could kit us out. After several glasses of Champagne, H-J produced his wardrobe. He was a much smaller man than either of us but somehow we squeezed ourselves into trousers and sports jackets which came far short of the wrist and ankles and set off with General Spiedel, who was in civilian clothes anyway, for the banks of the Seine. Here the Paris Boat Show was in full swing, about the first time since the war.

H-J then unfolded his plan. His wife had a place on the Tweed with excellent fishing and he had worked out that it would be a great idea to fish the Tweed from a Pedallo of which there were several in the show. We would carry out a trial to see which was the best and therefore H-J and General Spiedel would race Admiral Sherbrook and myself to the Pont des Invalides and back. The next thing was to persuade the exhibitors to lend us their craft and, nothing daunted, the race started. I don't remember who won but I rather fancy that we did as the General was a very large man, about twice the weight of H-J, and they had the utmost difficulty in steering a straight course. The trials completed and all of us rather damp, H-J took us off to a very expensive restaurant for an excellent dinner, still wearing our rather damp borrowed plumage. In fact he had to give the maitre d'hotel a hefty tip to get us in as we looked like clochards. At dinner the General announced that he now knew how the British won the war, 'You are all Blotty Mad'! (On a more serious note, I was pleased to find some 15 years later that the forces that we agreed, and I had worked out, were still what the Germans had and were still reckoned to be correct. It is always nice to get something right).

From time to time it was necessary to go to meetings at SHAPE near Versailles. General Eisenhower had left to become President of the USA and he had been replaced by General Schyller but his Chief of Staff, General Al Gunter had stayed on. Here was a remarkable man indeed as he seemed to have a photographic memory which included names and faces. Early on in my time at Fontainebleau I had been introduced to him briefly but forever after, if I were to pass him in a corridor he would say, 'Good morning Johnson' or whatever was appropriate at the time. Other visitors to SHAPE shared the same experience. It was said that he knew the name of every single person working in the headquarters and there must have been over a thousand. Every new arrival had to have his or her photograph taken for security reasons and a copy would be sent to Gunther's office and that was it. A wonderful facility to have.

That Autumn there was another big paper exercise. Marechal Juin had been most unhappy about the previous winter's exercise at Soisson and for this year it was decided that mobile headquarters should be exercised. This may have been fine for the soldiers and possibly for the Tactical Airforce but for the Navy it was a total disaster as we sat in tents in the middle of Fontainebleau Forest trying to make do with field telephones and despatch riders. The only positive result was that Admiral Jaujard and the Airforce Commander were able to persuade the Marechal that the whole idea was ridiculous and that henceforth we would rely on our new purpose-built underground Headquarters and Communications Centre. This was quite an impressive set-up and had the potential to work well.

Ted Wils, with whom I shared an office, was relieved by a very nice Dutch Royal Marine Officer, Major der Jong Outraadt. He had an amazing story to tell. At the fall of Holland he and his twin brother were taken prisoner by the Germans and shipped off with many others by train to prisoner-of-war camp. On their way through Germany both jumped from the train but, in making their escape, became separated. My friend searched for a day for his brother without success and, fearing that he had been recaptured, set off to make his way to France. He spoke French well and eventually made contact with an escape organisation who sent him on, from somewhere near Roscoff, to Falmouth in a fishing boat. This was in 1940 and he joined the free Dutch Forces.

Nothing was heard of his twin brother until one day when Outraadt was having a drink in a pub near Dover, where he was stationed, he suddenly saw his brother propping up the same bar! It transpired that his brother had made his way through Austria and Hungary to the Ukraine where he joined the Soviet Army as a tank driver and fought against the Germans. However, when the Germans started to be pushed back, he left the Soviet Army and made his way to Murmansk, where he shipped aboard an Allied merchant ship and so back to England. Arriving at the beginning of 1944 he was sent to join the Dutch Marines at Dover and this was his first day there. I never met the brother but this story does bear out the belief that there is some special bond between twins.

The winter of 1953 was another cold one with plenty of snow and we had some exciting trips to work in the Bond Mini. While ordinary four-wheeled cars went comfortably along in the ruts made by other cars, the Mini's centre wheel had to perform a sort of mountain course along the rough snow in the middle and there were several occasions when I had to get out and push. That Christmas there was a fancy-dress ball in the officer's mess and Mary and I set about making ourselves into a rather smart Regency couple, Mary with a very high waisted dress and I with a smart green silk tail coat, which I had made out of my dressing gown. When it came to the judging we were furious to find that we had been disqualified because we had hired our costumes and they wouldn't be convinced otherwise!

I had confidently expected to be promoted to Commander towards the end of my time at Fontainebleau and was extremely disappointed at the end of December when nothing happened. However in January 1954 all the British Naval Officers serving at SHAPE and NAVCENT were summoned to Versailles to met the Second Sea Lord, Admiral Davis (responsible for all naval personnel). There he harangued us saying that their Lordships considered that all officers serving on NATO staffs were wasting their and the Navy's time; consequently no reports on officers coming from Allied staffs would be considered by promotion boards. From H-J down we were all furious and horrified. We had worked jolly hard to make the new NATO command a success and there was no doubt whatsoever that the RN officers were held in very high regard by the officers of other nationalities.

I asked to have a heart to heart with H-J who was incredulous at the 'Little Englander' attitude of The Admiralty Board, which incidentally was the exact opposite to that of the Army and Air Force Boards. However H-J said that the only answer was to go somewhere where they would have to take notice. I'd had a Command, done a Staff job, had nearly 5 years seniority as a Lieutenant Commander and therefore I would have to go to sea as First Lieutenant of something big. Thus it was that I came to be appointed to the largest ship in the Royal Navy, HMS *Ark Royal*, building in Camell Laird's yard at Birkenhead. I was to be relieved on 25th May and join *Ark Royal* on 2nd June 1954.

Before finally leaving France we decided to see as much of the country as we could and in the Easter Holidays we left the children with Joan and set off on a tour which took us down the west side, through the foothills of the Pyrenees, to Lourdes and Toulouse, along the coast to Nice and then back by the Route Napoleon to Gap. We then went on through the Jura mountains to Strasbourg, and Metz before turning west again to Fontainebleau and home. The winter snows were just melting when we came through the Alps and it was a difficult and adventurous journey but well worth doing.

Once back, there were lots of things to get sorted out, pack up all our things and decide where we should send them. Michael was to start school at Winchester Lodge, a prep school in Torquay, and I would go up to Birkenhead and look for somewhere for us to live for the six to eight months before *Ark Royal* was completed and commissioned.

Hester had become engaged to Dr Rowland Elphinstone and we promised Granny Bull that we would supply the Champagne for the wedding and would bring it with us. This was an added complication and in all this there was the usual round of farewell parties to say good bye to all our friends both French and English. My relief was a bachelor called Davies, a fluent French speaker with property and a vineyard in Algeria, inherited from his mother who was French. Having turned over the job to him we regretfully said goodbye to Maison Tolstoï, the le Loups and Noisy-sur-Ecole and, after having loaded the car with bottles of Champagne stuffed into every corner and under the seats, we set off for England. Shortly before leaving, Michael came out in spots. The Customs at Folkestone took one look at him and waved us through with our five dozen bottles of bubbly and we headed thankfully for 4 Gertrude Terrace and Exmouth.

Before leaving I had sold the Bond Minicar to an American lady who wanted it for her son but it needed a certain amount of care to keep it on the road. This it never got from its new owner and I heard from friends that it was soon wrecked by the son who probably thought it was a sports car. A sad end for the little car that had carried me safely to work for nearly two years.

Having installed ourselves at Exmouth, I set off by train for Birkenhead, leaving Mary to take a recovered Michael to Winchester Lodge, starting at Half-Term. David, now almost five, went to Miss Kemmys Jenkins to start his first school. Now there was no place for Joan who, with her faithful bicycle, returned to Little Bealings where she eventually became the village postwoman. Thus ended our 'best time' in France. The le Loups were faithful correspondents for many years and the Déroulèdes are our very close friends to this day.

In 2001 we were invited to Géneviève's 90th birthday celebrations in Paris and at a huge family lunch I was honoured to find myself seated next to the birthday girl. We also heard regularly from Admiral Jaujard and I well recall getting a letter from him when we were in Norway in 1957 saying that if ever I wanted a crew for my boat, he was my man. Sadly both he and his wife were involved in a very bad car crash shortly after this in which his charming wife was killed and he never fully recovered. Our time in France had been a wonderful experience and we were fortunate to have lived in such a warm and friendly village. Sadly I have not been able to do justice to all the happenings in Noisy nor to all the other good people working in the team that made up NAVCENT and the rest of the Command. That would need a whole book.

Appendix to Chapter 10

CORONATION OF QUEEN ELIZABETH II

By Joan Churchyard

Ever since I was a small child and saw pictures of the Royal family I had made up my mind that one day I would go to London and see them in real life. As passing years seemed to bring the Princess Elizabeth nearer and nearer to the throne, I was determined that if she ever became Queen I would be among the thousands cheering her on her way to her crowning. I had not the slightest idea how this was to be accomplished, for London was unknown to me and, having never seen a Royal procession, I hadn't a notion how to become one of the crowd, especially at such an important 'do' as a coronation.

At the time of the sudden death of our beloved King, George VI, I was making arrangements to accompany Lieutenant Commander and Mrs Johnson to France to look after their two small boys, Michael 6 years and David $2^{1}/_{2}$ years, and I naturally thought that that was the end of my hopes. The Queen's Coronation, however was not fixed to take place for another 16 months.

As 1953 dawned and one heard more and more of the wonderful preparations that were taking place for the great day, my desire to see it was increased a thousand-fold and I began to cast about in my mind as to how I might get across the channel to do so. I mentioned to Mrs Johnson how much I wanted to go and she said immediately, 'Well why not'?

So that was that and from early March my mind dwelt on how and where! I had no one in London with whom I could stay and made up my mind that if I wanted to see anything at all I should have to spend the night on the pavement. I need not have worried as, by an extraordinary piece of luck, Commander Johnson won two seats in a servicemen's ballot and asked me if I would like them for myself and Michael. IF I WOULD LIKE THEM! I could have jumped for joy. This of course altered the whole arrangements for, now being sure of a seat, I had no need to contemplate a night under the stars. Also I had to be accommodated where there was room for Michael too.

Mrs Johnson wrote frantically to all her friends and acquaintances in London asking if they could put us up. At last we heard from Mrs Pallot that she had booked us into the Teremore Hotel North Totteridge for two nights and she and Dr Pallot could have us for the remaining two. Commander Johnson was also trying to book our passage and came home to say that no places were available on the boats and would I mind going by air! Nothing could have pleased me more and both Michael and I were thrilled at the prospect of our first flight. We just counted the days to the Red Letter Day, 31st May.

After weeks of suspense 'The Tickets' arrived, together with maps of London and the underground and endless directions and suggestions as to what and what not to do. At the eleventh hour Michael went down with German measles and, though we knew that he would be all right to travel by the end of the month, what if I was to catch it too? Fortunately I escaped but on the 30th his mother came out full of it and had to retire to bed on the very day that all the naval personnel and their families stationed at Fontainebleau were to attend a Coronation Garden Party at our house, the Maison Tolstoï. It was a grand 'do' ending with Admiral Howard-Johnston proposing the toast to Her Majesty and we all drank her health in champagne.

After an early start the next day Commander Johnson drove Michael and me to Orly airport. One thing about the journey that sticks in my mind was that when we passed a fairground, Michael said 'Look Dad a fair! Can't I stop and have a ride on the roundabout', and he about to fly for the first time!

On arrival at Orly our baggage was weighed and labelled and, everything being found OK, we went to the lounge before being told that our plane was ready. Michael and I hurried across the tarmac hoping to get good window seats, which we were lucky to do. We took off just before 7 pm and what a thrill as we began to rise off the ground. We were soon passing over the Tour d'Eiffel. It was great fun to gaze down and see everything from such an unusual angle. After a most enjoyable flight with super supper trays thrown in and with me treating myself to a small bottle of white wine, we arrived at London airport. After a quick go through Customs (they opened nothing and took no notice of the bottle of whisky that I declared) Michael and I were on the airbus to Waterloo terminus and were then soon on the underground bound for our unknown destination. Michael was absolutely fascinated by this new way of travel and counted every station all the way to Totteridge. We reached the hotel soon after 10.30 pm and thankfully accepted hot cups of Ovaltine before falling into our nice inviting beds. We slept like logs, strange beds or no. The next day after a good breakfast we caught the underground to Charing Cross to spy out the lie of the land for the following day, for I was anxious to find the quickest way to our seats and just what time to allow to get there.

My first and only fright of losing Michael came within half an hour of getting there. We were by Admiralty Arch when I realised that he wasn't by my side. Horror stricken I decided to stay put and a minute later I saw his figure coming towards me. He calmly explained that he had been to look at some fountains. I was determined to tie a label on him whether he liked it or not. We had quite a successful tour of the route, made sure exactly where our seats were and walked up the beautifully decorated Mall to Buckingham Palace where we joined the milling crowds. We gazed at the cars of colonial rulers as they got stuck in the traffic and we got pushed and shoved from pillar to post but everyone was in the same boat and all took it with good humour. Even the good old British Bobby, who took the full force of Michael's ice cream cornet in his stomach as the crowd surged forward at the sight of the Queen's car, just smiled and took out his handkerchief and mopped up the mess.

After something to eat we made our way slowly to Westminster Abbey, looking so very resplendent in all its trimmings. Crowds here were as dense as at the Palace. I heard one elderly lady say, 'I took up my place here on Sunday and I'll stay here till she comes'. I hoped she would be able to stick it out, for if anyone deserved to see the Queen she did! While we were at the Abbey we saw the Duke of Gloucester and his two sons enter for a last rehearsal; I supposed Princess Margaret also came but we only saw her car. The weather now was not too good – rain and a terrific wind which was ripping some of the flags from top to bottom. Tomorrow we had to be up before the lark, so we decided to make our way homewards. The traffic was in a constant jam and the short journey took simply ages. There were masses of people everywhere and every bit of pavement was taken up with someone bedding down for the night – many of them with small children – and it looked like being a wet night too. No one seemed downhearted and as we passed every sort of 'tent' we heard sounds of merriment and song. I thought how lucky I was to be given a grandstand view on the morrow and a nice warm bed.

Arriving at Trafalgar Square, I just couldn't see where our turnings were because of the solid mass of people, so I asked a 'city' man for directions. He said, 'I'm going to Charing Cross myself, just follow me'. It was easier said than done but, tightening my grip on Michael, I just surged forward, keeping his back in sight, and by sheer luck we eventually arrived. I didn't know that we looked hungry, but when I thanked my guide he thrust a lunch box into my hand explaining that he couldn't take it back with him. Neither, for that matter, could we as neither of us felt hungry. I started wondering how I could dispose of it as it is against my nature to throw away good food. A solution soon presented itself, for as we stood waiting in the underground for the train, the woman porter was telling us the sad tale of little lost Willie and how his frantic Ma was on the platform with her three other children. Quick as a flash I said, 'Here take this box to the children'. The box changed hands and as we boarded the train the porter caught my eye and said how pleased the kiddies had been. I guess they soon polished off the ham sandwiches, chocolate and fruit, and I hoped they would soon find little Willie. Michael had been listening wide-eyed to the story of the lost child and said, 'Jo I will wear that label'.

Arriving back at the hotel I got Michael to bed as soon as possible, though sleep was far from him and, after a bit of supper myself, I got everything possible ready for the morning and turned in, determined not to go to sleep as I didn't think the alarm clock would wake me up at 2.30 in the morning if I did. I lay there hour after hour wondering how I would make it in the morning and then I found myself waking with a start at 2 o'clock. I had dropped off but other folk moving about and a baby crying had woken me up. I sprang out of bed and got everything ready for the great day. The rain was pouring down but, although I wished it would stop, it didn't dampen my high spirits for this was the day of days that I had been waiting for. When I was ready I woke Michael. I gently shook him twice and he opened his eyes, took one look at me dressed and ready to go, came to in an instant and was quite ready to be up at 2.20 am poor kid!

We could hear other early risers preparing to leave, so the moment I had Michael ready we went downstairs hoping for a lift. Our luck was in and they offered us a lift to the heart of the city. It was an extraordinary drive through the wet streets of London that early in the morning. They were Americans, who were at SHAPE, and they hardly spoke a civil word to each other but their small boy never stopped talking, though I couldn't understand what the 2 year old was saying. However we were more than thankful for the lift. There was not much sign of life in the streets but two bus-loads of Bobbies followed us most of the way. We were put down at a handy Tube Station; I thanked our benefactors profusely and hoped they would see the show OK.

The underground wasn't exactly crowded but there were plenty of people about and everyone looked wide awake for 3 o'clock in the morning. Two young girls in their Sunday best were talking excitedly about going to watch an ox being roasted on the common that evening. On arrival at Charing Cross we found it had stopped raining and we hoped that perhaps it would be fine for 'Her' and us after all. As we came out of the station we were greeted by an ambulance which was about to pick up a poor old man – not a very good start to our day. The old chap didn't seem badly hurt but I doubt he saw much of the great day.

There were not as many people about as I had expected and it was without difficulty that we made our way to Admiralty Arch and our seats, where we arrived at 4 am. We weren't allowed to our seats until six but there was plenty of activity going on and the time soon passed. Whilst waiting with many others I heard a woman grumbling about the crowd who had the cheek to plant themselves in front of her despite her being there all night. I suddenly realised that she was referring to our lot, so I explained that we were only waiting to be allowed to go to our seats, to which she replied, 'Seats! They're only for VCs and GCs'. So, brandishing my tickets, I said, 'Just you wait and see'!

Within a few minutes of this incident an official called to our crowd saying that those with seats on stand so and so could enter. So, making sure that the woman saw us, we made our way to the now longed-for seats. We were very much wanting to sit down but were not allowed to do so until the cushions arrived in about another half-hour. Only then could we go to our allocated places. At long last we were shown to our seats and were delighted to discover that we were only six rows from the front with a grand view of the road. We now removed our macs, put on our rosettes and prepared to see everything that was to be seen. We went to the refreshment tent, had hot tea and took fruit and seven-and-sixpenny lunch-boxes back to our seats. By this time the troops were taking their places; sailors in front of us and on either side of the Arch and Guards further up the Mall.

People were now arriving fast and the seats filled up. We had been told to get there early but other folk arriving at about 8.15 seemed to get through all right. Then we heard from people around us the wonderful news of the conquest of Mount Everest. The procession had now started to form up in the Mall, with the first of the cars almost opposite us. At first glance this just appeared to contain a vast amount of ermine but was, in fact, the Earl and Countess of Harewood in their coronation robes.

Once the procession started excitement mounted on excitement. We had plenty to claim our attention and keep us amused and the broadcasting from the Arch was giving us 'music while you wait'. There were 'royal' cheers for the two mounted police chiefs as they rode up and down the Mall. They were grinning broadly. There was also terrific applause for the little man with a wheelbarrow every time he appeared to pick up what the horses had left behind! We really thought that something was happening as an even greater roar travelled the length of the Mall. We looked and what did we see but a lone cyclist pedalling furious past and, no doubt, wishing the road would open and swallow him up.

The procession had now started and more and more of this wonderful scene met our eyes as great personages were followed by even greater ones 'til louder and louder cheering told us that 'Royals' were on their way. By far the most popular of the foreigners was the Queen of Tonga, who came by waving to everyone and looking as if she was enjoying it even more than we were, as also did the elderly Princess Louise about to see her fifth coronation, I believe. She too received a great ovation. Our lovely Duchesses with their families soon followed – the Duchess of Gloucester with her two good-looking boys and the Duchess of Kent with her two sons and her daughter who looked so like her mother. Even louder cheering heralded the approach of the beloved Queen Mother and Princess Margaret. Everyone stood up as they passed and I found myself looking right into their carriage, they looked so happy and very lovely. They were followed by our very popular Prime Minister, Mr Winston Churchill, looking happy and smart in his uniform of Admiral of the Cinque Ports. Mrs Churchill too was looking very nice and thoroughly enjoying her day. I was very amused by Michael's remark about her for he exclaimed in a loud voice, 'Do look at all Mrs Churchill's white curls – it must be a wig!'

The thunderous roar that now echoed from one end of the Mall to the other announced to one and all that the supreme moment had arrived and, eagerly looking towards the Palace, we saw the approach of the Queen's procession – a truly wonderful sight with the Windsor Greys, dressed overall, so gracefully pulling that fairy-like golden coach towards us. We all stood up waving and cheering madly and then this wonderful cavalcade was passing us. The Queen looked absolutely radiant and had a special smile for the Navy section and waved directly at us, or so we believed. She really was beautiful, a very Queen indeed, and here was I seeing her at last! The Duke of Edinburgh too, in his Admiral's uniform, looked superb and very happy. I had hoped to photograph them but unfortunately at the eleventh hour my camera had unaccountably stuck, though I had never had any trouble with it before.

The procession passed on to the tumultuous roar of the excited crowds and we seemed to hear them all the way to the Abbey. Our thoughts turned now to the inevitable cup of tea, so down we went to seek some refreshments. We certainly need it after all the shouting and mad cheering and I for one felt quite hoarse and parched. When we returned to our seats the rain had begun to fall but that couldn't dampen our spirits. We put on all we had got and sat down, determined not to miss anything that was going on and there was quite a bit, what with the Royal Parks lorries clearing up the mall, the mounted police still getting their cheers, as did the man with his little yellow barrow for the droppings. Then there was the constant coming and going of the St John's ambulances in Trafalgar Square, where people seemed to be dropping like ninepins. It seemed as if every time we looked, some poor soul was being passed over the heads of the crowd. Such hard luck for them after waiting for all those hours. It couldn't have been pleasant standing in a crush hour after hour and now with a steady downpour. We were thankful of our seats and Michael and I sat it out and, with my mac over our heads, we didn't seem to get wet. Food was once more in our thoughts and our seven-and-sixpenny lunch boxes were quickly devoured and quite good they were too.

About half an hour later two luncheon tickets were thrust into my hand by our neighbours, a very nice naval Commander and his wife. At first I tried to refuse but to no avail and in the back of my mind was the thought that maybe a proper lunch and in the dry would be rather nice, so thanking our benefactor we took the tickets and made our way into The Admiralty, where, because of a mistake, the previous sitting had only just begun. We had to wait for about an hour but, as the skies had now really opened, we were quite glad to be in the dry. When our turn at last arrived we were quite ready for more food and thoroughly enjoyed our meal of ham, tongue and salad and felt refreshed by it. It was still raining heavily when we returned to our seats and our nice neighbours lent us an umbrella, so now we were really all right, come hail or snow.

We listened to the Abbey service as we waited and which by now was well-advanced, so that we knew it wouldn't be long before the return procession. I was most impressed by the statue-like sailors who lined the Mall near us. They just never moved even though by now they must have been soaked to the skin. I was quite moved by two scenes. One was a St John's ambulance man going from sailor to sailor popping something into their mouths – presumably a glucose sweet – and, second, were some policemen who were going along the line mopping the neck and face of each rain-soaked man. One sailor opposite us had to fall out but he did so most ceremoniously, laying his rifle on the ground, saluting and marching smartly away while his place was filled immediately by a reserve. I was sorry for the other chap, who would miss the parade after standing their since 7 am, but Michael soon saw him sitting in the stand opposite and, pointing, said, 'Jo there he is', and lucky he was now to get a grandstand view.

We had heard the cheering getting nearer and nearer and, looking through the Arch, we could see the procession passing across the square and noticed some carriages stopping to put their roofs up. It seemed no time at all that the cavalcade was passing in front of us, led by a mounted officer. We were spellbound as the spectacle unfolded before our eyes and thousands of marching men and women passed before us to terrific applause, which they richly deserved. Then came the carriages with the now familiar faces and all were given a right royal greeting, none perhaps more than the Queen of Tonga who alone had kept the roof of her carriage down and, though soaked through, was still thoroughly enjoying herself and determined to see and be seen by everyone. The crowd really went mad when she passed and she certainly endeared herself to everyone's heart. Finally the coach with the Queen was almost upon us and everyone turned to Admiralty Arch as the golden Coronation coach came through. This time our crowned Queen was in the splendour of her coronation robes with Prince Philip at her side, he bending his head to get a better look at The Admiralty. We were able to see right inside the coach and I was interested to notice the Queen's simple little white handbag lying on the seat opposite her. Then the Queen passed on up the Mall on the last stage of the journey, with the tumultuous cheering of a million voices ringing in her ears.

We were all wondering what had happened to 'Winnie' and how he had passed without anyone seeing him, then up went the cry, 'Here he comes'. He was behind the Queen's coach instead of being in front. It seems that there had been trouble with the horses pulling his carriage and they had had to pull up. I thought he looked a trifle glum; no doubt he was angry at having lost his rightful place in front of the Queen. I read later that he didn't continue up the Mall but turned off on to Horseguards Parade.

All the excitement having now passed, we thought about getting away but were asked by the police to stay in our seats for half an hour to give the disabled, who were near Buckingham Palace, to get away first. Then we joined the milling crowds in the Mall. Goodness what a mess it was! People had rid themselves of every conceivable object, their sodden macs, cushions, Union Jacks, bottles of drink and packets of food lying everywhere. We soon realised that we hadn't a chance of getting near the Palace and as Michael and I were both weary we decided to make tracks for home and comfort. As we walked through St James's Park the jets roared overhead and we knew that the Queen was on the Palace balcony with all her family.

Arriving at Charing Cross Station we were told that the gates were locked and were advised to walk over the bridge to Waterloo, which we wearily did, catching a train with no difficulty. Michael was still as thrilled as ever with the underground. After we arrived at our hotel we gathered up all our things and Doctor Pallot collected us and took us home to his house 'Green Shutters'. We had supper, listened to the Queen's broadcast and turned in for what we hoped would be a good night's rest. But oh dear! What with departing guests, the noise of the TV beneath our bedroom which went on until midnight and Michael having urgent calls (due to the breast of chicken he had had for supper, he informed Mrs Pallot) and also the endless ringing of the telephone, there was just no peace; I went down to breakfast the next morning feeling and looking like nothing on earth. I certainly felt far worse than when I got up at 2 am the previous morning. That day I went shopping and returned to find Michael in the charge of Mrs Pallot senior. We had supper with her and her husband and had a nice peaceful evening before turning in to our much needed beds. How good they looked too and I am glad to say that nothing disturbed us that night.

Next morning, Thursday, I packed my bags once more, and also Michael's, and said goodbye to him as the Pallots were going to see him off that night by air for France. After two more days with a friend I travelled to Hampshire where I stayed a couple of weeks and then to Bealings to see my family. I enjoyed the few days at home and on 30th June began my journey to return to France. I could hardly believe how so very fortunate I had been to have seen and enjoyed all the wonderful sights. God Bless the Queen!

Author's Note:
Mary and I met Michael at Orly full of all his adventures, quite a thing for a seven-year-old. Now, fifty plus years later, he says that the only thing he can remember is the anguish of seeing his precious ice cream cornet lying on the ground with the best of it trickling down the policeman's stomach and he had hardly had a lick!

Joan Churchyard born in 1918 was one of four children. Her Grandfather had been a well-known artist living and working in Woodbridge. However, her father had served in the trenches in France during World War I and had been severely traumatized. He was never able to work and had to go into an asylum for the remainder of his life. Her mother was killed in a railway accident when Joan was about 12. On leaving school she went into 'service' at the age of 14. She was a quick learner and avid reader who profited from her experiences but until she came to work for us in Little Bealings she had never been outside Suffolk. In better circumstances she would probably have gone to university.

Michael Pallot was the son of Engineer Rear Admiral Pallot who had been at Pembroke Dock at the same time as my parents when Michael and I were about 3 and 4 years old. On leaving the Navy, Admiral Pallot took Holy Orders and came to Instow in 1935 as the Rector and Michael and I renewed our friendship. It was thanks to Michael P that I learnt about girls! He was a year older than I and keen to find out all about life. We had a lot of fun together. He went to Medical School and I into the Navy. Sadly he died when only 35. I think he had a heart attack.

H.M.S Zodiac at 30 knots.

Above (top) Our house in Preston.

Above left: Mary and David.

Above: Mike and one of our ducks.

Left: Joan with two well armed small boys, David with a pistol and Mike with a sword!

Above:
H.M.S. Zodiac with hands fallen for leaving harbour.

Left:
The Family Johnson at Instow, 1951.

ALLIED FORCES CENTRAL EUROPE
FONTAINEBLEAU

Below: Cours Henri 1V. Allied Headquarters. My office was on the 1st Floor to the left of the entrance.

Looking through the Main Entrance to the Army and Marechal Juin's headquarters at the far side of the Cours Henri IV.

Front row L to R: Cdr Smith, C de F Beau, Cdr Gowland, Capt Te Poorten, RA Cazalet, VA Jaujard, C de V Baudouin, Cdr Benson, A.N.Other, A.N.Other, Lt Cdr Wils, with the author on the end.

Above: Maison Tolstoï.

Below: The Le Loups Cottage at the bottom of our garden.

Above Left: Off to work, David gives Mike and me a push start.

Above: Monsieur and Madame Le Loup with David and their nephew.

Left: Everyone gets in the act with the Bond Mini-car including Diane the Le Loup's dog.

Below: Pain de deux livres!

Right:
Picnic in Fontainebleau Forest.

Below:
Joan with Mike and David. Once she and Mike rode all the way to Fontainebleau and back.

Above left: Mike and David in 'party best'. Above right: Granny Bull, Hester, Mary, and the two boys at Noisy. Below left: Brigitte and Kathrine Déroulède. Below right: Le Loup with an ever present 'Caporal Gris' in his mouth.

Above: Monsieur Mason, Garagiste. He fixed all things mechanical in the village - note his 1922 Peugeot and the chickens.

Below: The Washing Place on the River Ecole, where everything was pounded on stone slabs before rinsing-off in the river.

OBITUARIES

Rear-Adml Howard-Johnston

REAR-ADML 'JOHNNY' HOWARD-JOHNSTON, who has died aged 92, was one of the Royal Navy's foremost exponents of anti-submarine warfare.

This was a neglected art in the Navy before the Second World War, but one on which Britain came to depend in the Battle of the Atlantic. When Johnston (he added the family name Howard later because "there were too many Johnstons in the Navy List") specialised in anti-submarine warfare in 1931, it was no path to promotion.

At that time strategic thinking was still dominated by the battle of Jutland. Convoy was rarely exercised, being regarded as a defensive tactic. The Navy clung to the belief — totally unfounded in war — that ultrasonic detection gear (Asdic) was a complete defence against U-boats.

In this atmosphere of stagnation, Johnston had a series of appointments in destroyers and at HMS *Osprey*, the anti-submarine warfare school at Portland, where he displayed a lively and innovative mind. In 1936 he received an Admiralty commendation for inventing training devices, including the "Johnston mobile anti-submarine target", which introduced much-needed realism into exercises.

His first command, the destroyer *Viscount* in 1937, was fitted with a listening device designed for submarines, which the Admiralty had bought from German makers. Trials seemed to show that it was unsatisfactory for surface ships, and it was discarded. But Howard-Johnston (as he now was) was impressed. One day off Portland, *Viscount* picked up the Shambles Buoy Bell at a range of 10 miles, while doing 20 knots.

Promoted commander, Howard-Johnston went to Athens in 1938 as director of studies at the Greek Naval War College. He returned in February 1940 with the Greek Order of the Phoenix and an appointment to the Anti-Submarine Warfare Division in the Admiralty.

However, at the start of the Norwegian campaign in April 1940, he was sent to organise anti-submarine operations off the fjords, and took part in the evacuation of Allied troops and casualties from Molde and Andalsnes. He was awarded the DSC.

Howard-Johnston: expert

That June, he took passage in the destroyer *Wild Swan* with a demolition party and eight tons of explosives to blow up port facilities in St Malo. Despite the French armed guard, he carried out his duties, winning a mention in despatches.

In 1941 Howard-Johnston took command of the destroyer *Malcolm* and became one of the most successful escort group commanders. He once estimated that his group escorted a total of 1,229 vessels across the Atlantic. He was mentioned in despatches a second time.

On June 29 1941, when *Malcolm* was escorting the homeward-bound convoy HX 133, a small cloud of black smoke was sighted on the horizon. *Malcolm* closed in at full speed. The cloud contained the conning tower of a U-boat which had been damaged in collision with a merchant ship and forced to surface.

The U-boat, U-651, dived, but *Malcolm* blew her back to the surface with depth charges, and picked up all but one of her crew. Howard-Johnston was subsequently awarded the DSO.

In 1942 Howard-Johnston joined the staff of the C-in-C Western Approaches in Liverpool, where his first-hand experience of the U-boat war was invaluable in the development of Captain Roberts's celebrated anti-U-boat school.

From reports of U-boat attacks and evidence of escort captains, the school evolved better search patterns and attack manoeuvres, and devised counter-measures against such new weapons as the "Gnat" acoustic torpedo which appeared in 1943.

By then, Howard-Johnston was the Navy's acknowledged anti-submarine expert. Promoted captain, he returned to the Admiralty as director of the Anti-U-Boat Division and a member of Churchill's anti-U-boat committee.

Clarence Dinsmore Johnston (he disliked his baptismal names and preferred his nickname) was born on Oct 13 1903, and joined the Navy as a cadet in 1917, attending Osborne and Dartmouth.

In 1921 he went to sea as a midshipman in the battle cruiser *Repulse*, and later served as a lieutenant on the battleship *Barham* in the Mediterranean and the gunboat *Tarantula* on the Yangtse River.

After the end of the war in Europe, Howard-Johnston took command of the cruiser *Bermuda*, serving in the British Pacific fleet and with the forces occupying Japan. A Francophile with fluent French, he was delighted in 1947 to be sent to Paris as naval attaché. Three years later he was appointed in command of HMS *Vernon*, the torpedo and anti-submarine school at Portsmouth.

There he had a deeply traumatic experience, to which he never again referred. As captain of *Vernon* he was closely involved in the search for the submarine *Affray*, which failed to surface after an exercise dive in the Channel in April 1951. Among those lost were some sub-lieutenants on a submarine training course. They included Howard-Johnston's eldest son Richard.

Howard-Johnston was a naval ADC to the Queen in 1952.

His last appointment as a rear-admiral was as chief of staff to the Flag Officer Central Europe. He retired in 1955 and was appointed CB the same year.

Johnny Howard-Johnston had a natural gift for sea warfare and was an excellent small ship captain. *Malcolm* was not only a deadly U-boat killer but a very happy ship. Intellectually, he was a major contributor to victory in the Atlantic, which, despite Allied successes in the spring of 1943, was a battle bitterly fought to the end, with new and improved types of U-boat coming into service. The last British merchantman was sunk as late as May 7 1945.

Howard-Johnston was made an officer of the US Legion of Merit in 1946. Latterly he lived in France, where he took part in naval historical programmes on French television.

Howard-Johnston married, in 1928, Esmée Fitzgibbon; they had a son, Richard. The marriage was dissolved. He married secondly, in 1941, Lady Alexandra, elder daughter of Field Marshal Earl Haig. They had two sons and a daughter. The marriage was dissolved, and he married thirdly, in 1955, Paulette, daughter of the French painter Paul Helleu.

Antonio Ruiz Soler. In Madrid, aged 74. Classical flamenco dancer known as simply as Antonio *El Bailarin* (The Dancer). One of his best remembered performances was in Manuel de Falla's *El Sombrero de Tres Picos* (The Three-Cornered Hat).

Sonya Richmond. At Swansea, aged 63. Writer whose published works include *Commonsense about Yoga* and *Yoga and your Health*. Wrote articles about the Ukraine, her grandparents' homeland, and a novel *One and a dog* about growing up in Liverpool with her labrador, Paddy.

Ed Sciurba. In Florida, aged 89. Stunt-man known in the 1930s as "The Man with Iron Jaws" for his ability to bite coins in half and pull massive trucks down the road with his teeth. He still lifted weights in his 70s, but only with his arms. Dentures had long since replaced his once mighty teeth.

Obituary - 'Johnny' Howard-Johnston
February 12th 1996.

Ark Royal with a full range of aircraft on deck consisting of Sea Hawks, Sea Venoms, Gannets, and Sky Raiders.

H.M.S. ARK ROYAL

COMMISSIONING SERVICE

22nd FEBRUARY, 1955

at the Shipyard,
CAMMELL LAIRD & CO., (Shipbuilders & Engineers) LTD.,
BIRKENHEAD

Conducted by the Venerable Archdeacon
F. N. CHAMBERLAIN, C.B., O.B.E., Q.H.Ch.,
Chaplain of the Fleet

THE OFFICERS OF H.M.S. ARK ROYAL

present

H.M.S. "TRADITIONAL"

or

HARD-A-GILBERT.

ooo0OO0ooo

A COMIC OPERETTA IN FIVE FITS.

July, 1955

DRAMATIS PERSONAE.

Scarface Joe }	Skates paid off from H.M.S.	W.G. Sandey
Ben Backstay }	'Rattlesnake'	G.N. Pleasant
Tom Pepper }		G.L. Bruty
Bruiser Bill	Landlord of the Swallowed Anchor Tavern.	W.M. Wren
Jim	Potman at the Swallowed Anchor Tavern.	C.A. Johnson
Andrew Miller	Boatswain of H.M.S. 'Traditional'	N.S.S. Ward
Rupert Rowley	Son of Sir Anthony Rowley, Bart.	K.D. Clitherow
Sam Splice	Boatswain's Mate, H.M.S. 'Traditional'	S.C. Stephens
Captain Ranger	Captain of H.M.S. 'Traditional'	R.M. Young
Midshipman		J.R. Griffiths
King Howaru	Cannibal King of the Isle of Eatanchu.	P.G. Byrne
Ah Mahjong	His First Lieutenant.	B. Simons
Witchdoctors		{ F.L. Eddy { J.S. Wilson { C.J. May
	F.W. Baskerville,	
Chorus of Seamen and Mutineers:	A.J. Bellamy, J.G. Cannon, T.R. Cruddas, D.J. Cruickshank, M.F. Fell, E.T. Genge, R.W. Kearsley, W.E. Ward, G.R. Woolston.	
Chorus of Cannibals:	R.R. Hepple, D.G.R. Hunt, P.G. Regan, T.W. Roskill, F.G.B. Sheffield, A.G. Wooley.	
Polly	Adopted daughter of Bruiser Bill.	G.R.C. Fisher
Mrs. Ranger	Wife of Captain Ranger.	J.B. Spicer
Ladies of the Town: (also Cannibal Princesses)		J.T. Lord, E. Mason, A. Wallace

ooo0OO0ooo

Written and Produced by:	J.K. Watkins
Musical Direction:	G.R.C. Fisher
Band:	R.J. Peach - The Volunteer Band of H.M.S. ARK ROYAL.
Pianist:	R.J. Arthur
Stage Manager:	P.S. Wilson
Stage Construction:	W.A. Ruffell, P.G. Byrne
Scenery: (A solo effort)	C. Harden
Properties:	C. Oldham
Lighting:	H.L. Vaughan
Sound:	R.A. Foster
Make up:	W.M. Wren

and numerous helpers

ooo0OO0ooo

Above: Sea Hawks over the Ark.

Below: Tight squash in the hangar!

Above: A Sea Hawk being shot off from the starboard catapult, the chap with the funny hat is one of Ray Lygo's 800 Squadron running to man his aircraft and has the squadron's trademark Roman soldier's red brush on top of his helmet!

Above: This Sea Venom has just left the catapult at 120 knots. The 100mm circumference wire rope strop which connects the aircraft to the shuttle of the catapult has just detached and is falling into the sea. This was very costly and wasteful and several years later the U.S Navy came up with a device which stuck out in front of the flight deck by each catapult which retrieved most of them for further use. The wire has to be so large because of the huge loads involved in accelerating 10 tons plus of aircraft to flying speed in such short distance.

Above: Ark Royal entering harbour; no marks for the smoke.

Below: Warleigh, Tamerton Foliot, Plymouth - lent to Mary and I while the ship was in dock.

TOULON, le 29 Novembre 1955
Expédié sous le n° 18.226

MARINE NATIONALE
IIIᵉ RÉGION MARITIME
"Etat-Major"
"Cabinet"
N° 271 EM/CAB

-:- COMMUNICATION -:-

OBJET : Séjour à TOULON du 2 au 6 Décembre 1955 du Porte-Avions H.M.S. ARK ROYAL et des pétroliers RFA BLUE RANGER et RFA GREEN RANGER de la Marine Royale britannique.

1.- GÉNÉRALITÉS :

Le porte-avions H.M.S. "ARK ROYAL", Commandé par le Capitaine de Vaisseau D.R.F. CAMBELL et les pétroliers R.F.A. "BLUE RANGER" commandé par le Capitaine de Vaisseau A. JACKSON, O.B.E., et R.F.A. "GREEN RANGER", commandé par le Capitaine de Vaisseau A.E. MACKENZIE, séjourneront à TOULON du 2 au 6 Décembre 1955.

2.- HEURE D'ARRIVÉE - SALUTS - POSTES D'AMARRAGES

Les bâtiments britanniques se présenteront dans les passes à 8 h 30 A le vendredi 2 Décembre.

Le Porte-avions "ARK ROYAL" saluera la terre de 21 coups de canon avant d'entrer dans les passes. La batterie de la Piastre rendra le salut coup pour coup.

Puis, à l'arrivée en rade, le Porte-Avions "ARK ROYAL" saluera de 15 coups de canon la marque de Monsieur le Vice-Amiral BARJOT, Commandant l'Escadre à bord du GEORGES LEYGUES. Le GEORGES LEYGUES rendra ce salut coup pour coup.

Il n'y aura pas de salut personnel au canon à l'occasion des visites officielles.

Orders for Ark Royal's visit to Toulon.

L'"ARK ROYAL" sera amarré à l'appontement 5 W à Milhaud.

Le "BLUE RANGER" sera amarré à l'appontement 6 Est à Milhaud.

Le "GREEN RANGER" sera amarré au Quai d'Honneur.

3.- OFFICIER DE LIAISON :

Le Lieutenant de Vaisseau CHOVE, de l'Arromanches assurera les fonctions d'officier de liaison auprès du Capitaine de Vaisseau CAMBELL, Commandant l'ARK ROYAL.

Le Lieutenant de Vaisseau CHOVE ira, par l'embarcation du pilote présenter les souhaits de bienvenue du Vice-Amiral d'Escadre, Préfet Maritime au Capitaine de Vaisseau CAMBELL (tenue n° 2).

4.- VISITES OFFICIELLES :

Les visites officielles sont réglées comme suit :

10 h 00	Le Capitaine de Vaisseau D.R.F. CAMBELL fait visite à Monsieur le Vice-Amiral d'Escadre, Préfet Maritime.
10 h 15	Le Capitaine de Vaisseau D.R.F. CAMBELL fait visite à Monsieur EUDIER, Sous Préfet de TOULON.
10 h 30	Le Capitaine de Vaisseau D.R.F. CAMBELL fait visite à Monsieur le Maire de TOULON.
10 h 50	Le Capitaine de Vaisseau D.R.F. CAMBELL fait visite à Monsieur le Vice-Amiral, Commandant l'Escadre à bord du GEORGES LEYGUES.
11 h 15	M. le Vice-Amiral d'Escadre LAMBERT, Préfet Maritime rend sa visite au Capitaine de Vaisseau Commandant l'ARK ROYAL.
11 h 30	M. le Vice-Amiral BARJOT, Commandant l'Escadre rend sa visite au Capitaine de Vaisseau Commandant l'ARK ROYAL.
11 h 45	Monsieur EUDIER, Sous-Préfet de TOULON, rend sa visite au Capitaine de Vaisseau Commandant l'ARK ROYAL.
12 h 00	Maître LE BELLEGOU, Maire de TOULON, rend sa visite au Capitaine de Vaisseau Commandant l'ARK ROYAL.

There were 4 more pages!

Above: Queen Elizabeth the Queen Mother with the Captain and Mike Fell. The aircraft nearby is a Gannet with twin turboprops.

Below: The Seaman Chief Petty Officers and Colour Sergeant Royal Marines. Starting 3rd from left is my indefatigable C.P.O Whiting then Chris Dreyer, Dennis Cambell, J.J. and Chief G.I.

CHAPTER 11

H.M.S. *Ark Royal*
31st May 1954 – 15th July 1956

It was with more than a little trepidation that I set off on 31st May to join the small team of officers and ratings standing by *Ark Royal* as she was nearing completion at Camell Laird's Yard in Birkenhead. Ships being built for the Royal Navy were under the auspices of the Captain Superintendent Contract-Built Ships at Newcastle-upon-Tyne. His organisation was charged with having the right people with the right qualifications appointed in time to make sure that all is in order before a ship is commissioned into naval service. Some officers and ratings such as Engineers and Shipwrights would have been appointed several years in advance, to make sure that they would be absolutely familiar with the layout of machinery, and similarly the Electrical and Weapons engineers. Other very early arrivals were on the Supply side as they had the task of assembling the vast quantities of stores and spares that would be required. The Seaman or Executive side came on the scene much later and in my case I had seven months to prepare my part in this great enterprise, to bring the Navy's largest warship to life.

It had been arranged that I should stay at a small commercial hotel on the outskirts of Birkenhead until I could find a house or flat in the vicinity for Mary and the boys. The hotel turned out to be a pretty gloomy place but I was given a warm welcome by Bertie Faunthorpe, a Bidefordian and one of a pair of rather eccentric brothers. The other one, Peter, lived in Instow and was Commodore of the Yacht Club. Bertie, who was an Engineer and Submariner, was The Admiralty Overseer for Submarines building at Camell's but his real claim to fame was that he was the greatest living expert on catching prawns and had written and published a book about it. Both prawns and lobsters in the rocks at Abbotsham would quake in their shells when Bertie was about!

The following morning, the Glorious First of June, I was taken to the shipyard to make my number and meet the rest of the team. I was shown to the rather rummagy wooden shack which housed the *Ark Royal* offices. The Senior Officer was Commander Christopher Dreyer DSO, DSC and Bar, the Senior Executive Officer of the ship, a tall lanky man with piercing blue eyes, auburn hair and a grin like the Cheshire Cat. Christopher was some four years older than I but we had known each other when we were boys in Instow. He had been at Dartmouth with another friend, Vincent Russell, and in our youth Vincent, with his younger brother John, and I had fought many a battle in the sand hills with Christopher and his brother John. Later on his family moved to Limers Lane in Northam but before that, they lived at North

Yeo on the front at Instow. Their father, General Dreyer, had been in the Royal Artillery, but was famous for having invented the system used in all our big ships for controlling the gunfire of the main armament and known as the Dreyer Fire Control Table.

Christopher himself had had a most distinguished war service in Coastal Forces in Command of MTBs operating from Dover and later on in the Adriatic. Immediately before joining *Ark Royal* in June 1953 he had spent two years with the Swedish Navy advising on MTB operations. Having been in *Ark* for a year he was well-rehearsed in what he wanted for the ship. As First Lieutenant it was my job to see to the accommodation and welfare of the 2,500 officers and men of the Ship's Company, plus the usual jobs that go with being No.1 of a big ship, e.g. the Fo'c'sle or, in this case, the Cable deck with its massive nine-and-a-half-ton anchors, cables and capstans.

The Commander lost little time in telling me about the great ship, giving me a conducted tour during which it became abundantly clear that every effort was being made to make a silk purse out of a sow's ear. The *Ark* had been designed in 1938 and the keel laid in 1940; however building was stopped in 1942 when steel was required for more immediate tasks like building escort vessels and merchant ships. Building restarted in 1948 but in the intervening years much had changed, not least the aircraft themselves. Instead of the old Swordfish biplanes, whose wings folded backwards, the new generation of jets had wings that folded upwards, were some 5 to 10 times heavier and needed much higher take-off and landing speeds.

The *Ark* had been designed as a two-hangar ship, one above the other, with lifts fore and aft to bring aircraft to the flight deck. Neither hangar in the original build had sufficient height to take the new generation of aircraft. This meant that the ship had to be stretched upwards, each hangar increased in height by six feet – twelve feet in all. In British carriers the flight decks were armoured with $1^1/_2$-inch armour plating so that the raising of the decks created great stability problems and a huge amount of ballast was put into the bilges to compensate. The ship was finally launched by Queen Elizabeth, the wife of George VI, in 1950 but that was not the end of the major surgery. Two new British inventions had come to the fore: one, the Angled Deck which allowed aircraft to land without the risk of running into aircraft already parked; the other, the Steam Catapult which permitted the launching of much heavier aircraft at speed up to 100 knots. A third invention, adopted from the Americans, was the Deck Edge Lift. This again was supposed to give greater flexibility to the handling of aircraft and it too required massive rebuilding to get it in. In point of fact it was fitted on the port side, the same side as the angled deck, and as a consequence could seldom be used.

All this, together with modern radar, Mirror Landing Sights and improved arrester gear, again added to the weight and stability problem and gave *Ark* a displacement of about 60,000 tons as opposed to the 43,000 of the original design. With an overall length of 810 feet and beam of 112 feet, she was a big ship in her time but was soon to be dwarfed by the huge American nuclear powered carriers.

Now in the fitting-out stage, *Ark* was buzzing with activity and I was introduced to the various foremen, bowler hatted as their badge of office, who supervised all the various trades – shipwrights, carpenters, joiners, pattern makers, engine fitters, boilermakers and so on, each with their separate Union and woe betide anyone who trespassed on another's preserve. It was down tools immediately and we were to suffer a number of lightning strikes, one of which was caused by me – but more of that later. The next day I had lunch with my namesake, Mr Robert Johnson, the Managing Director of the Yard, a very pleasant individual who introduced me to some of the Senior Managers. At that time Camell Laird's was one of the biggest shipbuilding companies in the world and it would have been impossible to believe that by the 1990s it would have ceased to exist.

I shared my office with another Lieutenant Commander, John Varley, who was Mate of the Upper Deck, short title MUD. Just as I was responsible for everything that went on inside the ship, he was responsible for everything on the outside and together we started writing the Standing Orders for two departments. John was a large burly chap who looked like and, indeed, wanted to be a farmer, an ambition he achieved about a year later when he decided to leave the Navy. To help me in my work I had a Chief Petty officer called Whiting, who was to be Chief of the Mess Decks and who turned out be a hard-working and faithful all throughout my time in the ship.

After a few nights in my Commercial Hotel I became determined to waste no time in finding somewhere to live and began scouring the local papers. Not having a car made things difficult but I rang Instow with an urgent request to borrow my mother's sit-up-and-beg bicycle, complete with wicker basket strapped to the front handle bars. When it arrived on the train I was in business and, using the little suburban train which ran down the Wirral peninsular, I was able to use the long summer evenings to explore the various possibilities. Eventually I found a very reasonable first-floor flat in an old Edwardian style house in Hoylake. No 33 Cable Road belonged to a very nice Jewish family called Solomon who were most helpful. I moved in straight away; it was an easy walk to Hoylake station and 20 minutes on the train to Birkenhead, all very convenient. However, by this time it was the school summer holidays and Mary and the boys were either at Instow or Exmouth, so I was on my own until Mary and David joined me in the middle of September, Michael of course returning to Torquay and Winchester Lodge.

In our little office I was getting to know the other officers, including John Watkins, the Supply Officer and erstwhile rugger player of some renown. He first played for the Navy in 1933 and also played as wing three-quarter for Somerset and the Barbarians. He was still playing rugger after the war and Captained the Navy XV. Our Chief Engineer, Commander Cannon, had been with the ship since 1953 and was most helpful in my exploration of the ship and in explaining its many quirks. The office on the other side of mine housed a gaggle of senior specialists: Rene Cruddas, the Air Engineer; George Sivewright, the Gunnery Officer; the navigator, Jim Woolley, who had been at Pangbourne with me; and Philip Gordon-Warren, ex Fleet Air Arm, in charge of damage Control. I and CPO Whiting spent most of our days getting to know the ship, making notes and trying to work out who should go into what size mess and where.

The accommodation was on five different decks, the flight deck being number 1 and the messes on 2,3,4,5 and 6 decks and they came in all different shapes and sizes.

Those situated on either side of the hangers were long and thin, like railway carriages, and each housed about 30 men. Others, like those on 6 deck, were underneath the hanger and were much bigger, sleeping about 50, but with virtually no headroom because of the mass of pipes and ventilation trunking, which meant that someone of my height, six feet, could not stand upright. Fine for a bunch of Welsh miners but, for the average matelot, pretty grim.

The ship had been designed for hammocks but these were now a thing of the past and they had been replaced by tiers of bunks either two or three high, with the second bunk in a tier letting down to make the backrest of a seat during the day. All this tended to crowd the mess decks and give them a really gloomy appearance. Even the Petty Officers' messes were little better. Clearly, for those destined to live on 6 deck, morale was going to be a problem and these messes would have to be shared between the different departments – seamen, engineers and so on – to avoid ill-feeling. The Ship's Company, when everyone was on board, numbered 2,500 of whom 250 were officers. The Wardroom, too, was on 6 deck and though here some attempt had been made to box in the pipe work and cables there was still precious little headroom, about 7 feet at its best. While senior officers had good cabins on 3 deck, the junior ones and most of the aircrew were crammed into 4- or 8-berth boxes.

To this day I remember the sinking feeling when I added up all the berths and found that we were 300 short. I added them again and again but there had been no mistake and panic stations followed. The Yard had provided the number of berths shown on the original plan and no one had thought to tell them of the increased numbers that were now required to man all the additional equipment. This of course was the fault of the ship-design team at Bath. I immediately went to Christopher Dreyer who needed quite a bit of convincing that we were in deep trouble.

The problem was how to find 300 extra berths in an already overcrowded ship. Something had to go but what? Forward of the lower hangar was a large space known as the Torpedo Body Room. Here torpedoes for aircraft were to be stowed and serviced. But for which aircraft? As I suspected, none of the aircraft we were to embark carried torpedoes and so, with permission from The Admiralty, we were able to convert this area into a bunk space for 250. This went quite a long way to solving the problem and the remaining 50 were squeezed in here and there.

The present day sailor demands his own bunk with his name on it, complete with locker and reading light. This was my first encounter with bunks and how I longed for the old-fashioned mess with hammocks which were stowed away during the day, leaving plenty of room for everyone and plenty of flexibility but of course this could never be. However it was not all doom and gloom and there were many excellent messdecks and lots of other good features, such as the large and airy Dining Halls and excellent galleys with all the very latest equipment, and there was no doubt that everything was being done to make sure that that everywhere was as bright and well-decorated as possible.

All this brought on the next domestic crisis – the Heads, or lack of them, for junior ratings. I wrote a letter to be sent to Their Lordships entitled 'The Bum – Pan Ratio' in which I pointed out that the lavatories in the ship had been provided on a sliding scale which took no notice of the needs of nature. The Admiral has 3, the Captain 2, Commanders 1 each, senior officers 1 per 6, junior officers and Petty Officers 1 per 15 and junior ratings (i.e. the rest) 1 per 50 and that, by any standard, was insufficient. We considered 1 per 30 to be the very minimum and found Ministry of Health guidelines to back us up. I felt sure that with over 1,300 compartments in the ship, one or two could be converted to serve the basic requirements of man. In fact after my letter had done the rounds of Whitehall and Bath, two compartments in the vicinity of the forward heads were converted and mass constipation averted.

It was during this conversion of heads that I hit upon a good idea. At this time toilet paper came in the form of small square sheets of brown paper commonly known as Admiralty Brown. These fitted into little rectangular metal boxes fixed to the dividing wall of each compartment. Jack had the habit of going to the heads sometimes for a quick smoke and the remains of his fag would be stubbed out and left in the bottom of the little Admiralty Brown box and was extremely difficult for the cleaner to get out. It occurred to me that if the bottom of the box were full of holes, the fag ends would fall out and could be easily swept up.

I persuaded the foreman of the Sheet Metal Workers to drill holes in the bottom of all the boxes, which he did, BUT, in the officers heads the boxes were made of wood and the Sheet Metal worker who was drilling the holes was so carried away with his task that he drilled holes in the wooden boxes as well. This was a job that could only be done by Joiners. All work stopped immediately and about 1000 men of all trades walked off the ship. It took over two days of negotiations to get them back to work again and I was in the doghouse with Cammell Laird's Management team. So much for initiative!

We were determined that *Ark Royal* should be a ship of excellence and Chris Dreyer and I visited Eagle, which was similar to *Ark* but had been in commission for about a year, and another new Fleet Carrier, Bulwark, to see what we could learn. We came away unimpressed; both ships were scruffy beyond words, but how to do better?

Discussing it with CPO Whiting we came to the conclusion that to try and clean the many passages and other heavily-used compartments by day was a waste of time. We needed Night Cleaning and Painting parties to work while the majority slept and these must be made up of ratings from all Departments. We horse-traded with the Heads of other Departments for numbers and arranged for a special mess deck to be allocated where they could have a reasonable chance of sleeping during the day without being disturbed. In the event this worked out extremely well; it was both economical and efficient. We rotated the night workers every three months but if they wished they could stay on and, in fact, most of my night spray-painting party were there for the whole commission and very good they were too.

One of the difficulties with a ship of this size, with all its multiplicity of functions, was to keep everyone informed as to what was going on and also to prevent boredom. Commander Dreyer, along with the Electrical Engineer Officer, Commander Harry Vaughan, came up with the idea of closed circuit television. There would be a set in every mess and a small studio from which news and general information could be broadcast and in the evenings films would be shown. It was a grand project which had to be self-financing to the tune of several thousand pounds, a lot of money in those days but necessary to pay for the miles of cabling, TV cameras and some 50-plus large television sets. We managed to get a certain amount of sponsorship from the firms supplying the equipment and John Watkins, who was a pretty forceful character, managed to persuade the NAAFI to advance us the balance against future rebate from the takings of the NAAFI shops on board once the ship was up and running. Work was started with the object of getting as much as possible installed before the ship was commissioned. We believed that this would be a 'first', certainly as far as the Royal Navy was concerned.

It is very difficult for the layman to imagine what life is like aboard an Aircraft Carrier. Everyone has a job to do but only a very small proportion have a job which allows them to see what is going on outside the ship. For many, life is contained within this huge metal box. Take for example an engine room rating: his life is a progress from his mess to the engine room, to the bathroom, to the dining hall and back to the mess. None of this requires going on deck and, in fact, when flying is in progress the flight deck is out of bounds to all except those actually involved, i.e. the aircraft handlers and the air crew. With our television cameras we would be able to show what was happening on the bridge, on the flight deck, in the machinery spaces, in the hangars, in the galleys and so on. During exercises and every evening at sea there would be a briefing from the TV studio so that no one should feel out of the picture or not know what it was that we were trying to achieve. All this was to be a very great aid to morale and to the very real need for our people to feel all part of one company. I was delighted at having it as a part of my responsibilities.

It was super at the end of the summer holidays to have Mary and David at Hoylake. David started at a local private school, Minto House, which took 5-year-olds. It was not far from our house but for David it was all a bit daunting as it was quite a large school and all strangers. The ship was due to commission towards the end of February 1955, sailing for acceptance trials on the 25th, so we had just over four months before the 'grey mistress' would take over our lives. At weekends we were able to explore North Wales and Cheshire. We also endeavoured to get as many officers as possible, with or without their wives, to 33 Cable Road so that we could get to know them properly. Mary found a good friend in Lettice Watkins, who lived nearby, and also Philip Gordon-Warren's wife, who hailed from Bermuda. The kitchen in the flat was just about adequate provided we remembered to put enough coins into the meter.

At Christmas Granny Bull brought Michael up so that we could all be together. They came by train as far as Birmingham, where I met them with the car for a very slippery drive back on icy roads. However, that bore no comparison to Mary's drive south with all our belongings at the end of February in heavy snow.

At the beginning of December our Captain joined. Captain Dennis Royle Farquaharson Cambell DSC had joined the Navy in 1925 and, in 1935, qualified as a fighter-pilot flying Fairey Flycatchers and Hawker Nimrods, both biplanes. At the beginning of World War II he was in command of a squadron equipped with Skuas and had the distinction of shooting down the first German aircraft of the war near

Scapa Flow. Soon after that he became a test pilot at Boscombe Down. Except for a short period in command of a single-screw frigate, *Tintagel Castle*, in 1947 and 1948, his whole career had been centred around flying and I got the impression that it was quite a shock for him to find himself in command of the Navy's largest and latest warship.

He was a curious mixture: on the one hand he was extremely shy and reserved and hated 'pomp and ceremony' but, on the other hand, was extremely quick-witted and decisive. At heart he was a 'boffin'; it was he who had invented the Angled Deck, for which he was awarded several thousand pounds and which was quickly adopted by every Navy in the world that had carriers. However, he was a keen caravaner and was much prouder of having had published in the Caravan Magazine a design for a new form of portable privy that he had invented. He was a mathematician and belonged to a society that exchanged mathematical problems. As Officers of the Watch at sea were soon to find out, he had a predilection for mental arithmetic and in quieter moments at sea he would bowl them an assortment of brain teasers. As far as running a big ship was concerned, he was a complete novice but no one realized this better than he and he was quick to seek and accept advice BUT it had to be good and it had to be right.

At about the same time we were joined by Commander Michael Fell DSO, DSC and Bar, the Commander (Air) but more commonly referred to as Wings. His job in *Ark* was to conduct all air operations and to be in charge of the Squadrons forming our Air Group when they were embarked. Mike had joined the Fleet Air Arm in 1938 and had a distinguished war record as a fighter pilot, flying from Carriers and also commanding a Squadron in the Western Desert (North Africa). In 1951 and 1952 he had commanded No.20 Carrier Group of the Royal Australian Navy in HMAS Sydney when he was awarded a Bar to his DSC during the war in Korea. Dark, slim and suave with keen features, he was a very professional aviator who knew exactly what he wanted and got it. At the same time he was a charming and cooperative person and he and his wife Joan were a very popular couple.

When a ship has employed a good proportion of a town's workforce for the length of time that *Ark Royal* had, quite a bond is formed, so when the townspeople of Birkenhead said that they would like to give something to the ship I was delegated to go to a Council meeting in the Town Hall to say what it was that the Ship's Company would like. I had asked around and the general opinion was that it would be nice to have a piano. This would be kept in one of the Dining Halls and used for entertainment. In a ship with a complement as big as ours there were bound to be several who would be excellent pianists. I got up and said my piece to the Councillors, following which a fierce debate started over what sort of piano it should be and what might be the cost. In the middle of all this an Elderly Councillor stood up saying, 'We've got a bloody piano in t' parlour and no beggar can play it; I'll give 'em t' piano so let's give 'em a piece of silver'. And so they did – we had a fine silver cup for Football.

As Commissioning Day approached so the pace increased and, by Christmas, our advance party had increased to around 300. There was a whole warehouse full of stores and spare parts which all had to be moved on board and stowed in their right places. Our shack of an office would no longer hold us all so, as compartments were completed and accepted, we too moved into the ship. My cabin was on 3 Deck in the Senior Officers Cabin Flat, situated aft above the Quarterdeck. The ship was fitted as a Fleet Flagship so we had an Admiral's Cabin across the stern and cabins nearby for the senior Staff Officers. The Captain, ever modest, did not wish to move into the Admiral's Cabin and this enabled me to have the cabin earmarked for the Commander. It was a large airy cabin on the port side of the Cabin Flat with a sleeping section curtained off from the day cabin. Large aboard ship is very different from large in a house, but I suppose my cabin measured 18 ft x 9 ft, whereas a normal single cabin would be more like 7 ft x 9 ft, and I also had the luxury of a 'scuttle' (window). In the middle of the Flat were the Heads and Bathrooms and also the Main Keyboard, watched over day and night by a Royal Marine sentry. There were some 15,000 keys in the ship including duplicates and triplicates which needed strict control. I and the other denizens of the Cabin Flat managed to persuade the Captain of Marines that the Sentry should wear gym shoes at night so that we weren't kept awake by squeaky boots.

For watertight integrity a warship is divided into a very large number of watertight compartments and in this ship there was no means of walking from one end of the ship to the other below 4 Deck. Only one under-cover route existed and that was on the starboard side of 2 Deck so traffic along this passage was continuous, earning it the nickname 'the Burma Road'. It led, amongst other places, to the Island, a large structure on the starboard side about the size of a small ship which, besides carrying the trunking to the funnel and the main radar arrays, housed the Navigating Bridge, The Admiral's Bridge, the Flying Control, the Operations and Aircraft Direction Room, the Aircrew Ready Rooms, Briefing Rooms, Aircraft Handlers Room and, of course, the Captain's and Admiral's Sea Cabins. Immediately under the Island on 2 Deck was another block of cabins which housed, among others, the Ship's Chaplain Will Sandey, a very remarkable character. By having his cabin forward he reckoned he was accessible to anyone from the Lower Deck who might not fancy going into Officers' territory to see him. Often in ships one comes across the 'Wardroom Padre' but Will was very definitely a Ship's Company Padre and he hung on to the pre-war tradition of not wearing uniform. A uniform with no badge of rank was introduced for Padres in 1940 in case they should be taken prisoner.

In his younger days he had been a boxer and cross-country runner but now he had turned his attention to golf. Will had arranged for the ship's Chapel to be most beautifully fitted out with some of the furniture hand-carved in oak by that famous Yorkshire wood carver 'Mousey' Thompson, who signed his work by carving a mouse on each piece. Another popular place below the island was the aircrew snack bar 'Noah's Grill', which was open 24 hours a day when the ship was at sea and would turn out endless supplies of bacon and eggs, or whatever, for hungry young aviators or for anyone else if they could get in.

The remainder of the Ship's Company joined in February and we had an impressive Commissioning Service in the Upper Hangar when we all declared that with God's help *Ark Royal* would be a fine and worthy ship. That evening we gave a Cocktail Party on the Quarterdeck for all the local dignitaries and worthies of

Liverpool and Birkenhead. All the openings to the elements were smartly screened off by our very smart maroon and white striped side screens so, despite the month, it was quite cosy. The party was clearly a great success and it was a merry crowd that left the ship, bar one. After every one had gone I thought I should make the rounds of the 'cloakrooms' to see that nothing had been left behind. Looking into the Admiral's cabin, which had been used as a Ladies Cloakroom, I heard a faint voice calling for help. It seemed to come from the Admiral's bathroom and looking in I saw a pair of legs sticking up in the air. They belonged to a rather amply-built and inebriated female, with her hat cocked over one eye, who said, 'I'm stuck; I just sat on the edge of the bath and 'shlipped in. . . I'm shut up like a jack knife'. She was, too, but with a good heave I managed to extricate her, only to find that her husband had gone off without her and we had to organise a taxi to get her home. Perhaps her husband had left in a similar state. . .

At noon on 25th February the great ship left the building dock and slipped down the Mersey to the open sea. It is always a thrilling feeling when a ship comes alive: the vibration of the propellers, the constant hum of machinery and the feeling of movement all help to transform an inanimate object into a living being. At this stage we were still flying the Red Ensign, with Cammell Laird's men at the controls and the Trials Captain in charge until the Sea Trials were completed to everyone's satisfaction and the ship formally accepted into Admiralty service. That night we anchored off the Isle of Man and the following day, after a two-hour Full Speed Trial, our Captain, Dennis Cambell, signed the bit of paper accepting the ship. The White Ensign was hoisted and we proceeded to the Clyde. Here we came to anchor off Greenock and put the Cammell Laird team ashore. The ship was really ours at last. I had not been to Greenock since Mary and I had been sent up there in 1945 but it didn't look much different.

We had been in light draught for going down the Mersey and our first task was to take on a full load of fuel oil – several thousand tons. The result was quite comical. Being at anchor we had of course hoisted out the boats, put down the various ladders and swung out the lower booms, only to discover that the platforms for the accommodation ladders, the ends of all the lizards (mooring pendants for the boats) and the ladders from the booms were several feet under water, as was the black boot topping which marked the top edge of the anti-fouling. We sent for Mr Sims, the Chief Naval Constructor in charge of Aircraft Carrier design to come post-haste from Bath. He arrived the next day with his No.2, Mr Moss, and, together with the Captain and Chris Dreyer, we circled the ship in the Captain's motor boat. When we got back on board the Captain said, 'Well Mr Sims, what do you think'? Sims replied, 'Well, she came out a bit deep didn't she'. What had happened was that no one at Bath had told the builders about what the draught would be after all the additional work and increased weight that had been added to the ship since the original design. Pretty disgraceful really, but Mr Sims got his K and became Director General of Ships in due course, as did Mr Moss on Sims' retirement. Actually they were a very nice pair.

From the Clyde we went to Loch Ewe for four days to 'shake down' and then to Spithead for three weeks of Gunnery Trials and Radar Calibration and for various other things before going up harbour at Portsmouth on 24th March. During our weekend in harbour members of the *Ark Royal* Association presented the ship with a most superb silver Ship's Bell in memory of all those who had served in the previous *Ark Royal*. The bell was mounted in a beautifully constructed oak belfry on the Quarterdeck. The bell weighed two hundredweight and the money for it had been set aside after a meeting of the survivors of the third *Ark Royal*, in the Canteen at Gibraltar Dockyard, after she had been sunk in November 1941. The belfry was paid for by the Officers of the third *Ark*, led by Admiral of the Fleet Sir Arthur Power who had been her first Captain. For the event about 150 'Old Arks' turned up and were given a great day on board. One of the nice things about Ship's Bells is that they are used as Fonts for Christenings and it is customary to have the names of all those Christened engraved on the inside of the bell. I imagine that the bell is now aboard the present *Ark Royal* and must have a goodly number of names on the inside.

After the weekend it was off to sea for a few days and then to Plymouth, where we entered the Hamoaze and berthed alongside in the Dockyard for Catapult trials. Steam catapults had been developed by John Brown Ltd and their resident expert was Lieutenant Commander Tom Pickering. He had joined the Erebus at the same time as I did but was now retired from the Navy, was employed by John Brown and was in Plymouth to conduct the trials. Testing out a catapult involved launching huge baulks of timber – each the equivalent weight of a fully-loaded aircraft – over the bows, measuring the velocity each time, fishing them out and doing it all over again and again. Each baulk had a name painted on it in large white letters such as Flossie or Doris. It was of course essential that the catapults were entirely reliable before being used to launch real aircraft. I believe the launch speed had to be 110 knots each time and that is fast.

When we were in Plymouth many other things were going on: we ammunitioned ship, took on board even more stores and gave Easter leave. John Varley got his wish to leave the Navy and was relieved by a very nice Lieutenant Commander, William Loftie, who had been at *Ganges* when I was there. William had resisted marriage until this time when, just before joining, he married an exceptionally charming young bride, Caroline, whom everybody liked. She was quite a bit younger than William and very much a Chelsea girl. I think she found our ways a little strange.

Ark Royal had been equipped with a very comprehensive laundry, but of course it had to be manned by members of the Ship's Company. I think about 20 were required and we sent them to the Millbay Laundry to be trained, only to have them sent back after a couple of days for using bad language and upsetting the laundry girls. It seemed that each department had off-loaded their dregs into the laundry party as a good way of getting rid of them. The next time I asked for volunteers and the whole thing went a little better. It is vital to have an efficient laundry in a ship with our numbers and especially when going into white uniform, but that is another story.

This period in Plymouth was filled with a variety of activities, the completion of the storing programme, innumerable tests of equipment and, after the Easter leave period, our first experience of 'Paint Ship'. At that time it was still done by hand, with people suspended over the side on painting stages, and about 500 men were employed – quite an organisation – but it all went quite quickly, despite the weather, and at the end we felt we looked pretty smart in the company of other Carriers in port – *Eagle, Ocean, Triumph* and *Warrior*. Little did I imagine that one day I would be in command of *Triumph*.

One of the highlights of our stay was a Variety show, the BBC's 'Variety Ahoy', with a stage rigged in the Upper Hangar. The stars were Janet Brown who became famous for her impersonation of Prime Minister Margaret Thatcher, comedian Jon Pertwee who gained fame as 'Dr Who' in the 1960s and last, but by no means least, everyone's favourite pop singer, Alma Cogan. I had the added excitement of having her change in my cabin and had to help pin her into her dress. She was a delightful bubbly character and just about the whole nation mourned when she died of cancer in her early thirties. The show was acclaimed a great success and the first of many events to be staged in the hangar.

Mary and I were very lucky to be lent Warleigh, a very historic manor house, parts of which dated from the 11th century. It had belonged to the Radcliffes at Tamerton Foliot since the 16th century and the sister of the present owner, Walter Radcliffe, was Mary's Godmother. We had the house for a fortnight while they were away. Most of the house was Elizabethan but in the Norman parts the walls were about six feet thick and going from the Dining Room to the Library and from the Library to the Hall you had to duck your head for several paces. There are supposed to be secret passages from the house to the boathouse on the River Tamar and also to the Parish Church. And not surprisingly there was a priest hole. One of the joys of being there was that we were able to invite our friends up from the ship for a meal and to enjoy some of our baronial splendour, albeit borrowed.

At Whitsun the ship was open to the public for Navy Days and over the weekend 22,226 visitors came on board. Being 'Open to Visitors' is always a bit of a challenge: first, to stop people going where they should not go and, second, to stop things getting pinched. Of course it was not just the public who pinched things but people from other ships seeking to embarrass their chums by finding loopholes in the organisation. I think we came out of this one pretty well having some 'visitors' sneaking aboard Eagle and bringing back the Captain's telescope, pinched from his cabin. This gave much embarrassment to Tony Griffin, who was the Commander of Eagle and had to come and ask for it back, and to us 'Arks' some childish pleasure at having got one up on our rival.

In another sort of one-upmanship we hit upon the idea of getting Sir Peter Scott, the ornithologist and artist, to paint a series of murals for the Ship's Company Dining Hall, about eight panels in all each measuring about eight feet by four. As I had known Peter during the war and had indeed been nearly sunk by him when I was in *Verity*, I was deputed to do the deal and went to have lunch with him and his wife at Slimbridge, the bird sanctuary. He had had his house built by the side of one of the lakes there, with the largest picture window that I had ever seen. You had the greatest pleasure seeing the ducks swim past you only feet away while sitting eating an excellent lunch. The outcome of it all was that he agreed to paint the pictures provided that we sent him the panels already painted with the base colours, which he would choose. They were to be done on the canvas side of hardboard. In return we would give him an antique dining-room table costing no more than £100. The choice of subject for the murals would be left to him but would, of course, be ducks or geese, as this was what he did best and for which he had made his name as an artist. The finished result was absolutely splendid; it gave our rather drab Dining Hall a considerable lift and became a great source of pride. Several years later I heard that the panels had been removed as they were considered too valuable to be in a Ship's Company Dining Hall. What a pity!

Having completed all the harbour trials and storing, June 1955 saw us setting off for Gibraltar for a three-week work-up but still without our complement of aircraft. Nearly all the time was spent at sea practising gunnery, seamanship drills, damage control, fuelling at sea and flight deck drills handling dummy aircraft. Just before we got to Gibraltar, Christopher Dreyer was taken ill with some mysterious allergy and was flown home to Haslar, so I had to take on his job as well as my own for the four weeks but all went well.

All did not go well with the ship's laundry. On passing Ushant we shifted into white uniform which, of course, had to be laundered. Now, to make whites look reasonable a certain amount of starch has to be used but our laundry crew got it wrong. All the whites coming back from the wash were starched as hard as boards and it was impossible to prise open the legs of trousers to get them on. The second shot at it wasn't much better, so we sent an urgent signal to The Admiralty to get someone from Bergers, who made the starch, flown out from England to show us how to use it. It was impossible to run a ship with everyone's legs stuck together! Bergers reacted quickly and a very nice man arrived on the scene so that after a couple of days everything was back to normal. From that time on we had excellent service from the laundry and complaints were few and far between.

The ship was alongside in Gibraltar for a long weekend before sailing for home, so there was a mad dash for the shops and soon the ship was bursting with rabbits. Why they should be called rabbits I have never discovered but rabbits are what the sailors call presents they buy to take home as peace-offerings. Back once more in the English channel, flying trials started for real and our Commander (Air), Mike Fell, had the honour of making the first deck landing and catapult launch in a Seahawk jet fighter from 800 squadron. It was good to see the flight deck coming into its own at last and for someone like myself, who had had no experience of aircraft carriers, it was awe-inspiring – the sheer power of the whole operation and the great thump of the aircraft as a six-ton plane hits the deck and pulls out the arrester wire to full stretch. Also, the forces required to launch an aircraft can be judged from the need to use a wire strop of $4^{1}/_{2}$-inch circumference steel wire to hook the aircraft to the catapult. At that time the strops just dropped into the water and were lost, so that a new strop had to be used for each launch and we carried a huge stock of them.

At the end of the flying trials we went to Spithead for the weekend and the Wardroom gave a dance on board. Brigitte Déroulède, who was about 18 at the time, was staying with Mary at Exmouth and they both came up to Portsmouth for the party. I was worried as to how it would be for Brigitte but it turned out to be a memorable success as I had managed to find a suitable young midshipman to look after her and they had a whale of a time.

After that it was back to Plymouth for summer leave and to ammunition ship before embarking the squadrons in August. John Watkins had written an operetta called 'H.M.S Traditional' or 'Hard a Gilbert' with the music pinched liberally from Gilbert and Sullivan and performed by the Wardroom. Despite everything else that was going on, 36 of us had been bludgeoned into taking part, fully supported by the Ship's Company volunteer band under the direction of Mr Peach, one of the ship's Air Electrical Officers, who was a wizard on the trombone. It was put on for three nights in the Upper Hangar playing to full houses and voted a great success. Will Sandey, the Padre, played Scarface Joe; our enormous Bosun, Mr Byrne, was the Cannibal King; Surgeon Lieutenant Fisher was the heroine Polly (Fisher was the son of the Archbishop of Canterbury and caused a bit of a flutter by marrying a Roman Catholic); I played a slow-witted Devon lad who had joined the Navy to see the world – not too difficult!

It was during this period in Plymouth that I heard that the Yacht Club in Instow was looking for a new class of boat to replace the now very long-in-the-tooth Taw and Torridge One Designs. I thought that the 18-foot Jolly Boat designed by Uffa Fox for the Plymouth clubs would be just the thing; it had proved a great success and was simple, fast and reasonably stable. I invited a team from the Yacht Club which included the Commodore, Rear Admiral Franklin, the Sailing Secretary, Guinea de Crespigny, and others to lunch on board before going to see the boat in action. However despite a very jolly lunch they turned it down as they thought it was too racy for North Devon. – a pity, and I still think it would have been very good.

The summer leave was spent at Instow and then it was back to Plymouth to prepare for our departure for the Mediterranean where we expected to spend the next nine months operating our full peacetime complement of aircraft. This consisted of 20 Hawker Sea Hawk fighters, 20 de Haviland Sea Venom two-seater night fighters, 8 twin-engined Fairey Gannet Anti-Submarine aircraft, 4 Douglas Skyraider Airborne Early-Warning aircraft and 2 Westland Sikorsky helicopters for Air Sea Rescue – a total of 54 which would go up to about 80 in time of war. The middle of September saw us out in the Channel to embark our aircraft.

Aircraft, aircrew and the squadron fitters and engineers do not stay aboard a carrier when it is in harbour. For one thing, it was not possible in those days to operate aircraft other than when the ship was underway and steaming into the wind and, for another reason, pilots of high performance jet aircraft have to keep constantly in practice and take to the air almost daily. The consequence of this is that a carrier goes from a relatively tranquil state, with plenty of spare room, to a bursting-at-the-seams state with the sudden arrival of about 600 additional officers and ratings with all their gear. From the officers' point of view, the Wardroom, which had been fairly staid, would now be topped up with 100 or so keen and energetic young aviators and, for the first time since commissioning, the ship was about to become 100% alive.

Aviators believe that they are a superior breed and, of course, in many ways they are. The skill, dedication and courage required to fly a jet on and off a carrier is exceptional but in all other respects they are all part of the naval service like the rest of us. The job of the carrier's permanent crew is to run an efficient and welcoming ship for the aircrew but, what is most important of all is to make the squadrons and aircrew feel part of the overall team, understand that it is their ship and have pride in her and all she does. A Fleet Air Arm Squadron is a self-contained unit with its own Commanding Officer and traditions. The same squadron will operate from several different carriers using the ship as a hotel and garage, therefore your hotel and garage facilities have to be the best. That was certainly our aim and I think, to no small degree, an aim achieved.

Out in the Channel we got on with the process of embarking our squadrons. The first to arrive was 800 Squadron of Sea Hawks. Commanded by Lieutenant Commander Ray Lygo, they were distinguished by the Roman-soldier-type red-brush-effect crest glued to the top of their flying helmets, though it was rubber and not hair. Ray was quite a character; he had started life as a junior reporter on the Times newspaper before joining the Navy in 1942. After the war he stood as the Liberal candidate for Eastbourne, before being offered a permanent commission. He went on to become a full Admiral and, having spent quite a bit of time on loan to the US Navy, he had married a very nice American wife; we knew them both well. On retirement from the Navy he became Chairman of British Aerospace. Quite a guy!

The arrival of 800 Squadron was closely followed by that of their deadly rivals, 898 Squadron under Lieutenant Commander Jimmy Pearce. Their trademark was that they all put on bowler hats when getting out of their cockpits, that is to say all but Jimmy Pierce who donned a very smart black 'topper'. The next day Joe Honeywell's 824 Squadron of Gannets flew on, along with 849's Skyraiders. (After he retired Joe set up a very successful yacht brokerage business at Newton Ferrers and Plymouth.) Somewhat later the Sea Venoms of 891 Squadron arrived with Maurice Birrell in command.

During this time we had two weekends at Portsmouth, one when we went alongside the Southern Railway Jetty in the dockyard and the second at anchor at Spithead as the weather forecast was too bad for us to go up harbour. Unfortunately this was the weekend that I had invited my cousin Charlie Wainman and his wife Ann to lunch and having sent a picket boat to Ryde Pier to pick them up it was the devil's own job to get them ashore again without smashing anything. I think that they enjoyed their visit but I did not, wishing all the time that I had called it off, but there were no mobile phones in those days. The weekend we were alongside the SR Jetty, we catapulted off four Sea Hawks in quick succession as we were leaving harbour, which gave the inhabitants of Gosport quite a shock. I am sure that nothing so environmentally unfriendly could happen today but we had a BBC News camera crew on board and were determined to put on a show for them.

We sailed for Gibraltar on 3rd October and most of the passage was spent working up the squadrons and the flight deck crews and all that went with it. Our quiet life was well and truly over and we soon became used to the thump of aircraft landing on, arrester wires being pulled out and the rattle and judder of a ship going at high speed, especially so when your cabin was at the back end of the ship but, luckily for me, mine was two decks down from the flight deck.

Our closed circuit television was now fully operational. We had made a compartment in the bowels of the ship into a small studio and for the first time, in our Navy at least, it was possible to keep the company of a big ship entirely in the picture.

With receivers in every mess and in recreational spaces it was possible to show everyone exactly what was happening and therefore what was expected of them. Apart from films and cartoons we ran a regular news service, interviews, quiz shows, daily briefings on the ship's programme and outside broadcasts from different sections of the ship. Though our cameras were not quite up to BBC standard, they were good enough to give everyone a good glimpse of what went on in the engine room, on the flight deck, in the ops room, etc., and helped to make everyone feel part of the whole. Films, in fact, presented our biggest problem. The system worked by projecting the film on to a front-silvered mirror set at 45 degrees to the TV camera and, though this worked after a fashion, the pictures tended to be very much too dark and for some shots, taken in poor light, almost invisible. After a lot of desperate experiments I hit on the idea of lighting the image on the front of the silvered mirror with a very bright diffused light and this worked like magic. We all heaved a sigh of relief.

Sadly, just before we arrived at Gibraltar we lost our first aircraft. One of the Sea Hawks went into the sea on taking off and both pilot and plane went under the ship without trace. It seemed that the starboard catapult failed to reach full power and the aircraft never reached flying speed. The pilot was a young Lieutenant called Morse. That evening we held a short memorial service and then it was flying as usual. Flying from carriers has always been hazardous and it is Fleet Air Arm tradition to carry on as if nothing had happened. Nevertheless it was a nasty jolt for us all; perhaps the 'fishheads' (pilots slang for seamen officers) felt it more than the airmen.

Everyone was pleased to be alongside in Gibraltar for the weekend, everyone that is except Christopher Dreyer who was again smitten by his mysterious allergy and had to be put ashore. Once again I found myself having to do his job as well as my own. This time it was a little more arduous than before because we were going to practise night flying as well as day. It is impossible for the Captain to be on the bridge twenty-four hours a day and still be alert all the time that flying is taking place. So, being the senior seaman officer, in fact the only seaman officer with command and fleet experience, I was called upon to be the duty 'Captain' at night from midnight until 0700 so that Dennis Cambell could get some rest.

To be truthful, this was one aspect of my job which I relished as it doesn't come everyone's way to be in charge of the largest ship in the Royal Navy, dashing about the ocean with a group of screening destroyers and having responsibility for all routine alterations of course and speed, the deployment of the ships on the screen coupled with the attendant excitement of aircraft being launched and recovered. Also the bacon and eggs sent up from Noah's Grill, the ever-open food bar for airmen, were delicious. The downside was having to be around during the day and I evolved a routine of turning in at 1700 to be woken again at 2330 to start my day. Once in the routine it worked pretty well and, after a bath and breakfast, I was ready to chair the daily Heads of Department meeting which made sure that everyone knew what to be doing and when. After that there was the daily business of Commander's Requestmen and Defaulters, preceded by a briefing from the Master-at-Arms (the ship's senior policeman).

Whilst at Gibraltar we had a boxing match against the local garrison, principally the RAF and the Seaforth Highlanders, which we won comfortably. The aircraft were ranged on deck so that it was possible to set up a ring in the Upper hangar, with seating for about 500; the rest of the Ship's Company were able to watch on our television which worked extremely well. The ship's Welfare Fund had financed the installation and had borrowed several thousand pounds in the process, so it came as a great relief that our faith in the system had been vindicated and that the Welfare Committee, of which I was Chairman, had no quibbles in paying off the loan. On another evening William Loftie, Phillip Gordon-Warren and I all had supper at the Royal Gibraltar Yacht Club. The meal, which included delicious swordfish steaks, cost us each the large sum of four shillings and sixpence, though Phillip complained that his feet hurt walking back to the ship and that William and I were too mean to take a taxi. On the whole the weather at Gibraltar had been disappointingly cold and we looked forward to changing back into blue uniform on arrival at Malta on 29th October.

The passage to Malta was taken up with more day and night flying training with the emphasis on speeding up the landing and take-off intervals. The destroyer *Whirlwind* had joined us as to act as Crash Boat, taking up position close astern whenever flying was taking place. Our helicopters were the first line of rescue during the day but had no equipment or capability for flying at night. During the passage Dennis Cambell told me that I should probably have to carry on doing the Commander's job for some time as Christopher Dreyer, who had been flown to the Naval Hospital at Bighi in Malta, was to be flown home. John Roxborough, who at the time was the Commander of the Cadet Training Ship *Triumph*, had been due to relieve Christopher in February but, after discussing the matter with Mike Fell, the Captain had written to The Admiralty asking that I should be promoted to Acting Commander and that a new First Lieutenant be appointed and flown out to relieve me. I took this as a very good omen. However, Their Lordships thought differently. John Roxborough's appointment was brought forward to Christmas. It seemed that they were determined to get their pound of flesh from me and there was no prospect of short-circuiting the promotion system. I was very disappointed, as I knew that I could do the job, but I think John R had friends in court and he wanted to be promoted to Captain for which *Ark* was a good avenue.

On our arrival off Malta it was blowing a gale and the Captain rightly decided that it would be unsafe to enter harbour at 0900 as planned and that we would have to stay at sea. Berths in the Grand Harbour were between head and stern buoys and it would have been impossible for tugs to have held a ship of *Ark*'s size in position long enough to get secured. However, our senior meteorological officer, Instructor Commander Bellamy, said that there was a front coming through and that between noon and 1300 it would be calm. To everyone's surprise he was absolutely right and we were secured safely between our buoys by 1300, when it again started to blow a gale. It was widely believed that our Schoolie had a direct line to the Almighty.

For the first few days in harbour there was the inevitable round of official calls including that of the Commander-in-Chief, Admiral Sir Guy Grantham, an extremely nice chap whom I had met before in 1946 when he was Chief of Staff to Algie

Willis. His arrival on board went according to plan with the Royal Marine Guard and the volunteer band doing their stuff. His departure was a different story.

Our Captain of Marines was not one of the brightest and when the C-in-C reached the top of the ladder to go down to his Barge and turned to receive the official salute from the Guard, who at that stage should 'Present Arms', absolutely nothing happened. After a long and pregnant pause the Admiral said, 'Your Guard appears to be stuck', and stormed off down to his Barge and shot off. No one was best pleased and I sent for the Captain of Marines and asked him what the hell he thought he was doing. He replied, 'Well sir, I'd been saying to myself, 'Now he is saying goodbye to the Commander Air, now to the First Lieutenant and now to the Captain' and before I had finished he had gone'. I asked, 'Why on earth didn't you look?', to which he replied, 'Oh I couldn't do that, sir, Royal Marine Officers always face their front'. I gave up in despair.

A couple of days later after I had been visiting Christopher Dreyer in the hospital at Bighi, one of the Sisters asked me why *Ark Royal* was such a noisy ship and, if I went out on to the terrace with her, she would show me what she meant. *Ark Royal* was moored between two buoys just below the hospital and there was a continuous succession of bugle-calls, pipes (orders using a bosun's call or whistle), messages for people to go here or report there, all amplified over the Tannoy – the ship's loudspeaker system which had speakers all round the ship, both inside and out. In fact it sounded more like a busy London Railway Station than a warship. Though this was tradition, it clearly had to stop.

The main culprits were the Seamen and Air Departments and I concluded that if the technical side of the ship, who were in fact the majority, could get about their work without being 'piped' to fall in here or go there, so could everyone else. Having first cleared it with the Captain, I told the heads of Departments that from then on only emergencies would be broadcast over the Tannoy. Just about every sailor had a watch and it would be up to the Departmental Officers Chief Petty Officers and Petty Officers to ensure that their men knew what to do and when to do it. All messes received copies of the Ship's daily Orders and Departmental Programmes. After a week of getting used to the new routine, it worked like a charm. I believe too that 99% of the people appreciated being trusted to get on with their allotted task without first being 'Fallen in and Fallen out'. It also saved a great deal of man-hours and it was woe betide anyone found skulking. We were back to being the 'Silent Service'. (Our example was soon to be taken up throughout the Navy.)

After a week in Harbour we put to sea again for more practice, particularly night flying for Sea Hawks, all achieved without disaster, though there were a couple of near misses. The first came about through a missing pin in the ejector seat mechanism in one of the Hawks. The acceleration of the aircraft, on being catapulted, shot the ejector seat half way along its guide rail, leaving the pilot with his head and shoulders sticking up above the cockpit, unable to reach the rudder bar with his feet but just managing to hang on to the joy-stick. To make matters worse the drogue for the parachute also deployed, putting an enormous strain on everything. However, by using full throttle the pilot managed to keep flying-speed and, by some miracle, managed to land at Hal Far airfield without further damage other than to his nerves. Everyone reckoned that he had been a very lucky young man.

The second incident was at dusk when one of the flight deck tractors rolled off the flight deck, sinking immediately with no sign of the driver. There followed a full-scale panic, both SAR helicopters were scrambled and our attendant destroyer told to search the area. Meanwhile on the flight deck the Chief of the Flight Deck Handlers mustered his men and asked if anyone had seen Naval Airman So and So. One of the handlers piped up and said, 'He's in the chapel playing the organ Chief', to which the Chief replied, 'If I want someone to say something funny, my son, I'll send for a comedian'. But that is exactly what the missing person was doing. He had left his tractor with the brake off! End of panic stations and red faces all round. A few days later Lieutenant Bowers of 800 Squadron had the honour of making the 1,000th deck landing and was presented with a bottle of Champagne by the Captain.

At the end of November we sailed in company with our Tanker, RFA Blue Ranger for Toulon, our first 'foreign' visit, and everyone with the exception of the Captain was very excited at the prospect. Dennis Cambell was a very shy person, hated ceremonial – of which there would be plenty – and spoke no French. We arrived off Toulon at 0830 on 2nd December and fired the first of several salutes – a 21-gun salute for France which was returned gun for gun by the French battery ashore. This was followed by a 15-gun salute to Vice-Admiral Barjot in the cruiser *George Leygues*, the same *George Leygues* that I had accompanied in *Melbreak* on D-day off Normandy in 1944. Admiral Barjot was a super little man whom I had known as a captain in SHAPE when I was at Fontainebleau; he had been with the Free French Forces and spoke very good English. Not so the Préfet Maritime, the C-in-C Mediterranean area, Vice-Admiral Lambert. Lambert had been on the Vichy side, was known to dislike the British and purported to understand no English but I did my best to act as interpreter. However, at the luncheon in Admiral Lambert's house I found myself sitting next to Madame Lambert who was very charming, though the Admiral remained pretty po-faced throughout. It was, nevertheless, an excellent lunch.

That evening the Wardroom gave a cocktail party for about 300 guests which passed off very well. I was delighted to meet another old friend from NATO days Captain Picard-Destelan, who invited me and a couple of others to come for a drive on the Saturday and back to his house afterwards to meet his wife and family. On the Sunday we were lent a car and I took the Captain and Mike Fell on a sightseeing tour, ending up at a delightful little restaurant in the country for lunch, before going on to watch the Rugby match between our ship and the Hyeres Rugby Club. We did very well to hold them to a 9–9 draw as this part of France is the home of French Rugby. We also beat the French Navy at soccer but lost the sailing match which was sailed in *Requins*, a smaller version of the International Dragon.

The Ship's Company enjoyed the wine and all that went with it and, although we landed fairly strong patrols with orders to bring people back on board if a situation looked like becoming ugly, they had little to do and the usual Anglo-French punch-ups never occurred, which was a great relief. However, it was not all wine, women and song, as a comprehensive number of coach trips were arranged to tour the countryside and visit places like Cannes and Grasse. The main complaint was that the exchange rate was very bad and Jack found things ashore very expensive. The ship also received a goodly number of visitors, including a strong team from the Light Fleet Carrier *Arromanches*, who wanted to see all the latest equipment. We sailed for Malta on 6th December feeling that we had done a good job as well as having had a good time.

Life aboard a warship at sea is seldom like a cruise. It costs a great deal of money to take a ship to sea and it is vital that the opportunity to train and keep proficient is not lost; whether it be transferring stores or fuelling from supply ships, testing the defence systems or damage control or round-the-clock flying, seldom a minute is wasted. A Carrier's main function is twofold: one is to provide air defence to the Fleet and the other is to carry out air strikes against an enemy. Both these functions have to be carried out simultaneously and all from a 270-metre long airstrip which is little more than one aircraft in width, which moves up and down, rolls about and has aircraft parked on all those areas of deck not being used for flying. The area was increased by the introduction of the angled deck. This was done by building out an extension on the port side forward of the island – the huge bridge structure on the starboard side – which in turn allows the landing strip to be skewed to run diagonally along the deck and to port, so that the starboard catapult is available for launching aircraft at the same time that other aircraft are landing on.

Flying stations involves just about everyone in the ship. Twenty-four hours a day a Combat Air Patrol (CAP) of two fighters, either Sea Hawks or Venoms, are kept airborne, together with a Skyraider radar-carrying Early-Warning plane to extend the range of the ship's own radar, whilst Gannets, the A/S aircraft, are employed on anti-submarine patrols to extend the ship's screen. Other fighters are on deck ready to be scrambled, either with the pilots in the cockpit or in the Ready Rooms in the island nearby. In Flying Control is the officer in charge of general flying operations with his assistants, whilst those aircraft that are airborne are under the control of the Direction Officers seated in front of their huge radar screens in the Operations Room and who are also looking for bogies (hostile aircraft) which may appear on their screens. Down below the Armourers are ready to send weapons on the bomb lifts and others on deck fit them to the aircraft. On deck are fuelling parties, fire parties (dressed in flame-proof suits) and Handlers ready to fold and unfold wings and bring up from or send down to the hangars the aircraft as required for the operation in hand, using the huge lifts at either end of the flight deck. At night the whole deck transforms into a scene from Dante's Inferno with the dim coloured lights of the flight deck, marshals with illuminated batons directing the movement of aircraft on deck, the crescendo of jet engines being run up for take-off, the swoosh of the steam catapults and everything moving with practised precision and speed.

In the Galleys food has to be prepared and available for all those working through the night, the ship has to be kept clean and any equipment or machinery that becomes defective has to be repaired without delay. Down below in the engine rooms everyone is on their toes ready to bring the ship up to full speed on the instant, whenever it is necessary. It is vital to have sufficient windspeed over the deck, normally 30 knots from ahead to make landing safe. The Captain on the bridge, constantly watching the wisp of steam at the forward end of the Flight Deck that indicates the relative direction of the wind over the deck, alters course so that it is straight down the deck. And, while all this is going on, those not on duty are trying to get some sleep amidst the noise and clatter of the ship.

Our own activity has to be coordinated with the other ships in the force and, if operating with other carriers, one has to be always ready to land-on any of their aircraft – and vice versa – if for any reason a deck becomes out of action because of an accident or damage ('Cross Decking' in the jargon of the day). The target was to be able to operate aircraft continuously for four days and this we could do, though everyone was pretty whacked by the end and glad to have a twenty-four-hour 'shut down' before doing it all over again. During our second period of 'round the clock' Operations we had had a visit from 12 senior allied officers from SHAPE who were flown off to us for the day. One was a French General whom I had known at Fontainebleau. As we had no Admiral embarked I was able to give them lunch in the Admiral's cabin between showing them round the ship to see what we did.

Arriving back off Malta on 16th December we flew-off our aircraft to Hal Far before entering harbour and securing to our two buoys in Bighi Bay in the Grand Harbour. Once secured our thoughts and efforts turned towards preparing for Christmas away from home. For my part I had to turn over my Commander's duties to John Roxburgh who arrived on board looking very boot-faced as he had been whisked off *Triumph* in Gibraltar instead of returning home to England for Christmas and leave. Roxburgh was a saturnine sort of chap with a rather swarthy look about him. He had always been known as Randy Roxburgh, a nickname that he hated. He had had a very distinguished career in submarines, getting his first command at the age of 23. The youngest submarine captain in World War II he had been awarded the DSO, DSC and Bar. He had the reputation of being a difficult man and he was.

Being totally unfamiliar with carrier life and being thrown into the middle of a very hectic programme as Second in Command was no sinecure. He wished to know the detail and reason for everything and had myself and others in his cabin after supper until two or three o'clock in the morning, asking endless questions. This went on for about a week. He would put a bottle of whisky on the table before each inquisition and go on until it was empty. He drank most of it but was always up and on the job by seven o'clock next morning, bright eyed and bushy tailed. I could quite see how, during the war, he had stalked and sunk a number of ships including three submarines. Nevertheless the turnover went well and it was quite a relief to be able to shed some of my responsibilities. Happily, too, just before Christmas his wife flew out to Malta to join him and this took a bit of the heat off.

While all this was going on Mike Fell our Commander (Air), had to fly home suddenly as his wife Joan had fallen against an electric fire which set her clothes on fire and burnt her back very badly. She was in hospital in intensive care but was soon out of danger and began to make a slow but painful recovery. Mike was able to return to the ship just in time for Christmas.

Back in Plymouth, Mrs Woolston, the wife of Bob our Operations Officer, had organised a children's party for the *Ark Royal* families during which children could record Christmas messages for their fathers. This was well before the days when everyone had a tape recorder and was quite an undertaking. David who was six refused to say anything, much to Mary's annoyance, but Michael was persuaded with some difficulty to say something and it was great fun to hear his voice when the tape arrived and was played over the ship's broadcast system. There was also great excitement when all the sacks of mail arrived on board – several hundred of them – with everyone wondering whether or not they would get a parcel. I was lucky as I had several, including a super Christmas stocking from Mary containing all sorts of things and which made me feel very homesick.

In the wardroom and, indeed, in many of the messes, we followed the old practice of putting everyone's name in a hat and drawing them out to see who would give a present to whom. In this way everybody would have a present. In the wardroom the price limit was two shillings and six pence and I drew John Bellamy, the Senior Meteorologist. I gave him some seaweed to hang in his cabin and a bottle of Gripe Water in the event of too much wind. Getting the seaweed was hazardous as I had to scramble down the rocks at Sliema to find the right sort. My present was a little rubber dog with a long tube with a bulb on the end and every time you squeezed the bulb the dog hopped along.

On Christmas Eve we had a midnight service on the Quarterdeck and on Christmas day itself, a service of nine lessons and carols accompanied by the band. About 400 attended and the singing could best be described as lusty. After church came the traditional Rounds of the Mess Decks, led by the youngest rating in the ship wearing the Captain's uniform. Because of the size of the ship we divided the rounds into three, John Roxburgh taking one, Mike Fell another while I went with the Captain on the third. He was accompanied by his wife and four year old daughter, Lallage, who was thoroughly spoilt in every mess we visited. Actually, having the four year old with us was a huge asset as it avoided us having to drink the many tots of rum that had been saved for the occasion. Everyone was on their best behaviour and the messes were beautifully decorated. The mess judged to be the best in each of the three circuits was presented with a huge Christmas cake.

In my experience it is never possible to get through Christmas day on board ship without some unfortunate happening and this Christmas proved no exception. I was just going into my cabin after an excellent Christmas lunch when I saw something that looked to me like a body hurtling past my scuttle followed by a loud splash. I stuck my head out and saw someone swimming for the gangway and while I was watching this another body flew past. Sticking my head further out I could see several others including the Flight Deck Officer in the water and a dghaisa fishing people out. As it was sixty feet from the flight deck to the water I didn't think that this was a terribly good idea and shot up to the flight deck to see what was going on. There, to my horror, I found the Master-at-Arms – the chap who is responsible for keeping law and order – presiding over a sort of kangaroo court and sitting on a makeshift throne with a paper crown on his head. Here he was ordering a team of 'bears' such as you have in Crossing the Line ceremonies, to go and fetch so and so on some farcical charge for which the punishment was to be thrown overboard. I sent for the 'Master' and asked him what the hell he thought he was doing and he told me that he was the Lord of Misrule and that this was tradition in Devonport-manned ships and helped the sailors to let off steam. I let off a good deal of steam myself and put an end to it, thankful that no one had been injured or drowned.

Though the weather had been not at all good in Malta with a succession of gales, it had been far worse in England. Mary and the boys had gone to Instow for Christmas where poor Michael had spent his Christmas in bed with 'flu. However he recovered sufficiently to do some tobogganing on the hill behind my parent's house, before a very icy drive back to Exmouth, where everything was frozen up and Mary put her foot through the bedroom ceiling when trying to get to the tank in the roof. However, in all this she managed to send me a very super cake to celebrate our eleventh anniversary and which I shared with Patricia and John Roxburgh and Caroline and William Loftie. Several of us on board had been secretly hoping that we might have something to celebrate when the New Year's promotions were published on 31st December but Bob Woolston our Operations officer was the only lucky one. George Sievewright, the Gunnery Officer, was particularly disappointed because he reckoned that this would have been his best chance as he was leaving the ship. He had been a tremendous help to me in running the Ship's Office, in addition to his other job of being in charge of the ships guns, and was a very efficient chap.

Just after the New Year the Wardroom organised a dance on board and the Squadrons excelled themselves with the decorations. I had invited Tom Baird, from Shotley days, with his wife, together with the Davidsons. Tom had relieved me in *Melbreak*. It was an excellent party but I was feeling homesick and not in the mood, so I was glad when it was all over.

The following morning, when things were being got back to normal, I told the Captain of the Quarterdeck to take the piano back to the Ship's Company dining hall forward, where it lived. This involved getting it into the hangar, up to the flight deck on the lift, along the flight deck to the forward lift, then down and through the emergency door into the Sickbay and finally to the dining hall. About an hour later a white-faced Petty Officer knocked on my cabin door saying, 'You know that piano what you told me to take forward Sir... Well it looks more like an 'arp now Sir and I think you'd better come and 'ave a look'. He was quite right. They had parked the piano on the flight deck behind a jet which was in fact testing its engine and all the woodwork had been blown completely away leaving just the metal frame and, as he said, just like a harp. This was our beautiful piano presented to the ship by the Mayor and Corporation of Birkenhead. There was nothing to be done but to give the remains a burial at sea and look for another one. None came to hand in Malta but in Instow Marylee Pilkington had heard the story and very kindly gave us her piano from Little Hill South which we collected the next time we were in Devonport.

Christmas and New Year safely over, it was off to sea again for exercises off Malta and also to show off the ship and our capabilities to various V.I.P.s. The first was the C-in-C Admiral Grantham, followed by the First Lord of The Admiralty Mr Thomas M.P, with the Secretary to The Admiralty Sir John Lang and, finally, Admiral Sir Charles Lambe the 2nd Sea Lord. They were all flown out and returned in Gannets of 824 Squadron and so had the full experience of a deck-landing and being squirted off by catapult. Everything went very well except for one unexpected incident. Some of our Sea Hawks were flown off to engage a squadron of RAF Meteors who were attacking the ship when, during the dog fight that followed, one of the Sea Hawk pilots saw the Red Fire Warning light come on and immediately ejected. He floated down safely to land in the sea with his plane splashing down a couple of miles away. The pilot was fished out by one of our SAR 'choppers' almost before he had got wet. All practice dog fights are recorded on a camera, activated by the pilot pressing his joystick trigger which would normally fire the guns. This resulted in a very cocky signal from RAF Malta claiming one Sea Hawk shot down by camera fire.

Later in January we embarked the Flag Officer Aircraft Carriers (FOAC), Rear Admiral Arthur Pedder, with all his staff. Sea-going Admirals in those days led a roving life and transferred from ship to ship, with all their equipment and office records packed in wicker laundry baskets. Many of the larger ships were built with Admiral's quarters and offices and, when no Admiral was expected, everyone moved up one, the Captain into the Admiral's cabin, the Commander into the Captain's and so on. In *Ark* we had always expected to be a flagship from time to time so no removals were necessary and it was rather nice to have the empty spaces occupied at last. FOAC and his staff had come from *Albion*, another carrier, arriving in a formation of five helicopters all landing on the deck at the same time, quite impressive.

The following day he inspected the Ship's Company fallen in by Divisions on the flight deck, followed by a march-past with our newly formed Pipe Band making its first ceremonial appearance. We had borrowed a number of sets of bagpipes and drums – in fact a complete band kit – from the Royal Navy Piping Association, as one of our engine room ratings called Maddison had managed to recruit a number of fellow Scots and had got the whole thing going. Then in November we had been joined by a Dutch Lieutenant Commander, on exchange with the Royal Navy as Assistant Fighter Direction Officer, and to everyone's amazement he turned out to be an expert piper. He had learnt to play the pipes during WW II when he was stationed at Culdrose in Cornwall. We put him in charge and he quickly licked them into shape. Besides being very smart they were very good pipers and their pièce de résistance was their march-past to the Plymouth Albion Rugby chant, the 'Oggie Song', transcribed for pipes and immensely popular with a Devonport-manned ship.

We had FOAC on board for about two weeks while we exercised with *Albion* and *Bulwark*, both slightly smaller than ourselves and who were passing through the Mediterranean on their way to the Far East station. We were put through a pretty extensive programme and I was pleased that, despite having being relieved by John Roxburgh, I was still to carry on working turn and turn about with the Captain during the nights. At about this time I had a letter from Christopher Dreyer to thank me for looking out for him while he was sick and also to say that he had left the Navy and had started a job with Vospers in Porchester, selling newly built MTB's, patrol craft and motor yachts to any one willing to buy them but principally in the Middle East.

At the end of the fortnight FOAC went back to Albion and we returned to Grand Harbour to paint ship and get spruced up for a visit to Naples. Everyone was in high spirits as we learnt that we were due back in Portsmouth at the end of March. Before leaving *Ark*, Admiral Pedder invited about twelve of us, including the Cambells, to a super dinner party in his cabin. Little did I know that we were due to become good friends some years later but naval life is always full of surprises, some nice and some nasty.

At the beginning of February we received a letter from Clarence House to say that Queen Elizabeth the Queen Mother would be coming to inspect the ship while we were in Portsmouth. She had launched the ship all those years ago in Cammell Lairds and had always taken a keen interest in her. We were required to submit a detailed programme for the visit. John Roxburgh was most insistent that nothing be left to chance and the exact timing for everything had to be recorded by walking round the proposed route with stopwatches and clip boards; no intelligent guesses were allowed – all very sensible as, with the number of people she would be likely to talk to and the sheer size of the ship, there was plenty of scope for making a complete hash of it. The police too at Portsmouth also wanted exact times for start and finish as they would have to ensure security while keeping the route to and from the Dockyard clear without snarling up local traffic.

On another tack, Mary and I were planning what to do after Easter when I expected to be getting some leave. I had managed to save up some money while being away and had worked out that after paying school fees – at that time there was no help with education – we would have left over about £80 which would be just about enough to take the car across to France and spend about ten days in Austria or Switzerland. We were also waiting hopefully for new pay scales as the Forces had dropped well behind.

In the meantime The Admiralty had just published a Fleet Order abolishing the specialist branches such as Supply, Engineer or Electrical with their distinctive colours of white, purple and green between the gold stripes. In future all officers were to be on a 'General List'. On the principle that all men should be equal but some more equal than others, it was also decreed that executive officers like me would in future be known as Seamen specialists who, on promotion, would be split into two categories: those selected for Post List would be the ones to command seagoing ships; the remainder – the General List – would be delegated to command desks or shore establishments. This caused a great deal of bitterness and in *Ark*'s wardroom many of the engineer and electrical specialists refused to give up their coloured stripes. They felt that they were highly qualified and were proud to be distinguished as such in a crowd.

I believe that the whole thing was the brainchild of some ambitious Supply officers who, in one of their traditional roles as Captain's or Admiral's Secretary, had the ear of certain senior officers and Mountbatten in particular. Mountbatten was First Sea Lord at the time and his Secretary, Captain(S) Ronnie Brockman, shot up to Vice-Admiral, the first Pusser to reach such a rank.

The other change to be introduced at the coming 30th June promotions was that officers selected for promotion would no longer gain their new rank immediately but would be promoted provisionally and assume the new rank after six months. This was a welcome change as it would avoid people getting 'pier head jumps' and would allow the appointers a chance to get the right people in the right jobs without huge disruption. I also heard that my pay would be increased by the princely sum of £10 a month. The biggest increases went to the Junior Rates and to Petty and Chief Petty Officers, something that had been very long overdue.

After another short period of exercising we set off for Naples, passing through the Straits of Messina on 22nd February, almost a year to the day of our Commissioning. Stromboli was showing off as we passed and several of us were lucky enough to be taken on a sightseeing flight in Sea Venoms to see what a volcano looks like from the top; very impressive it was too. With hindsight this proved to be not such a smart idea as some of the highly abrasive volcanic dust which was flying about was ingested into the engines, doing lasting damage to their turbine blades. All the planes that overflew Stromboli had to have their engines changed and, on reading the findings of the subsequent Board of Inquiry, Their Lordships were not amused.

Arriving off Naples on the 23rd we embarked an Italian TV crew who were to make a film about flying from a modern carrier and we spent all day dashing about showing what we could do, with all the squadrons showing off like mad. The following morning we berthed in Naples at the Stazione Marittima. But earlier that same morning my chum Ray Lygo, the CO of 800 Squadron, had asked me if I was willing to join in playing a hoax on Jimmy Pierce and the pilots of 898. Ray had arranged for a bogus letter to be delivered to Jimmy, purporting to come from the Director of the TV Company that had been on board filming, which said that he had learnt from one of the cameramen that 898 Squadron was famous for sporting bowler hats and, as he had been so impressed by their flying skills, he would like to interview them in his Studio. This would round the film off nicely and of course lunch would be provided. Cars would be waiting on the quayside for them and would they be sure to wear their bowler hats.

Puffed up with pride Jimmy Pierce showed me the letter, saying that he already had permission from 'Wings', Mike Fell, to leave the ship before the ship berthed but would it be possible for me to arrange a boat to put them ashore. I said that I would see what I could do but it might be difficult. A little later I sent for him and told him that it had all been arranged and that we would lower a boat and put them ashore. Meanwhile Lieutenant Edward Anson of 800 and a fluent Italian speaker had already been landed and had lined up a fleet of very smart cars to take them to the 'Studio'. 898 made a brave sight as they stepped ashore in their best uniforms and bowler hats to be driven off at high speed to a carefully selected deserted Palazzo deep in the countryside. Arriving in front of the impressive portico of the supposed Studio they got out of their cars which immediately shot off at high speed leaving them bowler hatted, lunchless and lost some 10 kilometres from Naples and, as it turned out, none of them had any Italian money. They crept back on board at about 1600 with redder than red faces.

With only a month to go before our return to the U.K everyone was looking for presents to take home. Canaries and budgies seemed to be appearing on board in large numbers and soon every mess seemed to have several cages hanging up. Various trips had been arranged by the ship to take people to Rome, Pompeii, Vesuvius and other popular sites and these were well-taken up. The Wardroom were given some free seats for the Opera and James Woolley, John Bellamy, Francis Eddy, Bobby Kearsly and I all had the luxury of a box to see Madame Butterfly. The

San Carlo Opera House is a very fine building indeed and the singing was excellent. The Neapolitans certainly love their opera and the applause was rapturous after every aria. We were a little disappointed that Madame Butterfly was a size 20 and unlikely to see sixty again. Pinkerton was cast in the same mould but they both had splendid voices. We rounded it off with a splendid supper before returning on board.

Leaving Naples after a fairly packed weekend we went quickly back to Malta to embark Rear Admiral Richmond, the Second-in-Command Mediterranean (FO2) with his staff to act as Flagship for the Combined Fleets Exercise with the Mediterranean and Home Fleets, starting from 7th March. The exercise, which consisted of non-stop activity, flying by day and night, dodging imaginary atomic weapons and exercising replenishment at sea, started well but 8th March – my birthday – was marred by tragedy. I was doing my deputy Captain stint on the bridge when at about 0100 one of our Sea Venoms flew into the sea. We thought that the pilot might have misjudged his height as it was a very dark night.

We flew off some Gannets to search for possible survivors but as we launched the third one it just rolled over on leaving the catapult and crashed into the sea just ahead of the ship. I ordered the helm hard over to try and avoid it and we could see its tail light burning as it passed down our side. Marker flares and rubber dinghies were thrown overboard, by which time the Captain was on the bridge, but the plane was upside down when it hit the water and sank very quickly. We and *Delight*, a destroyer, searched the area for eight hours looking for survivors or wreckage but nothing was seen. After that it was business as usual but it was a very nasty experience, with five young men lost in their prime – two in the Sea Venom and three in the Gannet.

The rest of the exercise went very well and we had a very complimentary signal from the Admiral after he had disembarked at Gibraltar which read, '*Ark Royal* has had a strenuous five days of exercises in which she has done outstandingly well and I have felt proud to fly my flag in her'. In fact we had flown 467 sorties during the time which was pretty good going. Because of all the damage-control exercises going on and because for some of the time the ship was sealed to protect her from the supposed threat of nuclear fall out, simulated by using masses of tear gas to test our protective systems, I had arranged with one of the 'schoolies', Instructor Lieutenant Bill Wren who had been at *Ganges* with me, that all the canaries and budgies should be put in the School Room down on 6 Deck and inside the citadel until we were back in Gibraltar. However I noticed, when their owners came to collect them, that many of the canaries were in fact very young chickens. Jolly Jack with a skinful can be sold just about anything and this time it was day-old chicks.

I was very pleased to find Rupert Bray in Gibraltar; he was the Home Fleet Signal Officer in *Tyne* which was the flagship. We had a very good run ashore in Algeciras. Meanwhile, planning for the Queen mother's visit was going on apace and we had numerous meetings. We also had a Board of Inquiry into the loss of the two aircraft and their crews. I had to give evidence but with complete lack of wreckage it was impossible to establish the cause of either of the accidents that had cost five lives.

We sailed from Gibraltar on 20th March loaded with goodies, about which everyone hoped that the Customs would be kind. We had also done some last minute 'tiddlying' up for our arrival in Portsmouth. Another exercise was scheduled for the passage home and for this we flew the flag of FO 2 Home Fleet, Rear Admiral 'Dickie' Onslow, a tremendously popular and successful destroyer Captain during the war who had gained a DSO with no less than three Bars to it (equal to four DSOs). He was a great character and full of fun.

One morning at about 0430, when I was doing my bit on the bridge, all hell was let loose. We were ordered to fly off searches here and there and to re-organise the disposition of our screening destroyers several times, as well as steaming this way and that at high speed. We had just managed to cope when, after about an hour and a half of this organised mayhem, I was called to the voice pipe from the Admiral's bridge (situated one deck down,) and a voice said, 'Admiral here, is that you Johnson?' I replied, 'Yes Sir'. 'Well done', the voice said, 'That is what is known as taking the piss out of the Deputy Captain. Come and have breakfast with me when you come off watch'. And I did.

The exercise in which we were engaged, 'Dawn Breeze', came to an end with mock air attacks on the United Kingdom, defended of course by the RAF. On Monday 26th March we berthed alongside the Southern Railway Jetty in Portsmouth Dockyard to make the final preparations for the Queen Mum's visit on the Wednesday. Mary had taken a room in the Gwalia Hotel in Southsea and it was wonderful to be together again after six very hectic months.

The Royal visit went off extremely well with a March-Past of the Ship's Company on the Flight Deck followed by a brief tour of the ship and meeting with the Chief Petty Officers in their mess and with the officers on the Quarterdeck. She had been particularly taken by our pipe band and asked to be introduced to the person who trained it. When our bagpipe-playing Dutch Lieutenant Commander was presented to her she couldn't believe it and thought we were pulling her leg. When he told her that he had learnt to play the pipes in Cornwall she nearly fainted. She had clearly enjoyed her visit to the ship that she had launched in 1950. Later we received a very nice signal which read, 'I so very greatly enjoyed my visit to you yesterday. I was delighted to have been able to visit *Ark Royal* and I was very glad to find that in such a short time you have recreated that traditional spirit which made famous the other great ships which bore your name. It gave me great pleasure to see the Ship's Company march past to the stirring music of both your bands and I send my best wishes to you all. Elizabeth R.'

We sailed again on the following Wednesday, having given long weekend leave to half the Ship's Company. After flying off our Squadrons for the last time, we turned our hand to carrying out intensive sea trials for what might be the next generation of fighters – both supersonic – the de Haviland 110 and the Supermarine 113. An army of experts accompanied them. The aircraft were very much heavier and larger than previous ones but our systems seemed able to cope. Tragically the DH 110 was to disintegrate a few months later at the Farnborough Air show while demonstrating its low-level capability, killing its pilot and a number of spectators. Later a much strengthened version did get to sea with the Fleet as the Sea Vixen, a very successful two-seater night fighter. The Supermarine 113 never got into production, losing out to the very successful US Navy fighter, the Phantom, which was adopted instead. At the end of a week of these trials we entered Plymouth for a short refit and to give leave.

In May Mary and I set off by car for Switzerland, where we spent a glorious ten days staying near Wengen. There was still snow higher up but below in the valleys there was everywhere a mass of blossom. The only thing that impinged on all the beauty was the pong. This, it seemed, was the time of year when the winter's 'soil', having been carefully stored in huge wooden barrels, was spread amongst the fruit trees to fertilize the land. However, we were able to get away into the mountains and rise above it. It was the first real holiday that we had had together for ages and we made the most of it, returning home thoroughly refreshed.

Back in Devonport the dockyard was busy putting right all the hundred and one things that had come to light in a year's hard use. Many of the officers had been in the ship for two or more years and were to be relieved. John Roxborough was appointed to command the destroyer *Contest* and went off to do various command courses, leaving me in charge once more and to do another turnover, this time to Commander Ian MacIntosh. Ian was another submariner and had started his career in the Royal Navy with a bang. He was an Australian who had chosen to come to England in 1940 to specialize in submarines. On his way, the passenger ship *Brittania* was sunk by a German armed raider in the South Atlantic. The crew took to the boats and Ian found himself in charge of a lifeboat with 82 other survivors. Showing tremendous courage and seamanship, he sailed the lifeboat some 1,600 miles to Brazil, where he found a ship to take him to England; only 38 survived the ordeal. Ian was awarded the DSC and later in the war he won a DSO in command of a submarine in the Far East. He was a very nice chap and had a charming, if rather unusual, wife. Her parents had been missionaries in China, where she was born and grew up, and her party piece was to sing little Chinese songs, always providing that no one was looking. One consolation of John Roxburgh being away was that he and Patricia lent us their house in Yelverton, which was a big help.

June had been a nail-biting month for us, wondering who would be successful in the promotion stakes on 30th June but this time the ship did well. I, Francis Eddy the Fighter Direction Officer; James Woolley the Navigator; Joe Honeywell the CO of 824; and Maurice Birrell CO of 891 were all promoted Commander. Francis Eddy and I were both to be promoted immediately and the others provisionally selected for promotion in 6 months. To my dismay and anger I found that I had been put on the Dry list (General List), as had Francis Eddy and Maurice Birrell, while James Woolley and Joe Honeywell were on the Post List. I felt that this was a real kick in the teeth and rushed off to see the Captain only to find him seething with rage as he had been Dry-listed too. Some officers in the fleet resigned their commissions on the spot but I had never wanted to do anything else but be in the Navy so I decided to soldier on. As things turned out James Woolley never set foot in a ship again but I did twice.

Having said all this I was extremely pleased to have been promoted and went rushing off to Mr Gieves on Mutley Plain to get my uniform altered and to buy a 'brass hat' – a cap with gold oak leaves on the peak. There were great celebrations on board and at lunch time I was presented with a genuine highly-polished brass top-hat made in the workshops. It was a dead fit and it seems that the Shipwright Officer was so convinced that I would be 'made up' that he had pinched a cap from my cabin so as to be sure it was the exact size. Following my promotion I was relieved as First Lieutenant by a chap called Cyril Newton and took my leave of the great ship.

It had been a hard two years and a watershed in my career but I took away many lasting memories: the great loyalty of my little Welsh Chief Petty Officer Whiting who had worked like a terrier to keep the messdecks and the inside of the ship spick and span, a tremendous boost for the general morale; also the Chief Gunnery Instructor, C.P.O Lamerton who had worked long and hard to run the Commander's office, from which all the orders for the daily running of the ship flowed; the great spirit which pervaded the ship, especially when the Squadrons were embarked (she ran like a destroyer despite having more than two thousand souls on board); trying to control lively young aviators when presiding at Guest Night dinners in the Wardroom (We had in effect two wardrooms separated by a watertight bulkhead with a door between the two. This meant that the Mess President was in one, with the Vice President in the other connected by a microphone and loudspeaker, none too easy); but, above all, the loyalty and cooperation that I had received at all levels that had made everything possible.

On 15th July I was given a rousing send-off and went to Instow with the family for summer leave and to wait and see what was to come next.

CHAPTER 12

Joint Services Staff College
LATIMER
November 1956 – May 1957

Towards the end of an excellent summer leave I found myself appointed to the Joint Services Staff College at Latimer in Buckinghamshire. It was to be a six-month course, starting in October, and the search was on to find somewhere to live. Happily my parents remembered that Josephine Lang, whose mother lived in Instow, had married Peter Lobb and they lived in Chesham Bois, which was only about five miles from the Staff College. We immediately rang them up and they told us that, by some sort of miracle, there was a house next door to them which was often let to people on the course and that we had better come up for the weekend and have a look.

The house turned out to be an old Elizabethan barn which had been converted into two flats and it was the top flat that was to let. The whole place was owned by a Mr and Mrs Jopling (the Jops) who lived in London but came down for the weekends. They were an interesting and unusual couple. Mr Jop had started life in the Indian Civil Service. Retiring from it with a pension after World War One, he returned to London and read for the Bar. He was now an eminent, if elderly, Q.C. Mrs Jop had been a well-known soprano, Joan Elweis, and was a grand-daughter of the artist Millais. She had met her husband-to-be in 1926 and for their subsequent honeymoon Mr Jop had bought a 20 hp Rolls Royce Tourer. This was still their only car and it lived in a very ramshackle barn backing on to the Lobb's house.

Though the rent was rather more than we had bargained for it seemed a nice place to be. The Joplings were extremely nice and it would be fun to start with neighbours whom we knew. The Lobb's two daughters, Jane and Mary, were not too different in age from our two. Peter Lob worked as a Jobber on the Stock Exchange. His firm dealt or jobbed in oil. Jobbers no longer exist but at that time each commodity had its jobbing firms and it was their task to hold stock until bought by an investor; they also had to buy any shares that investors were selling and hold them until another buyer came along and then sell them on, hopefully, at a profit, but frequently at a loss so that Peter would be ecstatic one day at having made millions, only to lose it all the next day. He had inherited the firm from his father and found it an extremely stressful business.

We discovered that David could go to a pre-prep school nearby called Oaklands, run by a Mr and Mrs McCaughtrie. We moved in quickly so as not to lose too much of the autumn term. The flat consisted of a living room which ran the whole width of the barn, a double bedroom and a single one in the ancient part and then, at the north end, a new bit had been built on which contained another bedroom and the bathroom, underneath which on the ground floor was a kitchen and small dining room. There was also an anthracite boiler which did the hot water and central heating. Everyone was most welcoming and we were glad to be where we were.

Latimer was a rather splendid Victorian country house which had been taken over by the government in about 1946 to house the Joint Services Staff College(JSSC). In the grounds there were lecture rooms and study areas to take the two hundred or so students. Those who were not living with their families were lodged in the house itself. Besides the mix of Army, Navy and Airforce officers from the UK and Commonwealth, there was a small number from the US forces and also from the Police, Civil Service, Colonial Service and Industry. The students in each syndicate were as good a mix of backgrounds and interests as was possible so that when your syndicate was asked to produce a reasoned answer to such and such a problem there were always a number of views put forward, which made it all very interesting. We each had to produce a paper giving our own assessment of the threat to the country and its defence policy, which required a huge amount of research and even more writing. Fortunately Mary was a much better typist than I and took on the unenviable job of typing up some ten thousand words or so, much to my relief.

At about the same time that our course was assembling, the Prime Minister, Anthony Eden, was leading the country into the debacle of Suez after Colonel Nasser had taken control of the Suez Canal for Egypt. Everyone on the course thought Eden quite mad and the reasons for our actions totally spurious. It was argued by the Government that only the French and the British, who jointly owned the Suez Canal Company, were capable of running the canal, which was patently untrue. After about four days of war and untold damage to the canal plus needless loss of life, world opinion, led by the United States, caused the United Nations to demand our withdrawal and Eden's resignation. However, the canal was effectively blocked and, being before the age of super tankers, there was an acute shortage of oil, leading to petrol rationing. Though it was not as severe as during World War II, the rationing hit everyone. Luckily a friend of mine, Gordon Tait, who was also on the course and living in Chesham Bois, agreed to a car-sharing scheme. This was fine except that Gordon had a thing about seeing magpies. For the first magpie seen he would drive with his arms crossed and, for the second, he would cross his legs as well, all very alarming but we always seemed to get there.

As winter progressed we began to realize that the manor Barn had certain snags. Despite its conversion it was, above all, an Elizabethan barn with very thin walls and no insulation. I think it was the coldest and draughtiest house in which we had ever lived. Snag number two was quite different. Mrs Jop, now no longer a singer, had decided to take up the 'cello and practised assiduously at the weekends, sometimes by herself and sometimes with like-minded friends who were also learning. Their room was directly beneath our living room and, like the rest of the house, there was no sound-proofing and we were deafened by what sounded like calving cows!

However we were only going to be there a short time and Christmas was soon upon us. Michael came up from his school in Torquay and it was fun to be all together again. What with trips to London, to the Elphinstones at Loughton and the pantomime, plus parties round about, the days passed quickly and it was soon time for us all to go back to school again.

Some courses throw up a number of students who go on to distinguish themselves in later life but my course (Number 19), though very friendly and able, only really managed one – Hugh Brammell, a soldier who went on to become Chief of Defence Staff, though I don't think anyone would have tipped him at the time.

With the coming of spring the Jopling's Rolls came out of its shed and one of my tasks was to help get it started, using the crank handle so as not to drain the battery. On my first attempt I gave it an almighty heave only to be severely ticked off by Mr Jop who explained that Rolls Royces of that vintage never needed more than a gentle nudge. In fact such was the precision of the cylinders that only a quarter of a turn with the starting handle was needed to bring the engine to life. If the engine was warm it could be started with just a spark from the magneto. I never went in the car myself but Mary made several trips to London sitting up like the Queen on the back seat protected from the weather by the large glass dividing windshield and a bearskin rug.

There was one famous occasion when we arranged to meet the Jops at a Point-to-Point for a picnic lunch. It was on the day following the Latimer Ball. We had the Shirley-Beavans staying and had got to bed at about 4 am, only to be woken by Mr Jop at some unearthly hour because he thought he should make sure that we knew the number of his car in case we shouldn't recognise it in the car park!

David got on well at his school though everyone there was in awe of Mrs. McCaughtrie, who was very strict. The punishment for misbehaving was to be deprived of wearing the school tie, which was ceremoniously removed in front of the whole class. I think that David was only once sent home in disgrace without his tie.

The Staff Course concluded at the end of May and we set about packing up our belongings and wondering where we would find ourselves next. We didn't have long to wait before being told that my next job would be in Norway as Deputy Director of the Norwegian Staff College in Oslo. The exact date had not been decided but, in the meantime, I was to get in touch with the present incumbent, Commander Hugh Mullineux, and also try to learn Norwegian. We moved back to my parents' house in Instow and managed to get David into the junior bit of Grenville College in Bideford for the remainder of the summer term.

Chesham Bois and Latimer had been a good experience and we had made a number of friends, especially the Lobbs, so it was sad to learn later that year that Peter Lobb's firm had been unable to survive the continuing turmoil of the world's oil markets and had gone bankrupt, with Peter having to take a menial job with a firm of stockbrokers. However, all came out fairly well for them in the long run.

CHAPTER 13

Naval Staff College
NORWAY
1957 – 1958

The prospect of a summer in Instow was fine but the task of trying to learn Norwegian was daunting. I had received a long letter from Hugh Mullineux in reply to a letter of mine and it became clear that he expected quite a lot of me. He had helped found the Norwegian Naval Staff College in 1952, had been there ever since and the college was very much his baby; he spoke and wrote fluent Norwegian. He was living in a hotel at Vettakolen up behind Oslo, his wife having returned to England some time previously to prepare for his retirement. He would be in England in July and hoped that we would visit them in their home in Yately close to Sandhurst.

In the meantime we got hold of a linguaphone course in Norwegian and a book called 'Spoken Norwegian' and spent several hours a day trying to get our tongues round the various words and endeavouring to master simple phrases such as Bestefar og Bestemor er in spesestuen (grandfather and grandmother are in the dining room) or Unnskyld can De si meg veien til Oslo (excuse me can you tell me the way to Oslo) and, like French aunts, Norwegian aunts too lose their pens. Salvation came in the person of Getin Franklin, the Norwegian wife of Richard. She happened to be staying with her mother-in law, Helen, in Instow and as soon as she heard where we were bound she took us in hand with both pronunciation and etiquette.

It seemed that doing the right thing in Norway was enormously important. At dinner parties ladies could not drink their wine unless they were 'skolled' by a gentleman. To do this you had first to catch her eye and then, holding your glass level with your second waistcoat button, say, 'Skol'. Both should then drink but your eyes must still hold hers until she puts her glass down. Then, as a guest, it was very bad manners not to have a second helping of each course, so first helpings should be small otherwise you wouldn't have room. During the meal you had to make a little speech to say how lykkelig (happy) you were to be there and how snill (kind) your hosts were to invite you. It was necessary to take blomsters (flowers) to your hostess and above all, be punctual. The time that you were asked was the time you arrived, accurat (exactly). Then upon the next occasion you met your hosts it was mandatory to say tak fo maten (thank you for the meal) before saying anything else. Sadly her visit was fairly short otherwise we might have been better equipped before our arrival in Norway.

It was a relief when the school holidays arrived, as David's couple of months at Grenville College had been pretty horrific and included him nearly drowning in the school swimming pool. Hugh Mullineux was now back in England and Mary and I drove up to Yately to meet him. He was a very nice chap but quite a bit older than I, having gone to Dartmouth in 1924. He was somehow everything that I was not. A dedicated staff officer and teacher, not interested in outdoor pursuits such as skiing and sailing, could not help us with a house as he had been living in a hotel for the past year, nor could he advise us on what sort of car might be suitable as he always went by tram or train. He was extremely erudite and immensely proud of his achievement in setting up the staff college, rightly so, and it soon became obvious that he was very worried that I should not be up to the job as I had asked all the wrong sort of questions. Nevertheless he was very helpful in telling me about the other members of the staff and of Captain Høy-Petersen, the man in charge. However he did say that he would put the wheels in motion to find us somewhere to live and was sure that we would enjoy Norway as much as he and his wife, albeit in another way. As a result of our visit I was extremely worried about the whole venture and my ability to do the job.

There was no going back and we plunged on with our preparations. I had always wanted a Rover car. I had been told by the Naval Attaché in Oslo that we would be expected to have a British one and as Rover had a special reduction in Norway to compete in price with Mercedes, we bought a Rover '90'. We thought it was terrific, the epitome of luxury and reliability. How wrong we were!

At the beginning of August we loaded up the car and set off for Newcastle to catch the Fred Olsen Line ship 'Braemar' to Oslo. The ship was new and seemed very super. We arrived at the entrance to Oslofjord early in the morning and were extremely excited by the magnificence of the scenery as we steamed up the fjord in warm summer sunshine. The sun continued to shine brilliantly as we docked and came down the gangway to be greeted by Captain Høy-Petersen, a very upstanding Norwegian with piercing blue eyes. He welcomed us with a firm handshake and a Velkommen til Norge (Welcome to Norway). His English was excellent and he explained that he would take us straight away to the house that had been found for us in Snarøya. It was a little way out of Oslo but as we had a car he was sure that it would be suitable.

We were delighted when we arrived at Strömstangveien 20 to be met by Anna Bea and Allan Lyle. The house was a modern one and, like all Norwegian houses, built of wood. It was situated right on the edge of a small fjord looking across it towards Kolsos mountain. Snarøya had been a small island which had been joined to the mainland by a short causeway. The house itself had been recently divided into two flats and ours was to be the much larger upper one. The Lyles, the owners of the house, lived in the lower one.

We would have the garage which was part of the house and share the utilities room which contained a washing machine and a Norwegian essential, a mangle. Our flat consisted of a large living room with panoramic views. At one end there was a large stone fireplace and at the other a small but modern kitchen. There was a door out on to a large balcony. There was one double bedroom and two small single ones, though in fact all bedrooms in Norway are small as the Norwegians believed that bedrooms were strictly for sleeping; consequently there was no waste of space. Bathroom and lavatory were in the centre of the house as were all pipes and drains to prevent freezing in winter. The floors were all polished wood and we were under strict instructions always to remove our outdoor shoes in the hallway before entering the house. In addition there was a small landing stage and a mooring for a boat if I was to have one. I could not believe my luck. I think Mary and the boys thought it was pretty super too!

Allan and Anna Bea were to become our mentors in things Norwegian. Allan had had an English father and a Norwegian mother and had lived in Norway for most of his life; his English was good but not perfect. He was a director of a wood-pulp and paper-marketing company. He was very fit, active and a keen sportsman; during the war he had been in the resistance and had many adventures to relate. His wife Anna Bea was wholly Norwegian, but she too spoke good English. She was a diabetic and in consequence had no children, which was obviously a sadness for her. She worked in an office in Oslo.

I was given a couple of days to settle in before reporting for work. Norway is a country of extremes, very warm in the short summer and cold in the long winter. Life was organised to take advantage of these features and in summer work everywhere started very early and finished at 1500 to take advantage of the long summer evenings. There was no lunch hour; the main meal of the day – middag, the midday meal – was taken at 1600 or thereabouts.

Wing Commander 'Bunny' Currant, a much decorated Battle of Britain fighter pilot and my opposite number in the Air Force Staff College, came to see that we were all right and offered to take me in to work on my first day. The Currants were a charming family with boys about the same age as ours and lived at Hövik some distance away. The day arrived and, wearing my best uniform, I was driven into Oslo to join the organisation. The Army, Navy and Air force Staff Colleges were all situated within the walls of Oslo's ancient citadel, the Akershus Festning. The naval part or, to give its proper name, Marinensstabskollen was on the top floor of the building which also housed the Air Force College. We had our own lecture room and there was also one large room in the Army building large enough to take all the students when there were tri-service lectures. The Akershus had been the Nazi headquarters during the German occupation and the home of the dreaded SS. In the courtyard one wall was pock-marked with bullet holes where many loyal Norwegians had been lined up and shot. There was also a prison block where they had been confined and brutally tortured.

Besides our lecture room there were syndicate rooms for the students, offices for the staff and a sort of do-it-yourself canteen where you could eat your mid-morning snack and get coffee. Høy-Petersen had his own office as did I; Bjorn Helle, a Norwegian Commander, and Lars Tobiessen shared, whilst the college secretary Fröken Müller had a room of her own from which she ran the administration. I was officially introduced to all the staff and became Kommandur Yim Yohnson.

Eighteen officers were to join the college for the Autumn Term, fourteen Norwegians and four Danes, mostly Commanders and Lieutenant Commanders but also some Coastal Defence officers who had Army ranks and uniform. The course lasted one year and the students were mixed up to form three syndicates. Some of the work would be individual study and some designed for syndicate solution. My task was to make sure that the students had a good enough grasp of English to play a useful part in an English-speaking NATO staff. Høy-Petersen, Helle and I would each have one syndicate. Each week I was required to take a class in English grammar and the vagaries of English spelling and pronunciation. About 40% of the course would be in English and the remainder in Scandinavian. Norwegian, Danish and Swedish are all basically the same language but with different pronunciation. As it turned out we had two Danish officers from Jutland whose accent was so thick and guttural that nobody in the class could understand them, not even their fellow Danes who said that they spoke 'Potato Danish', meaning with a whole potato in their mouths.

I had a week to get myself organised before the start of the new term and had a busy time preparing new schemes and exercises to keep them occupied. Twice a week there were to be outside lectures on both military and civil affairs, very much on the lines of our own staff colleges. During the week I was taken to call on the C-in-C of the Norwegian Navy, Admiral Andersen. He seemed genuinely pleased to see me; he had been with the Norwegian forces in the UK during the war and had an English wife. Mary and I also had the opportunity to meet the other staff wives. Fru Høy-Petersen was very charming, tall and elegant and the only fly in the ointment was that both she and her husband were very dedicated members of 'Moral Rearmament', not our cup of tea at all. She spent a great deal of time in Switzerland at the movement's headquarters. The Helles were a delightful couple from Bergen. They had both been in Washington where he had been the Assistant Naval Attaché. The Tobiessens too were charming; Fru Tobiessen was a professional photographer and they had twin girls of about two of whom they were very proud.

While I was getting into staff college life Mary and the boys were getting used to Snarøya and the Norwegian way of life. Allan and Anna Bea were good teachers. Living as we did on the edge of a fjord it was an immediate necessity to get a boat of some sort. With the help of my colleagues during coffee breaks we scanned the advertisements in the newspapers for something suitable and cheap. We discovered a 4-metre pram dinghy for sale on an island about a mile from our house. It was going for £15 and the owner said that he used it every day to go to work on the mainland, he had just bought a fibreglass boat and so wanted to sell the old one. I agreed to buy it as I did not think that we could go far wrong paying £15 for a boat in daily use. He said that he always used an outboard motor and suggested that he should come into Snarøya, pick up Mary and the boys, take them back to his island where he would remove the outboard and they could row the boat home. This seemed a fine idea and they were duly picked up and driven back to the island at great speed, the engine was removed and they set out for home.

They had not gone far when they discovered that the boat leaked like a sieve and that it was only the speed for the short journey that had kept it afloat all these years. They just managed to make it back to the house with the water almost up to the gunwhales. When I arrived back that evening I was very depressed to find that the keel

Above: Summer at Strømstangveien 20 with Baccarat moored off the utstikke which is just to the right of the larger hut. We had the top floor of the house and the Lyles had the bottom.

Below: Winter. Srtømstangveien 20 seen from the road before clearing the snow from the drive which was a must each time it snowed. David is standing in front of our garage with his toboggan.

Above: Akershus Festning, the Marinensstabskollen is the building on the extreme right.

Below. Front row L-R: Tobiessen, Frauken Möller, Newton, Høy-Petersen, Johnson, Helle

Above: Family outing at Austlid.

Below left: David on our Spark.

Below right: Mary with cup for the Ladies Cross Country competition at Austlid.

Above left: Mary sailing Baccarat

Above right: David has a go

Below: Mike in his element.

Seil nr.		Tilb.kall. nr.
ON 72	«Sjuto». Bjørn Ulleberg, Oslo, rorm. 1., 3. og 5. dag Bjørn Ulleberg, rorm. 2. og 4. dag Tor Løken	35
ON 76	«Alfrich». Rich. Steen, Bærum	36
ON 77	«Tjangs». A. W. Kamfjord, Oslo	37
ON 79	«Pedro II». Jan Gregersen, Bygdøy	38
ON 80	«Omi». Carl Høegh, Snarøya	39
ON 81	«Silvana V». Oscar Fr. Blich, Oslo	40
ON 83	«Tjeld 2». E. Jarøy, Oslo	41
ON 85	«Pelican». Lars Walløe, Oslo	42
ON 86	«Bliss 6». Peter-Jacob Sørensen, Oslo	43
ON 91	«Vivo». Ole J. Hartner, Oslo	44
ON 93	«Torill 3». Rolf Carlem, Oslo	45
ON 96	«Rox X». Bjørn E. Iversen, Sarpsborg	46
ON 97	«Mugge». Johs. Engebretsen, Tønsberg	47

9de start.
Startflagg J (blått, hvitt og blått).
Avgang kl. 13.40.

18 kvm-klassen.

18 S 2	«Li-Li». Tore Lidén, Sweden	1
18 S 3	«Filur». Lennart Berg, Sweden	2
18 S 4	«Kristina». L. O. S. Hanson, Sweden	3
18 N 1	«Vega III». Rorm. H. Aas	4

10de start.
Startflagg K (gult og blått).
Avgang kl. 13.45.

12½ kvm-klassen.

| C 43 | «Baccarat». C. A. Johnson, Snarøya | 1 |
| 57 | «Tidig V». Bente og Carl Erik Ellingsen, Bergen | 2 |

Seil nr.		Tilb. n
C 62	«Astra». H. K. H. Prinsesse Astrid	
C 76	«Fram». H. K. H. Kronprins Harald, rorm. Mikkel Thommessen	
C 79	«See». Kåre Drangsholt, Oslo	
C 80	«Cinderella». Carl Aug. Ringvold jr., Oslo	
C 81	«Snow White». Per Borthen, Oslo	
C 90	«Jeppe». Fridtjof Jebsen, Bygdøy	
C 102	«Skårungen». Niels Torp, Bygdøy	
C 103	«Non Stop». Odd M. Brodin, Ljan	
C 112	«Gny». Bjørn Nygaard, Bergen	
C 113	«Fabienne». Cato Holmsen jr., Bygdøy	
C 115	«Xanthippe». Peter Chr. Solberg, Bygdøy	
C 116	«Fly». Finn Christensen, rorm. H. Walther Lange, Svendborg	
C 119	«Mosato». Brødrene Thronsen, Oslo	
C 122	«Raggen» Ragnar Moltzau	

11te start.
Startflagg L (sorte med gule felter).
Avgang kl. 13.50.

Andunger.

S 1	«Skarp». Per Seldén, Sweden	
S 5	«Monica». Gunnar Dahlsten, Sweden	
S 11	«Vivace». Nils-Bertil Faxén, Sweden	
S 10	«Sprutt». Olov Celander, Sweden	
N 1	«Bess V». Blakstad Seilforening, rorm. Roar Østdahl, Blakstad	
N 2	«Bess 7». Blakstad Seilforening, rorm. Kåre Johanesen, Blakstad	
N 5	«Husky». Odd Pram, Oslo	
N 6	«Sambo II». Thor Føyen, Blakstad	
N 7	«Kikei». Stein Føyen, rorm. Grete Føyen, Slemmestad	

Copied from my waterlogged programme! There were 16 entries in 12 ½ sq meters with Baccarat being the oldest as No 1 at the bottom of the left hand page.

1883   K·N·S   1958

KONGELIG NORSK SEILFORENING

DISTANSE-SEILAS
OSLO/HANKØ

K.N.S. INTERNASJONALE
JUBILEUMSREGATTA

Hankø 1958

Above: David, Mike in sun glasses, Anna Bea and Mary on the long walk to the Lyle's hut. The Finse Glacier is in background with top in the clouds.

Below: The hut. In winter it is totally under the snow. Mike, Mary and Anna Bea were to sleep here in very itchy reindeer sleeping bags while David and I walked back to Finse.

Left
Anna Bea opens a tin of prunes. Keeping 'regular' in the mountains is important!

Below:
Having tarred the bottom of the pram we are off to catch some trout. I'm told off to row.

Above:
Mike, David and friends fishing from our uttstikke. The long basket thing is an eel trap.

Below:
Taken without a flash at midnight on mid summer's day on the shore below our house.
L-R: Anna Bea, Allan, Mike ,Mary ,Kirsten Tjensvoll and David.

plank was rotten. One of our neighbours suggested that we could botch it, until the winter, with tarred paper stuck on with more tar. This we did, getting covered in tar in the process, but all to no avail. Allan Lyle, ever the practical do-it-yourselfer said, 'All you need to do is to put in a new keel'. I asked whom I should get to do it. He looked at me in amazement and said, 'Well you do it yourself. All you have to do is to take the old keel out, then I'll take you to the local sawmill where we'll get a new one cut, buy some copper nails and then you just stick it in.'

This was our first lesson in Norwegian self-sufficiency. The chap at the sawmills knew exactly what was wanted – did this sort of thing all the time – so with Mary on one side of the boat and me on the other, both armed with hammers, we quickly had the new keel copper-riveted in place and marvelled at our skill. With a drop of paint our pram was as good as new and Allan pronounced it Tet som pot (tight as a pot). Michael and David had great fun in it and playing with Arne, the boy next door, who also had a boat. Every Norwegian did!

Besides the boat there was much to do and see. We found our way to the English Church, St Edmund's in Oslo. The congregation was a mixture of English families and English who were married to Norwegians. The Ambassador and his wife, Sir Peter and Lady Scarlett, were there most Sundays. They were both somehow caricatures of the rather 'county' Englishman abroad, both very tall, slim, with rather long noses, long narrow rather pointed feet and rather aloof. I also made myself known to the British element in the NATO Headquarters at Kolsos and, in particular, to Vice-Admiral Sir William Pedder the Commander in Chief Allied Forces Northern Europe (the last time we had met was in *Ark Royal* when our ship's laundry had managed to lose all his clothes) and also to Captain Edward Ashmore. Strictly speaking I was in no way part of the NATO set-up though I would need their help and support when it came to arranging lecturers for the staff college. In all other respects it was important that we got on with assimilating the Norwegian way of life and become temporary acting-Norwegians.

Our term had started and I was beginning to find out something about the students and their background. Norway in the 1950s was not a wealthy country; the oil fields which were to transform their economy had not yet been discovered. At the time we were there the total population was about 3.5 million of which two-thirds lived in or around Oslo. The main industries were forestry, fishing, whaling, mining and shipping. Only one-fortieth of the country was cultivable, the remainder being mountains, lakes and forest. Their fishing fleet was the largest of any European country and their merchant fleet the third largest in the world. Above all, Norway was a maritime country with a huge coastline. After their experience in World War II they were ardent supporters of NATO, to which they looked for protection. Except for Turkey, they were the only country to have a common border with the then 'enemy', the Soviet Republic.

The Norwegian Forces relied on an 18-months' conscription for all fit males for the bulk of their manpower, with virtually only the officers and NCOs making the Services a full-time career. The Navy consisted of destroyers and submarines built in Britain between 1944 and 46 and Norwegian-built coastal patrol vessels and Motor Torpedo Boats. Promotion was slow and opportunities restricted so that many of the permanent Navy were seconded to the Merchant Navy for several years at a time to gain ocean-going experience. They also got paid a great deal better while doing their sea time in the Merchant Fleet.

Norway had a socialist and very egalitarian government. The salaries for anyone working in any form of state-run employment, be it civil or military, were all placed in wage bands which applied across the board. Thus, a tram-driver, postman, petty officer, medium-grade civil servant, lighthouse-keeper or policeman would all get the same pay.

For the officers, a Lieutenant Commander was in the same band as the driver of an express train and so on. The pay in the various bands was extremely low and my RN pay, which was nothing to write home about and which was paid by the Norwegian government, was much better than that of Høy-Petersen.

In fact just about everything in Norway was pretty strictly controlled. There were no chemist shops where you could buy a simple aspirin. Self-medication was considered bad for the health and only a doctor could prescribe any form of medicine, obtainable only from the state-owned pharmacies. Likewise only state-owned wine shops could sell alcohol. Vinmonopolet (The Wine Shop) was in every large town and there you had to go. When it came to actual wine there was a choice of two, Rödvin or Vitvin (red wine or white wine); if you wanted rosé you had to mix the two together. Having no choice saved a lot of bother and the wine list in restaurants was commendably short. I have to say the Norwegian wine buyers had good taste and the wine was cheapish and good. I could get a 'black market' supply of gin or whisky from the Embassy out of Tony Tyers's (the naval attaché's store cupboard).

Even cheese and biscuits, ost and snekkerbrö, were a standard size. The cheese came in oblong blocks so that when you sliced it with your ost hovel (cheese plane) you had a rectangular slice of cheese which exactly fitted your rectangular crispbread which you then covered with an exactly-fitting piece of greaseproof paper, which came out of a packet of such papers. All went into a rectangular tin container, again exactly the right size, which every Norwegian took with him to work. All this was extremely important and the source of great and calculated one-upmanship. From seven in the morning until four in the afternoon is a long time to go without food, hence the ritual of the mid-morning coffee break. Around eleven o'clock someone would say, 'So skal vi kaffen kom drinkken', and off we would go to the canteen. Sitting at small tables, each would carefully take out his rectangular packet from its tin and see if today Fru Helle had produced something better than Fru Johnson.

The Danish students were a different sort again. Having in the past ruled Norway for over four hundred years, they considered the Norwegians as backwoodsmen. They were well-paid, professional, much more sophisticated in their life style and much more party-people than the perceived dour Norwegians. However, both types fitted together extremely well so there was a noticeably happy atmosphere about the place and the students were keen to learn and do well in their course.

One of the things that I had not bargained for was the amount of work that I would have to do in Norwegian. The individual and syndicate work in English all came to me for assessment and comment, which was as expected, but I found that I also had to assess and comment on all the work done by my own syndicate (60%) which had been done in Scandinavian. This meant spending many long hours at home poring over a dictionary, trying to make sense of what had been written. Fortunately Allan Lyle was able to help me out when I was really stumped and in return I corrected letters and papers that he had written in English in connection with his business.

The other big challenge was during the lectures. One of the Directing Staff had to introduce the speaker and preside over the question period at the end. If the questions failed to come then the DS was expected to prime the pump with an intelligent question designed to lead to further discussion. This was normally the preserve of Høy-Petersen but, if he was absent then, as the next senior, it fell to me. I would sit in agony through a lecture in Scandinavian trying my best to grasp what on earth it was about other than what it said in the title. Though I made my comments in English everything else was not. It was all too easy to congratulate someone on his excellent talk on, say, 'The Control of Shipping in the Kattegat' when he had actually been speaking about the production of bacon in Jutland! Things did get better as the year progressed.

The summer holidays had come to an end and Michael flew home for the Autumn term at Winchester Lodge. The airport at Fornabu was quite close to us, so it was all very easy at our end, but in London he had to be met by an adult and we were very fortunate that Hester was living in London. David also started school at St George's, a small English speaking school, Fagerstrand, run by an English woman married to a Norwegian. It was on the Drammensveien, the main road into Oslo, and occasionally I dropped him off at the school on my way to work. More usually he was dropped at the bus stop near the General Store in Snarøya, which was directly across the fjord from our house. Coming back in the afternoon he had to walk from the bus stop, around the end of the fjord, to our house – about 1 km.

Though we had the pram I still wanted something more substantial with a sail and we looked longingly at the fleets of yachts that turned out for the races in Oslofjord at weekends. By far the most numerous and popular was the Knarrer, a very nice looking family boat with a small cabin, which was suitable for both cruising and racing. All the usual international classes were present too – the Dragons, Six metres, International One Designs and so on – but all, even the Knarrer which was supposed to be the poor man's boat, far too expensive. I think Mary and David would have quite liked a Snekke which lots of people had. It was a small motorboat with a cabin forward and a single-cylinder engine which thumped away making a rather reassuring noise that could be heard for miles.

Allan Lyle said that he would keep his ears and eyes open for something but, in anticipation of getting a better boat, he thought that the house could do with a better utstikke, a landing-stage that stuck out. He ordered two large steel girders, timber and cement and after much banging with crowbars and hammers we managed to excavate two holes in the rocky shore to take the inboard ends of the girders which were cemented into place. Then, with a large block of concrete to act as a cantilever and the planks placed crosswise over the girders, we had a really first class jetty.

On 21st September the country went into mourning on the death of King Haakon V in his 85th year. As Prince Charles, the second son of King Frederik VIII of

Denmark, he had married Princess Maude, the daughter of Edward VII, in 1896. He accepted the Norwegian crown and took the name Haakon V when the country became independent in 1905. The first King of Norway since the 14th century, he was much loved by the Norwegian people. A great anglophile, he and his family were evacuated to England in 1940, moments before the country fell to the Germans. He spent the war in London as Commander of the Norwegian Forces fighting with the Allies and worked tirelessly on behalf of his people. He was succeeded by his son Olaf who had been born in 1903 and had married Princess Marthe of Sweden who, sadly, had died of cancer in 1954. Olaf was also well-liked by his people; he was a keen and accomplished sportsman in the two fields dear to most Norwegians, skiing and sailing. A huge crowd lined the streets for the funeral, with Heads of State coming from all over the world.

In the beginning of October Allan Lyle said that he thought that he had found just the boat for us. It belonged to the son of an acquaintance of his, who had a margarine factory, Gregard Heje. It was a 12.5 square metre, quite elderly but which had been raced regularly and was going for £180, complete with sails and all equipment. The next weekend we drove down to Vikene near Hankø at the mouth of Oslofjord to visit Andersen's Boatyard where she was laid up. It seemed that she had not been in the water that summer and the hull, which was glued carvel strip planking, had some nasty looking splits which Herr Andersen assured us could easily be repaired. At the price it seemed a bargain and on 16th October we became the proud owners of C 43 *BACCARAT*. The 12.5 square-metre class had been designed in the early thirties as small racing yachts suitable for the children of wealthy yacht owners, something for them to sail while their parents raced their large expensive boats. There was an active class association run by a young man called Cato Holmsen and the boats were strictly one design – 7.6 metres overall, 1.7 m beam with 500 kilos of lead on the fixed keel which drew just over a metre. About 130 of these not-so-little boats had been built and there was usually a good turnout for regattas. Crown Prince Harald had C 76 *FRAM* and Princess Astrid C 62 *ASTRA*. The next thing was to find a proposer and seconder and join the KNS, The Kongelig Norsk Seilforening (The Royal Norwegian Yacht Club), which we did and looked forward to the Spring. Meanwhile, there were many other more immediate things to be done to get ourselves ready for the hard Norwegian winter. Mary knitted hard on circular needles to equip us all with thick sweaters and, with Anna Bea's guidance, we bought boots which could be used for walking as well as skiing, rag socks, strømpers (thick tights), stil lengs (long-johns), oilskin tops and bottoms and good gloves. Having come from drab old post-war England we were most impressed by all the bright colours of the outdoor clothes especially those worn by the children – bright reds, blues and yellows.

With winter coming our work routine changed to allow for the short days. The new starting time was 9 o'clock and we came home later in the afternoon for middag. All the boats were taken out of Snarøya fjord in preparation for the ice which would come in November; our pram was hauled ashore and turned upside-down beside the house. While the main channel through Oslofjord was always open, the shoreline and the smaller shallower fjords always froze over. Allan explained that in the usual pattern of things there would be little snow before Christmas so that it was important to enjoy the ice before the snow came – once the ice became covered in snow, that was the end of skating. We had all done a bit of roller-skating and looked forward to the real thing.

All the things we wanted and, indeed, needed to buy made things financially pretty tight, especially after buying *Baccarat*. Luckily Allan knew a place which dealt in second-hand skates and boots. Every Norwegian has skis and skates from birth to death so that there is a ready market. The freeze came as predicted and we had a wonderful time skating on these huge expanses of ice. It was still good for skating when Michael arrived for the Christmas holidays and of course he and David had no difficulty in keeping up with their peers. Mary and I found it a good deal more difficult! At weekends everyone turned out and you could skate from one village to the next. The thing to do was to open your coat so that it acted as a sail and let the wind carry you along which was glorious, the struggle back against the wind was not. While Mary and I were off on our expeditions the boys would play 'Bandy' which was a form of ordinary hockey played on ice rather than ice-hockey.

Apart from all this Mary and I were trying to get to know the staff and students and gave a series of small supper parties for them and their wives. Norway, even in 1957, had fierce drink-driving rules. Anyone caught driving with alcohol in their blood went to jail automatically and any Allied officer on the NATO staff would be sent home immediately. No doubt I would have suffered the same fate. We soon discovered that this was a wise precaution as every male Norwegian at a party seemed to feel a compulsion to finish every available bottle in the house before he left. In fact they would not leave until they had! Apart from being very expensive for us, they were not good for much the following morning in class and we soon learnt from their charming wives that the thing to do was to hide away anything that you thought they should not drink and, when their taxi arrived at the appointed hour, to bundle them all in willy nilly.

I had been told a few weeks previously that we might be getting an American officer on the staff and, sure enough, just before Christmas Commander Newton USN arrived on the scene. He was to share an office with me and help me in my duties. He was a nice enough fellow but was not destined to set the world alight. A Reserve officer, he had been called up for World War II and had spent most of his time in the Pacific in Landing Ships. After the war he had accepted the offer to stay on in the Navy as a regular. He and his wife were both from New England and were really surprised to find themselves in Norway. He had volunteered for a posting to Europe, preferably to London on the staff of the US Admiral there, and had ended up here. He had no previous experience of Staff College work or methods but seemed willing enough to learn. I found him an easy companion in the office but outside we had very little in common. He spent much of his time at the US Embassy and I later discovered that the real reason for his posting was to try and facilitate the replacement of the Norwegian Navy's all-British-built ships and equipment with American.

With Christmas came the snow and everywhere was white. One of the principle lessons about living with snow was quickly learnt. If you do not clear your drive and steps as soon as it has fallen you do not get to work without a major effort, so we quickly became adept with our snow shovels. I had put snow tyres on the car and driving back and forth to Oslo was no problem; in fact it was a good deal better as snow fills up all the pot-holes and makes for a really smooth ride. Apart from a few kilometres of main road in and around Oslo, the Norwegian roads were notoriously bad as they lacked the money to keep up the huge road lengths throughout the country and, indeed, roads made good in the summer frequently broke up again in the severe winter conditions. Snow-covered roads and frozen lakes made excellent substitutes for road maintenance.

Like most countries Norway has its own traditions for Christmas, particularly when it comes to Father Christmas. In Norway elves or little people, nissen, live underground or under rocks and, at Christmas time, children who have behaved themselves receive gifts from the Christmas elves, Julnissen, dressed in red just like our very much larger Santa Claus. Apart from seeing them portrayed on Christmas cards and in shop window displays we did not really know much about them, so you can imagine our total surprise when on Christmas Eve a white-bearded Julnissen and his helper arrived on skis at our door with a huge sack demanding in Norwegian if there were two boys in the house called Michael and David and asking whether they had been good. We were all completely taken in and it was some minutes before we realised that our two Julnissen were the Lyles. It made a fine start to Christmas and a memory to be treasured.

We all went to church in Oslo the following day before returning home to a rather traditional English Christmas middag. The Norwegians always ate lutefisk, cod prepared in a very special way until it was transparent, but we hadn't fancied it. We had invited the Newtons to join us as they were newly arrived and didn't really know anyone. We nearly had a major disaster when Mary slipped bringing in the turkey and the whole lot went on the floor, but after a quick wipe-off it was back on its dish and no one knew the difference.

The College had only a very short holiday, but just time enough to equip ourselves with skis. I had been given an old and rather heavy pair of ex-Army skis with Kandahar bindings, the boys each had second hand ones and Mary a brand new pair costing £12. They were all very different from the modern skis and could be used for both slalom and cross-country. The ski-boot was gripped on both sides at the ball of the foot so that the heel was free to lift for cross-country work. For really serious cross-country, lope, the skis were much narrower and lighter than ours. They were fixed only at the toe to special boots and were certainly not suitable for beginners. Allan Lyle was expert on them. The soles of our skis were wooden and had to be waxed according to the temperature of the snow so they would at the same time slide and grip without becoming clogged up. If you got it wrong you could find yourself with about 10 cms of snow stuck firmly beneath your skis.

While I had to go to work Mary took the boys to Holmenkollen, the mountain behind Oslo, for Michael to have lessons daily with ex Olympic skier Tom Mörstad. Mary and David would meet up with Dolly Pedder and the two Pedder boys, William and David. Dolly Pedder had done a bit of skiing in Switzerland so was able to help in getting them started. I used to try to practise very gingerly with my skis in some open spaces in Snarøya after I had come back from work. We had a book which told us what to do but the main snag in my case was that it was pitch dark which made it more than difficult to keep one's balance.

After I had been doing this for about a week Allan said that it would be a good idea if he were to take Michael and me down the ski run at Holmenkollen. It wasn't too steep he said and we would find it quite easy as the whole length was floodlit. What the locals liked to do after work was to take the tram which ran from the centre of Oslo to the top, put on their skis and come whizzing down the $2^1/_2$- kilometre run to the bottom, get in their car and go home. I agreed to go which, with hindsight, was stupid. Mike managed it without too much difficulty but after I had fallen flat for the twentieth time I gave up counting. The one certainty about downhill ski runs is that in due course you are bound to get to the bottom, and I did. The following day I was barely able to move and there was no part of my body that did not ache. I never tried to go down it again. However, by the end of the holidays both boys were managing well and Mike's lessons were to stand him in good stead in the years to come.

The holidays over, Michael flew back to England and Winchester Lodge, leaving us to try and improve our skiing. There were few resorts at that time with ski lifts and slalom courses. Cross-country skiing was the sport in which everyone took part, from small children, pulled along on sledges by their stor (strong) fathers, to grandparents and great grandparents. When the sun shone all the world and its wife turned out to enjoy the well-marked trails and magnificent scenery. Every weekend we too were out there with them, trying not to get mown down. Our favourite place was Solihugda, about an hour's drive from Snarøya. There were always lots of children on the nursery slopes close to the car park and we would leave David there while we went off to see how far we could get. Some things about Norwegians quickly became apparent when it came to cross-country skiing, langelöperren. They do not fall down, they do not lose control going downhill nor do they go backwards at ever increasing velocity when going uphill. Consequently they do not take kindly to having an idiot on skis in their midst. They do not get out of your way unless you can really scare them.

We discovered at an early stage that there was only one nationality on the slopes that they really feared and that was the Danes who, having no hills in their native Denmark, come to Norway in great numbers to try their hand at skiing. If, when hurtling down a track out of control with rapidly closing Norwegians ahead, you gave the warning cry of 'Danske' at the top of your voice the track would miraculously clear. Steering oneself out of the way was not really an option for the unwary beginner as the ski trails were narrow and well-used with two ski tracks worn deeply into the snow that acted like railway lines. To get out of them without falling over or running into a fir tree required an agility that we just did not have.

However, all was not gloom and we did make fairly rapid progress. It was not long before we were able to do 10 or 15 kilometres during an afternoon, always providing that we were able to peek and see what colour wax – red, blue, silver, etc. – that the experts were putting on their skis in the car park before setting out. Sunday skiing was always a great topic of conversation at the Monday morning coffee break at the Stabskollen and I would be questioned closely to see where and how far I had been. Somehow the experts always seemed to have done about 10 kilometres more than I.

One of the best ways of easing one's aching muscles after skiing was to take a sauna. The Lyles had one in their part of the house and quite often we would be invited down on Sunday evenings. It was quite an experience the first time. Allan's sauna consisted of a small room, about 3m by 1.5m, with slatted wooden benches each side and a small stove with hot stones at one end. Water is poured on to the stones to create steam and you sat on the benches in the nude, sweat pouring off, while drinking cold beer to keep up the body fluids. The idea was to raise the body temperature to such an extent that you could go out and roll in the snow to cool off or, provided that you had first cut a hole in the ice, jump into the fjord. Mary and I both chickened out of this, preferring to have a cold shower, but Allan and friends dived in on several occasions. Whether or not it was good for the heart it certainly made you feel very relaxed and fit.

At the end of February a trip was arranged for the Navy and Airforce Stabskollen to visit Copenhagen where we were taken round various defence installations and then on to Paris to visit The Supreme Headquarters Allied Forces Europe (SHAPE). The visit to NATO was planned for the Friday with the whole day spent at SHAPE; Saturday would be a free day and we would fly back to Oslo on the Sunday, leaving Le Bourget in the morning so as to be back in good time for work on Monday. We had a good visit to Copenhagen where my ego was boosted as far as my Norwegian was concerned when some Danes to whom I was talking thought I was a Swede. At SHAPE we were taken in hand by Major-General Sixsmith; little did I know that he was to be my boss the following year. After an interesting day we dispersed to various hotels and I went to visit the Dérouledes. André very kindly lent me his 2 CV for the Saturday. It was a totally new driving experience and enormous fun. I was able to drive down to Noisy to visit the Le Loups who were surprised and delighted to see me and hear all about our doings. Afterwards I went on to Fontainebleau to look up old haunts before returning to Paris.

Our Norwegian Airforce plane was due to take off from Le Bourget at 1000 on the Sunday but by 1030 no more than half the students had arrived. As the morning progressed taxis arrived by dribs and drabs disgorging the remainder of our students very much the worse for wear. Paris had been a totally new experience for them and the night-life and all-night bars had taken their toll. We got airborne eventually about noon but still minus two! I have never in all my life seen such a collection of hungover people. Their wives who had been waiting over two hours at Fornabu Airport were not amused by the sight of their suffering husbands when we finally arrived. The following morning many of them were still under the weather and Høy-Petersen gave them a tremendous dressing down saying that it was the last time that they would ever take the course to Paris. It was pretty disgraceful but they did go again the following year.

February is the coldest month of the year and David would come back from school with the laces of his boots frozen like iron and needing to be thawed out before they could be taken off. He and Mary were getting quite adept with our spark. This was a device used by all Norwegian housewives for shopping and taking small children about in the winter. It consisted of a wooden chair with a handle bar at the back and mounted on two steel runners. Going along the flat icy roads you stood with one foot on a runner and scooted along until you came to a down hill bit when you put one foot on each runner and shot along at great speed. Not so easy to stop!

One of the things that did not always whiz along when it should was our car. When the weather was really cold the brakes had a habit of freezing on and we twice had to be removed from the middle of Oslo. I wrote to Rovers to complain and all I received was a letter to say that no one had ever complained about this before. I had a similar letter when I wrote to complain that the car always jumped out of low gear when going down steep hills unless you held the gear lever firmly in place. Steering with one hand in icy conditions is not recommended.

In the middle of March we had the excitement of the International Ski-Jumping, Höpprenn, and Cross-country, Langrennen, at Holmenkollen. The ski jumping was what we really wanted to see and we managed, through the Helles, to get seats for Mary, David and me high up in the enormous stand nearly opposite the point on the slope where the jumper lands. About 100,000 people came to watch the event. Luckily we had been well-briefed on what to wear and take, including a pile of newspapers on which to sit to stop our bottoms getting frozen. It was a fantastic sight to watch the competitors launch themselves into the air from an impossible height, flattening themselves over their skis so as to fly as far as possible, leaving it to the last fraction of a second to get into the landing position. We soon became experts along with the rest of the spectators, criticising and applauding, especially for the Norwegians, and hoping that neither the Japanese nor the Finns would win. Despite our best efforts a Finn won the gold medal.

The best time for skiing in Norway is April when the days are beginning to draw out and the snow is still good. As soon as Michael arrived for the Easter holidays we set off for a week's leave, staying in a small hotel at Austlid in the Hardangervidere. Though there were some small slopes, the place was chiefly a centre for cross-country. The hotel was full and we were all four in the same room, which made it cheaper. It was a bit of a squash but we seemed to manage pretty well. Both the snow and the scenery were excellent and we had the thrill of skiing across great tracts of snow, no one else in sight and, looking back, your ski tracks were the only ones to be seen with not a person in sight on this huge plateau of snow.

Mike and David spent most of the time on the slalom courses while Mary and I went exploring. In one place we came across quite a large waterfall, completely frozen, as was the river, and glistening in the sunshine. It was at Austlid that Mary had her most dramatic fall, doing a complete forward somersault through the air and landing on her skis without damage.

Back in Oslo the snow was beginning to melt and the ice disappeared from the fjord; mid-April to mid-May is about the worst time in the year around Oslo. Everywhere was slush and mess as all the builders' rubble and litter that had been so conveniently covered in snow was now exposed to view and very untidy it was too.

The Norwegian National Day, 17th May, seemed to mark the end of this slushy period, everyone out in the streets in their national costumes to watch the parades of marching bands and students, flags everywhere. This was the day in 1905 that Norway had gained its independence from Denmark and Sweden and made sure that everyone knew it. Later in the month we arranged through the KNS to have *Baccarat* towed up to Snarøya along with strings of other boats that had been laid up in Andersen's yard. We were thrilled when she arrived looking a picture with her white hull and gleaming varnish. The only thing that was not so good was Andersen's bill. It was much more than I had bargained for and more than I could pay. I got Allan Lyle to write to complain and the bill was slightly reduced but was still too much. Luckily I was given a spare-time job translating some business documents and articles into English which raised enough cash to pay the bill and break even. On reflection it was all my fault as, in discussing the work required with Herr Andersen in Norwegian, I rather think that I missed out a nought here and there!

It was at about this time that we received another shock. I was asked to go and see the C-in-C of the Norwegian Navy who told me that unless the British Government could see their way to reduce the amount that Norway was paying for my services it would be impossible for them to keep me on for a further year. He explained that he had written to say that he would like to retain me but only if the cost were reduced. The Norwegians were willing to pay my normal Royal Navy salary which, the C-in-C pointed out, was greater than his, but it was all the extras which broke the bank. The British required an extra 25% of my salary as a pension contribution, their share of Michael's school fees and travel expenses, a large insurance indemnity in case I died on the job and, quite bizarrely, a clause in the agreement that stated that if I did die they would send my body back to England in a lead-lined oak coffin with solid brass handles and fittings. The total bill when added up was more than double my normal pay. In the case of Hugh Mullineux they had paid only his normal RN salary and these new conditions had come as a most unwelcome surprise. I saw their point. The Admiral said that they would continue to press their case and hoped to be successful. However Mary and I were full of gloom when I broke the news that evening.

At about the same time we had a visit from the Director, Colonel Napier Crookenden, and some of his staff from the Joint Warfare School, Old Sarum. They had come to lecture to us before going on to watch an exercise in North Norway with the Royal Marines. I had to look after them and took the opportunity to discuss my plight. His father-in-law had been a Minister in the previous government and he told me that my case would be brought up in the House, and it was. However, what I hadn't realised, in my isolated position, was that there was a Treasury-led cull going on of all military advisers around the world in a short-sighted attempt to save on Defence spending. Terence Molloy in Turkey and Geoffrey Kirkby in Pakistan were being similarly affected as were people in Libya, Nigeria, Australia, East Africa, Malaya and many other places.

While it is now argued, probably rightly, that selling arms abroad is immoral, in 1958 it was much more acceptable than it is today. The hard truth is that there is always some country eager to fill the gaps and in the 1960s there were none keener than the Russians and the Americans. With the withdrawal of British influence overseas it was only a very short time before Norway and Turkey went over entirely to American equipment, ships, aircraft, weapons and transport as did, in part, the Australians. Libya and Pakistan went Russian and East Africa, in part, Chinese. These are just a few examples but the policy had a vast knock on effect in the United Kingdom where tens of thousands of jobs in the defence industry were lost.

The 1960s saw the start of the run-down of British heavy industry and ship-building and, with the reduced market for defence products, the cost of equipping our own forces escalated as did the cost of research and development, so much so that our forces too had, in part, to go American particularly with weapons and aircraft. Many of our best research scientists also went to work on the other side of the Atlantic. However in the Spring of 1958 there was nothing that I could do except hope for the best.

Later on in May the Marinenstabskollen went on a visit to the North Cape to see at first hand the defence organisation there and the various problems with which it had to deal. We flew to Trondheim in the cargo bay of a C130 transport, not a pleasant experience as the noise and vibration were indescribable, not to mention the cold. The next part of the trip was delightful as we went on to Harstad in one of the little coastal steamers which take people, mail and goods daily up and down the coast, calling at all the small ports and islands on the way. At this time of the year everything looked magnificent and I was particularly struck by the enormous size of the fishing industry. At each place there were racks upon racks of thousands of cod hung up in the sun to dry. We spent the night at Harstad which was crowded with fishing vessels and where there is one of the highest tidal rises and falls – about 18 metres. We arrived at low water and it was a mountaineering exercise to get off the ship.

The following day we transferred to a small Norwegian Navy stores carrier for the rest of the trip through the islands to Tromsø where the Norwegian Airforce had a maritime reconnaissance base. They were equipped with Catalina flying boats which had been such a success in the Atlantic during World War II as they had terrific endurance and could stay airborne for about 18 hours. Some of the students went out on patrol.

We were accommodated in the airforce base overnight. In the morning we had to make our way to the operations room for briefing, a distance of about 500 metres. Though we were inside the Arctic Circle and the sun had shone nearly all the previous day, it had rained during the night and the ground was still frozen. The road to the Ops Room was a sheet of ice and the one memory that will stick in my mind for ever was the sight of the Norwegian members of our group, Høy-Petersen in the lead, skating off into the distance just as if they had been wearing skates and not shoes, while Newton, myself and the Danes slipped and fell about like a lot of clowns on an ice-rink, which I suppose we were.

The next day the Norwegian element went on to the frontier with Russia – all top secret – and the rest of us were forbidden to go. In any case I needed to get back to prepare for the week ahead and was offered a flight to Bergen whence I could get a train to Oslo. It was a two-seater Airforce trainer which was fine except that when we approached Bergen we were told that the airfield was closed because of fog and we were sent on to Stavanger only to find the same situation there. The pilot said that he would circle in case there was a clearance. There was and we went in to land. Shortly before touchdown I realised that the under-carriage was still up and shouted at the pilot. He gave a Norwegian expression that I had not heard before, opened the throttle and climbed away to avoid the mountains. This was the last of the clearance at Stavanger and, with very little fuel left he decided to try Kristiansand, touching down with about a litre of fuel to spare. We were both pretty shaken by the experience but the following day we made it back to Fornabu and home.

Since my arrival at the Stabskollen I had tried to change the way things were taught. Straight lectures on rather dull subjects like 'How to write an Operation Order', 'Choose a location for a mobile base' or make a communications plan quickly caused the students eyes to glaze over, especially in the afternoon. I found it much better to try and put points over in little playlets with the staff playing various roles, all quite strange to Newton and the Norwegians. Høy-Petersen was very dismissive at first but, after a couple of good performances by Helle, Newton and myself, became converted and was soon full of ideas of what we should do next. This was fine except for the fact that I found myself having to write all the scripts. In the end we managed to get the students themselves to present their solutions to certain group studies in the form of playlets in both English and Norwegian which they themselves wrote. Once over their natural reticence they enjoyed learning in this way. The idea was by no means original but one that I had picked up from the Joint Services course at Latimer where they did it very well.

With the arrival of summer we began to enter *Baccarat* in the various evening races and regattas that happened around Oslo fjord. She was delightful to sail and we enjoyed getting out in her as much as we could. Unfortunately the regattas, which took place usually on Sunday afternoons and were run by the many different sailing clubs, required quite a lot of time to sail to the venue, race for about a couple of hours and then sail home. It was all much too long for Mary and David, so for these events my crew was usually Allan Lyle. He was extremely keen and knew the geography which was a big help. There was usually a good turn-out in our class and though we had a lot of good races we never actually managed to win one or even finish in the first three. The main reason for this was our sails, which were of Egyptian cotton, and though they set quite well they were no match for the faster boats who all had Dacron mains and jibs and lightweight nylon spinnakers. Had I thought that I would have a second year I might have got new sails but they were very expensive, the material coming from the USA. In the event I settled for a new cotton jib, which was an improvement, but not enough to win races. However we were never in the last three either, so all in all we acquitted ourselves pretty well and had a lot of enjoyment.

We had several visitors: Katherine Floyd, David's godmother, from South Africa; my cousin Rodney Johnson, who arrived totally unannounced; and Ted Beckwith of Instow. Ted had been taken prisoner while serving with the Sherwood Foresters in Norway in 1940. He had come back to retrace his steps and to write an account for the Regimental Association in Nottingham. We took him for a sail which he thoroughly enjoyed. He told us that he had taken his Company through a long tunnel to get to the other side of a mountain and that as they came out they walked straight into a regiment of Germans and were taken prisoner.

In North Norway the sun is visible 24 hours a day from the middle of May until the last week of July and even in Oslo we enjoyed glorious long summer evenings. St Hans night, 23rd June, is a great celebration with parties and fireworks everywhere. We marked it with a barbecue by the water's edge and it was light enough to take photographs without using a flash.

1958 was the year that the KNS (Royal Norwegian Yacht Club) celebrated its 75th Anniversary and on 7th July Mary and I attended a very splendid dinner in the clubhouse at which King Olaf was the guest of honour. This was the forerunner for the International Jubilee Regatta at Hankö situated just outside the entrance to Oslofjord. The regatta was to run from Wednesday to Sunday but as I was working it was only possible for us to sail at the weekend. However, we thought that we should have a shot at it and I arranged for the boat to be towed down with the rest of the 12.5 square metres. We would drive down after work on Friday, leaving David with the Pedders. To be economical we decided that we should camp and I borrowed a tent from the Norwegian Army.

Full of enthusiasm we set off for Hankö and on arrival found *Baccarat* safely berthed with the rest of the fleet. Hankö was a beautiful spot with a large natural harbour absolutely full of yachts including the Norwegian Royal Yacht *Norge*. She had been built originally for Tommy Sopwith as the *Philante* to escort his challenger for the America's Cup, *Endeavour*, across the Atlantic in 1938. During the war she became the headquarters ship for working up newly commissioned ships in Tobermory and towards the end of the war was commanded by Robin Durnford-Slater; Rupert Bray was on his staff as the Signals Officer. She looked very elegant in her new role. We met several old friends including Peter Scott who was over to watch the fun. But the important thing was to find a camping site and this was when our problems began.

There were no camping sites as such but we eventually found a relatively flat clearing in a pine forest where we decided to pitch our tent. The clearing was covered in pine needles which disguised the fact that underneath the surface was rock which totally defeated out attempts with tent pegs. Not to be defeated we slung the tent between a couple of fir trees. It was then that we discovered that it was an arctic tent designed to keep out the snow, having a very small tubular entrance through which you had to crawl. Luckily we had our lilos to sleep on, or so we thought, but each had a slow leak and throughout the night we took it in turns to blow up them up. It was a great relief when breakfast time arrived and we could strike camp and go down to the boat, setting sail to join the great fleet of competitors ranging from the 12 metres down to the ubiquitous Oslojolles.

Our race didn't start until 1345 during which time the wind increased steadily to about force 5 kicking up a nasty little chop. There were sixteen starters in our class and we made a good star, but after the first round disaster struck. I misjudged a tack in front of a much larger yacht and was caught on port tack. As I tried to get out of the way the end of his boom caught in our shrouds and broke a spreader. We were lucky as it could easily have been the mast or other damage but we quickly downed the main and sailed home under the jib. It had been an extremely wet sail because of the chop and we were both soaking wet, dispirited and cold. Back in Hankö we found a boatyard which would make us a new spreader, but our regatta was over. With all our gear wet we decided that we could not face another night in a tent, so we packed everything into the car and drove back to Snarøya for a comfortable night before catching a bus back to Hankö to sail the boat home. This was my one and only lifetime experience of camping. The following day was a complete contrast with very little wind and bright sunshine and we had a delightful if lengthy sail home. On the whole it had not been one of our best adventures.

A much better adventure came about just after Michael's arrival for the summer holidays. Anna Bea offered to take Mary, myself and Mike to visit their lake which was up in the mountains about $7^1/_2$ kms from Finse. David was considered to be too young and he would have to be left behind. This was not at all popular with David and Anna Bea was eventually persuaded to let him come on the understanding that only Mary and Mike would camp in the Lyle's hut by the lake while David and I would come part of the way but would stay in the Finse Hostel. It was with some excitement and a little apprehension that we caught the train for Bergen which stopped at Finse where we got out. Even though it was mid-July it was pretty cold.

The idea was that we should spend the night in the tourist hostel and start the walk first thing in the morning, which meant about 0630. The two boys and I had bunks in the men's dormitory, Mary and Anna Bea in the women's. Finse is a great centre for walking and indeed most of the expeditions to the two Poles had trained on the glacier. The Lyle's lake was situated to the north east and in common with all the lakes at this altitude was unfrozen for about two months of the year, July and August. The lakes abound with trout and the main object of the trip was to catch as many as possible to bring home.

The day dawned fine and, after a good breakfast, we put on all our gear, including rubber boots, and started forth. Anna Bea and I both had maps and compasses as she expected David and me to turn back after several kilometres but David thought otherwise. He is nothing if not determined! It was a very rough and hilly journey and we waded across several recently unfrozen rivers which seemed to appear from under bridges of ice. It was clear too that herds of reindeer had been wintering in the vicinity as there were shed antlers and all the other signs about. We were sad to have missed them. After several hours of walking we came over a pass and saw the lake glistening in the sunshine about 300 metres below. We sped down the mountainside to reach the Lyle's wooden hut. This had been completely buried in the winter snow but when we opened it up we found everything as it should be and the contents, including the reindeer skin sleeping bags, were put out in the sunshine to air.

It was lunch time and we were all starving but the fly – or flies – in the ointment were the flies. They were there in their millions, having just hatched, and swarmed all over us which was pretty off-putting; however one just had to do one's best to disregard them and get on with the various jobs. It was of course the flies that fed the trout and after lunch we tarred the bottom of the pram dinghy and got it into the lake. It was about the same size as ours at Snarøya and we wondered how it got there. Apparently Allan and six others had brought it by rail to Finse dragging it over the snow on the level and uphill and using it as a giant toboggan when they came to a downhill bit.

Fishing is done by towing trout flies attached to otter boards which spread out on either side of the boat, about five or six hooks on each side, and one is expected to catch several fish at a time. Time was running out for David and me as we had the long trek ahead of us and I was anxious to get back before the evening mist descended, when we would have had a hazardous task to find the way. So, sadly, we had to leave the fishing and set off for Finse, arriving back weary, but pleased with ourselves, at about 1900 to tuck into a good supper and bunk down for the night. However the hut party did very well and Anna Bea and Mary each came back with about 20 kilos of trout in their backpacks with Mike carrying another ten. I think both Mike and Mary were quite glad to get back as sleeping in a reindeer sleeping bag with the hairy side inside was a pretty itchy experience which, together with the aggressive flies which settled on any exposed flesh, made life quite difficult for the uninitiated. Nevertheless it had been a wonderful and never-to-be-forgotten experience and we were all most grateful that Anna Bea had taken us. Allan was pleased to have the trout and immediately took them into the smoke house in Oslo. Some would be smoked and others made into a rather rich paste called (translated from the Norwegian) rotten trout, which was a great delicacy.

It must have been in August that everything started to go wrong. First, I was sent for by Admiral Andersen and told that despite their best endeavours they had been unable to retain my services and I would have to leave in September. Second, Allan Lyle had found a new love, an American who was a secretary in their embassy, and Anna Bea moved out to a flat in Oslo. It was sad because they had both been such very good friends to us and we were angry with Allan who was unrepentant. Added to this he wanted us to move out of our flat. We could move in with him downstairs which, in view of the short time remaining, was just about all right and we could also have the hut by the waterside. However there were so many things to do – boats to sell, goodbyes to all our many friends, the flat to be cleaned and washed (including the ceilings) – that where we slept was of little significance. The Stabbskollen gave us a splendid farewell dinner and I think I made quite a good farewell speech in Norwegian.

Finally the day came for our departure; the heavy things had all been put into packing cases and our various well-travelled trunks. I had heard that I was to go once again to France to join the Supreme Allied Headquarters Europe situated just south of Paris. I was wanted urgently but could have a week to get ourselves sorted out and back to England before taking up my next appointment. We piled everything into and on to the car leaving just enough room for one person in the back and three in front and set off for the docks, to be loaded aboard the *Braemar*. It was with a certain amount of horror that we found Høy-Petersen waiting to see us off and bearing an enormous cardboard box. We tried to look pleased and somehow managed to squeeze it in. It was a large model of a Viking ship which we were proud to have. We were all sad to be leaving. We had loved Norway, counting it our best place.

CHAPTER 14

Supreme Headquarters Allied Powers Europe (S.H.A.P.E.)
France
October 1958 – February 1961

It seemed that Their Lordships, having sent us off to Norway, were now bent on seeing that the family Johnson should remain abroad at all costs. Having returned with the family to Instow I was straightaway directed to SHAPE, which in those days was situated at Camp Voluceau, Rocquencourt, between Paris and Versailles, for a briefing and to meet my immediate future bosses, Major General Eric Sixsmith and Colonel Jack Kelsey US Airforce. They told me that on joining the Joint Exercise Planning Staff of the Organisation and Training Division (O & T) I would be expected to fly immediately to Norfolk, Virginia, to help plan and write the orders for the largest NATO exercise yet, Codename SIDESTEP. I would be over there for about six weeks so that any move of family or house-hunting would have to wait for my return. The date for my joining was 6th October so we were going to be pretty pushed to find a house, move in and be ready for the boys' Christmas holidays. I was also taken to meet the senior Royal Navy representative and Naval Deputy to SACEUR (Supreme Allied Commander Europe), Rear Admiral Nigel Henderson, who explained to me that while my situation was unfortunate that was how it had to be.

Back at Instow we planned for Mary to arrive in the middle of November. We would be booked in to a hotel in St Germain-en-Laye where we would have two weeks, paid for by The Admiralty, in which to find a house. So on 6th October I was once more back in France and almost immediately on the way to Norfolk in company with Colonel Kelsey and a French Lieutenant Commander aboard a US Airforce DC 6. It seemed to take an interminable time to reach the US Airforce Base outside Washington and then on to Norfolk by bus.

Norfolk, besides being the Headquarters for the US Atlantic Fleet, was the NATO headquarters for the Supreme Allied Commander Atlantic (SACLANT) and was manned by officers and men from all the NATO countries with Atlantic seaboards. We had each been allocated a room in the Bachelor Officers' Quarters (BOQ) – comfortable but quite different from our own Wardroom Messes, particularly as there were no stewards to look after us. The place was well-equipped with a laundry, ironing and cleaning facilities but basically you did for yourself; breakfast on the first day was an experience when you found yourself having to fill in an order form for the galley and deciding whether you would like your eggs sunny side up or shut-eye. My French colleague was very intrigued at the prospect of French toast.

We were quickly absorbed into the exercise-writing team and worked during the weekdays from eight in the morning till pretty late at night. To produce workable orders for a multinational exercise is no small task. To be of any use you have to be well-acquainted with the war plans of your own side, plus what Intelligence thinks are the war plans of the enemy, what forces the NATO countries have committed to Allied Commands in the event of war, what they are actually prepared to commit for an exercise and then make sure that the promises will be honoured. A scenario has to be agreed and accepted as plausible and then orders have to be written for your own side and also for the Commands and forces playing the enemy. (In exercise parlance, the Blue is your side and Red the enemy side though, to be politically correct, Red was changed to Orange.

Exercise SIDESTEP was to take place over a period of ten days and involve the NATO Naval Commands from Norway to the Mediterranean, plus Army and Air Forces for the Land Battle. While most of the play would be a paper exercise, there would also be live play with a number of merchant ships hired for the occasion to form the nucleus of convoys, movement of troops and aircraft and call up of Reserves – all in all, quite an undertaking. The exercises were scheduled for September 1959 and what we were doing at Northwood was just the tip of the iceberg. Once back in France we would have to write the orders for our own Command, bringing in all the smaller Naval Command areas such as Channel, Brest and Cherbourg, the Benelux areas and so forth.

The weekends came as a welcome relief and I had a chance to enjoy the very generous hospitality that was offered. The BOQ was pretty well dead at weekends and I was invited to stay with the Dickens family out at Virginia Beach, where they had a very comfortable house. (Peter was a grandson of Charles Dickens and brother of Monica.) Besides seeing quite a bit of the countryside I was introduced to the American way of life, at that time all new to me: colour TV, Supermarkets, golf buggies, huge fridges and freezers in luxurious kitchens complete with every electrical gadget – all extremely cheap to buy – and 45 rpm records. Donald Cameron from Shotley days was also in Norfolk with his wife and children but, sadly, they were not a happy family.

Jack Kelsey left after 2 weeks to return to France, leaving the two of us to struggle on. It was a quick learning curve; it had to be. However, I enjoyed the American experience, the first of several visits, but was glad when it was time to return to SHAPE and try and get our life organised in France.

Mary arrived in the middle of November and we stayed in a rather run-down hotel in St Germain-en-Laye while we tried frantically – or rather Mary did, as I was up to my eyes in work – to find somewhere to live. The SHAPE housing office was supposed to have a list of suitable properties but when it came down to it they had little to offer. The specially-built SHAPE village was full and the houses close to the headquarters realised huge rents. Mary was shown some really appalling places and, as time ticked by, we became more and more depressed. SHAPE itself was situated at Roquencourt, about 10 kilometres down the motorway from Porte St Cloud and about 5 kilometres north of Versailles. We had hoped that the Déroulèdes might be able to help as Généviève's family lived in Versailles and they did, indeed, offer us a very nice house on the escarpment beyond Melun overlooking the Seine but it was too big and too far away. In the end we decided to take quite a nice house, but far from ideal, belonging to a M. Rivet, a Parisian who imported tools from America. The house was No 8 rue des Robaresses at Andresy not far up from the station at Maurecourt. Again this was situated high up and had a splendid view over the Seine but was a 30 kilometre drive from SHAPE and with no other SHAPE families living nearby. It also meant that we would need two cars and spend a great deal on petrol if we were to survive. Fortunately the road was good, passing through Louviciennes, Port Marly, St Germain-en-Laye, through the forest to Conflans St Honorine, where the road crossed the Seine, and then on to Andresy. It was a long dark drive in the winter but in the lighter months the route through the forest was enlivened by the local prostitutes who advertised their wares by their smart red umbrellas.

The house itself consisted of three bedrooms and a bathroom upstairs, a large sitting room with a big covered veranda, dining room and kitchen on the main floor and a basement with garage, workshop and utility room, all very reasonably equipped and furnished, and also a small garden. I think that the Rivets had been using the house as a weekend retreat but they now had other interests and, provided we paid the rent, we could more or less do as we liked. In addition, on hearing that I was keen on sailing M. Rivet offered me the use of his fairly ancient 'Caneton' class sailing dinghy, appropriately named *Donald*, which he arranged to have delivered to the house. The 'Caneton' had been a popular class which had now been replaced by the similar size but infinitely more modern 5-0-5 which had been specially designed for the Caneton association by an English designer, John Westall.

From the notice board in SHAPE I found a little black Renault 4 CV for sale for about £80 which was to serve us well for the rest of the time in France. This meant that while I took the Rover to work, Mary had the little black beetle for nipping about, though it was not the little red sports car that she had always wanted. We were pleased to be settled in before the boys arrived from school for the Christmas holidays but it was too far away and difficult to find friends, especially for Michael and David. However, there was a very nice Dutch naval family, the Van Eeghens, with a boy and girl about the right age, who lived not too far away. Cor was a Commander and his wife, Maggie, was from Wales. General Sixsmith also had two boys, Angus and Edmund, who became good friends.

Just below us and near Maurecourt Station lived a retired Englishman, Frere-Ash, and his French wife. They were most hospitable but the wrong age group. However we were fortunate in striking up a lifelong friendship with a Norwegian Colonel and his Scottish wife, Reidar and Ivy Kvaal. They had met and married during the war when Reidar escaped to Scotland. Though there were no children by this marriage they loved young people. Mary and Ivy became close friends and did many things together. Ivy, who had arrived in France a little while before us, was able to introduce her to a number of other SHAPE wives and we soon had a little circle of friends.

While Mary was getting to grips with life in Paris, I was getting to grips with finding my way through the intricacies of life in SHAPE. Technically everything had to be done in the two official languages, French and English, but inevitably, because of the preponderance of English speakers and the large American contingent, anyone not fluent in English tended to be sidelined. My Division, O&T, had a Turkish General at the top who was fluent in neither French nor English and, as a consequence, the Division was run by his No 2, Major-General Sixsmith or General 'Six' as he was commonly known. General Six was a very perceptive, energetic and wiry Scotsman, a Cameronian. He had served in the 51st Division during the war and had seen a lot of action. He had the ability to give you a free hand to get on with your job and, provided you let him know from to time to time what you were doing, he would back you to the hilt. All the section had the greatest respect for him though the Americans never got used to his tartan trews.

In our own little exercise-planning set-up Colonel Jack Kelsey had his own office with a connecting door. He was a tall very erect New Englander who had been in the Army Air Corps before WW II and during the war he had flown bombers in the Pacific theatre. The Supreme Allied Commander Europe (SACEUR) was a US Airforce Five-Star General and Jack Kelsey, having served with Norstad before SHAPE, would not do anything that might let him down, so that everything we did was minutely and intelligently scrutinised to ensure that all was in order. Though he was a stickler for correctness, he had a good sense of humour and it was a pleasure to work for him. His wife, Eileen, was equally charming but they had children older than ours so were not much use for our two.

In my office were three other officers: the French Capitaine de Corvette who had accompanied me to Norfolk, a US Air Force Major and a German Army Lieutenant Colonel. The French officer had a national job in addition to O&T and we saw little of him.

Of the other two, Major Herndon Fauntleroy Williams from Atlanta Georgia was great fun; he had the deepest of deep southern accent and during the Korean War he been on exchange duty with the Royal Air Force in command of a British fighter squadron. He had done this extremely well and had been awarded the Distinguished Flying Cross. Not surprisingly he had a taste for speed and was the proud owner of a Porsche. In fact I did my first ever 100 mph+ as a passenger in his car. He had a very pretty wife but sadly no children.

The third member, Lt Col Alfred Martin, was from Hamburg. Alfred had fought on the Russian front in 1941 where he had been badly wounded, losing his right leg below the knee. After rehabilitation he became ADC to General Kesselring. In Italy in 1943 when, with his General, he was observing the Allied attack on Monte Cassino he again had his leg shot off but, luckily, this time it was only the artificial one. When the Army was disbanded in 1945, and finding himself with nothing, he started his own business laying tiles. He was greatly relieved when the German Army was reconstituted and he was accepted for Staff duties. He had a quick brain, an excellent command of English and was a very entertaining companion. He refused to let his disability get in his way and was an accomplished skier and tennis player. Sadly in 1965, having returned to Army duties in Germany, he was put in prison for supplying military secrets to the German magazine, Der Spiegel. He was an adventurer and I was sorry to hear of his misfortunes even though they were self-inflicted.

Jack Kelsey, Will, Alfred and I had lunch together most days in the SHAPE canteen. Being an American-style organisation the canteen was an all-ranks affair and you queued for your meal with Generals and other ranks, all very democratic and it worked. There was an officers' restaurant where you could have your family but it was a lot more expensive. Life in general was quite expensive and we had to make the most of our money. The exchange rate for French francs was poor so that every other weekend someone with a fast car, quite often Will, would drive to Switzerland with a load of dollars and sterling where the rate was very much better. For the first and only time in our lives we had a Swiss bank account.

Lynn, our secretary, was a platinum blonde USAF Top Sergeant from the Bronx. Of Jewish origin, she had an accent that you could cut with a knife but she was first rate at her job. She also had a predilection for fast cars and owned a Chevrolet Corvette, the American answer to the Jaguar. I once asked her how fast she drove; the reply was, 'Never more than 120 Commander.'

The SHAPE building itself was a truly ramshackle affair consisting of hundreds of prefabricated sections like shoe boxes joined together so that they stuck out like the branches of an espaliered fruit tree on either side of the trunk, a long central corridor. At the far end was a separate collection of boxes housing the Headquarters of the US Airforce in Europe. The Cold War was at its height and, though Britain had some nuclear weapons and the French were trying to develop their Force de Frappe, the vast preponderance of weapons and know-how was American. This was where nuclear war or retaliation would be planned and executed as far as the Tactical Battle was concerned. The security was absolute and only US personnel with special passes were allowed to enter. They were a law unto themselves and it was deemed impossible to get them to co-operate in any exercise planning or indeed give any indication as to how they would react to any given situation. They were quite arrogant in this, claiming that their instructions came straight from Washington.

I was determined to break this down as it made what we were trying to achieve ineffective. Jack Kelsey and I had a number of meetings with General Norstad on the whole question of co-operation and, while not in time for Exercise SIDESTEP, I did get co-operation for the following year and was able to obtain entry and hold planning meetings. Their eventual co-operation was greatly appreciated especially by the British-commanded 2nd Tactical Air Force stationed in Germany. I have always believed that it was for being able to break down the barriers between the US Air Force and the rest that I was awarded an OBE in 1960. In mitigation the organisation, by definition, has officers and men from all the countries making up the alliance. Consequently security vetting is more than difficult so that it is only fair to recognise the US reticence in sharing their secrets.

Besides the large numbers of officers and civilians employed in the headquarters, there were also several thousand soldiers, sailors and airmen working in signals, transport, medical and all the other supporting services. These were all housed at the other side of the motorway that ran past SHAPE in Camp Voluceau. Here too was the international Church to which we came from time to time. The building catered for all the major Christian denominations and on Saturdays it doubled as a Synagogue. On Sundays services were scheduled at intervals of 1 hour and 15 minutes, the 15 minutes being used to shift the scenery, the books and the congregations. It was all very slick with Crucifix and Madonna for the Roman Catholics, bare room for the Quakers and everything as required for the in-betweens. When one thinks of how many millions have been killed or persecuted for not conforming with the 'in' sect of a particular religion and then see how simply a little shifting of scenery and props can satisfy, it makes one think. However it was a long way for us to come on a Sunday and our usual place of worship was the British Church at Maisons Laffitte.

The Church there had been built at the end of the 19th century for and by the British race-horse owners for their trainers and jockeys working at Longchamp and had flourished during the inter-war years. Now, with modern transport for horses, life had changed but there were still a number of elderly jockeys who had made their home in France and it was amusing to see these tiny old men with their normal-size wives coming to the Church, which was now well-patronized by English ex-pats, American Episcopalians and the likes of us.

The Vicar and his wife were a charming couple, the Reverend and Mrs McNeil, who lived in the Vicarage alongside the Church. He had been a prisoner of war in Japan but, because he was a priest, he had been allowed to work as a gardener. Though skin and bones when released, he had managed to come through his four-year ordeal much better than some. He was also Priest-in-Charge of the Church in Versailles and because of the distance between the two, services were often taken by a layman. A very nice American was the No.1 choice and he used to preach. When he was not available I used to fill in but never attempted a sermon.

In the spring we took Mike, David and the two Sixsmith boys, Angus and Edward, to Val d'Isere for a week's skiing. It was all a bit different from our Norwegian experience and, while the boys made excellent progress, Mary and I took it rather gently but enjoyed the little luxuries like sneaking off from the Piste for a café Liègeoise or a bit of sunbathing. In the evenings we were fairly exhausted but the boys were up half the night playing cards. All in all it was a good week with nothing broken.

On our return M. Rivet arrived with the boat, *Donald*. It was in a fairly poor state and we put it into the garage to be stripped down and painted. I also had to put on new decking, which I did with fibreglass, and I learnt the hard way about fibre-glassing in the process. In the end she looked pretty smart but it had been an agonisingly sticky experience. When completed we took her down to Triel where we had arranged for a berth at the local yacht and boat yard belonging to a M.Mallard, which seemed rather appropriate.

Our first sail was an unmitigated disaster as I was caught by a 180 degree wind-shift as we came out the other side of a road bridge and capsized. Fortunately the buoyancy bags stopped her from sinking but Mary and I had to swim as hard as we could, pushing her to the bank, to avoid being run down by an enormous barge loaded with motor cars from the Ford/Simca factory at Poissy. However we had learnt our lesson about sailing on rivers near bridges and 300-metre long barge tows and did not do it again. Granny Bull, who was sitting by the car near the river bank, knew nothing of what had passed but wondered how we had managed to get so wet.

In fact we had a lot of pleasure with *Donald*. There was a memorable occasion when André Déroulède was sailing with me and Génévieve came rushing along the river bank shouting that their first grandson, Jerome, had been born. Great celebrations.

On the whole it was nice to be back in France where we felt quite at home. Andresy was a pretty little town; we had an excellent and faithful femme-de-ménage, Marie, and nice friends, including the Molloys and the Dunbar-Nasmiths, but it was never as intimate as Noisy and too far from SHAPE. It was the difference between being one of thousands living in suburbia and being part of a village. From the work point of view there was a notable change in the acceptance of NATO as a going concern and, unlike Fontainebleau, we were no longer pioneers. However the unexpected could always happen and did. When, in the summer of 1959, General de Gaulle withdrew all French military personnel from NATO headquarters, within a week there were no French officers working in SHAPE. This was caused by a fit of pique against the Americans who refused to recognise France as a nuclear power and also American criticism of the way France was handling the very considerable problem of Algeria, where rebel forces were fighting for independence in a bloodthirsty war.

During the summer we returned to Instow and Exmouth. Mike was to go to Pangbourne in September and needed to get all his uniform ready. In addition the boys wanted a boat of their own and at Exmouth we were able to find a rather elderly Yachting World Cadet which we took with us back to France on a trailer that I had acquired from a German Army Colonel. He had been part of the Auto Union Team Racing Team and had used the trailer to transport spare engines. It had a steel plate on the floor, which made it jolly heavy, but once that had been removed it became a very useful member of the family.

That autumn saw Exercise Sidestep played out successfully and then it was our task to analyse the results and, at the same time, prepare the major exercise for the following year. An important part of the system was to prepare and present a verbal 'wash-up' of the exercise to an audience, which consisted of all the various Force Commanders and their staffs, and this took place some three months after the completion of the exercise itself so that there was always a fairly considerable pressure on our little team.

I had become increasingly disenchanted with the Rover and decided to chock it up in the garage until we could take it back to England and sell it. In its stead we bought a brand-new Citroen 2CV, collecting it from the factory in Paris straight off the production line. It was a splendid little car, enormous fun to drive and would tow the trailer with the Cadet on top. Mary and I used it to go to the 24-hour race at le Mans. We found that by taking out the seats and putting up two camp beds it quickly converted to being a camper. We had been invited by the director of KLG plugs in France to watch the race from their box which was immediately over the Jaguar Pit. It was an exciting experience and we met all the Jaguar drivers including Roy Salvadori. Pit stops were not the eight-seconds events that they are today and the drivers would come up to our box, down a glass of champagne and set off again. Jaguar won the event.

September 1959 saw Mike starting at Pangbourne and, with David still at Winchester Lodge, there had to be a huge amount of to-ing and fro-ing over days out, ends of term and so on, and Mary made frequent trips to England but in all this Granny Bull was the mainstay of the organisation; without her, life would have been far from easy.

On the work side we seemed to be continually under pressure but there were lots of other things going on, including the construction of a full-size ping-pong table, of which I was extremely proud even though it weighed a ton. It fitted into the veranda well and also doubled as a large dining table for parties. In December we had all the excitement of the SHAPE Ball in the Palace of Versailles – quite an event. We gave a dinner party beforehand for the Erskine-Tullochs, Van Eeghens and others, with Marie helping. Versailles really came to life with all the uniforms and we danced till 4 a.m. in the Chambre de Battailles. During the Christmas holidays Mary did her best to drive some culture into two rather unwilling boys by taking them to see Paris. We also hired a television set to improve their French but they quickly discovered that you could watch the pictures with the sound turned off and listen to their favourite programmes on the radio at the same time, so that didn't really work either.

In February Jack Kelsey and I had to attend planning meetings in Naples, after which I was to go on to Malta. We discovered that we could exchange our air tickets for much cheaper tickets on the train and by doing so could take Eileen and Mary with us. We were able to stay in a nice hotel in Naples and, while Jack and I were working, Eileen and Mary were able to see all the sights, Pompeii and Vesuvius and also visit the wonderful museums. Both suffered the Neapolitan hazard of having their bottoms pinched on every occasion.

While the Kelseys went back to France, Mary and I had a wonderful weekend in Rome before I went on to Malta. One of the experiences that has stuck most firmly in our memory was walking down the Appian Way at dawn, with not a soul about, and visiting the catacombs. Mary had a good trip back to Paris and found herself sharing a compartment, which had four couchettes, with the English nanny of author Alan Morsehead's children, a Belgian priest and a variety of people who came in and out during the day including a very old Italian priest who had been in England during World War One.

In Malta I stayed in the then newly-built Phoenicia Hotel, all very modern and splendid except that I had a room near the top and, though it had a very luxurious en-suite bathroom, water seldom ran out of the taps. However, I discovered that if I set my alarm to 5.30 and turned on the taps, I could go back to bed until 7 when there would be several inches of tepid water in the bath. The meetings were productive and I was pleased to meet up with André Beau – now a Capitaine de Vaisseau – one of my old colleagues from Fontainebleau days.

That spring (1960) we took the Sixsmith boys with us again to Val d'Isère for a week of good skiing and all-night card school! We had taken the Rover off its chocks for the trip and had a worrying journey as it kept on overheating and we had to make frequent stops. It turned out that the garage had fitted the wrong type of plug at the last servicing. I was glad to return it to its chocked-up state when we got home. During the summer the Molloys left; Terence had decided that he had had enough of the Army and would like to be a schoolmaster, so he enrolled for teacher training at St Loyes in Exeter. We saw them a couple of years later and found him very happily ensconced as Headmaster of a small village school near Wincanton.

That Autumn I had a change of P.A; this time it was a male US Airforce Top Sergeant who was half Cherokee Indian. He was also a Chinese interpreter. I asked him if he could speak French. 'No', he replied, 'but give me six weeks and I shall be pretty fluent', and he was. I asked him how he managed it and he said, 'I guess, Commander, that if you live and sleep with a French girl for six weeks you're sure pick up the lingo'. He was a great 'operator' in every respect and managed to 'fix' just about anything and was a great help to me in getting the Autumn exercise and subsequent 'wash-up' organised.

We had a pretty constant stream of visitors at Andresy, with Hester, Rowland and Henry as a very new-born and rather sickly baby. When we felt that we could afford it, we would take suitable guests to the Lido in Paris where you got quite a good supper and a most tremendous floor show which featured the famous 'Bluebell Girls – much more fun than the very hyped-up and rather vulgar Moulin Rouge. Sadly we didn't feel rich very often. The 1960 Ball at Versailles was again one of the events of the year and this time we had a much bigger pre-ball party with sixteen seated round the ping-pong table and the faithful Marie doing the cooking. We had a thoroughly international group with the Kvaals(Norwegian), Bakelants(Belgian), Van Eeghens (Dutch), Williamses (American) and so on. It was a great success. As you entered the Palace, the Grand Staircase was lined with Spahis (native cavalry from Algeria). In full dress of colourful blue and red uniform under flowing white cloaks, white turbans and with drawn sabres they looked pretty impressive. (Sadly the regiment was disbanded in 1962.) Mary had a very super dress, just right for the occasion, and 4 a.m. came round all too quickly.

Christmas came and went with Granny Bull and Hester getting both boys to airports on time and at the New Year I was totally surprised to find that I had been awarded an OBE in the Honours List and we gave a big party at SHAPE to celebrate. Normally one gets these things at the end of one's service so I was extremely honoured to be awarded it while I still had many years to go. I was due to be relieved in the Spring and so it was arranged that we should go to the Palace at the end of February. We stayed a couple of nights at the Cumberland Hotel with both Mike and David getting off school for the occasion. Compared with collecting my DSC in 1945 it was a very Rolls Royce occasion. I found myself standing in the OBE queue next to the actress Margaret Rutherford who, at that time, was at the height of her career and a very amusing person both on and off the stage. That evening we celebrated by going to Drury Lane to see 'My Fair Lady' which we thoroughly enjoyed. After the show David went round to the stage door to get autographs from the principals as they came out. Next day it was back to school for the boys and back to France for us to pack up.

For some time I had been in contact with my 'appointer' at The Admiralty as, though I had found my time at SHAPE both busy and interesting, I was fed up with desk jobs and dearly wanted to get back to sea, which was why I had joined the

Above: Mary and I in Donald on the Seine at Melun where we kept the boat.

Below: David does a 'bob-a-job' on Mary's black beetle 4CV Renault in front of our house in Andresy.

Above: The Johnson Fleet. The whole of the house on the first floor had been made into a large conservatory, which was a great asset.

Below: Andresy and the road past our house. The 2CV has just come out of the garden gate on the left. In our time there the bit on the right of the road was open country as far as you could see, but is now a housing development with supermarket and the lot.

Above:
Inside the conservatory with Mary giving the boys breakfast.

Below:
Orly airport with the boys walking out to board the de Haviland Dragon Rapide, a biplane, which would take them to Exeter via Jersey and so back to school in Torquay.

Above: The boys with Augus & Edward Sixsmith.

Left: Dressed for the slopes - Val D'isere.

Above: We often visited the LeLoups at Noisy.

Right: Dressed for the Ball.

Above: General and Mrs Norstad arriving at the Palace of Versailles with a guard of honour of Spahis manning the Grand Staircase.

Below: Our table at the SHAPE Ball. L to R: JJ, Mary, Jean Bakalants (Belgian), Reidar Kvaal (Norwegian), Ivy Kvaal, & Madam Bakalants.

Above: HP leaving Singapore Naval Base. Every corner of the upper deck is taken up with equipment.

Below: Doing our stuff in Kilindini! D25 is Cavalier. A typical working scene.

Above: Admiral Sir Royston Wright, C in C Far East Fleet, looks round HP. 'Oblong' is explaining something obtuse, I and 'Dickey' Bird are behind. The chap on the right is the Fleet Engineer Officer. 'Shiner' Wright was the Quaterdeck officer in Vindictive when I was a Cadet. I was his 'doggie'.

Below: HP cleans up at the Fleet Regatta in Hong Kong. Chief Shipwright Atwood (seated) did very well in the sailing world. Back row L-R, Stratton-Brown, Paddy Langran and Guy O'Donnell. I forget the others.

Above: Crossing the line. King Neptune and his court stop the ship and come aboard on our way to Bahrein. The bears didn't pay too much attention as to whether you had crossed the line before!

Below: Jack Wigg's successful production of the Pirates of Penzance at the Singapore Opera House, showing the Policemens' Chorus with the Major General's daughters. Stan Haig and I are 2nd and 3rd (policemen) from the left.

Navy in the first place. This was difficult as, having been placed on the 'dry' list, desk jobs were what I was supposed to do. However, with some help from Admiral Talbot Eddison, the senior British naval officer at SHAPE, those in charge of our lives at The Admiralty agreed to see what they could do and, to my surprise and joy, I was appointed to join a rather queer sort of ship, *Hartland Point*, in July 1961, having first done a series of courses. *Hartland Point* was an Escort Maintenance Ship, quite different from anything that I had come across before but she was a ship and part of the Far East Fleet based on Singapore.

Back in France there remained only to turn over to my successor and pack up the house. We sold the little Renault 4CV beetle and Herndon F. Williams bought the ping-pong table. *Donald* was left in good order for the Rivets and, having said goodbye to all our friends, our circus set off for Devon, with Mary driving the Rover and me following on with the Citroen 2CV towing the Cadet dinghy on top of a trailer full of stuff.

On reflection, while the job had been a success, we were glad to be leaving. Andresy, though nice in itself, had been too far away from the centre of things and Mary had not been well, suffering from severe bouts of migraine. The boys had not been able to have any friends close by during the holidays and, though they had got on well with the two Sixsmith boys, they too were out of range for easy visiting. On the plus side we had been able to do and see lots of things, renew and cement our friendship with the Dérouledes and visit the Le Loups in their retirement home near La Ferté Alaise. We also made some lasting friends like the Kvaals and Van Eeghens and, though we felt thoroughly at home in France, it was time to get away. Before taking up my new appointment, I had a series of courses to do to get me back into what was going on in the real Navy. In fact most of May and June was spent at Woolwich, which at that time was the location of the RN Tactical School. Having no house of our own we alternated between Instow and Exmouth and wondered what the next eighteen months would bring.

CHAPTER 15

Far East Fleet
H.M.S. *Hartland Point*
11th July 1961 – 13th February 1963

My appointment to *Hartland Point* was 'unaccompanied', which meant that no provision was made for members of the Ship's Company to have their wives and families on the station. Eighteen months was now the standard separation time, having been recently brought down from two years. The area covered by the Far East Fleet went from Hong Kong to the Indian Ocean with Singapore as the main base and headquarters; the aim of the whole thing was flexibility. There was nothing to prevent you from bringing out your family at your own expense, though of course there was no guarantee whatsoever that the ship would be in port at the right time. However we decided that, whatever happened, Mary would come out to Singapore for at least three months during the middle of my time out there and that we would just hope for the best. It was still possible to buy a new car free of Purchase Tax, about 30% of the total cost and we set about selling the Rover and buying a Morris Oxford Estate which we would subsequently ship out to Singapore.

After four years of being together it was a great wrench to say goodbye to Mary and the boys and set off by air, courtesy of RAF Transport Command, to join *Hartland Point* in Singapore on 11th July 1961. For reasons now forgotten the flight was delayed by 24 hours and by the time I arrived in Singapore *Hartland Point* had sailed for Colombo. I had to kick my heels in Singapore before a flight was available to take me to Ceylon (now Sri Lanka) to join my ship as the Executive Officer or, the more usual term, 'Commander'. (Small ships have 1st Lieutenants as Executive Officers; bigger ships, with a Captain in command, have Commanders).

Tradition requires that you join a ship wearing your best uniform complete with sword and medals and this I did in my best white uniform, coming off to the ship by boat as she lay at anchor off Colombo. I was greeted warmly by the Captain, John Le Blanc Smith, known to every one as 'Oblong' Smith, who had only recently joined the ship. Even more delighted was the Commander, Derek Smeeton, the chap that I was due to relieve. After a rapid turnover he departed that same evening for Singapore and then on home to England, leaving me to get on with it. The Captain turned out to be a very pleasant and unflappable person, a navigator by trade and a couple of years older than I. Born and bred in Kenya not far from Mombasa, where his parents still farmed, he had come to England during the war to join up. On my first meeting with him in his cabin he said to me, 'I shall leave the running of the ship entirely to you, especially when we are in harbour, and provided you do it well I will back you all the way. You will find me a bit like God, ready to take the praise and the blame, but otherwise you won't see much of me'.

I soon came to realize that he had the most extraordinary lifestyle. Everyday in harbour he would go ashore at about 5 p.m. and return on board at about 4 o'clock in the morning. He would be up and about for 'Colours' at 8 a.m. and we had a daily meeting in his cabin at 10. After lunch he would get his head down until it was time to go ashore and woe betide anyone who woke him. He used to say that he did not enjoy sport and took his exercise dancing. I have to say that it suited him; he was always bright eyed and bushy tailed when on duty and thoroughly on the ball. He just didn't need much sleep. I thought that later on in the commission, when his wife came out to Singapore, that things would change but they were two of a kind and great fun. It all suited me very well.

From the run-of-the-mill Royal Navy ship, *Hartland Point* was a bit of an oddity. She was one of a fleet of merchant ships taken up from new in 1944 and fitted out to be part of the Fleet Train for the war in the Pacific. She was a British version of the Liberty ship, built in Canada. A ship of just under 10,000 tons, her holds were fitted out as accommodation spaces and workshops to take the vast amount of technical equipment required to mend and maintain the destroyers and frigates of the fleet. We had the machinery to make just about anything and to do this the Ship's Company comprised mainly of senior rates and very experienced officers of all the technical branches from blacksmiths to electronic wizards. Of a Ship's Company of about 450, 75% were artificers and senior rates. Except for those required for watch-keeping and manning the many boats, there were very few seamen. She was a bit of an ugly duckling with every inch filled with something or somebody. Powered by a steam reciprocating engine driving a single screw, she had a speed of about 14 knots. In harbour she could, and usually did, berth two destroyers or frigates on either side and was able to supply them with electricity, fresh water and whatever else was required, so had a great amount of auxiliary machinery and generators.

The officer complement was large and, to fit them all in, the cabins were tiny and all just about the same. The only difference was that some where outboard with a porthole, others were inboard and very stuffy. My cabin, which was one of the best and outboard, measured 8ft 6ins deep and 6ft 6ins wide (approx 2.5 by 2 metres). The bunk went fore and aft under the scuttle with a full-size chest of drawers underneath; also there was a kneehole desk, wardrobe and wash basin. Hardly room to swing the proverbial cat and a far cry from the large cabins that I had enjoyed in *Zodiac* and *Ark Royal*. With the exception of the Sick Bay and electronics workshops, the ship was not air-conditioned. However, I was pleased with my lot and on the whole everyone on board was there because they were good at their job and got on with it.

On board were a large number of Hong Kong Chinese. The cooks and stewards were locally enlisted and of course we had a Chinese laundry crew, tailor, shoemaker and barber. I had an excellent Leading Steward to look after me called Kwan Chip. He was expert in seeing that I always had the right things to wear, either on board or ashore, and once our car had arrived he would wash and polish it every day. I met him again several years later on Paddington Station. He had come to

England with his family to start a Chinese Restaurant. I hope it went well for him. To serve in the Royal Navy was a much prized job because, by comparison with normal wages, they were well-paid and were able to send money home to their families both in Hong Kong and mainland China. Enlistment was tightly controlled by the Chinese Tongs or secret societies in Hong Kong and those wanting to join the Navy had to pay a considerable sum of money before they could come in any safety for an interview.

My immediate colleagues were the 1st Lieutenant, Paddy Langran, the Commander (E) Stan Haig, Commander (S) 'Dixie' Dean and Commander (L), 'Dickie' Bird. Dickie was an electronics wizard; he had invented the latest computerised system for controlling the guns in all the new ships and had been sent to sea to make sure that it all worked. It was a revolutionary system replacing the largely mechanical systems that had done the job since World War One. He was also teaching himself Mandarin and doing pretty well. However, expert and charming as he was, he was also an alcoholic. Most of the time he was being good but every so often he would go on a binge and this, I discovered, was to lead me a merry dance in the months to come.

The ship remained off Colombo for about a week and then it was back to Singapore where I was reunited with my baggage and the Morris Oxford which had been shipped out. It was fun to find many old friends there: Terry Herrick, who was Captain of the Fleet; Raymond Lowe, who had been a Chaplain at *Ganges*; and Hamilton-Meikle, who had relieved Geoffrey Kirkby in *Melbreak*. *Hartland Point* was immediately surrounded by a clutch of Frigates and life was all go as I found my way around the ship, the Naval Base and Singapore.

We seemed to have been there hardly any time before we received an order to sail for Bahrein. It seemed that the agreement for the British defence of Kuwait, which had been signed in 1899, had been abrogated by an exchange of letters in June 1961 and now, almost immediately, Iraq was making claims of sovereignty over the State and was massing troops on the Iraq/Kuwait border. Britain immediately despatched an armoured brigade to Kuwait and also a number of frigates and minesweepers to protect the lines of communications and to provide gunfire support where necessary. These ships would require on-the-spot maintenance, hence *Hartland Point*.

We arrived in Bahrein at the end of August and it was HOT. Almost immediately we had ships alongside wanting things mended. It soon became apparent, however, that our lack of air-conditioning made our task impossible and we had a continuous stream of people suffering from heat stroke. You could fry an egg on the deck and the heat in the engine room was 140°F (60°C). So after a couple of weeks of giving it our best shot it was decided that we should transfer our efforts to Mombasa, much to everyone's relief and the Captain's joy.

It was nice to be back in Kilindini harbour again; it brought back memories of 1942 when the place was jam-packed with the ships of the Far East Fleet. *Hartland Point* was secured head and stern between two buoys so that ships could berth on both sides. It was a joy to be in an equable climate again and ships arrived to keep us busy. Oblong's family farmed nearby and he was quickly away. I renewed my acquaintance with the Mombasa golf course, much improved since WW II, and also found a friendly crowd in the Mombasa Yacht Club. A chap called Bentley-Buckle had started a small East African airline which was clearly going well and he had shipped out ten 5-0-5 dinghies from England to start a new class there. I was given the use of one when I wanted it and thoroughly enjoyed my first experience of sailing a modern planing dinghy.

Back at home Mary and Michael were agonizing as to whether or not Mike should go for a Naval Scholarship. This would give him an entry to Dartmouth and help towards paying a year's school fees. We agreed to go ahead on the understanding that we would refund the money if at the end Mike changed his mind about going into the Navy.

By the end of October the situation in Kuwait had calmed off, the speed of Britain's reaction had been effective for the time being and by November we were back in Singapore and I began to find my way around. I joined the Royal Johore Bahru Golf Club. There were several keen golfers in the ship and it was easy to slip across the causeway to J-B in the car for a round of golf and a meal afterwards.

After the experience of Bahrein I managed to persuade all the members of the Wardroom to club together to buy an air-conditioning unit, which made a world of difference. Several of the Chief Petty Officers' messes did likewise; they were not very expensive and, for a ship having all the expertise, not difficult to install. All the modern ships had full air-conditioning with a centralized plant as a matter of course.

We also found that, while we had a Chaplain embarked for much of the time, we had no Chapel. However, in the bowels of the ship was an air-conditioned space called the torpedo body room complete with expensive equipment for looking after torpedoes. As none of the ships in our care had torpedoes, I obtained Oblong's approval to pack all the kit away and, by draping mosquito netting to form an arched ceiling and installing chairs and an altar made by the Chippies, we had a pretty fair chapel which could seat 30 in a peaceful and quiet part of the ship. I wrote to the Vicar of Hartland to tell him what we had done and asked if he had any spare kit. He was more than helpful and the parish sent us from Stoke Church some brass candlesticks, a lectern and a cross for the altar.

In December the Fleet moved up to Hong Kong and we went with them, joining in the various exercises on the way. *Hartland Point* was always quite useful on these passages, acting as a convoy or the enemy, to be torpedoed by submarines, shot at by surface ships or bombed by aircraft. (Not for real of course). In Hong Kong we secured to buoys off *Tamar*, the Naval Base, so that ships could be berthed on either side. I also had my first experience of Jenny's Side Party, a wonderful team of women in a Sampan who would paint your ship in exchange for various waste items and do it very well indeed. Jenny had started her business in the 1930s and had glowing recommendations from just about any senior naval officer that I had ever heard of.

At this time the Dutch were having big problems in their one-time colonies of Java and Sumatra and I was delighted to find that Cor Van Eeghen was in command of a Dutch Destroyer refitting in the commercial yard in Kowloon and we had some good get-togethers. Also in Hong Kong was David Durnford-Slater from Instow, working for Jardine Matheson, with the job of getting cargoes to the right ships and I had him on board for a meal on several occasions. Never having been to Hong Kong before, I found a huge number of things to see and do. Such a different culture and the Chinese just never seemed to stop working day and night. *Hartland Point* was well-known in Hong Kong and most of the older hands in the Wardroom had friends ashore. Nevertheless the new boys such as myself were quickly swept up and taken off to see the sights. I found the New Territories particularly fascinating where the little walled towns and villages had not changed for hundreds of years.

I had bought myself a tape recorder and, as Mary and the boys already had a 'shoebox' one at home, we began an exchange of tapes instead of letters which went on for the rest of the time in H-P. Hearing people's voices seemed to make things so much closer. It was possible to telephone England from Hong Kong but it involved going to the Post Office Building in the centre of Victoria, booking a call and then waiting for hours for your turn. It was extremely expensive and not particularly good as it was by cable via the Pacific, USA and Atlantic; there was a quite considerable time delay and you had to allow a considerable pause for a reply to come back.

After Christmas the pattern of our operation for 1962 began to become clear and it seemed that after a further spell in Mombasa during February and March we were pretty certain to spend April, May and June in Singapore or round about. Mary and I planned that she would come out at the end of the Easter holidays and return in time for the summer ones. The time seemed to pass extremely slowly but at last the end of April arrived and we were back in Singapore. Mary got an 'indulgence' flight, thanks to the RAF.

> Mary now takes up the story:
> 'This was the first of three great adventures in my life when I set off entirely on my own without any of the family with me. I went for the night to Hester in Loughton and next morning Rowland drove me to Stanstead airport where I boarded an RAF Comet – one of the first post-war jet passenger aircraft. Sadly there had been several mysterious losses and they had been withdrawn from commercial flying. (The RAF continued to operate a later version, but flying only by day, so that special cameras on board could take photos of wings, rudders and so on to check for signs of undue stress and to try and solve the problem.)
> 'As we couldn't fly at night we stopped the first night at El Adam in Libya, an airfield in the middle of the desert where, except for a barbed wire fence all round, there was nothing but sand. The next day was to Bahrein and the third to Gann in the Maldives where landing and take off were quite tricky, the runway being built on a narrow strip of sand just above sea level, but we had time there to swim in the huge lagoon which is surrounded by coral reefs. Then at last to Singapore, where Jimmy met me and took me to the Rest House in Johore Bahru, where we were to stay. The heat seemed tremendous. (During WW II Gann had been a Top Secret fuelling base for our ships and known only as Port X)'

Great rejoicings!
The Government Rest House at Johore Bahru was a relic of colonial days, though it was relatively modern and situated near the water's edge with lovely views across to Singapore Island. It was wonderful to be together again and there were so many

things to see and do, all new and strange. From the Rest House we were fascinated to watch the fisherman sitting on top of their tripods in the water and casting their nets with such skill. In J B itself there were gardens, a beautiful Mosque and, often, a wonderfully noisy and colourful Chinese Opera set up in the Market Place, though the market itself was intriguing with so many strange things to see and buy. Then of course there was the social life in the Naval Base, shopping at Tangs and, when we could afford it, going to dine and dance at Princes in Orchard Road.

Thanks to having a car we were able to explore and took various people from the ship, often Dickie Bird, on picnics and walks in the jungle for which we were horribly ill-equipped. I was due for what was called Station Leave, about seven days and so we set off for Kuala Lumpur and the Cameron Highlands, staying in various Rest Houses on the way. On the coast we endured nightly bombardment by huge flying insects and cowered beneath our mosquito nets, while in the Cameron Highlands huge creepy crawlies walked the floor at night, but all seemingly quite harmless. The beauty about the Highlands was that it was cool and we went for some glorious walks in the rain forest.

One of the more memorable events was an evening spent with the Sarawak Rangers. I had formed a friendship with the Army Major in charge; they had been embarked in *Hartland Point*, and he had invited Mary and me to spend an evening with the Rangers, who were trained as jungle scouts for the Army. They were all Sea Dyaks from Sarawak and by tradition, head hunters. They had been brought over to Malaya with their wives and family. Here they had built traditional Dyak longhouses for accommodation, which consisted of one long communal room upstairs while underneath were pigs, chickens and other livestock.

We had been invited to a celebration meal in one of the houses and were fêted and plied with all sorts of food and liberal quantities of rice wine poured from Army-issue metal teapots. After the meal came the entertainment – songs and dances to the accompaniment of magical music played on a whole row of gongs. The dances were spectacular and performed by men dressed as exotic lyre birds. Because the floor was totally uneven the dances were in slow time with the dancers displaying wonderful balance with gestures of the arms and hands that would have done credit to a ballerina as they moved and postured. The tradition is centuries old with the costumes and headdresses passed from father to son. On the darker side the older dyaks were proud to show the rings tattooed on their fingers, each ring signifying a head taken.

Sadly the time in Singapore seemed to fly past and in June it was time for Mary to begin her voyage home. I had managed to get her a passage in the RFA Amhurst which was forecast to take about three weeks. Amhurst had started life as a Fyffe's banana boat trading to the West Indies and was equipped with cabins to take about twelve passengers. Taken over during WW II she became a fast ammunition ship and was now sailing on her last voyage back to England. I wrote ahead to friends at the various ports of call to make sure that Mary would be welcomed at each stop and I also equipped her with a bucket for the dhobying! This was the straightforward part. The first snag was that Amhurst was delayed sailing as she could not be given a Lloyds Certificate of seaworthiness because of the state of her boilers and the fact that she was carrying out-of-date ammunition. To make things good took nearly a week but eventually she was allowed to sail and Mary takes up the story:

> 'The officers on board were an extraordinary collection. The Captain, who was on his last voyage, had no desires other than to get back to his home in Plymouth and open an 'oggie' shop. The Chief Engineer was an alcoholic who spent the whole time propped against the bar. There were several families on board including a Mrs Dawe, who had come out to visit the beach where she had last seen her husband when he came to see her off just before Singapore fell into Japanese hands, and a Captain and Mrs Morrow, who had been prisoners in Changi jail. I spent most of the time on deck trying to dry out my Malaysian shells and doing a tapestry. I would walk round the deck about ten times a day as Jimmy had told me that ten times round equalled one mile. We stopped at Gan for about three days with engine trouble – this was lovely and I had some lovely bathes and saw a Moray eel – and then went on to Aden. The sea was wonderful and there were lots of fish jumping. At Aden I was met and taken home to a naval Captain's house, a friend of Jimmy's. After that we sailed through the Suez Canal which was amazing; there were ships laid up in the salt lakes and Arabs riding by on camels. On the way through I bought a camel stool and several other things but was too nervous to leave the ship in case I got left behind.
>
> 'The next stop was Malta where another friend met me and took me home. The ship was moored in Bighi Bay opposite the hospital. We did not call in at Gibraltar but sailed on and passed close to Cape St Vincent in a gale. The ship rolled a lot and I somersaulted completely over while sitting in an armchair in the Saloon. There was great excitement as we neared England and passed the Eddystone light, then on up the Hamoaze to Ernisettle where, to my great surprise, I saw Granny Bull with Mike and David in a picket boat coming out to meet me and my fourteen pieces of luggage! How she managed it I never knew, but it was wonderful. I had been away for three months. (I was horrified to see that Mike had grown out of all his clothes.)'

It was during these summer holidays that Mary rented Mrs Pollard-Lowsely's flat in Instow House and the family gained a new member. David had complained bitterly that he was not allowed to have a pet, saying, 'You wouldn't even allow me to have pet snail'. Friends of ours in Instow, the Nightingales, bred Shetland Sheepdogs and had recently had a new litter of puppies for sale and so it was that we acquired our faithful, intelligent Jenny, together with all the problems of having a tiny puppy in someone else's flat. Luckily Granny Lang next door let Mary use her garden.

Meanwhile *Hartland Point* had sailed for Trincomalee to establish an advanced base there for frigates still on patrol in the Indian Ocean. The Captain had been there during the war and knew several of the local Ceylon Navy officers. We were to be there six weeks and I had taken the car as I wanted to drive up to Candy and Nuralia to see friends (Patsy Paul from Instow and her husband) who were tea planters. This I did and it was delightful but one had to be watchful for elephants and huge pot holes on the appalling roads. Trincomalee is a huge enclosed natural harbour and in WW II had been humming with activity. Now there was just about nothing to be seen and *Hartland Point* and a couple of frigates had it all to themselves.

The Wardrooms had quite good fun: we did a lot of sailing in superb weather conditions and the ship fielded a good cricket XI. There was, however, a big problem with the sailors as the bars and other places closed at 2100 when there was a curfew, imposed because of troubles with the Tamil population. This caused great gloom until I found an answer. I got Oblong to send a signal to all the ships in harbour to say that ship's time was to be 2 hours different from local time, which meant that the curfew in ship's time was 2300 – end of problem.

At the end of a pleasant and, hopefully, useful six weeks we sailed for Penang. Long sea passages in *Hartland Point* were fairly leisurely affairs and we usually filled in the evenings with a Ship's Company Concert, rigging quite a good stage on deck, and different messes from the Wardroom down would put on turns. We had a good selection of talent including a Chief who was a really first class conjurer. Besides putting on little playlets, the Wardroom skiffle group was excellent and our navigator, Dick Percival-Maxwell was a wizard with washboard and thimbles.

We spent the weekend in Penang and Oblong and I were lent a car and driver for the day to see round the island, one of the jewels of that part of the world. Then on to Singapore. On arrival Stan Haig, myself and a couple of others were coerced to take part in an amateur production of 'The Pirates of Penzance'; Stan and I were to be policemen. We also thought that we would stage a 'Roman Night at the Baths' in the Naval Base pool. This caused a frenzy of activity. We made a triumphal arch out of oil drums and bits and pieces, our 'toothie' carved a number of impressive busts out of plaster of Paris with his dentist's drill – really very clever – and everywhere people were making themselves costumes. I made a Centurion's outfit, moulding the breast and back plates of papier mâché around my body, and lay in the sun to dry it out. Painted silver it looked not bad. I also made a helmet using a red-bristled brush as the plume. The actual party was a smash hit and, at its zenith, Oblong attired as Caesar was borne in on a litter surrounded by a dozen beautiful slave-girls feeding him grapes and libations. Needless to say everyone finished up in the pool.

The following day we were ordered up to Hong Kong and Stan and I thought we would escape 'the Pirates' but we were assured that we would be back in time. However while in Hong Kong in October I received a telegram from Mary to say that my mother had had a stroke, was extremely ill and was unlikely to recover. Oblong agreed that I should fly home immediately but, happily, by the time I arrived she was out of danger, although it was agreed that she would never be able to return home and would stay in a Nursing Home in Northam run by a Mrs Clark. This presented further problems as by this time my father was really very blind and not able to live at Croft alone. All this fell on Mary to organise and my father moved into the same nursing home so that they could be together. He was glad to be with my mother but at the same time hated being there with the loss of what little independence he had. My mother being out of danger, I returned to Hong Kong.

The ship was back in Singapore in November as we were due for a short refit and docking. We were also back in time for the show. The producers and also leading lights of the show were a couple called Wigg and when John Wigg was not doing his stuff as an Engineer Commander they lived Gilbert and Sullivan, travelling round the world with wicker baskets full of costumes, props and orchestral scores. They were very very good and John had a delightful tenor voice. We did 'Pirates' once in the Naval Base theatre – which was not air-conditioned and my moustache came unstuck with the sweat, much to everyone's amusement – and then three nights in the main theatre in Singapore which was air-conditioned. We had good houses and my policeman's lot was a happy one! My moustache stayed on and I didn't drop my truncheon.

In the midst of all this and before we went into dock we had an official visit and tour of the ship by Vice-Admiral Sir Desmond Dreyer the Flag Officer Commanding the Far East Fleet. The ship was looking pretty good and we received a nice signal afterwards which said:

> '1. I have heard nothing but good of the splendid work done by *Hartland Point* in support of the small ships and I was very glad to see for myself what you are doing.
> 2. Thank you for a most interesting visit.'

This was well-deserved praise for a Ship's Company that went out of its way to do a good job. Having up to four frigates or six minesweepers alongside for repairs or planned maintenance takes a lot of planning. As well as a weekly planning meeting with all heads of departments, I held a daily one to sort out priorities and any movements required. We had three cranes, one big one forward and two smaller ones aft, and ships had to be positioned correctly if lifts of machinery or stores were required. If you got this wrong you could hold up work right through the system, especially as ships in maintenance relied on *Hartland Point* for power supplies, compressed air and so forth. My daily meetings were 20 minutes well-spent and made people think ahead and about other departments besides there own. It was very interesting and enlightening to have a succession of ships alongside and one very quickly got to know which ships were well-run and which were not.

One morning about 10th December I was sitting happily in my cabin with the ship in dry dock when I was rung up by Bryan Durant, the Chief-of-Staff, who asked what I was doing. I replied that I wasn't doing anything much. He then said, 'Well you are now; you're to go as Naval Officer in Charge at Labuan this afternoon.' I asked, 'Where is Labuan', to which he replied, 'I'm not sure, but if you come up to my office straight away we'll find out'. I jumped into the car and shot up to HQ to find the Chief of Staff and Henry Leach, the Staff Officer Operations, poring over a chart.

It appeared that troubles with Indonesia and the taking over of the Shell Oil Refinery in Brunei by rebels needed immediate action to restore order. Troops and aircraft were being deployed and Labuan, which is an island off North Borneo and Brunei, was to be the base for unloading shipping and also the main airfield and Command Centre for the operation. I was to be the Naval Officer in Charge Victoria Harbour and was to sail with a small party of communications ratings in the cruiser, HMS *Tiger*, at six o'clock that evening. As a parting shot Admiral Durant said, 'Spend what you like'. In the meantime the C class Destroyer *Cavalier* was at Labuan with orders to secure the harbour and provide a communications link.

It is always difficult to know what to take and in the event I took a Wanchai umbrella, a pusser's zip grip and a .38 revolver. We all had khaki uniform and the communications ratings had portable radios and an Aldis Lamp plus Lanchesters, a type of improved Sten Gun. *Tiger* sailed at midnight complete with 42 Commando, the 1st Green Jackets, who had come down from Penang in 24 hours, and a regiment of Queen's Own Hussars equipped with Ferret armoured cars. I was lucky and was given the navigating officer's cabin back aft. Then it was full speed for Borneo. *Tiger* flew the flag of Rear Admiral Jack Scatchard, Flag Officer 2nd in Command FE Fleet, and her Captain was Peter Graham, an old friend of mine.

On the way the ship received a signal telling us to go to Miri to land the Green Jackets as the Oil Depot had been occupied by rebels. We arrived off Miri at first light on the 12th. The CO insisted on carrying out an assault landing using the ship's boats. I was sent for to come to the bridge and was asked what the beach gradient was. I had not the slightest idea, but the Admiral said that as I was the chap responsible for landing people I had better go ashore and find out. I thought that this sounded rather dangerous but I had no option, so, borrowing a tin hat, putting on my .38 and a lifejacket and equipped with a long bamboo pole to take soundings, I set off in the ship's whaler to find out.

The beach was fine with a gentle slope but, however, I had noticed some locals on the shore waving for me to come round the end of the jetty into the harbour. There I found a very substantial set of steps. Back on board I reported my findings but the CO insisted on the beach. Each soldier carried the most enormous pack besides his rifle and ammunition and as they jumped out of the boats about half of them overbalanced backwards to look like a lot of overturned turtles. Happily an inquisitive crowd of natives had arrived to see what was happening and quickly plunged into the water to pull the soldiers ashore. The second wave used the steps. So much for the assault landing... however, they quickly succeeded in restoring order in the oil depot and releasing the Europeans who had been confined to their houses.

At about 0900 we sailed for Labuan, arriving six hours later. On the way the Admiral said that I would never be able to do what was required of me on my own and that I should take his Secretary as my No.2, remarking that he would have 'bugger all to do if he stayed on board'. So that was how I acquired Lieutenant the Lord Rathdonald, an Irish peer and the biggest expert at scrounging that I had ever met. On landing we went straight away to the harbourmaster's office where Bill Black, CO of *Cavalier* had set up a small HQ. After a short hand over, *Cavalier* sailed for Singapore leaving me with my signals team and about a dozen Royal Marines. We had no camping equipment but the building was substantial and I decided that we should bed down there for the night. At about 2100 we realised that we were surrounded by a large number of not very friendly locals. I had already received a signal saying that 5 Marines had been killed and a troop of Ghurkas ambushed so that I was more than a little worried. Sailors and handguns are pretty lethal and not wishing to spark off a shooting match I took everyone's ammunition away and locked it up for the night. I have to say that I slept very little but by the morning the crowd had disappeared and all was well.

The official report (below) contains most of what happened so I shall add the things not included. On the first day my Sergeant rolled our commandeered Jeep into a monsoon ditch so no more transport. Ben Rathdonald found us adjoining houses for the whole of our little band, complete with cook amah and wash amah, and also a backyard full of chickens. This was a great relief. The Army had issued us with compo ration packs which were found, on opening, to contain only Christmas puddings.

Day two showed that we lacked room and visibility in the harbour master's office and I decided to have a wooden hut, to house us, built on the roof. Ben found a Chinese contractor whose workmen knocked up a sizeable hut in one go, taking not a single measurement and holding the pieces of timber with their toes and feet while sawing and planing with both hands. Also arriving to help came a most remarkable Australian, Major Franck, who was in charge of the Port Engineer Squadron which saw to the unloading of ships. He was tireless and appeared to do without sleep; when he felt tired he just lay down wherever he happened to be, put his cap under his head, slept for half an hour and was off again at full speed.

When *Albion* arrived a few days later Colin Madden, the Captain, invited me to lunch. In the course of our conversation I mentioned that I lacked transport and, to my delight, on the following morning I heard a great commotion and, looking out, saw one of *Albion*'s helicopters approaching with a Citroen 2CV suspended beneath. This was slipped outside our house and attached to the steering wheel was a bottle of Champagne and a note which said 'Happy Christmas from *Albion*'. We had wheels at last.

Labuan is a delightful island, an entrepôt, and at one time was important for its coalmines which were used to bunker ships. The mines run out under the sea but are no longer worked. There was a mixed population of Europeans, Chinese, Malays and indigenous natives. There are few roads in this part of the world and transport into the mainland jungle was by boat up the many rivers and creeks, in long slim canoes propelled at great speed by outboard motors. In Labuan there was a nursing order of nuns who were in great demand as midwives and, despite all the trouble and unrest going on all around, I could not dissuade them from going about their daily errands of mercy, travelling miles up river with no protection except their habits.

On Christmas day I went to the local Anglican Church. The congregation was representative of all the different races living on the island and on entry you were handed out books in English, Chinese or Malay. The service itself was a mixture of languages and when it came to the hymns everyone sang in their own tongue to the same tune. The church was packed and I have to say that it was one of the best services that I have ever attended. Being able to live together is what life is all about.

Above:
Jungle Jim and Jungle Mary. We had just watched the parang being made by a nearby blacksmith.

Below left:
Cdr Dickie Bird, Mary and Cdr John Tourney our Supply Officer in the jungle in Johore.

Above:
Andy Capp b'day cake made for me by the Bakery Staff in the main Galley

Left: I was fortunate in finding an Army Air Corp chum who took me up in his Auster and I was able to take a number of photos. HP has Lincoln and Carysfort berthed alongside for maintenance. We usually went to a buoy so that both sides of the ship could be used. I didn't believe in boat routines and we ran a continuous service with the boats of the ships alongside joining in .so that the usual wait for a boat was about ten minutes to fifteen minutes. Not too inconvenient.
Right:
These two coastal trading junks had just left Junk Harbour in Kowloon and were off to sea with all sail set. Junk harbour gave
shelter to some thousand junks.

HP wardroom set up a Roman night at the pool in the Naval Base which also had space for dancing and eating. We had given the place a make over with a triumphal arch made out of 40 gallon oil drums and a number of amphora and busts made out of Plaster of Paris by our dentist, Surgeon Lt Cdr Manning.

Above: 'Oblong' Caesar being born in on a litter. 'Dickie' Bird on left is a rather serious looking bearer. On the right and out of focus is Patsy le Blanc Smith, Caesar's wife.

Below: And of course, Slave Girls!

Above: As the instigator and organiser I believed I should be a Centurion. Sadly, around one in the morning, there was a slave riot and I was thrown into the pool where my cardboard armour went soggy! Authority lost. Caesar went the same way.

Below: Some more elegant Romans. Jack and Jonnette Wigg on the right.

Above: Chinese food stall Johore Bahru. The food was delicious but washing up usually was done in the nearest monsoon ditch.

Below: Hartland Point moored off the Naval Base, Singapore 1962

Above: Sad Day! Amhurst sails from Singapore in the rain - taking Mary back to England.

Below: The Government Rest House in Johore Bahru where we lived during Mary's visit.

```
                           ACTION
FDJA 065    P/L   JRB   TOR 2343Z      12 DEC 62
                            0743Z
DIST. STAFF X1 2 3 8 9 C1 4 5 B1 M1 S1 2 4 6 R1 WR
ACTION. CAPTS SEC.  NOIC
_____
DEFERRED   110935Z
FROM       FOCINCFEF
TO         TERROR, TIGER, CAVALIER, ALERT, WOODBRIDGE HA
           LINCOLN, CAPRICE, LOCH LOMOND, HARTLAND POINT,
           MULL OF KINTYRE
INFO       CINC FE, FO2 FEF, COMBRITBOR.
_____
UNCLASSIFIED. FOLLOWING ARE ADMINISTRATIVE ARRANGEMENTS FOR
DETACHED NAVAL PERSONNEL SERVING IN BORNEO.
2. COMMAND. ON ARRIVAL NOIC VICTORIA HARBOUR IS TO ASSUME
DUTY OF OFFICER IN CHARGE OF NAVAL PARTY ALFA COMPRISING ALL
NAVAL PERSONNEL ON DETACHED DUTY ON SHORE IN NORTH BORNEO
TERRITORIES INCLUDING OFFICERS SERVING ON STAFF OF COMBRITBOR
MAINTENANCE PARTY IN BRUNEI TOWN, COMMUNICATION RATINGS AND
R.M. PERSONNEL SERVING UNDER THE N.D.A. PROPER SHIPS ARE TO
DRAFT RATINGS TO TERROR FOR NAVAL PARTY ALFA. Q.R. AND A.I.
ARTICLE 1906 REFERS: APPOINTMENTS FOR OFFICERS WILL BE ISSUED
TERROR FORWARD NOMINAL LIST OF NAVAL PARTY ALFA TO NOIC
VICTORIA HARBOUR SOONEST.
3. NOIC DEPLOY NAVAL PARTY ALFA AS REQUIRES COMBRITBOR.
4. DISCIPLINE. NAVAL PARTY ALFA TO BE REGARDED AS FORMED
NAVAL UNIT ON DETACHED DUTY FROM TERROR.
5. PAY. TERROR RESPONSIBLE FOR NAVAL PARTY ALFA.
6. MAIL. MAIL FROM U.K. SHOULD CONTINUE TO PROPER SHIPS FOR
PRESENT. BEING FORWARDED THROUGH B.F.M.O. SINGAPORE TO QUOTE
NAVAL PARTY ALFA, C/O B.F.P.O. 605 UNQUOTE. NOIC VICTORIA
HARBOUR TO ARRANGE ONWARD DELIVERY.
7. THESE INSTRUCTIONS SUPERSEDE FEF. 753/19S OF 10 DEC WHICH
PLACED NAVAL PARTY ALFA UNDER ELECTRICAL LIEUTENANT (R) W.
EDWARDS OF MAINTENANCE PARTY IN BRUNEI TOWN. NOIC VICTORIA
HARBOUR PASS TO THIS OFFICER.
                     ACTION 110935Z DEC 62
```

This was my Brief for going to Brunei and Labuan.
COMBRITBOR is Service language for the Commander British Forces in Borneo.
FOCINCFEF is the Commander in Chief Far East Fleet.

From: Brigadier J.B.A. GLENNIE, DSO, OBE

Headquarters
BRITISH FORCES COMMANDER BORNEO
British Forces Post Office 605

Telephone: BRUNEI 624

Reference: DO/JG/8

20 December 1962.

Dear Johnson,

On handing over command to General Walker I would like to thank you and all your staff for your superb efforts in handling all HM Ships and Army and Merchant Shipping in a somewhat chaotic situation. I am afraid I have not had time to see you as often as I would have liked and that due to shortage of Army staff you have had to function without much help from us.

I hope we shall be able to give you more help with the stepping up of our command and staff.

The very best of luck to you during the rest of your stay.

Yours sincerely,

Jack Glennie

NOIC – Commander C.A. JOHNSON, OBE, DSC, RN.,
Victoria Harbour,
LABUAN.

*I was delighted to receive this letter from Brigadier Glennie.
He had no easy task himself, and chaotic it was too.*

It was a most interesting experience and everyday I would go up to the Headquarters at the airfield to find out the general picture and to report my goings-on. The airfield was at its runway limit for handling the heavily-loaded Beverly and Hastings transport aircraft and one of the Hastings ran off the end of the runway into a swamp, never to be recovered while I was there. With Ben Rathdonald's help and a very hardworking little team of communicators we seemed to keep our bit of the show on the road pretty well and I like to think that we did a good job. However, I was not sorry to leave for Singapore on 4th of January, having been relieved by a chap called Venables.

Back in Singapore it was a matter of getting *Hartland Point* out of her refit and ready to sail for Hong Kong on 10th January, leaving the car to be shipped home. I was to be relieved in Hong Kong on 13th February 1963 and flew back home to Stanstead to be greeted by Mary, Jenny and a lot of snow. It was good to be home but I had enjoyed my time in *Hartland Point* – not a beautiful ship but a jolly useful one.

COPY The Naval Officer in Charge,
Victoria Harbour
LABUAN

The Flag Officer, Commander in Chief, FAR EAST FLEET. Singapore
(Copy to The Commander in Chief Far Eastern Forces)

4th January 1963

Sir,
Report of Proceedings

I have the honour to report on my activities as Naval Officer in Charge, Victoria Harbour since taking up this appointment on Wednesday 12th December 1962 until my relief by Lieutenant Commander J.R. Venables, Royal Navy, on 4th January 1963.

2. I arrived at Labuan at 1500 in HMS *Tiger* and straight way went to the harbour master's office where the Commanding Officer of HMS *Cavalier* had set up a small headquarters for the control of the port. A V/S station had been established on the Signal Tower and in addition thee was an R/T link between the tower and Labuan Airport as the Royal Navy had accepted the responsibility for its defence there being no RAF Regiment available. HMS *Woodbridge Haven* arrived at 1600 and it was decided that her complement would not be able to fulfil this commitment. In consequence I asked *Tiger* to land her Royal Marines for airfield guard duty. This they did until they were released by the Station Commander on Monday, 16th December when they returned to Singapore.

3. *Cavalier* having re-embarked her miscellaneous parties sailed at 2000 for Singapore, leaving Woodbridge Haven as Guard Ship and communications link. She was ordered to provide guards for the Shell Oil Jetty and Installation and also armed men for boat patrols in the local Marine Department boats.

4. My party consisted of myself, Lieutenant the Lord Rathdonald and eight communications ratings. We accommodated ourselves in the Signal Tower.

5. It was clear from the start that my main task was to establish priorities for the handling of ships and cargos with the object of causing the minimum accumulation of ships waiting to unload. In this I was helped most ably by the harbourmaster, Captain S.K.Young and Major R.Franck, Royal Australian Engineers, the Port Commandant in charge of Army movement.

6. Labuan is the entrepot for this coast and has one good jetty with good access and go down space completely adequate in normal times for the working of the port. However it can only accommodate one ocean going merchant ship on the outside of the wharf and shallow craft on the inside, the latter provided there is not an onshore wind blowing at the time of berthing. Normally no movements are undertaken at night as there are no tugs. However by working the port round the clock and assisted by fine weather it was possible to handle all the ships with only minor disruption of local trade.

7. One of the principal difficulties was caused by the absence of any cranes in the port, the only one being a small 5 ton crane mounted on a lighter with insufficient lift to reach the upper deck of a destroyer or the jetty, consequently the arrival of Woodbridge Haven, HMS Alert and HMS Blackpool with vehicles on the upper deck provided a slight problem. However the Straits Steamship Company's Kenynoac was berthed on the wharf and the Master made her derricks available to unload Woodbridge Haven and Alert while Wave Sovereign provided the same service fir Blackpool. The difficulty was resolved by the arrival f a 12 ton crane in the LCT Ardennes on 14th December.

8. The War Department chartered LST Empire Kittiwake and the Army manned LCTs *Ardennes* and *Arromanches* all arrived on the 14th and while the Kittiwake discharged her vehicles and stores by derrick, the heavier vehicles in the LCTs were unloaded over the beach at Ramsey Point where the beach itself was firm and had a good exit. However the gradient was too steep for the $1/2$ ton vehicles to wade as the entry was too steep and they were none of them waterproofed.

9. It was fortunate that when *Albion* arrived on the 15th December there was available in the port a flat topped lighter to act as a catamaran for the LCTs which took part of her deck park of vehicles ashore. Because of the slowness of *Albion*'s one and only crane, the off loading of vehicles was a painfully slow business and the remainder had to remain embarked until 17th December when operational commitments allowed *Albion* to anchor off Labuan for the night. By this time our LCT fleet had been augmented by a Z lighter borrowed from Brunei and for which there was no skipper. Captain Mack of the RFA Fort Charlotte volunteered his services until the proper skipper could be found.

10. During this first week ships were unloaded with remarkable speed and efficiency by Number Ten Port Squadron Royal Engineers working day and night, however by 19th December the initial rush had passed and the moment to moment operations began to turn into something resembling a planned programme. It was decided provisionally that the Brigade Maintenance Area should remain in Labuan and as the transport aircraft began to run out of engine hours more and more reliance was put on shipping.

11. A better hard having been found at the other side of the town, it became possible to instate a roll- on roll- off supply service to Brunei using an LCT and this has continued, being entirely satisfactory, though it needed a little persuasion at the start before the idea caught on.

12. During all this time Woodbridge Haven provided invaluable service as a communications link and also in providing armed men to go on nightly patrols in boats supplied and manned by the local police and Marine Department. A type 691 VHF set was installed in the shore Signal Tower and this has proved invaluable in working the ships in Harbour and with *Albion* when operating in Brunei Bay. Other communications have been based on the local Post Office telephone and radio telephone which has operated most efficiently throughout the emergency and without which operations would just not have happened.

13. For really smooth working of the port it has been found necessary to have a signal station and a temporary lean-to type office has been thrown up on the roof of the Marine Department and Customs Building.

14. Apart from controlling the daily movements of shipping in the port the NOIC has had to cope with a variety of things including arranging for the repair and slipping of boats chartered and damaged in operations around Brunei, organising boat patrols, fielding Naval officers and ratings stranded at Labuan on their way to or from their ships, collecting and distributing mail and stores for HM Ships and RFAs, arranging passages for RN and RM personnel and being a judge at the Labuan New Years Day Water Sports.

15. While nothing new or revolutionary has come to light as a result of the operation as it affects shipping, a number of things have been forgotten since World War II and many lessons can be relearned. To remark on the more important ones which apply to any brushfire type of operation:
(a) NOIC It is most desirable that a Naval Officer of sufficient standing be appointed as NOIC of any port which is suddenly called upon to handle naval ships, Military cargoes and RFAs. He should be senior to the Port Commandant and work with him and the Harbourmaster so as to obtain the harmonious working of the port. He will need an assistant.
(b) Communications It is essential that there should be an agreed joint service communications outfit for operations such as this. NOIC was dependant on the services of a guard ship for communications outside the port area, this is an uneconomical use of a warship and is not satisfactory as it will be rare if the ship carrying out such a function can be berthed alongside, consequently signals have to be re-passed by light or by hand. An UHF harbour intercom net has proved invaluable. It is suggested that suitable caravan/trailer type vehicles be fitted out as mobile communication links with a cryptographic capability and included in the initial vehicle load.
(c) The Army's Navy The LCTs run and manned by the Army were splendid and did a most useful job of work as did the LSTs on charter. They suffered from one important weakness – Communications. It was unfortunate that the Army LCTs had landed their UHF radios in Singapore Dockyard for repair and modernisation but regardless of this they are not able to compete properly and the LSTs being Merchant Navy manned had only merchant ship communications with all its known limitations. For an operation such as this, all military owned and chartered craft must be able to work on a common naval communications net while proceeding to and working in the theatre of operations. In addition they should be fitted with R/T and have a V/S capability. It is strongly recommended that a small complement of RN communication ratings be placed on board all such vessels when employed in combined operations.

(d) Off Loading Vehicles from a Commando Ship It was by chance that a suitable lighter existed at Labuan to enable other craft to berth on *Albion* to off-load her many and assorted vehicles. Lighters of the size required are rare and it is for consideration that some form of inflatable and portable catamaran be developed and carried in Commando ships for this very purpose.

(e) Waterproofing of Vehicles This seems to be a forgotten art, but when operating in areas of minimal port facilities much greater flexibility for landing vehicles would have resulted and a lot of time saved if waterproofing had been carried out.

(f) Naval Transport Soldiers and airmen when cast ashore are either accompanied by or followed immediately by their vehicles and life is geared to everyone having his own. Beggars can't be choosers and to borrow one is extremely difficult. There seems no reason why the Royal Navy ashore should not be on wheels with the best of them and provision should be made accordingly.

(g) Port Intelligence It did not appear that we knew as much about the ports and beaches in the theatre as we might have done and because the ports were British run in the first place all the information required must have been known by someone. It would seem that some buffing up of the organisation for collecting and disseminating this information is required and this information should be in one handy book for the user.

(h) Statistics During the period covered by this report some 2000 vehicles and 3,500 tons of military stores have passed through the port. This excludes troops, their kit and stores pre-loaded into vehicles.

SUMMARY OR LESSONS LEARNT
(a) An NOIC is required early in any port required to handle a military force.
(b) Communications. A pre-packed communications outfit with crypto is required. This could be housed in a trailer or caravan.
(c) Army Run Craft. All military run craft must be able to work on the same communications net as the Navy. Naval signalmen should be embarked.
(d) Off Loading Vehicles from Commando Ships. Some type of ship borne inflatable catamaran is required to enable lighters and other craft to berth alongside.
(e) Waterproofing of Vehicles. This should be done if there is any likelihood of beaches being used to disembark. It should be able to be done on passage to the scene of operations.
(f) Naval Transport. Naval parties deployed ashore should have their own transport as a matter of course.
(g) Port Intelligence. More up to date and accurate information on port capabilities is required in a hand form for the user.

I have the Honour to be,
Sir,

(C.J.A.Johnson)
COMMANDER
Royal Navy

CHAPTER 16

Senior Officers' War Course
GREENWICH
1963

Mary met me at Stanstead with Jenny. We spent a few days in the Pedders' flat in Chelsea and went to see both boys at Pangbourne, David having gone there in September 1962. We also went down to Instow to see my parents.

I had been appointed to Greenwich for the Senior Officers' War Course, a six-month course for Captains and Commanders. It ran each week from 1000 Monday to noon Friday, with work in the evenings, which required living in the College. We needed somewhere to live and were offered Naval married quarters, at Littlehampton, which had belonged to the Naval Air Station at Ford, now closed down. It was good for weekends.

Having enjoyed sailing GP 14s at Singapore, I decided to have a boat of my own and bought an Albacore (15 ft One Design). There was a good class at the Arun YC. We did pretty well in it and, with Mike crewing, came second in the Southern Area Championships.

Selection for promotion to Captain in June brought great relief and rejoicings. My parents were both delighted too. I was to go to The Admiralty, starting in October.

We quite wanted to buy a house in the Emsworth area but couldn't sell Croft while my parents were still alive, nor was it mine to sell. We made several visits to Instow as my mother was not at all well.

Mike joined BRNC Dartmouth as a Cadet in September and we started looking for a house in London, to move there before going to The Admiralty. It was not easy but we eventually found a hiring in Golders Green – a pretty good house belonging to David Douglas-Morris, brother of my term-mate Kenneth, at 556 Finchley Road and decided to take it and move in the same month.

We discovered that they sailed Merlin Rockets on the Welsh Harp so we joined the RAF Sailing Club (which was affiliated to the Wembley SC), sold the Albacore and ordered a new Merlin. It was a restricted class and I chose a Star Rocket design.

The house at Finchley Road was separated from the main road by a wide verge with trees. It had four bedrooms and a decent garden at the back. A short walk took you to Golders Park and then on up to Hampstead Heath – ideal for Jenny – and also only a short walk to Golders Green underground and a quick trip on the Northern Line to Whitehall.

It was quite an upheaval leaving Littlehampton, getting Mike off to Dartmouth and David to Pangbourne and moving my things out of Greenwich. It had been an interesting course but now it was time to move on.

CHAPTER 17

The Admiralty and Ministry of Defence LONDON 2nd October 1963 to 10th September 1965

I had been appointed Assistant Director of the Naval Tactical and Weapons Policy Directorate in the Admiralty and my Director was Captain Dick Janvrin. Along with Naval Plans, DNTWP was in the hierarchy of policy-making.

I found that it was a bit like going back to school after a long summer holiday and meeting all my friends. Most of my opposite numbers had been Cadets or Midshipmen at the same time as I; some had progressed faster and some more slowly. My Deputy Director was Teddy Gueritz from *Barham* days. Brian Longbottom and Peter House were there and, across the passage, in Plans were Peter Ashmore, John Roxburgh, Martin Lucy, John Harkness and Ted Lee. The Deputy Chief of Naval Staff and our joint boss was Rear Admiral Peter Hill-Norton, who had been my mentor during Sub-Lieutenants' courses. I was to relieve Teddy Archdale who said that he had never quite understood what he was supposed to be doing. This didn't surprise me in the least.

My office was right over the front entrance to The Admiralty and opposite The Admiralty Board Room, a magnificent room which had hardly changed in the last 300 years, beautifully panelled and with an ornate wind vane mechanically linked to the vane on the cupola on top of the Admiralty building. In the corner were the handles for working a semaphore when, before the days of telegraphy, Their Lordships could signal to the fleet anchored at the Nore or Spithead. During my first days there I was taken to meet the First Sea Lord, Admiral Sir Caspar John, and the First Lord, Lord Carrington. I also met the other heads of Directorate. Both my Directorate and Plans had the authority to call on any of the others such as Air Warfare, Communications, Underwater Warfare, and so forth, for technical advice and briefs.

My particular responsibility was for Amphibious Warfare, Air Support and Helicopters. I was also the Naval member on the NATO committee for standardisation, which took in not only weapons but also more basic things like screw threads, the British being one of the worst offenders with some 17 different sizes of thread. The first real task given to me was to produce a review of our amphibious capabilities and show how, if necessary, they could be improved.

Mary and I seemed hardly to have got ourselves settled in the house, and I in my new job, when my father rang to say that my mother had had another little stroke but, having been to Instow just before moving house, I decided not to go down just yet. Sadly, my mother died on 27th November. I got leave and we went down to Instow for the funeral, which was in All Saints Chapel. Mike came up from Dartmouth. My mother had wished to be cremated and the only crematorium in Devon at that time was at Torquay, which is where we went, taking my father with us. The Chapel in Instow was packed and all went well but it was a sad occasion and a terrible strain on my father. He did not want to stay in the nursing home but nor could he return to Croft and he agreed to come and live with us in London.

I drove the car back, leaving Mary the unenviable job of sorting out Croft, shutting it up and bringing my father up to London by train. It was several days later that I went to Paddington Station to meet them. My father put on a brave face but he was utterly devastated by the whole affair and started to go downhill. We were able to give him quite a nice room at the top of the stairs and Mary arranged for help during the day, including one nice young man who declared that he was an anarchist and I thought we should not employ him.

After Christmas my father suffered a couple of little strokes and he died on 2nd February 1964. In accordance with his wishes, he was cremated with minimum ceremony at the Golders Green Crematorium. Later we put up a plaque on the north wall of Instow Churchyard to commemorate both my parents, thus starting a fashion which quickly caught on. One of the consequences of all this was that, for the first time in our lives, we owned a house. At that time it was probably worth £1,800-£2,000 and we decided to keep it and find a tenant but first it had to be cleared of family things, refurbished and generally made lettable.

Back at the Admiralty it was all change. Mountbatten, who was Chief of the Defence Staff, had decided that there should be much more unity at the top and that the Admiralty, War Office and Air Ministry should lose their independence and, not before time, become the Ministry of Defence, with the very modern Board of Trade building becoming the shared home of the three services. The more senior bits were to be housed there while the rest would be mixed in around the old buildings, according to their specialist functions, so that members of the three services would work alongside their opposite numbers. On top of all this there was to be a smallish Defence Staff with a largely coordinating role.

The move was a highly complicated piece of planning, to be completed to a strict timetable over about three weeks. It went with surprisingly few hiccups. The new building was divided like layers of cake. It had six floors and the greater your importance the higher you were housed. On the sixth floor were the Chief of Defence Staff, the heads of the three services and their political bosses – the Minister of Defence and the Secretaries of State for the three services, together with their top Civil Servants (the Mandarins) – and the Vice Chiefs of Staff. On the fifth floor were the Deputy Chiefs and Assistant Chiefs of Staff. Both Naval Plans (DNP) and Naval Tactical and Weapons Policy (DNTWP), together with Army and Air equivalents, were also on this floor.

There were also a number of changes at the top: Admiral Sir David Luce became CNS, replacing Caspar John; Vice-Admiral John Frewen became VCNS; Rear Admiral Frank Hopkins became DCNS; and we had a new Assistant Chief of Naval Staff, Rear Admiral Michael Pollock. In our own division Captain Terry Lewin replaced Dick Janvrin as Director of DNTWP. I was indeed lucky as I could not have had a nicer team of bosses. I also found myself with some additional jobs and a PA.

My new jobs were pretty wide-ranging. I had to take under my wing the policy for the Defence against Nuclear, Chemical and Biological Warfare and also to be one of the Chiefs of Staff's Briefing Team, sometimes referred to – more in hope than anything else – as the Three Wise Men. The other two were John Owen, a Royal Marine from Plans, and Alistair Jaffray, a Civil Servant and Assistant Secretary to the Board. As the Briefing Team we had to provide written briefs for the Defence Committee Meetings, Inter-Service Meetings and the Overseas and Commonwealth Defence Committee, chaired by the Prime Minister. In addition we had to provide answers to Parliamentary Questions, which involved not only providing the answer to the written question but also answers to anticipated supplementary questions.

The trouble with this was that things didn't start to happen until about five o'clock in the evening and then there would be a flurry of activity, finding answers, getting agreement and then getting it typed up. I had a PA called Jean who was quite good but didn't like working late as she had a husband. However, in emergency Terry Lewin would allow me to use his PA, a gorgeous redhead called Betty who had no such ties. She could type at an incredible speed and in a matter of minutes could make a mass of scrawlings on bits of paper, cut and stuck together, into something that looked really well-prepared. Even so it meant that it was very difficult to get away before seven o'clock and frequently later.

Another task was to write speeches for the CNS and VCNS, though one always left the giver of the speech or lecture to put in humour where required. John Frewen was excellent and memorised everything, however detailed, but you had to be jolly careful that your facts were right.

Another side to the PQs was the very much more detailed business done by Select Committees of Parliament, particularly when it came to getting the Defence Estimates approved. This is an annual game played by all the various Government Ministries against the Treasury. The Whitehall Mandarins regard it as a game of chess and, depending upon the success of your moves, you may at the end of play get most of what you asked for. Your player is, of course, the Member of Parliament responsible for your particular department. In Defence it is the Minister of Defence who is responsible for the overall amount allocated to the Armed Forces but that has to be fought for by the Ministers of each of the three services. In our case it was the First Lord, who at this particular time was Lord Carrington, a charming and clever chap who had been a Subaltern in the Guards Armoured Brigade during WW II but who didn't know one end of a ship from the other.

The guardians of the rules and the principal players are the top Civil Servants, the Secretaries and Under-Secretaries. They all had double firsts from Oxbridge and at meetings would throw in little jokes in Latin to remind the common soldier, sailor or airman that they were very clever. Our task was to put the minister in to bat with a good grasp of what it was hoped to achieve. He was supported by his Under-Secretary and a little team of people like myself, armed with a mass of supporting papers from which you could dig out vital bits and pass little notes forward to your batsman.

I was introduced to an essential 'play' in the game called 'the Wedge'. This is something that you put in your budget, fully justified and costed, for example an additional frigate, which after a long battle with the Treasury you are prepared to cut so as to save money, knowing all the time that you didn't need it in the first place and at the end of the day you would come away with what you really wanted for the running of the Navy for a further year. I think that it is highly probable that every ministry in Whitehall had a 'wedge'. For successful wedge-playing it was essential that no one outside the team, especially neither of the other two services, knew what your wedge was and when, or even if, you were playing it. It all sounds rather childish but it worked. In that particular year we had Lord Carrington all briefed up and then there was a Cabinet reshuffle; he went and was replaced by Lord Jellico, so it was back to the beginning again.

Taking up far more time and energy was a battle being fought between the Navy and the Air Force for quite enormous amounts of money. The Air Force had put in a requirement for a new long-range attack bomber and, indeed, the prototype of the TSR2 was actually built and shortly to begin flying trials. During his time as CNS, Caspar John, a very distinguished aviator, had set his sights on building a new supercarrier on a par with the Americans' CVA01. Every effort was to be made to get it into the Defence Estimates and the new CNS, Admiral Luce, was equally determined that it should succeed.

Our team was led by Henry Leach, head of Naval Plans. I was told to come up with some scenarios to show how vital it was to have naval carrier-borne air power, while at the other end of the fifth floor the RAF were producing scenarios to show that with the TSR2 they could reach any likely target more quickly and effectively than carriers could ever do. My best scenario was the defence of the Falkland Islands from invasion by Argentina. However, when this was submitted to the Foreign Office for approval as a possible situation, we were told in no uncertain terms that the United Kingdom had been trying to get rid of the Falklands to the Argentines for some years and that in no way would we try to defend them. [I wonder whether Terry Lewin and Lord Carrington remembered this in 1982 when Terry (then Admiral and Chief of the Defence Staff) and Peter Carrington (then Foreign Secretary) went to war over them during Margaret Thatcher's Government. Peter Carrington resigned soon after the start.]

On another occasion the Navy scored a great moral triumph over the Air Force when it was discovered that, in another island defence scenario, on the maps used for the presentation of their case they had physically moved a particular island some 200 miles closer to their nearest operating base so that it would be within range of their aircraft.

Though assisted by Ray Lygo in producing lots of facts and figures as to what our new carrier would be able to do, I thought that the whole thing was stupid for the following reasons; first, the proposal was for one carrier only but, in fact, three would be needed in order to be sure of having one available whenever required; second, we had not the manpower to man it without denuding the rest of the Fleet (I think the complement was to be 4,000 including aircrew); and, third, it was enormously expensive, requiring a huge increase in Defence spending which was totally unwarranted. This was an unthinkable view to take and none of my mentors would give it a second's support, although I did have two allies.

One who supported me publicly was the Director of Army Plans, Brigadier FitzAlan Howard, who was a delightful chap and who realised that, if either or both the Air and Navy proposals got the green light, there would be nothing left in the pot for the Army. The other was Vice-Admiral Frank Hopkins who, as Deputy Chief of Staff, was also the senior serving Fleet Air Arm officer. He told me that privately he agreed with me but publicly he could not be seen to be letting the side down. I used to have lunch with Geoffrey Thatcher once or twice a week. He was Secretary to the First Sea Lord and I tried hard to get him to put my doubts to the great man but the answer was always the same, i.e. that Sir David Luce would have to resign if the bid for CVA01 were withdrawn and this he would not do.

Happily for this long-running saga, which had caused, amongst other things, a number of very late nights at the office, the whole thing ran into the buffers when, in October 1964, Sir Alec Douglas-Home lost the election to Labour. Harold Wilson was elected with a majority of four, Denis Healey became the new Minister of Defence, both projects were thrown out of the window and a new Defence Review was ordered.

Going back in time to the domestic front... We had gone down to Instow during the Easter leave period and found a lot of things to be done in Croft before it could be let and, in particular, we found a massive infestation of woodworm. The house had to be treated with Rentokil and, while I was back in London, Mary and David slept out on the veranda for several nights while it was done. Croft was later let to the MOD as a hiring, which seemed to work pretty well.

Also in the spring we took delivery of my new boat, a Merlin Rocket built by Wyche & Coppock; its number was 1666. It was a Star Rocket design so we call the boat *Betelgeuse*. Having joined the Welsh Harp Sailing Association via the RAF's membership, we took it down to the Club for launching. Being brand new it drew an admiring crowd so, having got it into the water and round to the jetty, I stepped on board and immediately capsized. I had never sailed a Merlin before and had no idea how tippy they were. However, it was the first capsize of many and Mary and I took a little while to get the hang of the beast. There were many other excitements as we got used to sailing on such a small stretch of water where, to be competitive, a spinnaker would be hoisted on a leg of 200 yards or less. We got pretty good in the end but at that time no one had wetsuits and the water was cold. Perhaps it took up too many of our weekends but London was pretty dead on a Sunday.

We were, of course, well-placed to nip down to Pangbourne to see David, who really wasn't enjoying it much, but he too liked London. We found ourselves quite popular as a place for people to come and stay, though I was against having any long-term lodgers as I did not wish to get tied down. Mark Morris was with us for a bit, as was Jane Edgcumbe, Mireille Constant, Sally Bartlett, Beatrice Fourcade and others. Beatrice was studying Anglo-Saxon and couldn't understand why we couldn't help her with her work.

Granny Bull came to stay several times and it was a quick flick round the North Circular to Loughton to see Hester and Rowland. We also had one disastrous visit from my Godmother, Elsie Piggott. We had taken her to the theatre and on our return we could not get into the house. Burglars were actually in there and had bolted the front door; they made their escape while we were wondering what had gone wrong. Though they left a lot of stuff lying on the floor and dropped in the garden, they still got away with a number of nice things, including several family miniatures, a pair of silver candlesticks and a very pretty 17th century porringer. We have always thought it was because we had taken our nice bits and pieces to be valued for insurance purposes and someone in the business had passed on a list of what we had to the local burglars. It was a sad affair as the things were irreplaceable but we were able to buy a dining room table and eight chairs, when the insurance company paid up, which have served us well ever since.

Hampstead Heath was a super place for walks and Mary would take Jenny there every day. There she met a good friend in Helen Ostler, who was blind but who walked on the Heath to give her super guide-dog a bit of freedom and exercise. In fact we had quite a good social life with friends at the MOD, my cousin Charlie Wainman who had a flat in Eaton Square, the Shirley-Beavanses at Much Hadham and the Taits and MacIntoshes in Chelsea.

The only person whom we never got close to was Terry Lewen. He ran two separate lives: he had a house in Kent, a wife who did not like the Navy and a handicapped son. Whatever the situation, he left the office no later than six-thirty and that was it. Having said that, he was tremendous to work for and always ready to delegate and let you get on with your job. He had a brain like a computer, aided by a photographic memory, which was quite extraordinary. He worked at lightning speed and could run rings round his peers, helped always by the remarkable Betty, his PA.

We also had good friends in the Thatchers. Geoffrey had bought an old Gosport Ferry and had had it towed round to Putney where, by great ingenuity and hard work, they had turned it into a very desirable floating home in which they lived for next to nothing. I think that their biggest single expenditure was the £600 that they paid for the old ferry.

For my part, the only break during the often hectic working day was lunch. About once a week I went for a pub lunch with Geoff Thatcher at the Sherlock Holmes but, more often than not, I would have it in the MOD or old Admiralty restaurant which was quicker and cheaper and gave me time, if the weather was nice, to go for a quick walk in St James's Park or along the Embankment. If the mood took me, I would go exploring. I had noticed that there were a number of unmarked doors in the basement of the MOD which led into tunnels containing masses of wires, pipes and so forth, linking the various buildings in Whitehall. Going down into these took me all over the place and I found myself coming up in the Foreign Office, War Office or wherever. Though security was tight and you couldn't enter any of these buildings by the front door without showing your pass, there was no check on this little underground world and it was quite fun to walk out through the front door of some strange building and discover where it was that you had come to the surface. In the many times that I did this I never met another soul, though of course the maintenance teams must have had a map and inspected the tunnels regularly.

Earlier on in 1964 I had had to work out a real live problem. In Southern Rhodesia Ian Smith had declared Independence and there was rioting in Salisbury. The Government wanted to know urgently whether it would be possible to fly a battalion of troops into the country by helicopter from ships in the Indian Ocean. As the chap with the Joint Operations chair, I got the job. As always the answer was required by yesterday and I had to call on all my contacts to try and get an answer which, in effect, was 'Yes, but. . . .' The trouble was that to get the range the numbers carried in each Wessex helicopter made it a very risky thing to undertake, especially if there were to be any resistance to our soldiers on landing, as each wave of helicopters could not carry a viable force. On these occasions the Chief of the Defence Staff likes to put on a positive show to avoid the criticism that the Taxpayer is putting up all this money and yet when you are asked to do a simple task you cannot do it. In actual fact the troubles were political, not military, and took a long time and much anguish to resolve.

My study into our amphibious capability had gone through pretty well and had thrown up some interesting facts. One which I felt pretty strongly about from my brief experience as NOIC Labuan was the fact that the Army had considerably more Landing Craft than the Navy. In fact they were running a sizeable little maritime force of their own, which appeared to be under no one's operational control. My chums in Army Plans knew nothing about it – 'Something to do with the Sappers', they said. I arranged to call on the Chief Engineer, a General who had his office at the opposite end of our floor. He was very nice about it and said that it was something that they had acquired at the end of WW II. He wasn't sure why they needed it and threw in the fact that, in their budget, they were planning and had had approval to build five new and rather large ships. These were in fact the Sir Lancelot Class of Landing Ship of some 5,000 tons each.

I explained all this to John Frewen, who told me to write a paper about it. This I did, having managed to get a copy of the plans and specifications out of an unsuspecting Army Department. [In the MOD no one wears uniform so that there is nothing to distinguish you as Navy, Army or whatever. Thus, provided you could find out who looked after what, you could walk into the appropriate office and say that so-and-so wanted to have a look at this 'whatever' urgently and walk out with the appropriate docket, take a copy and give it back with profuse thanks.]

My paper proposed that these very adequate ships should become part of our Amphibious Force and would complement the two new Landing Ships (Dock), *Fearless* and *Intrepid*, that were about to join the Fleet. The staff in the MOD gave my proposals a fair wind, though made a fuss about the manning commitment, but in Bath the constructors and others put up all sorts of objections because (a) they hadn't designed them and (b) they were being built to Merchant Navy standards. The arguments for and against rumbled on but I was delighted to learn, about a month after I left the MOD, that it had been agreed that they would be taken on to the Naval strength but manned by the Royal Fleet Auxiliary – not the best solution but a very satisfactory one. They played a vital role in the recapture of the Falklands and in many other operations around the world and they and their replacements continue to do so today. The LSL Sir Galahad, lost in the Falklands, has been replaced by a new and better one so I feel that in all this I got something right.

It was in October 1964 that Labour came to power under Harold Wilson. Denis Healey took over as Minister of Defence and a very nice young MP, John Mallalieu, became Secretary of State for the Navy. Like me, he would never take the lift to the fifth floor and always ran up the stairs – one of the few opportunities for taking exercise that one got. I enjoyed my briefing sessions with Denis Healey very much. He had had a distinguished career in the Army during WW II and had studied military affairs ever since. He was interested to get to the bottom of things and you could be sure of a searching and intelligent quizzing every time you were summoned. He had a routine of lying on his couch in his office for about an hour after lunch each day and you were normally called in at about three o'clock, by which time he had thought through exactly what he wanted of you.

I had a succession of meetings with him concerning the replacement for the now scrapped TSR2. We were again involved in a wrangle with the RAF, who wished to purchase the F111 from America. It was a new breed of attack bomber with swing wings and a good internal bomb load which, it was claimed, it could carry at high speed and high altitude over a long range. It could also be equipped to carry out low-level ground attack missions, carrying a variety of rockets or bombs – on the face of it a good all-round aircraft. However, from the Navy's point of view, it was a non-starter as it was too big and heavy to operate from carriers.

What the Navy wanted, and indeed needed, was a new low-level ground or anti-ship attack aircraft, capable of carrying a varied weapon load over a good range and able to be adapted to operate from the deck of a British carrier. The trouble was that the number of aircraft needed by the Navy would not justify a production run and so it was essential that the RAF had the same aircraft. We wanted an aircraft already turned down by the RAF, the Buccaneer. Compared with the F111 it was a solid, conventional, low-tech aircraft but it would do the job. How could we win?

By luck I attended a presentation given by RAF Plans on the F111 to demonstrate how they would use this aircraft. During this, someone from the manufacturer showed a film of the prototype of this aircraft in action. It was all very impressive and it was only sometime later that I remembered that the film showed that, when the F111 was used in the ground-attack role, this aircraft had its wings extended as in the landing and take-off mode, because all the weaponry was hung in pods under the wings. This must surely mean that the plane could not fly at anywhere near its designed and much vaunted speed when used in this role. It was on the ground-attack role that the RAF had made their case for having this very expensive plane. I went to my air adviser, Ray Lygo, who agreed with my assessment and couldn't think why no one had raised this before.

With Frank Hopkins's permission, I arranged a day to see Denis Healey to put our case. He was convinced and subsequently sent for the Air staff to explain. They were adamant that they were correct but, to resolve the matter, a small Navy/RAF team flew over to Washington for discussions. It was a very quick flip there and back by RAF Transport Command VC10. The RAF had got it wrong and were given a rough time by the Chief of the Air Staff, who was in a bad mood anyway as they had forgotten to load his luggage on to the plane. A second VC10 with his luggage on board was despatched as soon as possible, so all was well. We in the Navy contingent flew home the next day, well-satisfied. Buccaneers were ordered for both services and a version is still operational, though of course the naval ones went out of service with the demise of the big carriers in the 1970s. As with most things in life, they were not the best aircraft but a good compromise.

My other trip to America was to do with my responsibility for Defence against Chemical and Biological weapons, something not taken very seriously in the Navy. It was arranged that I should visit the US Army's trials station at a place called Dugway in Utah. I went with another chap from Plans, called Simmonds, whose real reason for going, I discovered during the flight, was to see his daughter who was about to marry a Mormon in Salt Lake City. We spent one night in Salt Lake City, which was pretty deadly, and were then taken by Army transport about 100 miles west, out in the desert.

One of the remarkable things about the desert was the fact that nothing changes. Thousands of 'carpet-baggers' made their way across this desert at the end of the 19th century, on their way to California and gold, and we were shown where the tracks of their wagons still remained, as if they were made yesterday. Many hundreds died from lack of water and yet now all around are lush meadows and green golf courses. It seems that some few hundred feet under the desert are vast reserves of water and, with artesian wells, the desert is now being turned green.

Dugway itself was most interesting; the Americans, like us, had been trying to perfect an agent which would make people unconscious or disorientated in an instant. We all knew how to kill people with chemical weapons derived from the Germans at the end of WW II but a disabling drug would be far more effective, especially for dealing with hi-jacked aircraft. Several types were explained to us and we watched their use on herds of goats but nothing was really effective. Some solutions were effective but too slow, while the instant ones tended to be lethal where the recipient was not in good health. I think that, of the hundred goats that we watched, 98 recovered in about 5 minutes but 2 died. We also saw several sorts of stun weapons demonstrated but none was foolproof. As far as I know, the search for the instant but temporary knock-out drop continues to this day. I also discovered that the Americans were way ahead of us with protective clothing and had got masks through which you could talk intelligently and be understood.

One of the things I had to do was to find and appoint a new Trials Officer to the RM Trials and Training Base at Instow. I thought that it ought to be shut down for economy reasons but then I thought I might like the job myself. In the event it was circulated to Royal Marine Officers about to retire. Not many wanted to live in far-away Devon but there were a couple whom I interviewed, one of them being Major Jimmy Powell. He had been in *Dauntless* with me and therefore was selected. It turned out to be an excellent choice for every reason.

It is very difficult to recall at this stage all that went on but I have several vivid mental pictures: of going down to the City to watch Churchill's funeral cortège coming up past the Mansion House and then dashing back to watch the remainder on television; of taking and leaving David in a huge crowd to see the Beatles; of picking up Pip at Golders Green Station and giving her a lift down to Exmouth; of Mike arriving back from a cruise to the West Indies with a grazed face, arms and legs, having come off a moped in Bermuda; of Mary and me going to Norway in the spring of 1965 to stay with Alan Lyle in his hut at Geilo and falling flat on my back with a dozen eggs in my rucksack; of being invited to lunch by John Frewen and, on arriving at his flat, being told by Lady Frewen that she had run out of money to put in the meter and that nothing had been cooked.

My stint at the MOD ended on 10th September 1965. It had been a good experience and my eyes had been opened to a new world but I had little desire to become one of the Whitehall warriors. It had been a busy time and in the two years at the MOD I had worked with a large number of people and made good friends in all three services. I gave a farewell party to all those who had worked with me and I think we had about 80 guests. The work had been frenetic at times but, by and large, living in London had been a good experience.

Whether it is to be judged as a compliment or not, I was, as had happened on leaving *Ark Royal*, relieved by two people – a Royal Marine, John Uniacke, for the Joint Warfare part of my brief, and a Captain called Cairns for the rest. I had been appointed to Portsmouth with the task of trying to sort out the Damage-Control School. I wasn't thrilled with the job but looked forward to the change and to getting in some sailing. We packed up the house in Finchley Road and moved to No.11 in Freestone Road in Southsea, belonging to Instructor Rear Admiral Darlington.

Note: Of some of the people mentioned, Peter Hill-Norton, John Frewen, Michael Pollock, Ray Lygo, Henry Leach and Frank Hopkins all became Admirals; Terry Lewin became an Admiral of the Fleet and a Peer, John Owen a Major General, Alistair Jaffrey Secretary to the Admiralty and FitzAlan-Howard the Duke of Norfolk.

CHAPTER 18

Nuclear, BIiological & Chemical Defence
H.M.S. *Phoenix*
8th October 1965
to 26th October 1967

I have to confess that I was not wild with excitement to be appointed to the NBCD School at Portsmouth. I was told the usual story, that the place was run down, needed new ideas and, of course, as I had had Nuclear, Biological and Chemical Defence under my wing at the MOD, who could be a better choice for the job? It was also pointed out that I had nearly been sunk on a couple of occasions during the war so I should have a feel for Damage-Control. I was not convinced. However, I have always liked being in Portsmouth; we knew a lot of people and I should be able to get plenty of sailing, so in the end I went to my new job fairly willingly.

We had quite a job finding somewhere to live. There were no Married Quarters for Captains. Nearly everyone in the Navy, except us, owned a house in the Portsmouth area and we needed to find a suitable hiring. Number 11 Freestone Road just about fitted the bill. It was the end house of a little Victorian terrace, just off The Circle in Southsea, and as an end house it had been extended to give quite a decent size drawing room but in all other respects it was pretty poky with few mod-cons. In a way it was a smaller edition of 4 Gertrude Terrace with the same inconvenient kitchen out at the back, which gave on to a small garden taken up mostly with strawberries. However, it was enclosed and good for Jenny. It also had a garage and off-road parking. At that time we had the Morris Oxford Estate, the 2CV in which I went to work most days and also, of course, the Merlin Rocket.

When you are living at home you don't write letters to one another and diaries kept at the time have gone astray, so that I have few dates on which to hang a cohesive narrative. It seems best to deal with different aspects separately and so I shall start with the job, then family and finally sailing.

I took over the NBCD School at Cosham from a chap called Swann and found it to be in a sort of time-warp. At the time the school was a subsidiary of HMS *Excellent*, the Gunnery School, who administered, fed and paid us, but in all other respects we were a bore and were treated as a poor relation, though Arthur Power (son of the Admiral) an old friend and Captain of *Excellent*, was always most helpful. Many of the staff were elderly and had been there for a very long time with very little enthusiasm for the job. The school was quite a large establishment in area and consisted of a number of single-storey buildings. It had been used for accommodation during WW II and now the buildings were used as classrooms, messes, offices and so forth. At the rear was a section of a ship 'mock-up' which could be flooded and used to teach damage-control. I also found that I owned Horsey Island. This was a narrow island, about a mile in length, stretching out towards Porchester and connected to the school by a bridge. Along the centre of the island was a long lake which had been built for torpedo testing and which was now used for training divers. Halfway along there was a large radio station with very high masts and a multitude of aerials, for which I was responsible, and at the far end was the Fire Fighting School. Everyone in the Navy had to pass through the NBCD School at least once and the fire-fighting bit once in a commission, so there was no shortage of pupils. It was what happened to them that worried me.

My Commander, an engineer called Ted Bennington, had joined about the same time and was full of ideas; the difficulty was to get them implemented. Admiral Varyll Begg, the C-in-C Portsmouth, whom I had always found pretty intimidating in the past, was clearly on our side. The process was started to shift some of the old and bold and to get some younger people appointed. None of this could happen overnight but it was a start. I felt that we lacked identity and I put the wheels in motion to have more independence with a ship's name of our own instead of just a string of initials. I thought that *Phoenix* would be an appropriate name and, shortly after Admiral Frank Hopkins had relieved Varyll Begg in 1966, we were officially commissioned as HMS *Phoenix*. This helped enormously with the new image.

In the meantime we finalised drawings for a new, bigger and better damage-control training unit which could be heeled to alarming angles, while water poured in in vast quantities through shell holes, burst pipes, etc., all of which pupils would have to staunch. I had to go to meetings in Bath at regular intervals with the warship design and equipment committee and everyone was most helpful in giving the new unit a fair wind; money was found for the work to start at the end of 1966 and it was completed in 1967 shortly after I had left.

Other things put in train more quickly were the addition of new units at the fire school, to give people better understanding of the use of breathing apparatus, and also the conversion of a number of disused houses on Horsea Island so that they could be used for training sailors in giving effective aid in the event of civil disasters, such as earthquakes or acts of terrorism. We were also active in trying to make a stand over materials being used in the construction of new ships. Both the Canadian and the US Navies had had some pretty horrendous fires caused by the aluminium, used to save weight in the superstructure, burning very easily. This was because of the amount of magnesium added to give stiffness and prevent corrosion by salt water. We were using the same alloy and the naval constructors were loath to change. They were convinced, finally, but too late to prevent serious fires in ships hit by bombs during the Falkland war in 1982. It takes a very long time for change to feed through the system and what is built into a ship is there for its life.

In actual fact the job proved far more interesting than I had imagined. I was a fairly frequent visitor to Porton Down, the experimental establishment for Chemical and Biological Weapons. At the time the production of these weapons had been halted but it was still very necessary to keep up to date with all the possibilities and the scientists there were fully engaged in trying to produce antidotes to the various things that could be inflicted upon you and in particular to find something that could be either swallowed or injected to protect against the effects of nerve gas. We also organised and took part in several exercises off Portland when ships were attacked from the air. Coloured droplets were used to simulate chemical agents and the object was to see how many droplets were likely to stick to a ship or be ingested by the air-conditioning systems. In addition we tested different types of ship against simulated nuclear fallout.

I also had the chance to see how other navies set about their training and had an interesting visit to the US Navy's Damage-Control School at Treasure Island in San Francisco. There they had an old WW II destroyer in a covered dry dock which they could flood and list. It looked extremely good but, because it was a complete ship, it was actually quite limited in what could be done. Our system of having fairly simple boxes to represent ship sections, which you could heel, roll and simulate damage with a great deal of reality, was to my mind a much better bet. However it was good for ship-stability exercises, though again, because the ship was in a fairly tight-fitting dock, nothing very violent could be done.

I made several visits to the French Navy in Cherbourg and lectured to their Damage-Control School staff on nuclear, biological and chemical defence. They sent an aircraft to Lee-on-the-Solent to pick me up. At the time I gave the lectures in French, which I think must have been all right as I was invited back to do a similar thing again. On the damage-control side the French had an old British 'Bay' class frigate moored in shallow water in the harbour in which they would simulate damage and, if the sailors were ineffective in their damage-control measures, the ship would eventually sink to the bottom. As it was in a drying berth they would let all the water run out at low water, close the various stopcocks and refloat the ship on the next tide, all ready to start again – very practical and rather typically French – but when I went on board the whole thing was horribly damp and smelly like a badly looked-after public lavatory.

On the face of it I came to the conclusion that once our new unit had been built we would have a much better system than either the French or the Americans. The effectiveness of the whole system rested with the ships themselves. Some Captains were much keener than others in making sure that their ships' companies came along to *Phoenix* for training whenever possible. It was our job to try and keep the training methods up-to-date and effective. I think, with the equipment available during my time, we were moderately successful and that the new stuff being installed would and, in fact, did make a vast improvement.

On the family front we decided to have Jenny, our Shetland sheep dog, mated and she went to kennels near the Rufus Stone on the edge of the New Forest. Great excitement followed when she had five puppies. As they were pedigree we gave them kennel names, all beginning with T. One of them, Tijuana, went to the Gooseys, an Australian couple and friends of Mike as John was in the same term at Dartmouth. Some time later when the Gooseys returned to Australia they decided that it was impossible to take Tijuana back with them and, happily, she came back to live with us. Mother and daughter were great companions both to themselves and to us.

Mike left Dartmouth to join Maidstone and then Tartar as part of his training before going to Portsmouth for Sub-Lieutenants' courses. He had been doing well on the sporting scene both with the Navy Ski team and at Rugger. There were very strict rules at the time about the amount of money you were allowed to take abroad and Mary thought of various ingenious ways of hiding additional amounts. Disaster struck on the Rugger front when Mike, who was playing wing three-quarter for the Navy against the Metropolitan Police, tripped over a stray dog which had somehow got on to the field and badly damaged his knee. Though he had an Orthopaedic Surgeon from London to try and put it right, the techniques of the day were nowhere near as good as today and it has been a source of trouble ever since. It also meant that he had to do quite a bit of his Sub's courses with his leg in plaster.

While at Portsmouth, Mike celebrated his 21st Birthday. We arranged a party for it in the Mess at *Phoenix* and had a very good Group called The Blue Jeans who made the party go with a swing. I think there were about 60 at it and it took a lot of fixing to find the right girls for the 30 or so boys. We had a houseful and Minty Dodd came as a partner for David. She caused great excitement as she had a paper dress. At the end of his courses Mike went off to join *Fife*.

David took his 'A' levels in the summer of 1966 and, as he had passed, we decided that he should leave Pangbourne. This brought about a furious series of letters from the College demanding a year's school fees on the grounds that we had not given a term's notice. We refused to pay as we argued that they should be expecting their pupils to pass exams and therefore leave after 'A' levels as there was nothing to stay on for. They did finally accede but with very bad grace and I think I gave them £100. At the time we didn't have a year's school fees available as we were already committed to altering No.4 Gertrude Terrace. David did, in fact, continue his studies at Highbury Sixth Form College to try and get some better grades and it was nice to have him at home. Having the 2CV back after a testing time with Mike at Dartmouth, Mary used it to teach David to drive and I think he passed his test at the first attempt. He also showed his talent for the stage, playing No Good Boyo in Whale Island's drama group's production of 'Under Milk Wood' directed by the dentist there.

At the time David thought that he would like to be a Chartered Accountant and in the autumn of 1967 I arranged with Mike Shirley-Beavan of Binder Hamlyn, a well-known firm of Chartered Accountants in the City, to take him on as an articled clerk. David and I went to the Southampton car auctions to buy him a second-hand car. We came away with a Wolseley which looked pretty good and went well, but after about six months it was apparent that the seller had done a pretty clever cover-up on the bodywork and rust began to appear everywhere, which goes to show that car auctions are not for the amateur. We arranged for him to stay in digs in London run by a Miss Beaufort, whose grandfather had invented the windspeed scale, but after a short while he moved to Notting Hill Gate, sharing a flat with another Old Pangbournean called Sach.

Being articled in a firm like Binder Hamlyn was not all jam as the other articled clerks were all much older than David, most of them having been to university first. Mike S-B never warned us about this and had we known I don't think we would have taken up the offer. I suppose on his side, he was just trying to help an old friend. Sometimes the old boy network is not the best. However to be launched on London at the age of 18, without enough money, and to have done well in the job for two years says a great deal for David's character and ability.

Granny B was having a difficult time in Exmouth. No 4 was becoming too big and too expensive for her to run and it was a case of either finding another place to live or altering the existing one. At about Christmas-time 1966 Granny agreed to have the house converted into two flats and sell one of the flats to cover the cost of the conversion. We said that we would provide the capital and would be paid back after the second flat was sold. Granny suggested a firm called Meadows in Exmouth to draw up the plans and oversee the work as they had done several other similar jobs nearby. It turned out that the architect was a chap called Plunkett-Cole who had been about a year senior to me at Pangbourne. The project got off the ground in February 1967 and, after a huge amount of correspondence, visits, etc., to agree exactly what was to be done, work started in August and the job was completed by end of November. Though there were several shortcomings, particularly over the shared entrance, it was a great improvement and Granny had a decent kitchen in place of the awful, cold, lean-to that was there before. She was delighted to be back in her own house for Christmas. The work had cost over £3,000 and the next step was to sell the top flat to recoup the costs. The flat was sold to the Hallidays in April 1968 for about £4,000. When all was done and solicitors, builders and everyone else paid we actually made a slight loss, but the end result was well worth it. With hindsight we should have let the top flat as within four years the housing market went sky high and when the Halllidays sold the flat to the Greens in 1973 they got about £18,000 for it.

We also got involved with my Spurrell Uncle and Aunt at Bishops Waltham. My Aunt Kitty died soon after we arrived in Portsmouth and about a year later Uncle Oliver had a stroke and had to go into a nursing home. As his nearest relation we got involved with keeping an eye on the house, visiting him in the nursing home and so forth. However, when he died it was found that, because they had no children and he had left everything to his wife who had predeceased him, his will was invalid. The solicitor advertised for relatives in the newspapers and over thirty came forward, the estate being divided between them – a good lesson in the importance of keeping wills up to date.

Also at this time Aunt Elsie, who was over 80 and living alone, had to give up her very unsuitable house in Clifton Terrace in Winchester and move into a nursing home. Cynthia Bull and Aunt Iris at Twyford did the moving, but of course Mary also got involved and on a couple of occasions had her to stay in a nursing home near to Freestone Road so that she could take her out or bring her home during the day. On a happier note Uncle Christopher celebrated his 80th birthday and we all went to a big lunch party at a hotel in Southampton.

One of the reasons that I had been glad to come to Portsmouth was for the sailing. Being the owner of a Merlin Rocket I was able to join the Hamble River Sailing Club. As a club it had little to offer on the social side as it consisted of a large shed-like structure with rather grotty changing rooms at one end and a tower at the other for running the races. After racing you could get tea and buns and that was it. However it was home to some of the best dinghy sailors in the country, many semi-professional being sail makers, designers and generally working in the industry. There was quite a strong team from Proctor Masts which included Olympic and Americas Cup helm John Oakley.

Numbers were limited by the spaces in the boat park and the two classes sailed were Merlins and National 12s, both development or restricted classes. Racing was on Saturdays and Sundays starting at 1430 and on Wednesday evenings after work. It was for us another steep learning curve as, though the Welsh Harp had made us pretty nippy, coping with a Merlin in the Solent lop was another thing altogether. We soon discovered that everyone had wetsuits. They were very expensive to buy and not readily available, so most people had made their own. All you had to do was to buy a sheet of neoprene, some contact adhesive, a roll of tape for the seams and some zips. There were no patterns, so we got the sizes right by lying down on the floor in the drawing room on huge sheets of brown paper and drawing round each other. They worked pretty well, our suits didn't look much different from the rest and we were pretty pleased with ourselves.

When it came to the racing it turned out that Mary wasn't heavy enough to keep the boat up and I needed to find a bigger crew. Luckily my Commander's son, Clive Bennington, was on his last year at Portsmouth Grammar School before going into the Navy and was keen to have a go. He was available only at the weekends but nevertheless he turned out to be pretty useful and we did quite well. On the downside it meant that Mary became a sailing widow left on the shore at the Hamble with Jenny. There were some excellent sailors in the Merlins at the Hamble including David Thomas, self-taught naval architect who designed the very successful range of Hunter yachts, and Stephen Jones, designer of Merlins, National 12s and International 14s. David Thomas had a German wife and their young son was a very enthusiastic dog-walker for Jenny.

The races were run by a remarkably efficient person called Kippie Robinson. She managed the starts of three classes, hoisted flags, hooted hooters and worked out handicaps with remarkable efficiency, each weekend, entirely unaided. The club had no social life but did jolly good teas after racing. If you wanted anything more you migrated to the Bugle. However our Welsh Harp training had sharpened me up and at the end of our second year we came away bearing a satisfactory quantity of silverware.

There was another side to sailing which got me very much involved. In about March 1966 I was telephoned by Otto Steiner, who had just taken over as Assistant Chief of Naval Staff, to ask if I would take on the job of Naval Sailing Selector from him. After much persuasion I agreed, especially as he offered me his Secretary, John Barker, to give me assistance if and when required. I agreed to meet him at the Whale Island Sailing Centre and reckoned that I would have quite a job to keep up the image when he arrived in a most beautiful Bentley Continental which he parked next to my 2CV. But that was typical Otto. He was actually a very nice chap and most helpful. The job entailed finding the best sailors for inter-service and other team events in dinghies and small keel boats and then making sure that they were available – not so easy especially if they were serving in ships. The best source of material came from our own naval inter-command competitions with teams being entered by Portsmouth, Plymouth, Scotland, Fleet, Naval Air and Royal Marines; normally Commands entered two teams each of three boats. On top of this were helms and crews with well-known pedigrees.

It was obviously sensible that I should also take on responsibility for running the Portsmouth Command teams which I took over from Arthur Power, the Captain of Excellent. Having embarked on this I then found myself lumbered with the job of being Chairman of the Establishments Yacht Replacement Committee, which turned out to be not as bad as it seemed as there was a pretty dire shortage of money to replace more than one yacht in two or three years. Each of the major establishments had a yacht for recreational sailing and for racing off shore; the problem was how to choose a competitive compromise. We were lucky in *Phoenix* as we were able to use the Whale Island yacht, *Braganza*, in which Mary and I had some good evening sails, and also sailed her a couple of days in Cowes Week.

Apart from the hassle of trying to get people available to sail for the Command and the Navy, I enjoyed the selector's task. I had some excellent helms to choose from. For the dinghies I had: Rodney Paterson, Olympic Gold Medallist; ERA Peter Colclough, who for many years was the British and European 5-0-5 Champion; Peter Bruce who later became one of the key members of our Admiral's Cup team; Chief Shipwright Atfield; Jim Saltenstall, who became the British Olympic coach; and several other top helms. We used to field two teams, an A and a B team each of three helms; I usually sailed in the A team and enjoyed sailing against the top helms of the other services and clubs. At that time the Army had Stuart Jardine, another Olympic helm and the RAF had two that were very hard to beat, Newman and McWilliams. The latter became one of the top sailmakers on leaving the Air Force and I had him make the sails for our Poacher class yacht, *Champagne*.

In 1966 Rodney Paterson, who was a submariner, came to see me to ask if I could arrange for him to have three months' leave to compete in the Olympics in Acapulco with crew Ian MacDonald-Smith. I straightaway went to see his boss, the Flag Officer Submarines in HMS *Dolphin* to see if this was possible. FOSM at the time was Iain McGeoch, himself a very keen sailor, who said that he would do his best. In the event Rodney was given three months on half pay and won a Gold in his Flying Dutchman, *Superdocious*. Rodney was always a great embarrassment when we went to sail boats provided by another club as the first thing he would do was to alter all the rigging tensions and, taking out a large sailmakers needle, he would insert black wool wind-indicators all over the sails. Despite the fact that he nearly always came first, people just don't like their boats being mucked about by a stranger and I had to spend a lot of time apologizing.

The keel boat racing used to take place at the Seaview Yacht Club in the Isle of Wight. The Club kept a fleet of Mermaids, a little smaller than a Dragon and, in fact, very much the same as *Baccarat*, the boat we had in Norway. Provided you obeyed their rules and didn't bust anything, the Club was most hospitable and it was great fun to go over there. For these races I had some other equally experienced helms to call on, such as Surgeon Captain Bob Mooney, Captain Bill Pillar and, again, Peter Bruce. We had two very successful seasons there and my one regret was that I never managed to win the Royal Yacht Squadron Gold Cup. This was for the best individual helm and the first year it was won by Mac Williams and the second by Stuart Jardine. Mary and some of the other wives would come across and there were some amusing and idiosyncratic members to talk to. The food was always superb and both the Navy and Portsmouth Command won most of their matches.

Our two years in Portsmouth were quickly passed and it was time to move on, this time to Scotland where I was to be Chief of Staff to the Flag Officer Scotland and Northern Ireland in Rosyth. I was by now thoroughly involved with sailing and the problem was what sort of boat to have. I discovered that there was very little dinghy sailing in the Forth and it was necessary to have a keel boat. The best sort to have was a Dragon but this was far too expensive and I decided on a compromise. Flying Fifteens were raced from Burntisland on the shore of the Forth and selling the Merlin gave me just enough to buy a rather elderly Fifteen and order some new sails. It was not really such a good idea but I am not sure what I could have done for the better. However, to Scotland with a Flying Fifteen it was! We bade farewell to Freestone Rd and set off north of the Border to return to my birthplace!

CHAPTER 19

Flag Officer Scotland & Northern Ireland Rosyth
23rd November 1967 to 23rd August 1969

I had been appointed to be Chief of Staff to the Flag Officer Scotland and Northern Ireland, Vice Admiral Sir John O.C. (Jock) Hayes KCB, OBE, whose Headquarters were at Rosyth. Besides this national command he was also the NATO Commander Northern Atlantic (COMNORLANT) – an area which went from approximately north of the Humber to north of Norway and west to 30°W – and Commander Northern Channel Area (COMNORCHAN) – the North Sea from below the Humber to The Naze and across to Holland. We were to have an official residence, Donibristle House. All this seemed a leap into the unknown as we set off for Scotland with the two dogs in the Morris Oxford, towing the Flying Fifteen complete with dinghy on top, our heavy stuff, pictures and other belongings having gone on ahead by furniture van. I was to relieve Allister Gilchrist whom I had last met when he was Captain of *Chichester*, a diesel frigate, when I was in *Hartland Point*.

Scotland is a long way from Portsmouth and it was with great relief that we arrived safely at Donibristle, to be welcomed by the Gilchrists who were to put us up for the night. The next day Allister turned over the job to me, his wife explained the mysterious workings of Donibristle to Mary and then it was all ours. Donibristle House or, to be strictly correct, Donibristle House (West), was quite a place.

Situated on the shore of the Firth of Forth to the East of Inverkeithing, it was originally the female servants' quarters for the Great House which had been destroyed by fire in 1912 and never rebuilt. It belonged to the Earls of Moray and in 1914 the then Earl, who had been keenly interested in flying, let the estate to the Navy for the peppercorn rent of one shilling a year to build an airfield for the newly formed Royal Naval Air Service and so it had remained. Initially our house had been occupied by the Captain of the Air Station while Donibristle House (East), the male servants' quarters, was lived in by the Dowager Lady Moray. The two houses were connected by a tunnel about 100 feet long which Patricia Ashmore remembered cycling through on her trike in the 1920s when staying with her grandmother. Donibristle (East) now was occupied by Captain Paddy Hanmer, a bachelor and Captain of HMS *Cochrane*, the base ship for Rosyth.

In our time the airfield had gone, sold as a building site, and the hangers were let to the Distillers Company who stored in them countless empty bottles and cases of all known brands of whisky. Nevertheless the approach to our house was impressive. The driveway was about a mile long, coming through woods and fields round to the front of the house where there was a wide terrace with the sea on one side and our house on the other. Ours was the larger of the two houses as the female servants outnumbered the males. In addition we housed the kitchen for the great house, a huge room with a balcony running round and occupying two storeys. It had a great iron range with turnspits and the like for roasting great joints of meat. The kitchen had been connected to the main house by another tunnel of similar length so it would seem unlikely that food ever arrived hot. However this tunnel had been sealed off long since. The foundations had been dug out of solid rock and on the side of the courtyard opposite the great kitchen were large caverns intended as mangers for cows so that the milk was always fresh, but now made into quite useful garages for cars.

It was on these same rocks below that the Bonny Earl of Moray had been driven out of his mother's house, with coat tails burning, to be murdered by the Earl of Huntley and his followers in 1592. It was always said that Donibristle House was haunted and there was certainly one bedroom into which the dogs would not go.

The first thing that I had to do was to meet the boss, 'Jock' Hayes, a tall and rather aesthetic looking chap, very charming and with a passion for classical music. He lost little time in telling me that it was his job to go out and about and meet the people and it was my job to run the shop, which is what I did. The 'shop' in fact consisted of two halves: one was run from the Admiral's Office in Rosyth Dockyard; the other was managed from the Maritime Headquarters in a large underground complex at nearby Pitrivie which also housed, above ground, the office and Headquarters of the Air Officer Commanding Scotland and N.Ireland and the NATO Command, Air Vice Marshall 'Johnnie' Johnstone, a very distinguished and successful wartime fighter pilot. My opposite number there was his Chief Staff Officer, Group Captain Saunders who also responsible for the Joint Staff Mess and accommodation.

With the exception perhaps of the coal industry, the Royal Navy was the largest employer of civilian labour in Scotland at this time, probably about 12,000, of which some 8,000 worked in and around Rosyth Dockyard, and then of course there were all the staff at the various stores, armament and fuel depots, plus all those in the naval establishments around the Forth and the Clyde. We had in our command the Naval Base at Rosyth, HMS *Cochrane*; the Artificers training College, HMS *Caledonia*; the minesweeping base at South Queensferry, HMS *Lochinvar*; the Fisheries Protection Squadron; and Claverhouse, the RNVR HQ and flotilla in Edinburgh. On the other side in the Clyde we had HMS *Neptune*, the submarine base, and the main depot for Boom Defence. Over in N. Ireland there was the Joint Anti-Submarine School in Londonderry and the N.Ireland RNVR flotilla in Belfast. In England, going down as far as Grimsby, we had scattered about a number of high-powered radio stations. So I had quite a wide-ranging job with endless variety.

The Joint Maritime Headquarters ran the operational side of the picture. We had operational command of naval ships in our area and I had a Staff Officer Operations, Commander Peter Shevlin, to run the day-to-day business. It is important to remember that at this time the 'Cold War' was at its height and all Soviet moves had to be countered; we had a joint briefing every morning for myself and my Air Force opposite number. Away to one side in the bunker was a sort of 'holy of holies' where only a very few were allowed to know even what it was about, let alone enter, and inside a plot was kept of every Soviet submarine at sea in the Atlantic and northern waters. This derived from an ultra top-secret Anglo-American device able to detect the movement of all submarines – fascinating and very important to our security, bearing in mind the significant number Soviet nuclear-missile-firing submarines kept on patrol.

On the air side there were the daily reconnaissance flights by the huge Soviet four-engined long-range aircraft codenamed 'Bears'. These had to be countered with our fighter aircraft if they looked like coming too close. It was impossible to carry out an exercise at sea of any magnitude without a Soviet shadow, either submarine or E-LNT (pronounced Elint) trawler bristling with aerials or even, for larger exercises, one or two warships. Another problem was the number of Eastern Bloc fishing vessels, which put into remote inlets ostensibly to carry out repairs, all of which had to be examined. There was also a Soviet fish factory ship which used to hang around for weeks on end and cause enormous speculation as to what she was really up to. It may all seem very childish, with hindsight, but at the time it was considered vital that the Soviets should not be allowed to get away it.

In addition to all this there was a constant fish-war taking place both off Iceland and in the North Sea with boats from other countries fishing in areas allocated to our fishermen. I remember on one occasion being woken in the middle of the night by the duty 'Ops' officer asking permission for one of our fishery protection ships to fire across the bows of a persistently offending Dutch trawler who refused to stop. I gave permission with the added rider, 'For God's sake don't hit it'. All in all there was more than enough to keep me occupied and life was seldom dull. If it did quieten down then something always popped up, like the frequent problems posed by the tugs in Londonderry. The crews had to be either all Protestant or all Roman Catholic so that if some one fell sick and had to be replaced in emergency, say, by a catholic in a protestant tug, the whole lot would go on strike, which in turn meant that naval ships could not sail or had to remain at sea until it was sorted. I used to get extremely angry when this happened but to no avail except to allow me to let off steam.

In the Navy you are not given a stately home in which to live just for your own pleasure or as some sort of reward. Not at all. You have it, plus staff, in order to: further the Navy's position; to keep a good working relationship with the local population and in particular with people who have influence in the area; to have to your home the various officers under your command so that you can get to know them better and they you; to be a hotel for visiting 'firemen'.

This was our first go with staff and just about all the weight fell on Mary. In the house there were some rooms on the ground floor for staff but we lived on the first floor where we had a very nice drawing room, a comfortable sitting room, a dining room with a table for 12 and a not very brilliant but adequate kitchen. On the next floor we had our bedroom and dressing room and four other double bedrooms, one of which was *en suite* and kept for the more important guests. The top floor had a number of maids' rooms but was unused and unfurnished.

To look after all this we had a Petty Officer Steward, a Steward who came from *Cochrane* from time to time and an Officers' Cook, a young and spotty-faced man of 20 who lived in. For a young chap he was really remarkable, cooking for large dinner parties and for us every day and doing extremely well. His only failing was on pay days when he would 'go ashore' and get sloshed. We also enjoyed the services of a very nice full-time gardener who took care of the extensive grounds and the cricket pitch. I had the luxury of an official car and driver, Harry Cardno, who kept the quite elderly Ford Zephyr in immaculate condition, washing and leathering it every day in all conditions even though he had the most dreadful chilblains. Harry, I think, was greatly disappointed in me; he liked to have a bet on the horses every day and, while my predecessors had liked the same and sent him off to Dunfermline every lunch time to place their bets, I was not that way inclined. Very dull.

Mary of course had the car and, having decided the menu, would go most days into Inverkeithing with the PO Steward to do the shopping ('to do the messages', as the Scots would say). There was always quite a lot to get because, besides feeding ourselves, we had also to feed the staff and provide quantities of tea, milk and sugar – all very expensive unless you kept an eye on it. One of the cook's jobs was to stoke the boiler. This was a piece of industrial archaeology, situated in the cellars, which heated the house and the water by consuming half a ton of coke a month but it worked. On pay nights I found it just as well to do it myself as the Chef's aim at getting the stuff into the furnace was usually not good!

The Admiral had a very nice house on the outskirts of North Queensferry, St Margaret's Hope, but much of the time he spent at his own home, Arabella in the Black Isle just North of Invergordon, which suited me fine. His Secretary, Commander Bill Higgins used to come to all the Staff meetings and kept him well-informed as to what was going on. One of the very first things that I had to organize was a search for two airmen whose plane had crashed off the Moray Firth. One of the warships taking part was HMS *Fife* in which Mike was serving as the Sub-Lieutenant. Sadly they were not found.

In December I had to go and inspect the Boom Defence Depot in the Clyde. The Captain in Charge, Clyde, was Ernie Turner DSO, DSC, a very distinguished WW II submariner whom I had known before. He and his wife had invited us to lunch and Mary and I had our first experience of being chauffeur-driven for our day out and felt very grand. Harry was an excellent driver and always knew exactly where to go and what to do. In all the time in Scotland I don't think that we were ever late. Sadly he was to die of lung cancer a couple of years after we had left. He was an inveterate smoker.

Mary's first cousins Nick and Cynthia Bull were living and working in Edinburgh, Nick at Ferranti where he was one of the 'boffins' working on weapons guidance systems. They had two children: Diana was 4 and Christopher about 18 months when we arrived. It was good to have them there and I think that they were very pleased to have us. They were able to introduce us to life in Edinburgh and, most importantly, Cynthia taught us Scottish Country Dancing. This was absolutely vital as you were very poorly thought of if you could not do an Eightsome reel. Luckily I had had a bit of a head start as I had gone to Scottish Dancing classes when I was in

Singapore at the Sailing Club in the Naval Base. Having been born in North Queensferry it was expected that I know all these sorts of things. On our arrival in Rosyth the Dunfermline Times had banner headlines saying 'Scot Returns Home', even though I had left at the early age of 18 months and had not been back since.

Both the boys were able to come for Christmas and we had a dance for the young in the old kitchen, which, despite the stone floor, made a splendid party room. Somehow Mary managed to collect some 30 to 35 of the right age group, which everyone thought miraculous, and the evening went very well and launched both Mike and David into the local scene. Meanwhile I had started work on the Flying Fifteen; she was called *Splinter*, well-named as, on rubbing her down, I discovered plenty of cracks. I had her in the old stable block, a rather magnificent building with a large stable yard in the centre. It was all falling into decay but at one time there must have been stabling for some 30 horses. *Splinter* was in one of the carriage sheds which was still waterproof.

You reached the stables by walking past the other house eastwards along the Forth, passing the small private harbour with its breakwater and quayside. It was from here that the Earls of Moray would have been rowed or sailed across the Forth to Crammond, where horses and carriages would have been waiting to take them on to Edinburgh. Sadly the harbour had largely silted up but I did keep a RNSA dinghy there during the summer, principally for the use of the Chef who was keen on boats and liked to go fishing. Going on past the stables, towards Dalgety, the path took you through a most magnificent avenue of rhododendrons, some thirteen or fourteen different varieties and colours. In the opposite direction from our house lay a small wood in the midst of which was the Chapel, which belonged to the house but which had fallen into decay, and further on again you could walk out to a promontory which gave you an excellent view of the Forth Bridge and from where you could look down on the seals on the rocks below.

January also saw the start of our fairly unremitting social programme, beginning with Rear Admiral Peter Ashmore and the Dutch Naval Attaché coming to stay, and the usual round of lunch and dinner parties for the local Provosts and Sheriffs and also the leading lights of the area, together with our own staff and their wives, Commanding Officers of visiting ships plus the ships and Establishments in our own Command. All this put a lot of work on to Mary and our hard-pressed staff but our young Chef managed to cope remarkably well. I am sure that we got some entertainment allowance but never enough and we were always out of pocket. While many of the people we had to put up were passed on to us by the Admiral, others were those such as one's own staff and all the others from the Command whose confidential reports I had either to write or to sort into some order for promotion. I needed this opportunity to get to know them better and having them to the house was sometimes the only way of meeting them and getting to find out something about them and what made them tick.

In February we had David for about three weeks as his firm was doing an audit of Coates Cotton in Glasgow. He was able to use the house as a base and also shoot some of the pigeons which plagued us. He was an excellent shot and we all enjoyed pigeon pie. It was good to have him and I believe that during the audit he distinguished himself by finding an error of £1 million in the Coates account. One of the advantages of living in Scotland was that if the snow was good we could put our skis on top of the car and head off for Glenshee, which was becoming quite a popular resort, and while David was with us we were able to go and get some good skiing on a couple of weekends. The main disadvantage was that, instead of the nice run-outs at the bottom of the slope that we had become accustomed to in France, there was usually just a mushy area of mud and melting snow and a burn (stream) if you didn't stop quickly enough. Meanwhile in Exmouth, Granny B was looking to find a buyer for the top flat and having cold feet about it, particularly not knowing what sort of people she might have living above her.

One of the things that I had to do from time to time was the annual sea inspection of the local ships. This was quite fun and involved going aboard with a team of specialists in the various aspects – gunnery, sonar, damage control, replenishment at sea and so forth – all of which had to be tested. We would have a meeting the day before, to finalise the timing and the events that would be sprung on the ship, and follow up with another once we had got ashore to assess how they had coped. One had to be quite careful not to create total chaos otherwise the whole thing could be jeopardised and the credibility of the assessment would be lost – quite a delicate balancing act but my Staff Communications Office, Colin Maitland-Dougall, was excellent at calling in the air attacks, or whatever, at just the right time.

Hester, Rowland and the children all came to stay during the Easter holidays and thoroughly enjoyed living in regal state. The children particularly liked being able to go just anywhere and also the excitement of the tunnel between the two houses. They also had a lot of fun with the go-cart that we had knocked up thanks to a good set of pram wheels. From our front gate you could get a jolly good downhill run of about 400 yards, which with no brakes could be quite exciting.

In April we took the Flying Fifteen to Burntisland where we had put down a mooring inside the breakwater close to the Burntisland Boat Club, a wooden hut built at the inner end of the breakwater. There were about a dozen Fifteens, some kept out of the water in cradles and hoisted in just for the races which normally took place on Saturday afternoons. The members were a pretty dour lot and I can't say that we were welcomed with open arms. I think that they were very suspicious of our English accents. However, some of them had beautiful boats which they sailed very well. Never having sailed a Fifteen before, I had a lot to learn. The first was being disappointed to find that despite the fact that there was a heavy iron keel, Mary and I were not heavy enough to keep the boat upright. Uffa Fox had designed the shape of the keel quite differently from a normal keel boat so that it would plane easily on a reach, which was fine, but the down side was that unless you sailed the boat bolt upright it just would not go to windward. Fortunately I was able to find a keen and fairly heavy RAF Squadron Leader at the headquarters called Jock Wherry and with his aid we didn't do too badly but, though we had some seconds and thirds, I don't believe that I ever managed to win a race. It would have been better to have had a Dragon at the Royal Forth at Leith but they cost a lot of money which we didn't have.

Besides the sailing at Burntisland I found myself Branch Captain of the Forth Branch of the RNSA and also on the RNSA's Central Committee which required trips to London from time to time. These meetings were in the evening so that it was generally possible to fit in business at the MOD at the same time, which was useful. Ian McGeoch had taken over as Commodore of the RNSA in place of Frank Hopkins. It was at the Spring meeting that we were able to welcome RNSA member and ex-Southsea greengrocer, now Sir Alec Rose, as Honorary Life Vice-Commodore. Sir Alec had been knighted for his circumnavigation of the world in his ketch *Lively Lady*, at that time a feat of great bravery and endurance. Just over a year previously Mary and I had been to see him off on his adventure from alongside the pontoon at Whale Island. He had proudly shown us his 'garden' of onions up in the forepeak. His theory was that they would continue to shoot all the time of the voyage so that you could eat the leaves and thus have green vegetables every day to keep you healthy. It certainly worked. He was a really charming man with a great sense of humour.

The sailing centre in the Forth was in Lochinvar, the minesweeping base on the south side of the Forth, just upstream of South Queensferry where there were a number of Bosun dinghies. We had some very good sailors and we tried to organise races every Thursday evening including inter-establishment team races. The ace helms consisted of Lieutenant Peter Bruce, Surgeon Captain Bob Moodie, Chief Shipwright Attfield and several others. In fact that summer I took a team down to Portsmouth for the Inter-Command Regatta with every hope of lifting the trophy but sadly there was flat calm on each of the three days and consequently no sailing.

It was in the Spring that we had Mike for several weeks. He had had an operation in London for his gammy knee and it had to be rested. Also at this time David rang up to say that being a Chartered Accountant was not for him and he was going to Bath University instead. We were shocked at first as we had thought that he was doing pretty well but it turned out to be for the best in the long run.

In June Jock Hayes was relieved by Vice Admiral Ian McGeoch, CB, DSO, DSC. He and his wife Somers were very different from the Hayes, being very much more down to earth and approachable. Having said that, the new boss was quite a hard task-master and wanted everything done 'now' and correctly. I think we had a good understanding. He had been a very successful wartime submarine Captain, spending most of the war based on Malta until his boat was sunk in 1942. He and his crew managed to abandon ship and were put in prison camps in Italy. After about three months he and another officer managed to escape but were recaptured near Genoa.

Back in prison camp they escaped again and this time made their way to Spain by suspending themselves on some homemade netting underneath goods trains and, though undetected by border guards, they arrived in very poor shape, lacking food and water. It was on the later stage of the trip that a stone or something flipped up hitting McGeoch in his right eye which resulted in the eye having to be removed. He always wore a glass eye and in his younger days was famed for having a selection of these which he would put in for parties; one had a nude girl, another, a union jack and so forth. Now that he was an Admiral these, sadly, never appeared.

We dined out Jock Hayes in the Mess at Pitrivie and I had fun in my farewell speech to him, congratulating him on being the first West Indian to reach the rank of Admiral. His father had been a doctor in Jamaica, where he was born and grew up.

These last years in Scotland he had been working hard to get himself accepted as a true Scot and so I was able to congratulate him on winning the ultimate accolade of being also the first West Indian to be elected to that elite Corps, the Royal Company of Archers and the Queen's Bodyguard in Scotland. To get there you had really 'made it' socially and had the privilege of wearing a dark green tartan kilt and plaid with a blackcock's feather in your bonnet, plus of course, a bow and arrow. Who could ask for anything more.

Mary found herself quite involved with the local wives organisation called the SWANS. The Chairman of the association was Mrs Ridley, wife of Terence Ridley who was the Rear Admiral in charge of Rosyth Dockyard. They were a charming couple and great fun. The SWANS were very active in visiting and generally looking after the wives of all those who worked in the base and needed help. Many of the workers lived in the large council estates near the Dockyard. One day Mary was visiting a house on one of the estates when she was asked in by a woman who was quite distressed and who invited her to come upstairs to see her mother, only to discover that the good lady was dead. Once a year there was a big summer fair to raise money and Mary was given a list of people who usually gave items to be sold. One was a farmer whom she called upon to pick up his contribution. He had forgotten all about it but immediately went out to the yard, quickly killed four chickens and presented them to Mary just as they were. She and the Chef had quite a game plucking them and our rather small kitchen was full of feathers and fleas.

Scotland is a popular place for visitors in the summer and, after giving a buffet lunch for thirty so that people could meet the McGeochs, we had a visit of two French destroyers, the French Naval Attaché, Hester and Rowland plus children and, the day before their departure, the Déroulèdes. Mary and I went to the airport to meet them when, to our horror, four people got off the plane instead of two. They had brought André's very nice nephew and his wife from Grand Rosignol. We were pushed for space but thankfully the Maitland-Dougalls offered to put them up which was a great success. I was having a busy time so we lent André the Morris Oxford and let them get on with it.

Now that the Hallidays were well installed and various little differences sorted out, (they wanted a balcony which we couldn't agree to), Granny B was able to come up to Scotland for a long visit. She just loved it at Donibristle and the staff were very good to her. She was enchanted by the situation and inspired to take up painting again, something that she had not had time to do since she was married.

In September we had a big maritime exercise which ran for about 10 days. We had to run the Blue Force while Northwood ran the Orange. There were a good number of ships and aircraft involved, plus a paper convoy exercise going on at the same time. The latter involved bringing in a number of Reserve officers and ratings mostly from the Edinburgh RNR at Claverhouse. They had been for fortnightly training at Pitrevie for months before-hand so knew what to do. I think that the exercise itself went pretty well and we managed to avoid getting many ships 'sunk' by the large number of Orange submarines. The main problem was the Soviet surface ships, submarines and aircraft that shadowed the force at very close quarters and there were some near-collisions but of course there was no way that one could tell them to go away. The oceans are free for anyone's use.

That September David started at Bath University. We were pleased that it was all settled but little did we think that it was going to be his home for the next five years.

I was not able to take the usual leave periods but Mary and I were able to make it up by taking several days at a time to go and explore Scotland and had some lovely visits to the Great Glen, Glencoe, Loch Lomond and Skye and also around and about in Fife and Perthshire. We used to set off in the car with the dogs and take pot luck, which in ninety-nine per cent of the time turned out just right. Christmas went well with all the usual parties and the Admiral got his 'K' in the New Year's Honours List and was now Sir Ian. He said that he felt a complete fraud but I know that they were both very pleased. In January we had the most tremendous gale which funnelled down the Forth and blew down some 150 trees in our wood. Luckily the house suffered no damage though many were not so lucky. Needless to say I slept through it, quite oblivious to what was going on.

I was determined to do something over the winter to improve *Splinter*'s performance and, as working in the stables had not been a success, this winter she was moved to one of the main stores in the dockyard where I was able to take the keel off and turn her upside down. The store was used as a garage for the small mobile cranes and I discovered that they could all easily be started, so at weekends I had great fun being a crane driver and moving the boat just how and when necessary. We had one near-disaster with Jenny in the dockyard when she went into a drainpipe after a rat and couldn't turn round to come out. We got her out after about two hours with no lasting damage except to our nerves.

The Admiral, besides being Chairman of the RNSA was himself a very keen yachtsman and wished to encourage sail-training. We had attended the commissioning of the *Malcolm Miller*, a three-masted sail-training ship donated by an Edinburgh business man in memory of his son who was killed in a road accident. Clearly the powers-that-be would not sanction anything of this size and I was asked to put up a proposal for a suitable yacht which could be built in reasonable numbers but without too much expense. I had fun drawing up plans for a 45-ft ketch which would take about 16, plus a skipper and mate. I had gone for a fairly stable craft with an easily-worked sail plan but the Admiral reckoned that it would not be exciting enough for the people who were to sail it and I had to try again. This time I proposed a 50-ft boat with much finer lines and a bigger sail plan and it was eventually sent forward with supporting arguments. After several meetings in London the three services agreed to ask some recognised yacht designers to come up with proposals and costings. The result was the Nicholson 55, of which some eight were finally built.

Sir Alec Rose and I had the honour of breaking the first hull out of its mould in 1972. This was the Navy's yacht *Adventure* which was to have a distinguished career, taking part in several Round-the-World races before eventually being presented, by Prince Charles, to the Russian Naval Sailing Association in 2003 in St Petersburg.

At the beginning of the year and as a forerunner to Defence economies we were told that naval sea-training would be moved from the Moray Firth to Plymouth and, of course, from our Command. Everything in future would be based on Plymouth and in the approaches to the Channel. Apart from losing most of our ships and part of our raison d'être, it seemed to us madness to try and do sea-training off a highly-populated coastal area and in one of the busiest shipping lanes in the world, whereas in and off the Moray Firth you could do pretty well what you liked without getting in anyone's way and, importantly, there were available good airfields and uncluttered airspace. Our Air Force half of the Headquarters were equally furious with the idea.

The main instigator of the idea was my old boss, Terry Lewin, now a Rear Admiral and Assistant Chief of Naval Staff and also Chairman of a 'Way Ahead' Committee. We put together a pretty strong case and made several sorties to London to argue it. The fact was that our case was pretty unassailable from a practical point of view and we won the day. The Admiral was delighted and so was I. However, though I may have won the battle, I lost the war. Terry Lewin became an Admiral of the Fleet and Peer of the Realm. I did not. In addition some years later, when Terry was Chief of the Defence Staff, it was agreed that Sea-Training should be moved to Plymouth, where it is today.

In April the troubles in N. Ireland seemed to get considerably worse and our operations in Londonderry, where we had the Joint Anti-Submarine School, were brought to a halt by strikes; the Protestants would not work with tugs manned by Roman Catholics and there was fighting and damage. I flew across to Ballikelly, the RAF airfield for Derry, to try and discover what could be done. I was horrified on being driven into Londonderry to see British soldiers, fully armed, patrolling the streets. I had never thought that I should see the day that this should be necessary. Sadly, this was to become a familiar sight for the next thirty years but I was not to know that. We managed to cobble together some sort of agreement for the tug crews, chiefly, I think, by threatening to man them with Navy personnel, and things returned to a degree of normality. We also made it known that it was our intention to relocate the whole school to the Moray Firth with the consequent loss of local jobs.

I had heard from the Naval Secretary that I was to be relieved towards the end of August by Captain John Murray and that I should be appointed in Command of *Triumph*, refitting in Singapore in November. I was to relieve Peter La Niece who had joined the Navy at the same time as I did. I was delighted at the prospect of getting back to sea. Locally, the sailing season was upon us once again with *Splinter* back in the water at Burntisland and looking very smart but whether I was going to be able to sail her any better was another matter. I was also determined that on the naval side we should take a strong team down to Portsmouth for the various Inter-Service and Inter-Command events and bring back some silver after the frustrations of the previous year when there was no wind on any of the days that we were there. In the event we had mixed success with our team of 12. In the Inter-Command series, sailed at Seaview in Mermaids, we won the Robertshaw Cup convincingly, a first time ever for Scotland.

The helms and crews were: Lieutenant Peter Bruce (*Caledonia*) crewed by Chief Shipwright Attfield (*Caledonia*) and Instructor Lieutenant Wilson (*Caledonia*); myself with Captain Bill Pillar (NSPO Glasgow) and REA Searl (*Lochinvar*); Lieutenant Commander Colin Maitland-Dougall (FOSNI) with Inst. Lieutenant Green (*Neptune*) and Lieutenant Commander Hales (*Bronington*); Surgeon Captain Bob Mooney (*Cochrane*) with Lieutenant Jordan (*Dreadnought*) and Lieutenant-Commander Reeves (*Cochrane*). Peter Bruce was to become a key figure in Great Britain's Admiral's Cup team while Bill Pillar ended up as Governor General of Jersey. Wilson turned up in the 1970s as part of the design team at Appledore shipyard and, for a short time, was my crew in an Osprey. He left to become Peter Bruce's business partner in a yachting business in Lymington.

Of course it is always difficult to get the people you want but on this occasion the various ships and establishments had cooperated fully with the result... Success! I Captained almost the same team in the Inter-Service competition but we lost by a couple of points to the Royal Air Force as one of our boats was disqualified for passing the wrong side of a danger mark. It was fortunate that Mike's ship was in Portsmouth and he was able to come and crew which was a big asset.

Mike brought Philippa Crabtree up for a weekend in the minivan and she had an exciting time driving it round the grounds, practising for her driving test. The minivan had rendered yeoman service and was used to its limits before being superseded by an MGB, which was to be Mike's pride and joy.

The social scene ran on at a fairly intense pace with visitors both family and official, garden parties at Holyrood House, Princess Alexandra at *Cochrane* and so on. We had made good friends of the Army in Edinburgh and one of the most memorable events was as principal guests at an evening 'do' in Edinburgh Castle. We were at the saluting base on the Castle Green when the gates opened and out marched the massed bands of the Scottish regiments, pipes skirling and kilts swinging – very difficult to beat. On a smaller scale we had Angus Sixsmith to stay and persuaded him to play his pipes down by the water's edge below the house while we had a dinner party which he did very well. Earlier in the year Mary was out of action for several weeks when she tore her Achilles tendon when Scottish dancing; it just happened in a flash and the only cure was rest.

One of the tasks which came my way during my time in Scotland was to be the spokesman for the Command when various events or disasters were to be reported on radio or television. For the TV interviews the BBC would set up a camera in my office and fire off questions which I would do my best to answer. Normally there would be a short discussion first as to what line the interviewer would pursue and all would be well. Back in the studio and before the actual broadcast the interviewer would ask the questions again in front of a camera, so that when the item went out during the news, it would appear to the public that I was actually there with the interviewer. This was done to save money as otherwise they would have to bring two cameras, cameramen and everything else.

However, on one notable occasion, when we were having more than the usual problems with nuclear protestors at the submarine base in the Clyde and in particular with attacks directed at the American nuclear submarines based there, I was required to answer questions on safety and policy with and in direct opposition to the views of the ultra left-wing, old Etonian Member of Parliament for West Lothian, Tam Dalyell, a thorn in the Government's flesh. I thought that I had done pretty well but when it was broadcast I was made to appear a complete idiot as the questions which looked as if they had been asked in a live broadcast had been changed deliberately back in the studio to suit the interviewer's left-wing sympathies and anti-nuclear views. I was horrified when I watched the six o'clock news and so indeed was the Prime Minister, Harold Wilson, who was on the phone as quick as a flash to ask what the hell was going on. When told about the unscrupulous changing of the questions, he sent immediately for the Director General of the BBC and threatened to sack him. The following day the MOD issued instructions that in future no interviews were to be given unless there where two cameras present and a tape recording of the whole interview.

David was up in early July at the end of his first year. His course was a 'sandwich' one which meant finding a job for business experience. He had hoped to find a place locally but had no success. Luckily my cousin Charlie Wainman, who owned a number of businesses in the Isle of Wight, was able to place him in a job with J Arthur Dickson in Cowes, one of the largest producers of post and greeting cards in the UK – not wildly exciting but it filled the bill. Mike was on leave at the same time and it was nice to have both boys together. They had both made some nice friends locally and seemed to have a pretty good time.

Granny B was up for a final visit and in July we had all the Elphinstones for a week at the end of term. The Chef and I had made quite a good job of mending an old folding canoe, which I had found in one of the cellars, and Henry thoroughly enjoyed paddling around in it. At other times the Chef used it to go fishing but without much success. Somehow the summer passed in a flash especially as, on the work side, we had had a large number of visiting ships which in turn sparked off a swarm of Soviet intelligence gatherers in the shape of submarines, fishing vessels, E-LINT trawlers and the ubiquitous fish-factory ships. They seemed to hang around for ever and all had to be taken care of, if only to show that we knew exactly why they were there and what they were up to – all quite time-consuming and often very frustrating.

August was soon upon us and it was time to say goodbye to our many friends, both civilian and in the three Services, and also to our very loyal staff who had served us extremely well. We often wondered what had happened to our excellent and very individualistic young chef and feared that life in a large galley aboard ship would not be a success. Of course there was the inevitable round of parties 'to say goodbye to the Johnsons'. It had been an interesting experience and a worthwhile job but Mary had found it a lonely one from time to time, for, though Donibristle House was a super place, it was really very cut-off and quite spooky when one was there on one's own. Now it is all unrecognisable, having been sold to developers. The whole area is a huge housing estate with its own school and shops and the house has been divided into very expensive apartments. Perhaps we had had the best of it and my relief, John Murray, and his wife were to be the last of the Navy to live there.

Triumph was an 'accompanied' appointment and so Mary would be able to come with me to Singapore in November. The problem was what to do in the meantime. We had planned to take back Croft but the tenants were anxious to stay on for a further year and new tenants were not that easy to find. My 'Command' courses were centred on Portsmouth and fortunately we were offered a largish flat in a married quarters block in King's Crescent in Old Portsmouth. Any port in a storm, so, after sending all our pictures, ornaments and other unwanted bits and pieces off to store, we set off for Portsmouth with the Flying Fifteen in tow. This was fine for us but the real losers were Mike and David who were about to be deprived of a base for all their belongings and, from November, would have nowhere to lay their heads when on leave. Neither boys took kindly to the idea of being finally shoved out of the nest to fend for themselves and, on reflection, we had been pretty hard-hearted about them. We felt that they were both grown men and should be able to look after themselves, which of course they did very well.

ORDER OF SERVICE

FOR THE COMMISSIONING OF

Her Majesty's Ship Phoenix

In the presence of

Admiral Sir Frank Hopkins, KCB, DSO, DSC*
Commander-in-Chief, Portsmouth

AND

Captain C. A. Johnson, OBE, DSC
the Commanding Officer

Below:
Reading the Commissioning Warrant.

Above: Admiral's Inspection. Talking to members of the Ship's Company.

Below: Phoenix Staff. My Commander Ted Bennington is on my left.

Top: Mike was now doing his Sub Lieutenants courses in Portsmouth. Skiing, in Norway and France, had stood him in good stead and he was a member of the Naval Ski Team. His best discipline was the Downhill. Mike is 3rd from the right.

Upper left: Sailing our Merlin Rocket inland with Mary as crew. When she was based in the Hamble my crew was usually Ted Bennington's son.

Left: Summer leave. Mary and I crossing the finish line.at Instow. Freddie Johns' ferry to Appledore in the foreground.

Above: Bruvvers!

Above: Donibristle House.
We lived in the house to the left and the C.O. of Cochrane in the one on the right. Though the facades match, the one on the right was L shaped and thus a lot smaller. The two houses were joined by a tunnel which also served the Great House burnt down before WW I and never rebuilt.

Below. Lunch Party at St Margaret's Hope. L-R: Us, My Secretary, Lady Hayes, Sir Jock Hayes, Capt & Mrs Gerrard-Pearce, AVM 'Johnnie' Johnston, Winnie Ewing (Leader S N P), AN Other, AN Other, Erskine (Flags), Bill Higgins (Admiral's Secretary).

Above Left: Mary in front of the ornamental wrought iron gate leading to our lawn. The whole thing was made in Holland and presented to the Morays by Wiliam of Orange.

Above Right: David turned out to be a crack shot with pigeons.

Below: Every young officer's dream, Mike with his MGB

Above: Mike and I sailing the Flying Fifteen out of Burntisland Harbour.

Below: Donibristle House. The cars are parked in what used to be byres for cattle so that the Great House should have fresh milk on tap. They are cut out of solid rock and made good garages. Our entrance was between the two tubs which used to serve the giant kitchen.

Above: Triumph leaving the Straits after re-commissioning.

Below: Mary cutting the Commissioning Cake with the help of the Master-at Arms and his sword. The Chief Cook watches anxiously. However it was a masterpiece.

Above: Some of Triumph's families that attended the ceremony.

Below: The truly magnificent Commissioning Cake, with the ship's Battle Honours. The first ship to bear the name Triumph was in the 16th century.

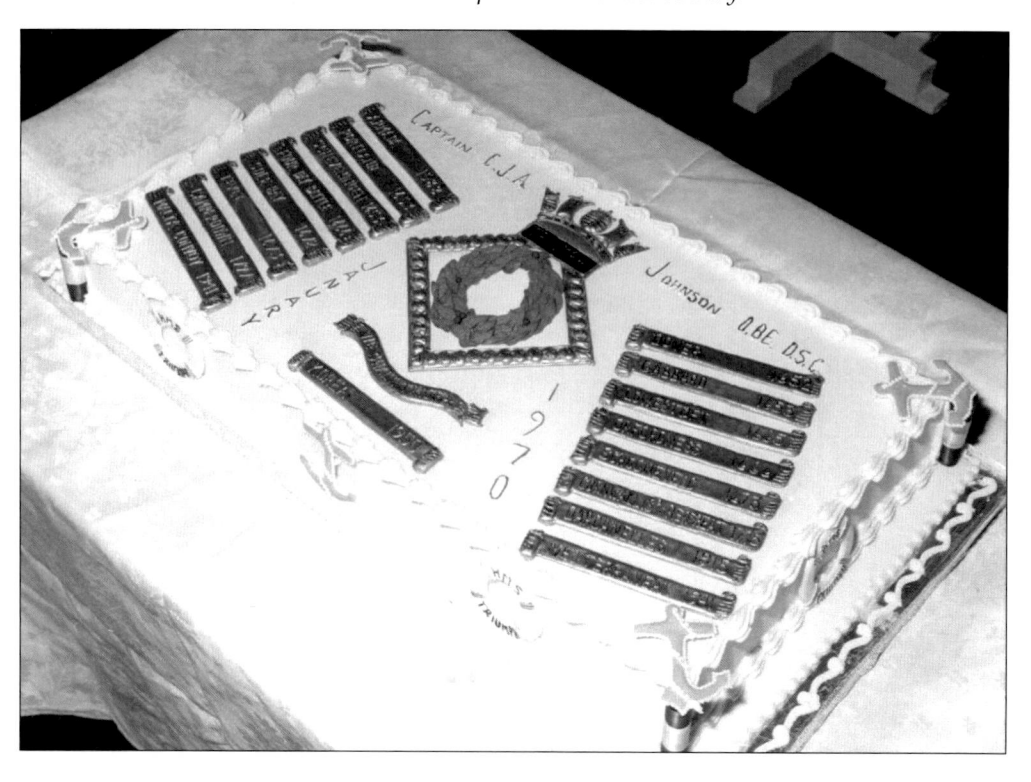

Above: Triumph leaving harbour and giving a good view of the flight deck.

Below: Two of Triumph's 8 Landing Craft (Assault) LCAs.

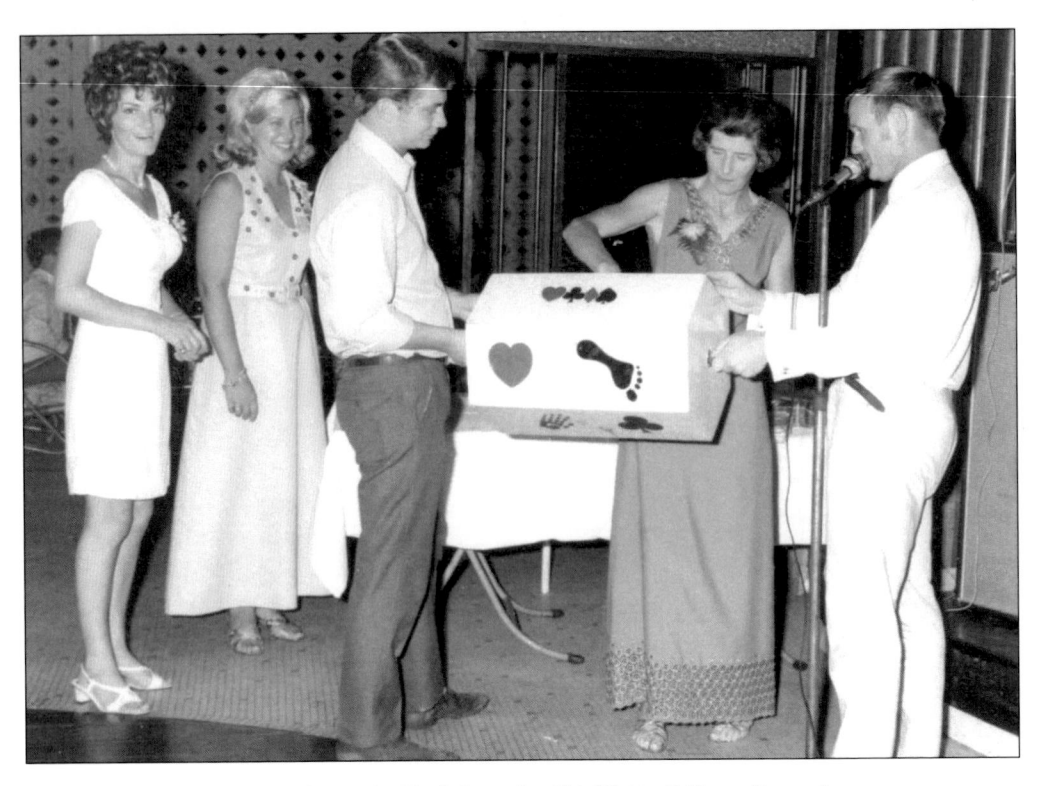

Above: Mary draws the Tombola at the Chief Petty Officers dinner dance.

Below: David enjoying the ease and luxury of my day cabin. A slight contrast to Bath University

Above: Refuelling at sea. A steady course is essential, hence the two black balls at the yardarm.

Below:
A junk cutting it fine. Having been around for a thousand years they think they have right of way!

Above A flight of Wessex returning to the ship.

Below: Landing on.

Triumph in dry dock in Singapore. Carriers and Cruise liners have very fine lines and you may wonder how they float the right way up! On the chocks it is just possible to stand up under the keel.

Above: Our house at Kenya Crescent in the Naval Base. It was an old-style colonial house, basically a large, airy bungalow on stilts so as to keep cool in the days before air conditioning.

Below Left: Mary in my cabin onboard. It was the age of the mini skirt.

Below Right: The indispensable Min who saw to our every need.

Above: Heading north at maximum speed for Bangladesh (East Pakistan) flood relief. We were loaded up with every sort of thing including these army lorries and drums of motor fuel.

Below: Fearless hadn't enough fuel for the high speed dash so came up alongside for some of ours.

Above: December 5th 1970. Mike and Philippa (Crabtree) were married in Littleham Church.
The Reception was in the Royal Marine Mess at Lympstone.
Below, left: We made it, Hoorah!

Above: David, dressed for the part.

CHAPTER 20

H.M.S. *Triumph* FAR EAST FLEET 19th Nov 1969 to 19th April 1971

We were delighted to be going out to Singapore, but many things had to be done first. The Flying Fifteen was eventually sold to someone in Belfast and I had to tow it up to Liverpool and put it on the ferry in the hope that it would arrive safely at the other end. It must have done, as I was paid. The dinghy I kept and stowed in one of the Bray's barns at Ropley. Jenny and Tijuana were taken to boarding kennels at Chelfham, just outside Barnstaple – not the usual sort of kennels as they were to become part of the household and the boys would visit them from time to time. A few days before we left Mike had a very bad go of tonsillitis and had to go into Haslar; luckily David and Rosemary Bray helped to clear out the flat and David drove us to Brize Norton (RAF Transport Command) on 18th November and we were off.

The actual flight was very comfortable; being a 'senior officer' we had the RAF equivalent to First Class. We made several stops for fuel, the first at Muharraq in the Gulf and the second in Gan where we were delayed for 24 hours. It was annoying in one way but we were able to enjoy the wonderful swimming off the reefs. On arrival in Singapore we were met by my Commander, Peter Everett, who very kindly took us to his house for the night. Peter, whom I had known before, had been left over, so to speak, from the last commission to see the ship through her refit since my predecessor, Peter La Niece, had gone back to the UK some weeks previously, leaving me his car – a very elderly Opel – which I had arranged to buy for £10.

The following morning Peter and I went down to the ship, while Mrs Everett took Mary to the flat they had found for us in Leonie Gardens, just off Grange Road in Singapore. It is always very exciting joining a new ship and more so if it is yours. In dock *Triumph* looked enormous though, in actual fact, as Carriers go she was quite small. She was one of a number of Light Fleet Carriers built at the end of World War II. She had seen active service during the Korean War where she had been Flagship of the British Fleet. With the advent of newer and bigger aircraft the class became redundant and *Triumph* began a new life as the Cadet Training Ship for budding Naval officers, while others of the class were sold off or scrapped. One went to France as the *Arromanches* and another to the Dutch as the *Karel Doormann*, both having been extensively modernised and fitted with angled decks. The Karel Doormann eventually went to the Argentine but played little part in the Falklands war.

In the mid-sixties *Triumph* began her third and last career. Her hangar was fitted out as a giant workshop with every sort of equipment for maintaining destroyers and frigates, while a new hangar which could take 4 Wessex helicopters was built on the flight deck, leaving a small flight deck forward of the island. Further aft were a selection of boats and cranes. Without the aircrew the spare accommodation could take either two Fleet Maintenance groups or a Royal Marine Commando unit, while the davits on either side of the upper deck had been altered to take a number of LCAs (Landing Craft Assault. The ship herself was just over 600 ft in length with a flight deck width of 90 ft. Displacing just under 20,000 tons, she had a top speed of 25 knots from steam turbines driving two shafts.

With the Fleet maintenance group the complement was just over 1,000. The ship had a 'married accompanied' status and I discovered that there were some 350 wives, plus children, living in Singapore. Mary and I had quite a large family to look after. People serving in ships were not entitled to married quarters and families had to house themselves around Singapore island as best they could. Mary found herself President of the *Triumph* Wives Club (the TWINS) which provided a focal point for the many young wives who had never been away from home and somewhere to bring their problems, which were many and varied.

That first morning I was able to meet all the Heads of Departments, who were an excellent bunch, and also my Secretary, Lieutenant Mike Ellis, who informed me that I was to call on the Flag Officer Far East Fleet, Vice Admiral Sir Derek Empson, at noon. Luckily my PO Steward, Botrill, had found all the right gear. The Admiral, who was ex Fleet Air Arm was charming and told me that, as the last of the Commando Carriers had left the station and would not be replaced, Triumph would spend a large part of her time with the amphibious forces. This suited me just fine and would be much more interesting than maintenance work, which would be achieved by leaving our Fleet Maintenance teams ashore to make use of spare workshop capacity in the dockyard. Diana Empson lost no time in taking Mary under her wing and arranging for her to meet the other wives. The Empsons had two small adopted children and Mary and Diana were to become very good friends.

Back in Triumph I was delighted with my quarters. The ship had been fitted out as a Flagship and, with no Admiral embarked, I occupied the Admiral's cabin, which extended across the whole breadth of the ship and was situated at the after end of the Senior Officers' Cabin Flat just above the Quarterdeck. From Port to Starboard it consisted of my galley with a Petty Officer Chef, a large day cabin with a dining table which could be extended to seat 12, a sleeping cabin and a bathroom, all very tastefully furnished and air-conditioned. My desk was in one corner of the day cabin and, in the other corner, there was a sofa and armchairs. I was well pleased with my lot.

Our flat in Singapore belonged to an Indian Merchant Navy Captain and was spacious and airy. One of the conditions on taking the flat was that we should take on the owner's Malay servant, a young girl called Rubia, which was fine. What was not so fine was that we had also to take on his Golden Retriever bitch. It was a friendly dog and wanted love. The moment you sat down it would leap on to your lap and start licking your face – not much fun in the Singapore heat to be engulfed by a hot, heavy, hairy love-sick pooch. However it all turned out pretty well; Mary soon got to grips with shopping and it was only to be for a short period. With the run down of the military in Singapore, it was likely that a senior officer's house would become available to rent in the Naval Base.

The refit ended on 16th December and it was good to have the ship to ourselves, with every one turning to with a will to get everything up to scratch for the Commissioning in the New Year.

At about this time I was confronted with the first tragedy concerning one of our families. One of my Chief Artificers shot his wife and then himself. It transpired that his wife, who was a very attractive woman, had been taken up by the eldest son of the Sultan of Johore. This had been going on for quite a little while until her husband could stand it no longer and had shot her when she came home at about 3 o'clock one morning. All this had great political connotations and it was vital that the press didn't get hold of the story. Luckily everyone cooperated but it was a very sad beginning.

On a much happier note, we had to press on with arrangements for Christmas. We had the Naval Base Carol Service on the flight deck and some 1,400 came – rather more than we had expected – but it went well. Afterwards Mary and I entertained about thirty guests, which included the Admiral and his wife, with a buffet supper in my cabin. On Christmas day itself we had a service on the Quarterdeck, after which Mary and I did the rounds of the mess decks – quite a test as there were a lot of them, all very hospitable and excellently decorated. There was a real family atmosphere as the men who were on duty were able to have their families on board for Christmas dinner. We were glad to escape for a picnic lunch and to play tennis to work it off before going out to a family dinner with the Moffats (he had been the Church of Scotland Padre in Rosyth) later that evening. Mary also found herself having to go to the Wives' Club party, all pretty hectic but she had been able to get several dresses made and so was all right for things to wear.

The ship's routine was such that work started at 6.30 am and finished at 1 pm, it being too hot to work in the afternoons. However, there was always plenty of activity in the evenings; Triumph had a very good football team and one was expected to turn up to watch matches and other events. Of course all the sports facilities were floodlit so in many ways it was the best time of the day, being reasonably cool. I had also joined the Red House sailing club and was able to hire a GP 14 on a semi-permanent basis. There was quite a decent class of them and we were able to get some good racing. Back in England Mike had gone to Austria to ski, while David spent Christmas at Exmouth with Granny Bull. On New Year's day Mary and I celebrated our silver wedding by going out to dinner in the Starlight Restaurant at the top of the 'Malaysia', a very smart new hotel with about thirty storeys. It was great fun and there was an excellent dance band and cabaret.

Our Commissioning Ceremony was on 6th January. The Ship's Company mustered on the Flight Deck along with many of the families and a number of guests, which included the Chief of Staff, Ian McLaughlan, and his wife. After the service I talked to the Ship's Company to tell them what the ship was going to do and also what I expected them to do. That done, Mary, with the help of the Master at Arms and using his sword, cut the very splendid Commissioning cake which the Chefs had made. Everything seemed to go very well indeed; the sun shone and I was very proud of my command and rightly so. I was delighted to get a signal from Admiral McGeoch wishing us all success.

Six days later we left harbour for sea trials and my first go in the driving seat. A ship in dockyard is dead, but once she is under way she becomes alive and Triumph was no exception as we glided down the Straits and then off to the East for full-power trials, exercising various emergencies, replenishment, flying off and landing helicopters and all the rest. I personally needed to see exactly how the ship handled as did my Navigation officer, Andrew Pearson. She actually handled extremely well, though one had to allow for the fairly small horsepower in a relatively large ship.

Replenishment at sea is always a bit of a challenge: the supplying ship maintains a steady course and speed, about 12 knots, and my job was to bring Triumph up alongside with 50 feet between the two ships and to keep her there while hoses and jackstays are passed across between the two ships. The secret is to come in at a decent speed and angle and then take the speed off quickly while getting on to a parallel course. Once in position it is best to have two people to keep the ship in position, one to steer and the other to keep the revolutions absolutely right. I had not had a go since *Hartland Point* which, with its single screw, was a different kettle of fish altogether, but happily we got it right first shot. Ships' Companies tend to judge the captain by his ability to handle the ship, so having passed the first hurdle my next was to bring her alongside in Singapore. Luckily there was hardly any wind and we got the 90-degree turn into the basin just right and back alongside without tugs, which was nice. We were berthed starboard side to, which in a carrier is the easy side as it is the same side as the Island and consequently you are ideally placed to see what is happening.

Our new Chaplain, Ray Jones, was waiting for us on the jetty. A Welshman and a very live wire, he and his wife had had a pretty hectic flight out with four children under six. We also had a very good Free Church and Church of Scotland Padre, Peter Brown. The Chaplains were carried not only for Triumph but also for the destroyers and frigates on the station, but we did have a very well-appointed Chapel down below which could seat about 30 people. Before joining the Navy Ray Jones had been a curate in Bideford for three years, quite a coincidence. Both he and Peter Brown turned out to be a great success with the Ship's Company.

In the beginning of February I took the ship up to Hong Kong, exercising with various ships on the way. We berthed alongside the outer mole of the Naval Base where Peter Higham, the Commodore Hong Kong, was waiting to greet us. As usual the first couple of days were taken up with official calls but it was good to be back and see all the changes that had taken place since 1963. It was amazing that so much had changed, with skyscrapers now dwarfing the old colonial buildings that had been such a feature only seven years ago. I believe too that the population had increased by about a million.

For many of the Ship's Company it was their first visit and everyone was eager to get ashore. One of my first callers was Jenny of Jenny's Side Party who welcomed me warmly, anxious to be given the job of looking after our paintwork and the removal of 'gash', which of course she was. Mary had arranged to fly up with Mrs Dixon, the Supply Officer's wife, a couple of days after our arrival. They were staying in a Hotel in Kowloon and I had also brought up our ancient Opel car so that we would have our own wheels. A good idea but the car objected strongly to the Hong Kong hills!

Our main purpose in Hong Kong was to carry out maintenance on the ships based there, which kept the Fleet Maintenance Unit (FMU) busy. At the same time we had a good opportunity to get to know the local leading lights, both civilian and military. To this end Mary and I gave a couple of very enjoyable dinner parties, one of which resulted in being invited for a day's sailing in Jardine Matheson's very super 50-ft yawl.

Our visit also coincided with Shrove Tuesday and we organised the annual pancake race round the Naval Base. This attracted the local television and I found myself being interviewed by a very charming Chinese reporter and asked to give a demonstration on how to toss a pancake. Happily I managed to catch it and avoided losing face!

While we were in Hong Kong we got confirmation that a house in the Naval Base would be available by the time the ship returned at the beginning of March and at the end of the visit Mary flew back to Singapore to get the flat packed up and to move in. This she did, but we had made no allowance for the Civil Service mind. It seems that because the house had been occupied by a Commander, it had brown furniture and no carpets. Now that it was to be occupied by a Captain everything had to be changed, whether we minded or not. Captains had to have white furniture and decent rugs plus repainting to match. However all was eventually arranged as per regulations and we moved in, about two days after berthing in Singapore, in the first week in March.

The house, at the end of Kenya Crescent, was one of the old Colonial-style houses – a large bungalow on stilts with big rooms, overhead fans and grills or rattan blinds for windows, the whole object being to keep cool. The beds were all four-posters with mosquito-netting which had to be tucked in at night. There was a largish garden in the front with a variety of tropical plants and trees, including a banana tree. At the back of the house and connected by a covered way was a tiny cottage for the staff. In our case and because I had the full works on board, we decided that we could get along with a cook amah.

To get an amah we had to go with the system, i.e. an amah would be chosen for us by the senior Chinese servant on the base who would pocket the fee paid to him by all those seeking jobs. He ran the Tong and was all powerful. This is how we came to have a very delightful young Chinese girl called Min. It would seem that this was her first job on her own and she knew little about cooking, neither did she have much English but she was clean and willing and could always go round to another amah to find out what it was that Missy (Mary) wanted. The kitchen itself was pretty basic and the legs of the tables and store-cupboards had to stand in little bowls of water to prevent everything being eaten by ants when you weren't looking. It was wonderful to be able to unpack at last and get a sense of permanence.

However, sleeping was a problem, especially for me as on board I lived in air-conditioned comfort. After a very short time we bought a second-hand and rather noisy air-conditioner for the bedroom, had glass put in the windows and enjoyed a good night's rest. To make things even better, our new Volvo Estate had arrived from Sweden and we had a reliable and comfortable car, though it took us both a little time to get used to the automatic gear-box with several near-disasters through not leaving the car in 'Park' with the engine running.

Peter Everett and his wife left for home on 9th March, to be relieved by Max and Betty Walker from Rosyth. I was glad to start again with a new Commander who would do things as I wanted them done rather than what had pleased my predecessor.

Back in England everywhere was covered in snow and there were continual strikes, which was worrying as we had booked for David to fly out to join us for a couple of weeks towards the end of March. However, all went well and he arrived on time. He had wisely brought little with him in the way of clothes but a quick visit to Triumph's excellent tailor and the Sembawang shops soon had him fully equipped. Mary had met a nice Army Brigadier whose son was coming out at the same time and had arranged for them to go on a trip into the jungle up-country for several days, to the Tasek Bera area of Pahang . The area there is largely water and inhabited by aboriginals and all sorts of birds and animals so, after the initial rail journey, much of the trip was by boat and camping at night.

While David was up-country I took Triumph to sea for a week in company with *Intrepid*, Captain Jim Eberle, for exercises with 45 Commando (Colonel Roger Ephraums) embarked. Tom Stocker, the Commodore Amphibious Forces, was in charge in *Intrepid* which was equipped as a headquarters ship for this sort of thing, with lots of communication facilities including satellite – quite a contrast to Triumph where the communications set-up was basic. On our return Mary and I took a couple of days' Station Leave to go up to the Cameron Highlands and enjoy walking in the forest in cool fresh air for a welcome change. Keeping active in the tropics always requires a bit of effort. In Singapore it was my custom to walk down to the ship every morning, before it got too hot, and arrive on board just before seven o'clock in good time to change and have breakfast. In the late afternoon we usually played a round of golf or tennis. The base had quite a good little course which suited my standard. We had some really good golfers on board, one of our Chief ERAs having a single figure handicap, but they played at the Tanglin Club, a championship course.

As Vice Commodore of the Red House Sailing Club I used to race a couple of days a week in the GP 14 that I had rented. The local dockyard people had bagged all the newer ones but the rather elderly one that I was allocated turned out to be not too bad and we had some good results. Mary was my usual crew but, for inter-ship and inter-service events, my Petty Officer Cook was very keen and, though a good deal heavier than Mary, was a very useful chap to have. He was keen to be an officer and I was pleased to be able to put the wheels in motion for this to happen. In the 1990s, when Appledore Shipbuilders were completing several ships for the Royal Navy, Mary and I were delighted to welcome Lieutenant Commander Taylor and his wife to Instow when he was down inspecting the galley arrangements of the new ships. He was a first class chef too!

David returned to Bath at the end of April and at the beginning of May I took Triumph up to Penang to liase with the Ghurkhas who were stationed there, taking some helicopters with us. Mary flew up to join me there. Penang was and is a delightful island, though the approach to the anchorage and the anchorage itself were fairly nail-biting as there was very little water under the keel and one gets no marks for running aground. I found myself launched into a pretty full social programme starting with a very successful lunch party for the Chief Minister and his wife, Dr and Mrs Lim. Like Singapore, Penang is run by the Chinese and very well too. We were also well-looked-after by the Ghurkhas who are always a very super lot.

Just before we sailed I 'choppered' into the Ghurkha barracks for a farewell do for Admiral Hill-Norton, the C in C, who was doing the rounds of his Command to say good-bye before taking up his new job as First Sea Lord. Needless to say they put on a very fine show. I think I attended no less than four farewells 'does', including one in his house, before he actually went. He was relieved by a very nice Air Vice Marshall.

We sailed for Singapore on 10th May, Mary flying back to be greeted by a smiling Min who had spring-cleaned the house in her absence. I was quite glad to leave Penang as the weather had been pretty foul with a lot of wind which kicked up a very nasty short sea in the anchorage. Happily my Coxswain was pretty good and my motor boat remained unscathed but not so with some of the others. The ship normally berthed alongside so there was little occasion to practise boat handling and, as a consequence, I was always very relieved when all liberty men were safely back on board but the shipwrights had a busy old time making good the damage.

The war in Vietnam was still going and various American ships would come down to Singapore for rest and recreation. When they or other foreign ships visited the Naval Base it was normal to nominate one of our ships as host. This came our way quite often and we hosted several American destroyers, a cruiser, a French frigate and a US Coastguard Cutter commanded by a delightful Captain from Seattle called Abney. We used to enjoy these visits as it was a chance to meet new people and to appreciate how they dealt with their various problems. Apart from the usual naval hospitality, Mary and I would invite the Captain and several other officers up to our house for an informal supper – which Min always managed to produce – after which we sat out on our balcony, lit by little oil lamps, and put the world to rights.

At the beginning of June Mike started his Long Gunnery course at Whale Island, which meant that he would be in Portsmouth for a year. At the time I don't think either of us knew that this would be the last Long (G) course. All was about to change with the advent of Principal Warfare Officers (PWOs). However in Triumph it was off to sea again and up to Hong Kong for a week. Mary organised a wives' coffee morning and they all came down to the Base to wave us off.

In actual fact it was a wet and windy trip and at 1800 on the second day out we came across a tanker called Fair Transport, obviously in difficulties, and stopped. We made a lee so that we could send a boat over to see what the trouble was, secretly hoping that she would need a tow and we could get salvage money. However, it transpired that three large pipes from the tanker's engine were split and we sent over a repair team to remove them, bring them back on board for repair and then fit them back so that she could resume her voyage. She had an all-Chinese crew and was registered in Monrovia, so no come-back for us. All this took until 0230 the following morning and we had to do a 'full-power trial' to make our ETA in Hong Kong, arriving alongside at 1500 and, as far as I was concerned, having had very little sleep.

Whilst in Hong Kong I was able to buy a little jade horse for David's 21st and also a Singer sewing machine for Mary, which left me broke, so that I was delighted when the ship's tailor Mr Yu invited me, the Commander, the Chief, the Padre, the Supply Officer and several others to a slap-up Chinese meal in one of the best restaurants. The Chinese on board always feel that they have to do this sort of thing, first for 'face' and, second, to make sure in their minds that they won't get the sack, not that there was any danger of that in Mr Yu's case as he was first class. Indeed, as I write this, many years later, I still have a number of his excellent suits in my wardrobe.

When we returned to Singapore at the end of June, Mary had started dress-making classes with an Indian tailor and the new sewing machine was quickly put to good use as Mary became expert at knocking up dresses for herself and shirts for me. I specialised in buttonholes! Since the arrival of the new Chief of Staff, John Templeton-Cothill, brighter planters was the order of the day, 'planters' being the general term for what men wore for an informal evening out, consisting of long trousers, cream shirt and tie, but not any more! John himself was a colourful character; I had tried to teach him ship-handling back in the fifties without a great deal of success. A bachelor, he shared a château near Avignon with another bachelor and ex-First Lieutenant of mine, Dick Clayton. After Singapore John left the Navy, married a very nice woman about his age and became a director of Sotheby's in Paris.

Towards the end of July we had the visit of the French ship Chevalier Paul, which we hosted. They were a delightful bunch and Mary and I had a lunch party on board for the Captain and a couple of other officers, the French Ambassador and his wife, plus my Commander Max Walker and his wife Betty who was French. The Chef surpassed himself and it was fun to be speaking French again. It was altogether a very happy visit.

The next week Mary was off on her Grand Tour of the Pacific. The Admiral was to make a tour of his area and also have talks with the other naval Commanders on the way. The RAF provided an aircraft for him, Diana Empson and some of his staff but there were still seats to spare and several others, including Mary, were invited to go along for the ride. The trip took her to Brisbane, Fiji (where she stayed with her cousins Meg and Frazer Griffiths – Frazer was head of the Treasury there) and then on to Hawaii via Guam. They had five days in Honolulu, where Mary was looked after very well by the Abneys. He had been Captain of the US Coastguard Cutter that we had hosted earlier in the year when she visited Singapore for R & R. As they left Honolulu they were all given garlands of flowers. All in all she was away for ten days, returning via Wake and Manila, a trip of some 14,000 miles. I was extremely jealous.

It was about this time that I received a personal and confidential letter from Ewan Raikes, the Naval Secretary, to tell me that I would be relieved in the New Year and be appointed as Chief of Staff to Admiral ********** in the rank of Rear Admiral, and, as is usual in these cases, not to tell anyone except my wife. We were of course overjoyed – this was what I had worked and hoped for so you can imagine my utter disappointment and anger when some six weeks later I received another letter to say that Admiral ********** had been diagnosed with cancer, so was unable to take up his appointment, and that his replacement wanted another chap as his Chief of Staff. However, he would give me a very nice job instead as Commodore of the Barracks at Portsmouth, which he was sure that I would enjoy. It took me several days to calm down. I would have liked to have chucked the Navy there and then and I suppose that I should have instantly resigned.

The trouble was that I was enjoying the best job of my life and didn't wish to do anything to curtail it. After a lot of discussion with Mary I decided to carry on; I would take the maximum pension that I could from the Navy but I was never going to work for another employer. On retiring I would do my own thing or bust. On reflection and many years later you realise that you have to accept that this is how life near the top works. In my time Admirals were always given the choice of picking their own team, certainly their Chief of Staff and Secretary, people with whom they had worked together and who knew their ways and vice versa. If you picked a winner you could go on up together. Sadly my horse was a faller.

While all this was going on, life went on apace. Mike flew out to stay with us for a week during his summer leave; it was good to see him. He was keen to learn to water-ski and my Secretary, Mike Ellis, organised this but Mike soon discovered that water was a lot harder than snow and, though he succeeded, he was black and blue by the end. He had various chums in Singapore so we had a big supper-party at the house and all Min's relations turned up to help. On the Sunday we had a Confirmation Service on board taken by the Bishop of Singapore who, with his wife, stayed on for lunch afterwards.

Back home there had been a General Election with victory for the Conservatives and shortly afterwards we had a visit from an all-party Defence Committee led by Bill Deedes – later Editor of the *Daily Telegraph* and now Lord Deedes. They were brought on board by the new C-in-C, Air Vice Marshall Burnett, and I gave them a tour of the ship, with a briefing on what we did, which I think quite surprised them as, by now, we had done so much with the Amphibious Group that we proudly sported the Combined Operations badge on our funnel, as did *Fearless* and *Intrepid*. Later, at lunch, they were able to meet many of the officers and we hoped that they went on their way well-satisfied. We were certainly impressed by their interest and depth of knowledge.

Shortly after Mike had left, David arrived, having spent about four weeks at Santander University learning Spanish. It seemed that the course had been good but he was very short of money, which was our fault. In Singapore most of his acquaintances from the previous visit had already gone home so that he had a fairly quiet time until he went back to Bath at the beginning of October.

About ten days after Mike had flown home our phone rang at about 3 o'clock in the morning. This was Mike to say that he and Philippa Crabtree were going to get married at the beginning of December, so it was all systems go from then on, with plans for Mary and me to fly home for the wedding, guest lists with Granny Bull, wedding presents and all the usual palaver. However, weddings were happening in Singapore as well. My Damage-Control Officer, Lieutenant Tom Allen, was marrying a very nice Queen Alexandra's Nursing Sister, Jane. As she had no relatives able to come out to Singapore she asked me if I would act in loco parentis and give her away and this I gladly agreed to do. The wedding was in the Dockyard Church which was quite close to our house, about two minutes in the car. Mary and Min helped her dress but, as we were ready absolutely on time, I suggested that we should wait five minutes to build up a little tension. Little did I know that the dockyard workers had chosen that very moment to go on strike and we were held up by the crowd for about ten minutes, with emotions running very high indeed. Fortunately all ended well; it was a splendid wedding, with a reception in *Triumph*, and everyone was very happy. We still keep in touch with our honorary daughter.

Aboard we were getting ourselves ready for a trip to Hong Kong and then on to Japan. Amongst other things I was advised that I had to have gifts to present in Japan when calling on different authorities as an exchange of presents was part of the ritual. I was advised that Malt Whisky was very acceptable and so I had to spend a lot of money buying half a dozen bottles of malt whiskey in Singapore and then getting the shipwrights to make a presentation casket for each bottle. I was horrified later when presenting them to find that the Japanese drank it with ginger ale!

Before leaving we were faced with an Admiral's inspection. These inspections happen usually once in a Commission and involve an inspection of the Ship and Ship's Company, with everything clean and tidy and everyone in their Sunday best,, followed by a second day with the ship being put through its paces by the Admiral's Staff to test the reaction to different emergencies, winding up with some special scenario worked out by the Staff to try and catch us out.

The inspecting officer was Rear Admiral John Templeton-Cothill, the Chief of Staff. All went really pretty well and the final big set piece on the second day was a terrorist attack on the ship carried out by members of the Royal Malaysian Navy acting the part of terrorists. John T-C was on the bridge conducting affairs and I had let him have my bridge chair while I stood at the back of the bridge. I could hardly contain myself as I watched a 'terrorist' creep silently up to the compass platform to place a bomb under the Captain's chair. John T-C was blissfully unaware and when the thunder flash went off underneath him he shot some six feet into air. Though we were all laughing hysterically, he somehow didn't see the funny side. Never mind we had had our money's worth. In actual fact we got a very good report so all was well and the ship received a very nice signal from Admiral Empson.

At the end of September we sailed for Hong Kong arriving on the 29th. Going alongside I gave myself – and anyone else looking – a very nasty fright. Just as I was making my final approach we were hit by strong squall and the ship started to be blown sideways on to an American cruiser moored alongside. The tug, which was between me and the jetty to give us a shove if needed, thought that it would be the jam in the sandwich and shot off out of it. It looked certain that disaster would follow. I needed to get the ship resting against the pontoons of the jetty up ahead to stop the sideways movement. I rang down for full speed ahead on both engines and got a splendid response from the engine room. We surged ahead, which stopped the drift, then it was full speed astern to bring her up and, though we hit the first pontoon with a fair thump, the only things that got bent were the gash (rubbish) chute and my pride. It was the only bosh shot that I made during my time in the ship and it could have been a very expensive one. Roger Wyke-Sneyd, the new Commodore Hong Kong, who was waiting on the jetty to greet me, was not very impressed by my performance and neither was I.

We had only a short time in Hong Kong before sailing for Sasebo on the island of Kyushu, the southern island of Japan but I had time to have the Bazalgettes and the Wyke-Sneyds to lunch and to meet the new Governor, Sir David Trench. He was a super chap and in his younger days had been in the Hong Kong Police and spoke fluent Cantonese, which must have been a great asset.

At this time, too, the build-up for Mike's wedding was going apace, with letters about guests, wedding presents, how we were going to fly home, how much it would cost and whether or not Mary could get her fur coat out of store.

Before sailing on 2nd October we embarked the band of the Royal Welsh Fusiliers, who were delighted with the opportunity to visit Japan and who would be a great asset to us. We had a pretty horrible trip up, force 9 part of the way and constant rain; in addition we had to make the passage at 18 knots to get there on time. Everyone was extremely seasick and it was jolly cold too. The band wished they had never volunteered. We arrived in Sasebo at 0830 on the 5th amidst glorious sunshine, no wind and the band playing as we berthed alongside in the Naval Base, which was shared by the Japanese Defence Force and the US Navy. I was immediately launched into a pretty hectic schedule:

    0845 Press conference with 24 Japanese journalists
    0930 Call on Admiral Mitzutani (with bottle of whisky in casket)
    0950 Call on President of Sasebo Chamber of Commerce(another bottle)
    1010 Call on Mayor of Sasebo (another bottle)

Later that morning my calls were returned and then in the afternoon it was the turn of the Americans (no whisky!). The Captain of their base lent me an old Chevrolet for my own use while we were there, which was excellent. At 1830 we gave a cocktail party and afterwards I had Admiral and Mrs Mizutani, the Mayor and Mrs Tsuji, Captain and Mrs Shaw USN and a couple of others to supper. The Japanese ladies wore the most beautiful Kimonos but spoke no English and did a lot of giggling, especially when it came to knives and forks, though the Chef had done his best to avoid their having to cut things up. It all seemed to go pretty well and the Mayor of

Sasebo's main topic of conversation was how he could buy a pair of Purdy shotguns and how much would they cost and he didn't seem at all put out by the huge price that I gave him.

The next day, with my Cox'n driving, I took Max Walker and David Dixon on a trip around the coast. The countryside was a cross between Norway and Switzerland, really delightful with little fjords, fishing villages and oyster farms. Then, on the following day, I took my secretary Mike Ellis to explore inland which was even more attractive. Everyone was busy with the harvest and, as the fields were all terraced on the steep hillsides, it all had to be cut by sickle and stooked up as, I felt sure, it had been for a thousand years. We also visited a huge and very ancient Shinto shrine.

There was a big ceremony going on and it was fascinating to see the priests in their gorgeous robes and tall black hats. It looked like a scene out of 'The Mikado'. One had to wonder how it was that people who lived in such a beautiful country could have been so cruel but then, when we drove through towns or where there were a number of building sites, there were gangs of women all dressed in the same sort of uniform and the same went for the factory workers. Before going on this trip I and several other officers had been invited out to lunch by Admiral Mizutani and the Mayor at a restaurant perched on top of a hill behind Sasebo. Situated at about 1200 feet it had a wonderful panoramic view of the countryside. The lunch was out-of-doors and, thankfully, we were given chairs as I would never have managed had we sat Japanese-style on the ground. All the food was cooked on stoves in front of each table. The restaurant was part of an edible-fungus farm and so we ate all sorts of odd-looking things besides meat, prawns and other vegetables, but it was all delicious.

We sailed for Hong Kong on 7th Oct, with everyone on board having thoroughly enjoyed their visit. The Chaplain, Ray Jones, had done a splendid job in organising coach trips so that well over half the Ship's Company had had the opportunity to see the country and visit some of the many places of interest, including the reconstructed city of Nagasaki (wiped out by an atom bomb in 1945). Just to be on the safe side Ray had had himself blessed at the old Shinto shrine for 300 yen – about 10p in sterling today. I was concerned about typhoon Irma between us and Hong Kong but luckily it veered out of our path and the passage back was a great improvement on the one coming up.

We arrived in Hong Kong at 0730 on the 12th and almost immediately started embarking 40 Commando in preparation for sailing at 1630. In the meantime Jim Eberley (Captain of *Intrepid*) and I had to attend an exercise-briefing so that we should know what to do. The briefing was given by Derek Napper, Commodore Amphibious Forces (COMAF), and Pat Ovens, Brigade Commander of the 3rd Commando Brigade. Once at sea it was all go, with helicopters pouring in and out, the first landings taking place in the New Territories quite close to the Shaw Studios which Mary and I had been invited to visit earlier in the year. The activity went on until the 15th, both by day and by night, which meant not much sleep, but it was all good clean fun. The imminent arrival of Typhoon Jane put an end to it all, as it became too windy to operate choppers, and *Intrepid*, *Llandaff* and *Triumph* were ordered to take shelter in Mirs Bay, a well-sheltered inlet on the North side of the New Territories. We had quite a job getting all our troops and choppers back on board.

The following day COMAF ordered us all to sea to steam off in an easterly direction so as to get behind the typhoon. We spent a most uncomfortable twenty-four hours rolling around and I could see no point in going on as, from the noises coming from the heavy equipment in the hangar, I had grave fears that something would break loose and we would be in serious trouble. I signalled COMAF in *Intrepid* that I was fed up and would like to go back to Mirs Bay, which I did. It was a great relief to be back in a snug anchorage though, of course, main engines and everyone were kept at immediate notice to shove off out of it in the event that 'Joan' turned our way. It didn't and a little later I had a signal from *Intrepid* asking if there was room for him too! There was. However, we did not have to wait too long for the weather to improve and on the 18th we were back alongside in Hong Kong, disembarking all remaining troops and gear ready to sail the following day, Typhoon Kate permitting.

Back at Singapore Mary was having a busy time getting messages to the link wives so that everyone knew what was going on and it worked very well. We managed to keep the mail going through all this and Mary and I were corresponding every day, mostly about Mike's wedding – now only six weeks away.

We arrived back in Singapore on the 22nd and everyone was delighted to be home again. Typhoons excepted, it had been a very successful trip; it had done the ship a lot of good and we were feeling very pleased with ourselves. It was shortly after this that I received the bombshell that my promotion to Rear Admiral was off. However, the imminent return to England and last-minute planning helped to take our minds off it. I had leave to go home and Mary and I were booked to fly to England on 2nd December, returning on the 12th.

Life, though, is full of surprises. On 18th November the news broke that huge areas of Bangladesh (East Pakistan) had been flooded by the south-west monsoon, tens of thousands had lost their homes and many were dead. The British Government had promised immediate aid and *Triumph* and *Intrepid* were ordered to take it there. My plans for going home for the wedding had gone down the chute and we decided that Mary should go home by herself. It was all a dreadful disappointment but nothing compared to the disaster that we had been called upon to help.

Jim Eberley had just been relieved by William Staveley and COMAF was up in Hong Kong, so I was senior officer. There followed twenty-four hours of frantic activity as we embarked helicopters, lorries, bridge-building and well-digging equipment, about 100 inflatable boats with outboard motors, aircrew, a squadron of Royal Engineers, a field hospital and goodness knows what else. In addition we loaded 1,000 tons of rice in sacks, plus clothing and medical supplies. The rice had to be brought on board by our sailors and stowed in passages or wherever there was space. I was getting quite worried about topweight as things were piled upon us and, in fact, our draught increased by just over a foot. The Ship's Company worked tirelessly until everything was stowed securely and, meanwhile, the same thing was going on in *Intrepid*. It is amazing how sailors always react so well to a challenge.

We sailed in company on the evening of the 20th. Mary had come down to see us off and she looked such a lonely figure standing there on the jetty. It really was unfortunate as we had been looking forward so much to going home together for one of the most important occasions of our life. There must be something about us and weddings.

The 21st found both ships steaming at full speed, 25 knots, for the Ganges Delta, a distance of some 1,600 miles. We expected to arrive at about midnight on the 23rd. We had on board, besides the aircrew, some 350 Army personnel and a full house of newspaper reporters who immediately installed themselves, as reporters do, at the Wardroom bar.

We had flown mail ashore on passing Penang and in the mail that came back was a letter from Ewan Raikes, confirming my appointment as Commodore of the Barracks at Portsmouth and suggesting that we should ring his office to fix dates while we were in England. I passed this on to Mary as soon as I could.

Because of our dated communications 'fit' William Staveley suggested that I should transfer to *Intrepid* but, as I had a small Command chopper in *Triumph*, I elected to stay put and pop over as required, knowing that when we arrived at our destination both Derek Napper (COMAF) and Pat Ovens (3rd Commando Brigade) would be joining *Intrepid* and taking over command of the operation. Anyway, I always enjoyed any excuse to get airborne. I held several planning meetings in *Intrepid* and we worked out how we should go about our task. One of the big problems was distance. The depth of water off the Delta was uncertain and very shallow which meant that we would have to anchor several miles off, making the journeys for our landing craft long and difficult. While we could land immediate aid by chopper, any heavy stuff would have to go by boat and we decided to set up a forward base ashore where boats crews could check in and refuel if necessary.

One of the (doubtful) advantages fitted in *Intrepid* was satellite communications, which meant that we were constantly receiving phone calls from Whitehall. Ted Heath, the Prime Minister, phoned several times to ask how we were getting on and to wish us well. We also had to set up a special briefing facility so that the 'gentlemen' from the media could file their dispatches.

The weather was excellent – clear blue skies, little wind and a long low swell. From the air both ships looked magnificent as we made our way northward at full speed and I felt really proud of my command. The Chief was jolly pleased too as *Intrepid* couldn't keep up the pace and had gradually to drop astern. We had sad news on the way that the wife of one my artificers, MEA Hodgkiss, had died suddenly and without any reason. He and his wife were a charming couple and we had had them to lunch with the Bishop of Singapore not so long before. It was my job to tell him and the poor man was quite shattered. I arranged that on our arrival he would be flown ashore in the Wessex helicopter that was flying into Dacca to pick up Derek Napper; he would then be flown back to Singapore. We arrived off the Delta at midnight on the 23rd and dropped anchor. Everyone needed a good night's rest before the activity started at first light. The great disappointment of the Ship's Company was that when they turned to in the morning, all rearing to go, there was absolutely nothing to see. From the highest point in the ship the low-lying coastline was just a thin featureless blur on the horizon, though there were some buoys to mark the passage up river.

Everyone turned to with a will, getting boats out and loaded. Our job was to get ashore what we had brought up and then help with more supplies which were being flown into Dacca. It was a huge problem. I flew into the little town of Patuakhali, where the Pakistani Army and the local civil authorities had set up their headquarters and where Pat Ovens had established his HQ alongside. Derek Napper had flown off to *Intrepid* and we were glad to see him as neither I nor William Staveley were much impressed by Oven's organising abilities and had been getting more and more frustrated. We got a good insight into the problem as we flew in over the disaster area.

It was such a huge area that had been affected and the bit that we were responsible for covered 1800 square miles of paddy fields divided into small holdings, absolutely flat with various bits of the Ganges running through it from North to South. The whole region was criss-crossed by a myriad of small waterways, dykes and ditches. There was not a road in the place, all communication being by boat and these had nearly all been destroyed and the jetties washed away. Now, as we flew in, the floods had subsided leaving the survivors and the remains of the paddy and livestock.

Seeing it from the air it didn't look too bad, many of the huts were still standing and there were quite a few people and livestock to be seen but, of course, what had actually happened was that the entire rice crop for the year had been washed away just before harvest time, leaving only the stalks standing. Thus, though outwardly it looked all right, there was nothing for the people to eat and there wouldn't be until the next harvest in six months' time. The people lived almost entirely on rice and their pitifully small income came from selling it. It seemed that those who were saved were the ones whose houses had survived the 150 mph winds or who had clung to palm trees or bits of floating timber. I did not see any human corpses but there were numbers of dead bullocks floating about and some were seen drifting past the ship.

Our job was to get the food to the main dumps, where it would be guarded by the Pakistani Army, and from there distributed by helicopter and boat to the villages, homesteads and islands. We had sent off a flotilla of boats under the command of one my officers and I was left wondering if and when we should see them again. We were 20 miles off shore and it was another 35 miles up river to Patuakhali. Meanwhile the Army were off-loading their gear into a couple of large landing-craft that we had brought, plus some from *Intrepid*. Later on that day we were joined by a RFA supply ship so there would be no shortage of stores or aviation spirit. With everything having to come to a halt at sunset, we were all able to enjoy a good night's sleep or rather all except the boats' crews up-river.

Meanwhile, Mary was in the air on her way back to Exmouth and all which that would entail.

The following day things seemed to have settled down: the multitude of boats had found their way back to the ship for reloading and I was able to get rid of some of the media who were being a pain in the neck, as is their wont. We also had a surprise visit from the Ministers for Defence and Overseas Aid who had come out from England to see how we were doing. I think that they were impressed. They jolly well should have been as we were doing really very well and I was delighted to see the rice mountain rapidly decreasing as it was flown or ferried ashore.

On another trip ashore I was flown over the area by the Pakistani Air Force, accompanied by the local Army Commander, who explained what exactly was going on and, once again, I was appalled by the size of the problem and, not least, by the fact that this sort of thing happened so frequently. It appears that, up until the fifties, there had been a large area of coastal mangrove swamps and forest which had protected the hinterland but, to accommodate their ever-expanding population, these had been cleared to provide more land for cultivation with the consequential devastating effect.

There was no doubt at all that the people were thankful for the help that we had brought; the only thing that really annoyed me was that the locals wouldn't unload the helicopters unless we paid them, even though they were starving! Meanwhile our medical teams were kept very busy dealing with locals injured in the disaster and our sickbay was kept full. Having been an Aircraft Carrier it was well-equipped and we had about 10 beds. It was really a mini-hospital with an operating theatre.

It was in the morning of the 27th that I received a signal from Derek Empson, Commander Far East Fleet, which said, 'Let your Commander have a go at driving the ship and go home for your son's wedding'. I was overjoyed and immediately sent off a telegram to Mary, in Exmouth, to say that I now expected to be home for the wedding. The news also brought on panic. How was I going to get there, what did I need to take, what did I have to do before leaving and, above all, how was I going to pay the fare? This was before the days of Credit Cards and I certainly didn't have enough money in the bank to pay a full single fare from Dacca to London via Karachi. The last day to arrive in Exmouth would be 4th December, the day before the wedding, which meant that I would have to leave Dacca at the latest on the 3rd. I had four days to get myself organised or perhaps, if things went well, less.

The first thing I had to do was to write a report of proceedings for COMFEF which in turn meant getting reports from the various heads of departments and also from *Intrepid*. While this was going on my Secretary had the task of finding out all about flights and costs and my Leading Steward had the task of getting out my best blue uniform, and all that went with it, and weighing it.

The news quickly got round the ship that the skipper was off home and this also filtered through to the media lot. To my great delight the reporter from the *Daily Mail* said that he could give me his ticket from Karachi to London provided I took back two cans of film without telling any of the other reporters so that he would scoop the news. This I agreed to do, but not without a great deal of worry about what the cans really contained. One certainly couldn't risk that sort of thing today.

Then I arranged to draw a month's pay in advance so that I would be all right from Dacca to Karachi. Next we concocted a fairly official looking piece of paper which read:

'TO WHOM IT MAY CONCERN. This is to certify that Captain C.J.A. Johnson, Royal Navy, is required to proceed on duty from HMS *Triumph*, at sea off Chittagong, to the United Kingdom and to proceed via Dacca, East Pakistan.'

Max Walker signed it as Commanding Officer and we impressed it with the ship's stamp. I was ready for the off.

Everything finally sorted, I got the command helicopter to take me to Dacca on the afternoon of the 29th. I booked into a hotel near the airport, ready for the flight to Karachi the following morning. Having got my ticket and having time to spare, I went for a walk into the country. Here it was undamaged by the storms and everything was green and lush. I was fascinated by all the little homesteads and the colours of the wild flowers and, in particular, the birds – the bulbuls and so forth all with beautiful plumage. But everywhere was so poor and, going into and out of the hotel, you had to face a barrage of professional beggars.

However, after a rather sticky night (no air-conditioning), it was breakfast and off to the airport. The flight to Karachi was in an old Dakota or DC3, which stopped at airports on the way and it was amusing to see who got on and off. Apparently it was a festival of some sort so people where going home to visit their families and were carrying all sorts of presents in the shape of vegetables, chickens (dead) and goodness knows what. There was a woman sitting next to me from whose basket a white sticky liquid slowly oozed on to the floor. We arrived on time in Karachi and I joined the queue for the BOAC flight to London with all my bits and pieces.

All was fine until I got to passport control. I showed them my piece of paper from *Triumph*, but it didn't work. I explained that I had come to save their country, but no good. My passport had not been stamped on entering the country, therefore I couldn't leave because I hadn't come in! I was holding up the queue as I argued with the passport wallah and everyone behind me was getting touchy. Finally someone from the back of the queue whispered in my ear that the magic words were 'crew change'. I took the hint and said that I was crew change. My passport was stamped immediately and, without further question, I was off.

After a good flight to London I bussed to Reading and then caught the train to Exeter, where Mary met me. I was tired, jolly cold, but delighted to be home. We had all arranged to stay at West View just along the road from No. 4 Gertrude Terrace.

This was still in the happy days when the bride's parents were expected to pay for just about everything and the Crabtrees had done a wonderful job. It was a lovely service in the church at Littleham – beautifully decorated – with everyone looking their best, followed by a tremendous reception arranged at the Royal Marine Mess at Lympstone. It couldn't have been better. Adrian Brunner did a good job as best man and had organised a good arch of swords for Mike and Pip as they came out of the church. They eventually left the reception looking very smart in a Rolls and, after a night in an expensive hotel, were off to their flat in a part of the Brunner parents' house near Portsmouth, before going on a late honeymoon to Paris during the Christmas leave period. Our contribution in all this was to give a large dinner party at the Imperial Hotel, which seemed to go pretty well. It was a mixture of Crabtrees, Bulls, Elphinstones, some old friends and, of course, us.

The following day, Sunday, Mary and I were off on the return flight to Singapore, leaving Granny B holding the baby, so to speak. It was a pity that it was all such a rush. David drove us to RAF Lynham where we would catch a VC 10 to Singapore. We set off in fine style with David saying that he knew the way. He did, but not to Lynham and we had gone quite a long way before we realised that we were heading for RAF Brize Norton, another Transport Command airfield which David had been to before. Disaster! It looked as if we would never be at Lynham in time and of course there were no public telephones in sight. However we had to go past Bath, so we called in on Geoffrey Kirkby and asked him to ring Lynham to tell them we were delayed and to hold the plane until we got there. In actual fact we arrived at just about take off time and were met and bustled out and on to the plane, which took off without more ado. Phew!

The following day we were back in Singapore, with Min to greet us. *Triumph* was back in the Naval Base with three frigates alongside for maintenance. She had sailed from the Delta soon after I had left. Having unloaded all the extra Army personnel, boats and the stores that we had taken up, there was little more that she could do. In fact everything was back to normal, as if we had never been away, except that everywhere that one went in the ship there seemed to be grains of rice which had leaked from the sacks. It was several months before we finally got rid of these little white souvenirs. Of course it was a great morale boost for the ship and we were all proud of what we had achieved.

The post mortem had shown that Mrs Hodgkiss, the wife whose sad death occurred while on our way north, had died from a brain tumour which had been quite unexpected. Her funeral had taken place while we were in England. Sadly she was just one of about ten deaths that occurred during our time out there – mostly children and wives – but one of the saddest occurred just before Christmas during a football match. A young rating was playing for the ship's First XI and his wife and tiny baby, who had only just arrived out from England, were in the stand to watch him play. It was near the end of the match when a rain storm with thunder and lightning started, nothing unusual in Singapore. Play continued, but just as this young chap was about to take a corner kick, he was struck dead by a bolt of lightning. It was unbelievable. We were all numbed by the event. One of the *Triumph* wives turned up trumps and took care of the young widow and her baby until her late husband's parents were flown out from England for the funeral. But life had to go on and the 15th December saw nine children baptized at a Family Communion on board.

With Christmas upon us we once again had a huge gathering for the Carol Service and the Midnight Service on Christmas Eve was taken by Ambrose Weekes of Shotley days, who was now Chaplain of the Fleet. It was a candlelight service and the Quarterdeck, beautifully decorated, looked lovely. Somebody had made a splendid crib with very well-carved figures, really brilliant, and some 200 came to the service. On Christmas Day itself Mary and I survived rounds of the messes. We had our own meal in the evening with an assortment of people from the ship. Min had prepared it all and it was excellent. It was the first time that she had done a Christmas dinner so she was very pleased that it went well. Back in England we heard that people were suffering a succession of power cuts and postal strikes so we counted ourselves lucky indeed.

In the middle of January Singapore was bracing itself for the Commonwealth Conference, with all sorts of things arranged. Mary and I were invited to a reception at the Commander-in-Chief's house so that we could meet Ted Heath and Sir Alec Douglas-Home, the Foreign Secretary. We both thought that Sir Alec looked very tired. I had a long talk with the Prime Minister on sailing, especially his early days racing 'Snipes' on the South Coast. He seemed a real leader and pretty tough with it but, at the same time, he was easy to talk to and had a great sense of humour. I thought that he would be a great chap to have as PM and just the sort the country needed but sadly he didn't have great success. I think that the Unions were too strong for his type of politics.

The end of the conference coincided with Chinese New Year, a time for great celebrations and wonderful fireworks. Min presented us with a special treat that all the Chinese have at this time, Moon Cake. It looked all right but tasted absolutely filthy, or so it seemed to us, and I had to lose it surreptitiously in a monsoon ditch at the bottom of our garden.

The time was fast approaching when we had to start making arrangements for returning to England and we sent the Volvo off in a RFA at the beginning of February but, of course, we still had the old Opel so that we were not carless. Many others in the ship were also getting relieved, fifteen to eighteen months being the time allowed for married accompanied personnel. In fact our trip to Hong Kong at this time was to be my last. Many of the wives went up by air for a last visit but Mary had managed to fix up a trip aboard the RFA Landing Ship, Sir Galahad, which was to call into Miri in Brunei on the way, while I took the Opel up in the ship. We had had the brakes fixed so that it now behaved pretty well.

By now, of course, we had many friends in Hong Kong and it was sad that we were going to be saying goodbye to them. Whilst we were there the Empsons came up on a farewell visit and the Admiral flew his flag in *Triumph*. This meant that I had to clear out of my cabin for a couple of days so that he could entertain the local VIPs on board – no real hardship as we were staying with the Bazalgettes and, in any case, I always had my sea cabin as a retreat if necessary.

Hong Kong had just built a new and very smart Opera House and we went to see a production of Madame Butterfly. It was extremely well-done, with all the Japanese parts sung by Chinese and the Americans played by Eurasians – such a difference having the right-looking sort of people and it made the whole thing so real. The following night we saw a traditional Chinese Opera played in English, also fun, with superb costumes. The only fly in the ointment during this visit was that Mary had her handbag stolen out of the car while we were standing alongside it. We had got out to look at a very tall pagoda in the New Territories and while I was taking a photograph the bag disappeared, despite the fact that there was no one in sight either before or after. Chinese Magic but very annoying.

Triumph sailed from Hong Kong on 10th March, while Mary flew back with the Empsons via Bangkok, all arriving at Singapore on the 13th. Leaving the berth at *Tamar*, I had a nasty shock as I realised that my Navigation Officer was in no way fit to carry out his duties. Because of a medical condition Andrew was not allowed to have alcohol and some idiot had slipped him a 'Mickey Finn', with the result that he was hopelessly drunk and had to be taken below. Normally I could rely on him to give me courses to steer, distance to the next turn and all the vital information necessary to get a big ship out of a very busy harbour. I was up the creek without the proverbial paddle, added to which it was raining and jolly windy. It was back to basics, with me rushing to and from the chart table and the officer of the watch filling in the gaps. It was an anxious twenty minutes and I was thankful when we reached the open sea. Otherwise the trip back to Singapore passed without incident.

Before we went our separate ways, Mary asked me if there was anything that I wanted in Bangkok. 'Please bring me a kite', was my reply, as the Thais were famous kite makers and I looked forward to being presented with one on arrival but it was not my lucky week. Mary had bought me a splendid kite and special string but found that she hadn't room to bring it with her on the Empson's plane. She had given it to a friend to bring but, sadly, it never arrived. I have the string to this day.

Back in Singapore, with just a month before the arrival of my relief, we began the inevitable round of farewell calls, parties and visits, making arrangements to take back 'Croft' (our house in Instow) and getting all our bits and pieces packed and ready to ship home. We had a wonderful firm of Chinese packers who wrapped everything individually in masses of paper tied up with string and threw it off the balcony to the waiting van below. We had bought quite a few bits of china and precious objects and all of them were to arrive home totally undamaged. Meanwhile I had a lot to do on board with reports on every officer to be written, final inspections and so forth, in preparation for handing over to my successor, John Forbes, on 19th April.

For me it was a sad time. This was to be my last chance of going to sea and enjoying that special relationship that one has with a Ship's Company that cannot be repeated anywhere else. As Captain I have always made it a habit to walk about the ship during working hours, talk to people at their place of work about what they were doing and why, about their homes and families, their hopes and ambitions and so forth and in doing so I would get to know a lot of people and, hopefully, they got to know me. Of course Mary too had had a very good rapport with the large number of wives and families that had come out to Singapore. I always wished that I had her facility for remembering everyone's name and, more importantly, the names and ages of all their children. I think that together we had made a pretty good team.

Sadly the 19th arrived all too soon and, after receiving my relief on board, introducing him to the officers, giving him a quick turnover – which included selling him the Opel for the same £10 that I had paid for it – I had the honour of being 'cheered ship' by the Ship's Company on the flight deck and then rowed ashore in one of the ship's whalers by my Commanders. The ship was at a buoy and they pulled me to the Red House steps. Then came the horrid realisation that, as the boat pulled away back to the ship, the curtain had fallen on one of the best episodes of our life. Now it was a question of finally clearing out of our house, bidding farewell to a tearful Min and flying home. A slight consolation was that, for the first time in our lives, we actually had our own house to go to.

Extract from *Triumph* Wives in Singapore (TWINS) Magazine for March 1971:

'Bouquet'. Captain and Mrs Johnson are leaving at the end of this month. We have all, in *Triumph*, been sadly aware of this fact. Over a number of months we have steadily 'Grown accustomed' to their faces and we will miss them both enormously. Mrs Johnson in particular will be missed by all the *Triumph* wives, whether they have had direct or indirect contact with her. She has been such a thoughtful 'Mum' to us all – in a kind, gentle, understanding and very discreet way she has done a tremendous amount for the wives and the ship, always ready to listen or to help. 'The nicest Captain's wife one can dream of and so easy to talk to' is the cry I have so often heard. And how very true too. Yes indeed *Triumph* won't be the same without her and following in her steps will be a very difficult task for whoever attempts it. The Officers and Wives of Portsmouth Barracks are lucky people, a fact they will soon appreciate as we, in *Triumph*, have done.

'During the past 16 months it has been our privilege to have her as our guardian angel, Mrs Johnson, and it is indeed a sad time when we now have to say 'adieu'... none of us wish to say 'goodbye'.

'Mrs Johnson has been a tower of strength to each and every one of us, her help, advice, assurance has been readily given although at times surely Mrs Johnson herself must have felt as though she had 'had it'. One can but admire such a staunch, humble, stalwart Captain's wife.

'Mrs Johnson, from all *Triumph* wives, our sincere thanks. God bless you and every best wish for the future.'*

*Author's Note. I would like to say 'Hear Hear'!

CHAPTER 21

Commodore Royal Naval Barracks
PORTSMOUTH
15th June 1971
to 25th October 1972

Arriving back in England from Singapore was quite a contrast, back to normality and rather nice. The first thing was to collect the Volvo and make our way down to Instow. Having been 'let' for nearly ten years everything was pretty run down, so there was plenty to do, but of course the very first thing was to collect the dogs from their 'holiday home' at Chelfham, just the other side of Barnstaple. We wondered if they would still recognise us but we needn't have worried. The moment Jenny and Tijuana saw us it was just like we had never been away and as soon as we opened the car they jumped in and immediately sat in their usual places ready to be taken home. I think that they had had a pretty good time really, for, though the place was advertised as boarding kennels, they were allowed in the house as well as having good country walks, so we were delighted to find them so fit and well. In Croft we fixed them up with a couple of old armchairs in the garage so that they had very comfortable and snug beds which they loved.

We had about six weeks to sort ourselves out before starting the next job at Portsmouth. I had to get my uniform altered and get some additional and costly bits and pieces, such as a dress uniform tailcoat and trousers, and also waited anxiously for all our gear to arrive so that we could unpack and start again. I had several helpful letters from the outgoing Commodore, E.W.Ellis, telling me what to expect. Happily everything did arrive on time with nothing damaged and on 14th June we arrived at Anchor Gate House in Portsmouth, ready to take up my new job on the morrow. The Ellises had, of course, moved out to give us a clear run.

I was not pleased to have the job and was not looking forward to it in any way. I was still carrying a large chip on my shoulder, so the first surprise was to find that we had moved into one of the best houses in the Navy and to be greeted by a delightful staff. The house itself had been built during the Napoleonic wars, by French prisoners of war, to house the Admiral in charge of all the hulks which lay in Portsmouth harbour and which housed these French prisoners. Situated near Unicorn gate, it had about one-and-a-half acres of garden surrounded by high walls, a tennis court and lots of out-buildings. Perhaps the only snag was that on the other side of one wall was the Naval Detention Quarters but this was to disturb us not one iota.

We had an elegant drawing room, a dining room that could seat 16 guests and numerous bedrooms and bathrooms. Mary and I had a very comfortable bedroom with dressing-room and bathroom. In the bedroom was the most splendid dressing-table you could imagine. White with huge mirrors which somehow provided an all round image of yourself whether you liked it or not. The dressing table had at one time belonged to Princess Alice, one of Queen Victoria's daughters, and the backing of each looking glass was solid silver. In fact there were many antiques in the house which had come at some time or other from the old Royal Yacht, *Victoria and Albert*.

As for staff we had a Petty Officer Steward, a Leading Steward as my valet, a Wren for Mary, a Chief Cook and a Petty Officer Cook, my Cox'n who was a Seaman Petty Officer and who drove the official car and, finally, a civilian gardener. Our first reaction was, 'This is jolly nice but its going to cost us an arm and a leg'. Which, of course, it did!

Next morning, 15th June, life began in earnest. At ten to nine my car was waiting outside the front door with my Commodore's pennant (a cross of St George with a red ball in each of the two squares nearest the mast) flying from the mini-flagstaff on the bonnet. This was to take me to the Barracks parade ground where I was to inspect the Guard of Honour, meet the Heads of Departments and find out what it was that I was supposed to do. Dressed in my best suit with sword and medals, I was greeted by the outgoing Commodore, the bugler sounded the Alert and I was invited to mount the dais to take the salute while the Guard presented arms. I was totally surprised when suddenly the Band struck up with some resounding bars from 'Iolanthe'. Nobody had warned me and I certainly hadn't realised that I was entitled to, and indeed got, a musical salute. While this was going on, my Broad Pennant was broken out at the masthead where it would remain until I myself was relieved. After I had come down and inspected the Guard, I was introduced to the various Heads of Departments and I was pleased to see several old friends including a sailing chum, Surgeon Captain Bob Mooney, the PMO; then it was up to my office to sign the books and meet the staff, while my predecessor bade his farewells and departed to pastures new.

I had a light, airy office on the upper floor of The Commodore's Office block and my window overlooked the Parade Ground. Next door was my Secretary's office and across the corridor that of my Personal Assistant. My Secretary, Lieutenant Commander Devonshire, had been there for the previous Commodore and was soon to be relieved but my PA, who was a Civil Servant, had had the job for a number of years and knew exactly what I was supposed to do and when. She was also an excellent shorthand typist and brilliant at warding off the unwanted. Between the two of them they explained who did what and produced a formidable programme of calls and meetings to start me off.

I found that I was in charge of:

RN Physical Training School and sports facilities
RN School of Education and Training Techniques
RN School of Management and Work Study
RN Divisional School
HMS *Victory* (the ship)
RN Detention Quarters
The Naval Family Welfare Branch
The *Navy News* (The Navy's newspaper)
Some 3000 Married Quarters
The Naval Dental School
Naval Sick Quarters
Navy Days
Overall charge of some 6,000 Officers, Ratings, WRNS and civilians
I was Vice Chairman of Portsmouth Dockyard Management Committee

I was Chairman of:

The Portsmouth Branch, RN Benevolent Trust
South Africa Lodge Orphanage
The Royal Sailors' Rest (Aggie Weston's)
The Victory Housing Association
Portsmouth Branch, Royal Naval Sailing Association
I was Rear Commodore of the RNSA and Selector and Captain of Navy sailing teams.
I was the Navy's 'Chief Magistrate', dealing with all cases which could not be judged by officers in command and below the rank of Captain.
I was expected to take all the 'odds and overs' which the C-in-C didn't want or didn't have time to deal with.

I reckoned it was enough to keep me going.

My first call, of course, was on the Commander-in-Chief, Admiral Sir Horace Law, who was one of the nicest chaps you could wish to meet and his wife was equally charming; she had arranged a party for Mary to meet some of the other wives and made her very welcome. They were both quite old, as people go in the service, as the Admiral had achieved the ultimate in staying on in the Navy long after his contemporaries, having been promoted on his last shot to Commander and, again on his last shot, to Captain. He was due to be relieved in the New Year. After the C-in-C, there was Peter La Niece, my predecessor in *Triumph* and now Flag Officer Spithead.

Back at Anchor Gate House, Jenny and Tijuana were getting themselves set up and used to their new domain. The great excitement for them was that directly outside the gates to our drive was the headquarters of the Dockyard cats. The cats were part of the establishment, some thirty being on the books to control the dockyard rats, and it was outside our gates that they were fed. The cats of course were a sort of force majeur but, provided they didn't come into our garden, a sort of uneasy truce was maintained. In general they had a splendid time with lots of people around to spoil them.

The day-to-day running of the barracks itself was done by the Commander, another Commander Walker, and he was President of the Wardroom Mess, which was largely a hotel for officers doing courses at the various establishments within my

Above: Anchor Gate House, built by French Prisoners during the Napoleonic wars.

Below: The outgoing Commodore introducing me to my officers. These two are Surgeon Captain Bob Mooney, a very old friend from sailing days, and my Commander, Geoff Walker.

Above:
R.N.S.A. Dinner.
Admiral McGeoch (Commodore) introduces Roy Mullinder (RN Sailing Coach) to Prince Philip.

Below:
Mary Elphinstone, Mary, the youngest rating and Geoff Walker at work on the Christmas pudding being mixed in a Rum Tub while I look on!

Above: The C-in-C, Admiral Sir Horace Law inspects Divisions.

Below: Mary and I being welcomed aboard by the Captain of the Italian Sail Training Ship Admirante Vespucci while she was visiting Portsmouth and whose ship we were hosting.

Trying to look how a Rear Commodore of the Royal Naval Sailing Association should look, however I see that I am wearing my Hamble River Sailing Club tie.

Above: My very beautiful Merlin rocket 2237 "Kiriain Three' which I raced at Hamble S.C.

Below: One of the nice things I did from time to time was to present medals on behalf of Her Majesty. Here I have just pinned on a British Empire Medal and am presenting the citation.

*Above: Introducing Jon Pertwee (Dr Who) to the crowd.
The girl on the right is the actress who played his scatty assistant.*

Below: Jon talks to the multitude of fans!

This real-size 'all singing, all dancing' and exterminating Dalek was made by the Victory Chippies.

*Above:
Inspecting the Victory Sea Cadets. We also had a Royal Marine Cadet Unit and the two were great rivals.*

Left: Mary and I in the garden of Anchor House dressed in our Sunday Best!

Bringing the Lord Chancellor Lord Hailsham into dinner past the Guard of Honour of Victory's Sea Cadets armed with Cutlasses in Nelsonian style.

Left: End of the Road. Greeting my successor John Lea.

Below: Being towed 'out to grass'! They had organised a Bosun's Dinghy on a trailer with my Rear Commodore RNSA Burgee at the masthead. Centre on the tow-rope is Surgeon Captain Bob Mooney and on his left is my Secretary Lieutenant Commander Charles Hooper.

Mary and I sailing our little Cat-rigged schooner Champagne at Instow.

Above: Mary and I cut the Diamond Wedding Cake - 1st January 2005.

Below: From Small Beginnings!

command as indeed were the barracks generally. We had large accommodation blocks which were allocated to ships refitting in the dockyard and thus, in addition to those permanently on the staff, we had a continually changing population. At this time there was a huge amount of rebuilding going on, with the old, early 20th century, accommodation being replaced by modern facilities, where ratings would have their own cabins and some degree of privacy. One of the first to enjoy the new facilities were the WRNS who had purpose-built accommodation with single cabins for everyone.

It was a daunting task to get to know all the various heads of departments and organisations and Mary and I set about having weekly lunch- and dinner-parties to meet them and their wives. Lunch-parties were normally short affairs, ending promptly so that every one could get on with their work, whereas the dinner parties were much more leisurely, though we did try and see that everyone had left by 2300! We were indeed fortunate in having an excellent staff and Mary had a daily meeting with the Petty Officer Steward who would come to the Study, which was also her office, to decide the menus. Into all this we were able to mix our own friends and also meet some extremely interesting people from all walks of life, from Lord Seebohm (the Chairman of Barclays Bank), judges, MPs, Bishop Warlock, the Roman Catholic Cardinal who lived just around the corner and innumerable foreign officers who had come to see how the RN did it.

As I went round my command one of the things that left a lasting memory was the small naval town of married quarters at Rowner. Here there were schools, playgrounds, welfare facilities, shops and a medical centre, together with all the problems of inner city life as the Ministry of Defence had followed the fashion of the time of building high-rise blocks of flats. I remember on my first visit being struck by the appalling lavatorial smells in the lift shafts, graffiti, lifts out of action, desperate mothers with small children, over-stretched Wren social workers and so on and so forth. Another ongoing problem was with the families who refused to leave their quarters after their husbands had finished their time in the Navy and we were continually wasting time and money in taking them to court in Winchester so as to obtain eviction orders. By contrast, we also had some very good and attractive housing for both officers and ratings and also some excellent Housing Association developments. These latter houses were run by the Victory Housing Trust and provided long-term housing for retired Naval personnel. Happily the high-rise blocks at Rowner have long since been pulled down.

Much time and thought was spent on dealing with defaulters and the RN Detention Quarters. The RNDQs were run by an old friend of mine, Commander James Woolley. The building was typical of civilian prisons but the staff were all Service personnel chosen for the job. There were also Prison Visitors appointed by the Home Office to see that all was run in a proper manner. What was different from a civil prison was that many of the inmates were there because they had chosen to take the path of disobedience to get out of the Navy. I had to visit the place on a monthly basis and it was really very well-run but the regime was tough and, to my mind, the system that caused me and other senior officers to send offenders there needed radical overhaul.

Fundamentally, it was the rules of the contract (engagement) between the Ministry of Defence and a rating entering the service which caused the problem. In 1971, as in the 1930s, ratings 'signed on' for either 12 or 7 years. If they wished to leave the Navy they could, after three years, buy themselves out. The fee for this was considerably more than the average rating could afford so, as an alternative, he would decide to 'work his passage'. To do this he either deserted or made himself a criminal. Those who deserted became 'wanted men'; they were hunted by the police, could not legitimately get employment and, of course, had no entitlement to any benefits. If they were not criminals when they started, they frequently took to crime to survive. If caught by the police, they were immediately returned to the Navy. Those who resorted to disobedience in the Navy fared little better. The accepted road to escape from their contract required three major offences. The first got six weeks in Naval Detention, the second earned twelve weeks and the third was often six months in a civil prison followed by a 'dishonourable discharge'. This meant that their service papers were stamped with a great red stamp and could not be used as a reference when applying for a job. Of course there were real baddies amongst them but, for the majority, their only crime was a desire to live at home with their wives and families. This was something that young people signing on at 18 never thought about.

After going along with the system for several months, I realised what a terrible waste of time and money it all was and determined to do something about it. After discussions with the Naval Psychologist (who, as part of his brief, dealt with offenders), Commander Peter Meryon (the head of Naval Welfare) and various other people, I was able to put forward recommendations for a totally new scheme where ratings would have recognised break points after 15 months, three years or six years, when they would have the opportunity of giving one year's notice to leave the Service. If at the end of that year they still wished to leave, they would have the right to do so.

My first hurdle was to get the blessing of Horace Law, the C-in-C. This proved much easier than I had anticipated. He was by nature a very caring person and immediately gave the scheme his full support. The next stage of getting Ministry of Defence approval was a very different matter. My previous boss from Singapore, Derek Empson, now the Second Sea Lord and in charge of Personnel, was fine. Not so were all the people who had to provide for the recruiting to replace the perceived wastage caused by the scheme, i.e. the Treasury who forecast increased costs and, of course, the traditionalists who could see nothing wrong with the present system. My proposals were a destabilizing factor that they could well do without.

All the objections were indeed true and well-founded but were not in the real world. Sailors in the 1930s were seldom married; now they were. The Services encouraged it by providing excellent married quarters. However, in the 1970s many wives had good jobs and were unwilling or financially unable to move to be with their husbands. We had to convince people that things were changing. We had the local MP for Portsmouth, Michael Judd, to lunch and persuaded him to put in his oar by asking awkward questions in the House. Eventually it all came together and before I left I was delighted to see these new measures introduced and, as far as I am aware, they continue to this day. As predicted by the critics, it did cause manning problems and it did cost money. However, this is the price one has to pay for present-day standards and expectations.

Whilst still on the subject of discipline, quite a new experience for me was having to deal with female defaulters. The Wrens got into almost as many scrapes as the sailors. I was unnerved at first to find that, when I told them off for whatever thing they had done, they almost invariably burst into tears. However, the First Officer Wrens, Hilary Jeayes, was unmoved and told me to stand no nonsense. She was a delightful character, but tough. She was the sister of a chap who had been at Pangbourne with me and was an excellent artist, amongst other things.

On an entirely different tack, one of the reasons that I had been looking forward to coming to Portsmouth was, of course, the sailing and I lost little time in getting organised. I found myself involved once again in both Command and Inter-Service competition in Bosuns and also in the Seaview Mermaids which were always great fun. I was lucky enough to have Jim Saltenstall as one of my crew in the Mermaids; he was an absolute ace at spinnaker handling and we did quite well. Jim, when he left the Navy, went on to be the Olympic coach for the British Youth team and, later, for the very successful England squad for Australian Olympics when England scored the highest number of medals ever. Also attached to the Barracks, in the newly-created post of Navy Sailing Coach, was Chief Petty Officer Roy Mullender. This was something quite new to me and I didn't know how to use him or really what qualifications he had for the job. He was a Fleet Air Arm Air Artificer and had been highly recommended by the chap who ran the FAA sailing team. I needn't have worried as he was a very strong character, full of ideas and a very competent sailor with no financial worries as he had married a very rich (and attractive) wife. My main task was to keep him in check and make sure that he told me what he was doing and when, but it took a little time before we saw eye to eye.

At this time the Navy had a very old-fashioned system for examining and qualifying people for boat-handling competence. I don't think that it had changed much since the 1930s. One of Roy's jobs was to bring it up to date for the current type of naval recreational sailing, now invariably carried out in Bosun dinghies or in the cruising yachts owned by the various naval establishments around the country. It was a coincidence that the Royal Yachting Association was also trying to do the same thing and had appointed a very competent chap, Bob Bond, to do this. Roy and he worked closely together and, after a lot of argument, we persuaded the Navy to adopt the new RYA grading and qualifications for Yacht Master and Dinghy Helm.

Later, in 1974, Roy Mullender skippered one of the Navy's sail-training yachts, Adventure, in the second RNSA/Whitbread Round the World race and did very well. Leaving the Navy the following year, he became sales manager for Topper dinghies.

On the personal side, I wanted to have a boat of my own. Ian McGeoch, now retired, had bought an International One Design in Cowes, where they had a class of them, and wanted me to go shares with him but I was not keen. I have never been a very good sharer! On Bob Mooney's advice I bought a much less up-market boat, one of the Victory class. These were a one design, open cockpit keelboat, about 21 feet overall, designed in the 1930s. There were about 20 of them at the Portsmouth Sailing Club and they raced in the Solent on Tuesday and Thursday evenings. They were very competitive. Many of the pundits like Bob had sailed them for years and, as I found out, they were very good at it and at knowing the Solent currents. They also sailed as a class in Cowes week.

One of the snags was that they needed to be sailed by three people and, while Mary made one of the crew, I needed a third. I was lucky in finding two very experienced sailors who could be called on: Les Wilkinson, the editor of Navy News and Surgeon Commander Bob Needham, the Barracks Dentist. I don't think that we ever quite managed to win a race but usually finished well up the fleet. One of the problems that our Victory had, which was common to many older boats in the class, was that she leaked like a sieve where the side planks met the stem post and a lot of time was spent, when she was in her berth at King's Stairs, trying bung up the leaks but without lasting success. However, it was good to get away on Thursday evenings, when possible, as the week between 0800 on Mondays and 1600 on Fridays was booked for pretty well non-stop activity until it was time to go to bed. Both Mary and I had separate diaries, which had to be carefully coordinated, and my PA would produce a schedule of what we were supposed to be doing when and what we should wear.

At weekends it was very much up to us. Normally we would let the staff off and have the house to ourselves which was rather nice. David was at Bath, not far away, and would sometimes turn up but often we would pack the car up and go down to Instow. We found that we could leave to come back to Portsmouth at about 1900 on Sunday evenings, which gave us two good days. At that time we had no boat of our own there and I managed to hire a Wayfarer from someone who had gone away and had left it upside down and unloved in the corner of a garden at Littleham, so for a very small outlay we were able to have boat, which we returned at the end of two years in very much better condition than we had found it.

However, I still wanted something for the weekends that we were at Portsmouth and I was unable to resist the lure of having another Merlin at the Hamble. I found a very new and beautifully-kept Merlin, that was up for sale at a very good price, and didn't believe the owner when he told me that the reason for selling it was because he couldn't get her to go to windward. It was a Proctor XIX, the latest Proctor design, and I was sure that I would be able to tune the rig correctly. It turned out that he was right and I was wrong as she couldn't compete with the latest Morrison designs. However, she was good off the wind and faster than many of the older boats. I had some good racing with David Williams's son as crew and, while we didn't win much, it was nice to be back there amongst the experts and semi-professionals who made up the class.

Mary and I took the Victory to Cowes week at the beginning of August; the boats were towed across and we had arranged to stay in a B & B and then fend for ourselves. It was the first time that I had really had the opportunity to take advantage of my membership of the Royal Yacht Squadron and it was quite an experience to see what went on. There were about sixteen Victories taking part and we were one of the last classes to start so that there was quite a bit of hanging around. The weather wasn't brilliant and we did not do very well. However, it was something that I had always wanted to do and it was just nice to be part of the scene, both on the water and ashore.

The Squadron Ball was quite a grand affair and, as local Branch Chairman, I was responsible for the RNSA Cocktail Party which was quite a headache. It had the reputation of being the best party of Cowes week and a strict organisation had to be set up to fend off the gate-crashers. Luckily the sun shone and it went well. I was astounded at the amount drink that some of our elder members knocked back.

One of the perks of the job which came our way was being invited by the C-in-C to dine aboard Victory in the Admiral's cabin. These were always very special occasions with interesting guests. The cabin itself was exactly how it was in Nelson's time and it was impossible not feel moved by the experience. It was always magical and, for Navy Days (for which I was responsible), I had the privilege of being able to invite guests on board for the grand finale of the day when the Royal Marine Band would Beat a Retreat and I took the salute from the Quarterdeck.

Navy Days themselves required tremendous organisation and publicity. Apart from the object of letting the public see what the Navy was all about, it was also the principal fundraiser for Naval Charities. The event was usually staged over the August Bank Holiday and the object was to attract about 100,000 visitors over the three-day period. To do this I had a Lieutenant Commander on my staff whose sole job was to plan it and make it work. The chap I had was a retired officer who had been doing it for about six years and doing it very well. It was a full-time job and often a frustrating one when ships or display teams, upon which he had relied and planned, were pulled out at the last moment for operational requirements. One of the biggest headaches on the day was the presence of small children. A large team of Navy wives were pressed in to run a crèche for toddlers while their parents and older children went round the ships. In addition, it served as a base and reception point for children that had got lost. It was by no means unusual at the end of the day to be left with several children whose parents had gone home without them. After all this we took a week's leave to go Instow and relax.

On our return we had Mike and Pip to stay and also David and various friends. Mike was now in Dido which was due to refit in Chatham. He and Pip had been allocated a very peculiar married quarter there in St Mary's Gardens, Khyber Road, which consisted of two terrace houses that had been knocked into one, but only in so far as they had knocked a hole through in the halls and also the landing. Otherwise they had two of everything including two front doors and two staircases. Ultimately they wanted to buy a house in the Portsmouth area and we tried to keep an eye out for one without much success.

Of course, Trafalgar Day was always a big event in Portsmouth, particularly so at the Barracks where, in the Wardroom Dining room, there are murals which run all round the walls depicting scenes from the battle. I believe that they had been painted by Wylie, the marine artist, and were extremely valuable. Planning for the Trafalgar Day dinner starts early to make sure that suitable guests are invited. This particular year the Mess Committee had decided to invite past Commodores and these included Admirals Horace Law, Fitzroy Talbot and Phillip Sharp. Roy Talbot had been No.1 of *Imperial* when I was a Midshipman and it was he and his wife who had kept bantams on the top floor of Anchor Gate House. Phillip Sharp had been a Divisional Officer in *Vindictive*, but I had come across both of them many times since and it was fun to see them again as well as several other old friends. The following day we all attended the annual memorial service aboard Victory.

Having a large and well-equipped Wardroom we were often called upon to host large dinners and another big one that autumn was the RNSA's Commodore's Dinner with Prince Phillip, Duke of Edinburgh, Admiral of the Association, present. Ian McGeoch, the current Commodore, was in the chair. Dinner Jackets are great levellers and it was good to see many of the Chief Petty Officers and Petty Officers, who had done so well with sailing in the Navy, mixed in with Admirals and other sailing glitterati. On this occasion I had no speaking duties but, as a rule, I enjoyed after-dinner speaking and my next chance in the Barracks was the farewell dinner to Sir Horace Law, when I had great fun with 'The Odes of Horace'.

The following week was a big occasion as the new Second Sea Lord, Admiral Sir Andrew Lewis, was coming to lay the foundation-stone for the new Commodore's block in the Barracks. The building was also to house the Administrative Offices and also to have a special Courts Martial room. All the local TV and press turned up. I had not met Admiral Lewis before but was told that he was a bit starchy. After he had done his stuff I had to make a little speech of thanks and, not knowing what to say, came up with a little bit of Gilbertian doggerel which ended, 'Straightly laid with trowel and mortar by the Second Lord who rules the water'. It seemed to go down well but I was embarrassed to see it hit the headlines in the local press and also on Southern Television. Such is fame.

It was fortunate that the ceremony was not interrupted by bomb scares which happened with monotonous regularity. The IRA were very active on the mainland at this time and, though 99.9 % were hoaxes, they all had to be taken seriously. They usually happened around midnight just after one had gone to bed, the most common being some drunken matelot ringing the police and putting on an Irish accent to say that a bomb had been planted in the Wrens' quarters, in the hope of seeing them turn out in their nighties.

Mary found herself very much involved with being on the committee of various charities, including King George's Fund for Sailors and local organisations such as Naval Wives. At the same time RNSA business also occupied me. I had for some time tried to get a scheme through the main committee to enable young officers and ratings to take part in top-class dinghy competition. This could only happen if the person concerned could own and campaign a boat of one of the internationally-recognised classes, which, with the constantly moving life in the Navy, was a very expensive thing to undertake. I was therefore delighted when my scheme, whereby an applicant with talent could receive an interest-free loan from the RNSA to buy his own boat, was finally approved and publicized. For financial reasons it had to be limited to one person a year and we kicked it off by buying Olympic Medallist Ian McDonald-Smith's International Finn for a young Lieutenant, Rick Pharoah, and I was excited to store it in our spare garage for the winter. It really was a most beautifully-built boat. The scheme continues to run to this day, with great success.

Another big milestone in the sailing scene was the advent of the Services Adventure Training Yachts. These were based on the scheme that Admiral McGeoch had launched when we were in Scotland and consisted of a number of 55-foot yachts built by Camper Nicholson and called Nicholson 55s. Each service was to have three. Sir Alec Rose and I had the honour of being asked to break the first hull out of its mould. This was the Navy's yacht Adventure. They were to be fully-equipped ocean-going yachts and would be based in the main at Gosport at a Joint Services Sailing Centre. The scene had already been set for a Round the World race and the RNSA had gone into partnership with Whitbreads, the brewers, who would put up the money. The race would be known as The Whitbread/RNSA Round the World Race; it would be for sailing yachts up to 60ft in length and the RNSA would provide the organisation.

I found myself being appointed Chairman of the organizing committee, which consisted of such pundits as Robin Knox-Johnston (the first person to sail round the world non-stop) and 'Blondie' Haslar (who started the Trans-Atlantic Races) and other well-known yachtsmen. I was not at all keen to have the job, as I knew nothing about ocean racing and didn't want to. Also, I thought that racing small yachts round the world was an unseamanlike thing to do and was bound to lead to loss of life. I was only too pleased when, after our second meeting, Whitbread offered to put up the money to pay for a retired Captain to take on the job and become the professional organiser in what turned out to be full-time job.

There was great competition to skipper Adventure on the first race and Roy Mullender was appointed for one of the legs as was Fiona Keene's (from Instow) husband, James Myatt, in the Army yacht. I was to be proved quite wrong as this race, which is still sailed every four years, is an important event in the yachting calendar and, while many yachts have been lost or broken, it has claimed few lives – largely due to costly sea and air rescues and the satellite monitoring of participating yachts.

Early in the December preparations were going on apace for Christmas and, in fact, Mary Elphinstone had helped to stir the enormous Christmas pudding in the Barracks' galley when she was with us for half term. There was the Victory pantomime in the barracks' theatre and we had Geoffrey and Daphne Kirkby to stay for the Winter Ball in the mess. Just before we departed on leave, we had a Christmas party for our staff in Anchor Gate to which twenty-nine came including, wives and children. Mary had cleverly found presents for each one. Everyone seemed to enjoy themselves and we counted ourselves fortunate indeed to have such a good lot of people working for us. That done, it was off to Instow for Christmas leave.

Back again in Portsmouth we had Mike and Pip and also David for the New Year's Eve Party and, a little later, Granny Bull and Con before she went back to school. Henry was by this time at Grenville and Hester and Rowland borrowed Croft from time to time to take him out. This year it was Mary's turn to chair the committee for the Summer Fête, which was to be the major fund-raising effort for the year for King George's Fund for Sailors and other charities.

Commander Geoff Walker had been relieved by Keith Dedman at the beginning of January. Keith was Fleet Air Arm and was full of ideas for this sort of thing. His first was to have an auction of antiques which people might have in their attics and he was able to persuade two well-known experts, who were frequently on television, to come and do it and we had them to lunch first. It was a great success and we made a great deal of money. We felt that we had some things to spare in the way of silver photograph frames which we put in the sale but later regretted.

I also released some unclaimed and unwanted items from the RN Trophy Store, which was within my domain. This was a real Aladdin's cave of stuff – silver and pictures which had been presented to ships over the years and for which there were no ships in commission bearing that name. Ships commissioning were allowed to come and choose pieces but many of the items had belonged to capital ships of the past and were much too large. There were also a number of floor-to-ceiling portraits of Admirals and other worthies, some of which we offloaded to the National Portrait Gallery. I had borrowed some silver for our table in Anchor Gate and also a magnificent tiger skin which we had in the hall. It had been shot by Mountbatten when Viceroy of India and the bullet used went with it in a glass case. I was very sad when the day came that we had to give it up. The one used by the bass drummer in the Royal Marine band at Eastney had got the moth and they needed a replacement.

One of the less popular of my establishments within the Barracks was the RN School of Work Study and I was constantly getting complaints from outside. There was nothing much wrong with the school or its trained practioners; it was just that it was new to the Navy and ships and establishments resented having people hovering around them, armed with clip-boards, stop watches and cameras, and then receiving a report as to how they might do their jobs more quickly or with fewer people. It was difficult to get past the 'we've always done it that way' syndrome and, as some of the reports went on up the line and were far from complimentary, I would get a lot of stick from my peers. However we stuck to our guns and eventually, but not in my time, time-and-motion studies became an accepted tool of management.

In March I was invited to take the salute at the passing out parade at the Royal Green Jackets' barracks in Winchester. We had a sort of twinning arrangement with the Green Jackets which went well at all levels. It was a beautiful evening and I was proud to do the job. Everyone was extremely well-turned-out and the drill exemplary. After a buffet supper in the officers' mess we were treated to the Regimental Band giving a magnificent rendering of the 1812 Overture with field guns firing blanks, fireworks and masses of flame-coloured smoke which was floodlit to give the impression that the whole place was on fire. This, together with tolling of the church bells, provided one of the best bits of musical theatre that I had ever seen.

The following evening we hosted a talk by Robin Knox-Johnston about his round-the-world marathon. The talk itself was in the theatre but we had a buffet at Anchor Gate first, to which Robin and his wife came, as well as the Laws, the McGeoghs, John and Priscilla Barker and Chief Petty Officers Mullender, Ellis and Mason with their wives. It was a very interesting talk; it had seemed a wondrous exploit at the time and everyone was thrilled to meet the man in person. It took Robin nine months to circumnavigate in his very solid ketch Suhaili. Now people like Ellen

McArthur do it in seventy days or less, but in very different types of yacht with every sort of aid imaginable.

In March too we hosted the Inter-Command Drama festival with a series of plays being performed in the Barracks theatre. This was an annual competition and special judges were brought down from London for the event. The standard was extremely high and fun to watch. In this particular year it was won by the Naval Air Command but I cannot recall the name of the play. We always had something going on as we had so many facilities, such as the Naval athletics stadium at Pitt Street, excellent playing fields and a county-class cricket pitch. The Physical Training School was one of mine. This was where all the naval PT Instructors were trained and kept up to date and it was always a great pleasure to go along and witness the extraordinarily high standards that were achieved.

It had long been the custom for the Commodore to see all Chief Petty Officers before they left the Service to thank them for all they had done and to find out if all was well. I found this most worthwhile and would have each one in for about ten to fifteen minutes, encourage them to let their hair down and enquire about their plans for the future. I was constantly amazed by the diversity of things that they had either started or planned to do. Every long-service person had a couple of months before they left the Navy, during which time they could choose from a great variety of courses which would help them in the future. Indeed, in the Barracks itself we had a vocational training school where ratings could gain qualifications as electricians, plumbers, motor-car mechanics, and building – all with 'hands-on' experience.

At the end of March, with the sailing season about to start, I found myself having to sail against the Civil Service at Littleton Lake near Heathrow Airport. It was a team race in Enterprises and I had done it before but this year there had obviously been a shortage of rain and the level of water was well down. The result was that the Navy team kept running aground on unmarked banks, which only the locals knew, and the whole affair was a bit of a disaster. But, on another note, the whole winter had been pretty terrible with strikes and power cuts, three-day weeks and inflation running at 17 % – so that a poor sailing day was a minor problem – and it did make life very difficult for Mike and Pip trying to buy a house. *Dido* was now back in Portsmouth and Pip at Anchor Gate.

Planning was now well underway for the King George's Fund for Sailors fête in June. 'Dr Who' on television was an immensely popular programme and was compulsory viewing for children and dads alike. Keith Dedman had contacts in the BBC and I had met Jon Pertwee, the Dr Who of the day, on several occasions so we decided to go for it. Jon was happy to come as he had been in Portsmouth Barracks during his wartime service. Keith managed get scale drawings of Daleks, the scary death-dealing robots, and we set the Barracks carpenters the task of making some full-size replicas. When the day itself came, we had Jon Pertwee and the actress who played his rather dumb assistant to lunch before we launched him on to the scene. He did the job splendidly, appearing in his full costume, which consisted in the main of an old naval boat cloak, and was pursued wherever he went by hordes of small children. The psychology had worked as we had reckoned that, if you could attract the children, the parents would have to come and Mary's committee were able to hand over a record sum of over £3,500, a huge amount by any standard, and all the other stalls and amusements did terrific trade.

Earlier on in May we had said goodbye to the Laws. Admiral Law had been relieved by Sir Andrew Lewis who had had only a very short time as Second Sea Lord. At the time Admirals seemed to be having a high drop-out rate through illness! Andrew Lewis had not expected the job but seemed delighted to have it and, despite adverse reports, I found him easy to work with. His wife seemed nice too when we met her a few days after her arrival at dinner aboard Victory. Dining in Victory, though super for the guests, was quite a problem for the staff as there were no means of cooking or heating anything on board the ship itself for fear of fire. Everything had to be brought ready for the table. The only constraint on the guests was that there were no heads (lavatories), the ship being in a dry dock, and everyone was warned to take the necessary precautions before arriving.

During the time I had been in Portsmouth there had been a number of moves to unify some of the institutions run in parallel by the three Services, with the very obvious savings in cost. One of the proposals was to shut down the Naval Detention Quarters and send everyone to the Army at Colchester. To this end I paid a visit to the Army DQs to assess the possibilities. I had to report that, while the move was perfectly possible, I considered it most undesirable. I was horrified at the routines that were carried out there, really mindless punishments, with Sergeants yelling their heads off. In our DQs the routine was strict but focussed on education and rehabilitation and certainly not running round all day with rifles and packs full of bricks. In addition we had just refurbished a disused staff building within the DQ precincts, for use by young offenders where they could be detained without coming into contact with old lags or druggies and picking up their bad habits. The C-in-C supported my case and the project was shelved for the time being.

Another unification move, which was implemented, was to make the RAF responsible for the furnishing of all married quarters and it wasn't long before someone from the RAF stores branch came to inspect Anchor Gate House. Some weeks later I received a letter saying that I would be glad to know that they would be able refurnish Anchor Gate House with nice new modern furniture. I wasn't glad to know in any way and was horrified at the prospect of having all the super period furniture dragged out and sent to the tip. I wrote a strong letter to say that in no way would I allow any of the present furniture to be removed and as far as I know it is still there. It certainly was in 1990.

I was determined to make the most of the sailing during the summer and most Tuesday evenings found us racing with the Victorys in the Solent, whilst on Sundays we were at the Hamble with the Merlins. In addition I was able to sail in the inter-service races at Seaview and also for the Portsmouth Command, with fair success. Ian McGeoch invited me to sail his International One Design in the Round the Island race; he and Pat Godber, secretary of the RNSA, would be my crew. We were all to meet up at Cowes in good time for the start and went off from the Squadron steps in the nanny boat in great style. However, once we had got on board, the Admiral discovered to his horror that he had left all the navigation equipment – parallel rulers, dividers, handbearing compass, pencils and so forth – at home. There was nothing much that we could do about it; we had a chart and a compass and Pat said that he had a box of matches to use to measure the distance, so we decided to go.

The start for the race was quite a challenge with several hundred boats taking part. It was a running start, but having had a lot of dinghy racing experience we were able to force our way to the front of the pack with some clear air and made a good start. We rounded the Needles in a nice force 3-4 and set about beating up the southern shore against the easterly breeze. Amongst the other things that we had not got was the tidal atlas but we decided to go offshore and take advantage of the east-going current. This was fine until we had got about half way when we ran into a thick sea mist. Without sight of land we were lost, despite Pat's dubious calculations with his matchsticks, and we decided that the only thing to do was to tack in towards the shore until we heard the waves breaking and then go about; this we did. After an anxious couple of hours beating up the shore we were thankful to hear the foghorn on the Nab Tower and, with the fog clearing, we began the run home. The wind had fallen to very light so we had difficulty in getting the spinnaker to draw and it was not until about six in the evening that we crossed the finishing line. We were pleased to see a number of boats struggling in behind us.

Once ashore we waited anxiously for the results and were over the moon when we discovered that, despite everything, we had won our class. However it was more by luck than good judgement and who knows what might have happened if we had had all the kit on board. It was the first race that Ian's boat had won and we had great celebrations in the Royal Corinthian YC, which was hosting the event. (The IODs were 33 ft overall, a one design version of a Six-Metre).

In June we hosted a visit by the Columbian sail-training ship, *Gloria*. She was a four-masted ship, square-rigged, and had originally been built for the grain trade from Australia. She seemed to be very well-run with a smart young crew of Cadets. I was interested in the Columbian Navy as it had been built up in the thirties by the uncle of a pre-war girlfriend of mine, a retired RN Captain named Trechman, whose son had been No.2 in *Imperial* out in Malta. *Gloria* had come over for the Tall Ships race which was to start in the Solent. There were a number of square-riggers, making a splendid spectacle at the start, and, as Andrew Lewis had asked me to take his wife out in his Barge, we had pole position.

Later in July I was once again involved with the Inter-Service and Inter-Command dinghy and keel-boat team racing series and, as a change from 1971 when we won the dinghy trophies, this year we won the keel-boats but again I failed in my ambition to win the RYS Gold Cup for individual Inter-Service helms, being beaten into second place by the RAF's Flight Lieutenant McWilliams who later became one of the top sail-makers with a sail loft in Cowes. Such is life. The cup had been presented originally by the Kaiser in about 1912, was actually gold-plated and would have looked good on the dinner table.

This year I could fit in only two days of Cowes week so I arranged to skipper *Braganza*, (Whale Island's yacht) on the Monday, when we would go to the Squadron Ball afterwards, and again on the Wednesday when Mary was able to take Pippa Williams across to Cowes in the C-in-C's Barge and afterwards host the RNSA Cocktail Party. *Braganza* sailed in Class Three (Ocean racers) and needed a crew of six, of which Mike made one. Because it was the leave period for many naval establishments, I had to make up a crew from a special course for NATO officers and had a real mixed bunch, all professed sailors but with language problems in an emergency.

Monday's race went extremely well and I had high hopes for Wednesday. The day started well enough and we were lying well up in the fleet when we came to the last mark of the course just to the West of Cowes. All we had to do on rounding was to down spinnaker and enjoy the short beat back to the finish but it was not to be. When I yelled, 'Down spinnaker', the Dutchman on the starboard sheet and the Dane on the port both let fly their sheets at the same time, with the result that the spinnaker wrapped itself round the forestay and nothing we could do would get it down. In desperation I got Mike to go up the mast to see what he could do but, despite valiant efforts, it was stuck firm. It was impossible to set the jib and we sailed ignominiously back to the finish with the spinnaker flogging itself to bits and our rivals happily sailing past us. Poor Mary, who was sitting on the Squadron lawn with Pippa Williams and expecting to see a triumphant finish, could not believe her eyes as this sorry sight appeared on the scene. I got a lot of tee-hees at the cocktail party; it cost me a fortune to get the spinnaker repaired and, most of all, a lot of lost pride.

The last weekend in August and, consequently, Navy Days were soon upon us again and we found ourselves playing host to yet another sail-training ship, *Admirante Vespucci*, full of Italian Cadets. *Vespucci* was specially-built as a training ship but had been given all the outward appearance of a three-deck ship of the line of about 1800, though much bigger and with good engines and plenty of space between decks. She was to be open to visitors during the weekend and we put up the Italian Naval Attaché, Rear Admiral Vittori, for the first night. He and Captain Ribuffo, the ship's Captain, were delighted to be invited to look round *Victory* and to be present when I took the salute in the evening. In fact we hosted a small party on board each of the three evenings of Navy Days. The Italians were an amusing and lively bunch and we went to an entertaining party on board.

Navy Days over and with no problems of any importance, we slipped away to Instow where we were joined by Mike and Pip and later by David, who had just come back from Norway. He had run out of money when he got to Oslo and had spent his last night there sleeping on a bench in Frogner Park. Otherwise, the trip had gone very well and he had seen the Lyles at Snarøya and brought back all the latest news.

We were back in Portsmouth on 10th September and, with only about six weeks remaining before I was due to be relieved, there seemed to be an impossible number of things to get through: final inspections and visits, writing officers' confidential reports, trying to make sure that all the projects that I had started would come to fruition, selling two boats and all the rest of it. I was thankful for a good supporting staff. At the end of September we were dined out by the C-in-C and Lady Lewis in *Victory*; the other guests at the dinner were the Earl and Countess Howe, Rear Admiral Sir Anthony Miers VC and Lady Miers and Sir Arthur and Lady Drew. Sir Arthur was a Whitehall Mandarin, the Permanent Under Secretary for the Navy.

Sir Anthony Miers or, to give him his more common name, 'Crapp' Miers was one of the legendry figures of WW II. A ruthless and successful submariner with a DSO and bar in addition to his VC, he had had the reputation in his younger days of coming aboard having drunk quite a lot and making members of his crew fight him. They never won. A term mate of mine, Percy Chapman, who was his First Lieutenant in his submarine for several years coped with this by keeping a revolver in his bunk and telling Miers that he would b*****y well shoot him if he didn't shut up and turn in. Apparently it always worked. Now a senior citizen and millionaire, having been one of the founder members of National Car Parks Ltd, you couldn't meet a more amiable chap.

I found myself sitting next to Lady Howe. Her husband was a direct descendant of Admiral Lord Howe, famed for his investment of Cherbourg in 1754 and his defeat of the French fleet off Cherbourg in 1794 on 'The Glorious First of June'. I was intrigued by the very splendid wrist ornaments that she was wearing, consisting of a velvet band on each wrist on which were mounted a number of beautifully enamelled oval miniatures which depicted the Admiral's victory over the French. They had been presented to the first Lady Howe by a grateful nation. She said that she felt that she just had to wear them for the occasion but that they weighed a ton. She had never dared to wear them before, in case they fell off and broke but all was well.

For this year's Trafalgar Night dinner the Mess Committee had decided to invite all the judges who had served in or had had connections with the Navy during or since World War II. They had managed to find twelve including the Lord Chancellor, Lord Hailsham, who had been First Lord of the Admiralty. Admiral Lewis was getting into quite state about it and kept ringing me to see if everything was going to be all right and I kept assuring him that all was fine. Hailsham and Lord Chief Justice Kaminski were to stay at Admiralty House while we put up three others with their wives – Sir John Brightman, Sir Henry Brandon and Sir John Donaldson. Mary had the job of entertaining these and other wives while I took their husbands off to dine

At the dinner itself my job was to make the speech of welcome and propose the toast 'Our Distinguished Guests' and Lord Hailsham had the task of proposing the traditional toast 'The Immortal Memory of Nelson and his Comrades'. The Commander, as Mess President, had the C-in-C and I had on my right, Lord Hailsham and on my left, Sir John Donaldson. Hailsham had the reputation of being a pretty fiery and unpredictable politician and, as Quintin Hogg, had got up to all sorts of antics in the House of Commons. I was quite nervous as to how it would be but I could not have had two nicer companions and very amusing too. All went well until it came to what I thought was my turn to get up and speak. As I was getting to my feet I felt a tap on my arm and Hailsham said 'Lord Chancellors always go first' and he did. I was completely thrown, but luckily he made quite a long speech which gave me time to think up a new beginning and I was able to have quite a lot of fun with a bowdlerized version of the Lord Chancellor's song from Iolanthe and also something about each of our other fourteen guests. It seemed to go down very well and I am sure that my blunder passed unnoticed amongst the other hundred or so people present. It was really a very jolly occasion; both Hailsham and Andrew

Lewis enjoyed themselves immensely and I wondered when they would go home. Mary's evening had gone well too.

The following morning we all had to appear in best bib and tucker aboard Victory for the traditional Trafalgar Day Service around the spot on the deck where Nelson fell, mortally wounded. Afterwards Mary and I had some very nice thank you letters and I was invited to a posh dinner at Lincolns Inn. I was amazed at the amount of port that Law Lords could consume! (Sir John Donaldson became Lord Donaldson, Lord Chief Justice; Sir John Brightman, Lord Brightman; Sir Henry Brandon, Lord Brandon; and all three Privy Councillors). Useful people to know but happily we have not had to use their services.

I myself was dined out in the mess on 24th October and handed over to an old friend, Commodore John Lea, an Engineer, the following morning. A little later I was ceremoniously towed out of the Barracks in a Bosun dinghy and then back to the house to change, say good-bye to the staff and depart. Suddenly it was all over.

Despite the fact that I had not wanted the job, it had turned out to be an interesting eighteen months with many new facets of life that I had not experienced before: fortnightly editorial meeting for the Navy News and its change over to colour, with the move to the all new Portsmouth Evening News Headquarters; chairing the RNBT meetings and seeing how this dedicated organisation really did help those in need; meeting the undercover members of the Navy's drug squad, specially selected Naval Patrolmen who risked their lives living with and looking like the druggies they were out to get and who reported directly to me; working to get planning permission and funding for sheltered housing for elderly and infirm naval pensioners; meeting and working with local organisations in and around Portsmouth and, in particular, the local police. Life was never dull and my secretary, Charles Hooper, made sure that I was always well-briefed.

Mary too had had a busy time. We had been warned that the appointment would be an expensive one and it certainly was. Quite apart from family and the friends who had been to stay or were living in the area, Mary had to arrange the feeding of the 5,000! Between the beginning of January and the end of October we had had 476 people to the house for lunch or dinner. Neither of us being drinkers unless we had guests, we managed to keep a fairly tight rein on the wine side of it, but Mary found that the amount of tea, sugar and milk used by the staff was prodigious. She chaired or was a member of several Committees and also belonged to an organisation which arranged visits to people having difficulty with their lives. All in all, I don't think that we wasted our time.

I was still being paid until the end of the year as, like everyone else, I had the opportunity to take a course in what might be useful in my future life. I was determined not to work for another organisation, so, with the prospect of taking on and doing up an old house, I and another old friend, Captain Stuart Farquharson-Roberts, joined a 'bricks and mortar' course near Farnham. It was run by the Army and included carpentry, plumbing and electrics, all of which have stood me in good stead.

So it was that we found ourselves back in Instow and wondering what to do next. At the end of December I received a letter from their Lordships thanking me for my service and another from the Naval Secretary pointing out that as I was still on the 'reserve' until I was 65, I would have a dormant appointment in case of war. Mine was to go to Narvik to take charge of convoys and I would be required to go for training with the Commodore of Convoy course every other year. I have been quite glad that war did not break out as I thought that Narvik might be quite a hazardous place to start from, even if I were to get there. And so it was that we settled into life at Instow, whence it all started, and wondered about what the future might hold for us. In the event it held quite a lot and we have had so much to be thankful for as you will see.

CHAPTER 22

Sense and Senility
1973 and beyond

It is now June 2007 and never in a thousand years did I think that I would be typing out a postscript to something that I had first written in the late seventies. I am conscious of the fact that there is quite a gap, but I shall do my best to fill it with as few words as possible. In 1973 there was a great deal of disruption in the country with endless strikes and inflation running at around 17%, not perhaps the best time to retire, but on the other hand in 1972 the Government had agreed to link the Forces pension to the rate of inflation for the first time but, because of my age, my pension would be frozen for two years until I was 55. We also had the advantage of actually owning a house in Instow so for the first time in our lives we would have our own roof over our heads. I had also made up my mind that I was not going to work for anyone else and we came to the conclusion that the right thing to go for was the holiday trade in North Devon which was clearly on the up and up. Everyone leaving the services has the opportunity of doing a course which would help them in the future. I did the very excellent bricks and mortar plus house maintenance course run by the Army.

With this behind me we thought we would buy a group of holiday chalets but got gazzumped at the last minute. Next we tried for a caravan site which looked really attractive until we discovered that the planning permission was dodgy. It seemed on reflection that the only thing that I knew how to do was to sail boats and we would start a sailing school at Instow. There had never been one here before and I set about buying some very second-hand boats. At the same time I enrolled at the National Sailing Centre in Cowes for a pretty intensive course and qualified as a Royal Yachting Association Coach. I now had a nationally recognized qualification and started the North Devon Sailing School in the summer of 1973. In the next couple of years I recruited and trained a number of instructors including John Pilkington, a childhood friend. A recently retired Sapper Colonel, he had, like me, come back to live in Instow and was a huge help. We had a good number of willing and not so willing pupils, the latter being children sent by parents to get them out of their hair for a week. We also acquired a small inflatable with outboard, which Mary drove as a rescue boat.

All work and no play makes Jack a dull boy. I needed to get a boat to race. The North Devon Yacht Club ran to several classes which raced at weekends, the class that appealed to me most being the $5^1/_2$ metre Osprey and I bought a second-hand one from Appledore. The Ospreys needed an agile crew who could trapeze and handle a fair size spinnaker. I was lucky enough to find one from Appledore Shipyard design section and we had a lot of fun, occasional success and a great deal of excitement.

Towards the end of 1973 I found myself elected as Commodore of the North Devon Yacht Club which had very recently moved to a new site, having bought the railway station closed by Dr Beeching in the sixties. A monster effort by the members had turned the site into a Yacht Club with a new prefab clubhouse and a long slipway made from old concrete railway sleepers stretching some 150 metres over the mud for use at half-tide. Having done all this there was no money in the bank. Anything that was required had to be done by self-help by a number of dedicated members but, despite our best efforts, money kept on slipping away. However in 1975 Miss Peggy Lines retired to Instow from being Managing Director of Hamleys, the world famous toy shop and I enlisted her help. What she didn't know about financial controls wasn't worth knowing and with her help as Hon Secretary she brought us into the black. At that time too there was a lot of pulling down and rebuilding going on and we acquired load after load of hard core to form a sizeable boat park. I served as Commodore for eleven years with huge support and forbearance from Mary.

Going back to 1974, two things happened, the most important being the house that I had always coveted in Instow came on the market. I had seen it in the final stage of building when a child. I had come to many parties in it while I was growing up when it was owned by the Durnford-Slaters. It had a wonderful outlook, an acre of garden, plenty of room for boats in the winter and a self-contained flat on the top floor which we could let as holiday accommodation and earn some money. The house was appropriately called Landfall, we are still living happily in it today, and there is plenty of room too for our children, grandchildren and great-grandchildren. When we bought the house it needed a great deal doing and, with my maintenance course behind me, Mary and I redecorated the house inside and out, borrowing long ladders for painting the third storey with Mary at the top of the ladder and me holding it steady. On top of that I had the care and maintenance of seven boats.

The second thing in '74 was that the then Rector persuaded me to be a Church Warden for the Parish Church on the grounds that there was nothing really to do. How gullible can one be? The other sucker was John Pilkington and between us we looked after the church, in my case for 19 years and John a year or two longer. During those years Mary and I must have raised many thousands of pounds to fight damp, leaking roofs, woodworm, death-watch beetle, sinking church organs and providing money for the ever-increasing Parish Share and Parson's expenses.

In 1975 I joined the Committee of the Barnstaple Sea Cadets and also the newly-formed North Devon Branch of the Society for Decorative and fine Arts, NADFAS, and had the honour of being its president for some 15 years until 2007. In 1975 too Mary took on the job of being the local visitor and organiser for the Soldiers, Sailors and Airman's Association, SSAFA; her area went from Bideford to the Cornish border and she was constantly being phoned for help with all sorts things from wigs to helping young service wives whose husbands had found someone else and they had been required to leave their married quarters having practically nothing of their own.

1st October 1977 saw David marry Alex Kerr, the daughter of Mark and Pat. Mark was a contempory of mine in the Navy and on retirement had taken up the post of Manager for the Clovelly Estates. We were delighted and, for the wedding in Clovelly Church, we had a houseful, with Mike – who was serving in Canada for two years – flying back with Philippa and their two children Amelia and Alexandra. Amelia, nearly 6, was a bridesmaid. David and Alex had bought a house in Reading, where he worked for a firm owned by Rupert Bray called Glossifilm and Alex in the Botanical gardens of Reading University. Initially we furnished their house with second-hand furniture from Instow for £25; we also did a bit of painting and decorating and fitted up a kitchen.

In 1979 Instow was officially twinned with Arromanches and Mary became a member of the Twinning Committee with the meetings being held in our house. The twinning still continues strongly and, though no longer on the committee, we still keep in contact with our French friends. However 1979 was not a good year for me as I was becoming more and more troubled with arthritis and in December I went into hospital for a new hip, with the second one being done a year later. This meant that I could no longer do the Sailing School and neither could I sail the Osprey. All the boats were sold off, except for the Mirror dinghy which we kept for the grandchildren. It was of course not really possible for me to do without a boat and in 1980 I bought a little sailing yacht which was a cat-rigged schooner with a lifting keel and which we named *Champagne*. With just two sails she was easy to manage and while we had a lot of enjoyment from her, it wasn't keen racing and the adrenalin was lacking. My surgeon had forbidden me to cruise off-shore and also to 'sit out' a dinghy. There had to be a way.

At the time several members had bought catamarans, which I had always looked down on as not being proper boats. However I had to eat my words and at the end of 1980 I bought a second-hand (but only just) Dart 15, a single handed catamaran. I had thought that cats were easy to sail but found I had much to learn and went swimming a number of times before I got the hang of it. With a couple of other single-handers we started a class which quickly grew in popularity and there are now over thirty in the yacht club. I really loved sailing it and had a fair amount of success and was pleased to share fourth place in the National Championships at the age of 73 in a field of some sixty boats in 1993.

Again on the sailing side, in 1980 I took on the organisation and training of the Cadet section of the Yacht Club from Charles and Pamela Gott. Cadet members were aged from 12 to 17 and the idea was to provide sailing instruction for them during the summer holidays when the tides were right. In reality this came down to 4 weeks but, with up to 80 Cadets on the books, it was a constant balancing act to get enough helpers and boats to meet the need. Somehow we always seemed to manage and I had a splendid team of helpers both on the water and ashore. Many of the Cadets had Mirror dinghies, as did the Club, but, though delightful boats, they do not like collisions and my boat-menders prided themselves in instant an expert repairs. Seldom was a boat out of action for more than a day. We became registered as a RYA teaching establishment of which I was the Principal, which enabled the children to get nationally-recognised qualifications, and so it remains today. I believe that I ran the cadets for 10 years.

I had written to the Chairmen of both Torridge and North Devon District Councils offering my services and experience and, as a result, was asked to form and become Chairman of a Forum to try and sort out the many conflicting problems affecting the Taw and Torridge Estuary. We would hold our meetings in the Council Offices and would have their support. With local naturalist Trevor Beer as Secretary, I invited each town and parish council bordering the tidal part of the estuary to send a member and also invited clubs and organisations using the river to send representatives. We had our first meeting in the N. Devon Council chamber early in 1981 and had a very good response. As well as the councillors, we had representatives from the fishermen, netsmen, yacht club, water-skiers, ramblers, RSPB, wildfowlers, MOD and others and so the North Devon Estuary Forum was inaugurated, meeting four times a year in either the Torridge or the N.Devon Council Chamber. We were able to put forward many ideas for the harmonisation of all the various activities and by the mere fact of having a meeting place for discussion between so many disparate organisations many preconceived ideas and prejudices were able to be ironed out. Indeed our organisation became a model for a number of other estuaries in Devon and Cornwall. The first place to follow our lead was the Exe Estuary. After 15 years in the Chair I turned it over to the very able Chairmanship of Mrs Rosemary Day and it has continued to grow in usefulness to this day.

Early in 1981 we had the joy of David and Alex's first child, Rosie, but no sooner had she been christened in Instow Church than the balloon went up in the shape of the Falklands War. Our son Mike was then First Lieutenant of the destroyer *Cardiff*. She was in the Indian Ocean at the time and was brought back through the Mediterranean to Gibraltar before sailing to join the Task Force. Pippa flew out to Gibraltar to meet him, as he had not made a will, and we went up to their house in Fareham to look after their three children. Charlotte their youngest was not yet at school. We listened agonizingly to the news, as various ships were hit by missiles, and at Amelia's and Alexandra's school there were several children whose fathers had been killed in the fighting. Happily, though heavily involved, *Cardiff* came through unscathed but it was most worrying time for us. *Cardiff* was the first ship to enter Port Stanley after the conflict and it was with great joy that Mike was able to meet up with his first cousin, Dr Mary Elphinstone, who by chance was in the Falklands as a temporary relief for a GP who was home in Britain on three months' leave.

Meanwhile David and Alex had moved to Bristol and we were once more, together with Alex's parents, back in the decorating business. David had got a new job in the management team of Lawson Marden, an international packaging company, but had rocked the boat by going off to do a MA at Manchester University. Happily his job was held open for him but Alex kept the show on the road by taking in lodgers and going off to work as a gardener, with Rosie in a carry-cot.

During the years I was often asked to speak at dinners and I also gave a variety of lectures to various organisations such the Devonshire Association, NADFAS (I was enlisted as a standby lecturer) and also various Clubs and Societies, mostly to raise money for the Church. I had devised talks on London Life in Victoria's time, The History of the Taw and Torridge Estuary, The Spanish Armada, World War II and so forth. I think the most challenging was in 1994 when Mike, now a Captain and Naval Attaché in Paris, offered me up to be the after-dinner speaker at the Free French Navy's dinner in Paris to mark the 40th Anniversary of the landings in Normandy. I stuck firmly to English and it seemed to go down very well. I found myself sitting next to a French Admiral who, in 1940, had been a Cadet at the French naval college in Brest and in 1941 had escaped with another Cadet to England, where they continued their training at the Britannia RN College, before going to sea as a RN Midshipman for two years, finally rejoining the French Navy after the war. He was a most interesting person. In 2005 I had another flurry of speeches, first on the bicentenary of Trafalgar when I had to give three in a row, all different, and second for the Centenary of the North Devon Yacht Club. Perhaps now I shall be allowed to hang up my speaker's hat.

Mary, whose mother was born on a ranch in Coronado, California, has a number of American cousins, several of whom with their spouses visited us and also we went there. They were a most interesting lot. One, an astrophysicist at the Johnson Space Center, designed a camera to go on the moon in the first landing which is still there. He also lectured astronauts on space and we met several with their wives at a dinner given for us in Houston, one of whom had done the first independent space walk. The husband of another had been a member of the team at Los Alamos, whose job it was to predict the effect of the first experimental atomic explosion and had got it wrong, with the result that he and Oppenheimer were much to close when it went off and they nearly got blown out of their socks.

I think it was in 1990 that I was invited to join the Management Committee of the Appledore Lifeboat and took on the job of organising the collection of money from about 150 Lifeboat boxes placed in shops, pubs and the like. It needed a team of about ten volunteers prepared to go round emptying boxes or placing new ones in the Appledore Lifeboat's area, which stretched from Fremington to Bucks Cross, along the coast, and many miles inland as far as Winkleigh. Mary and I did one of the rounds but finding willing and reliable people was no easy matter. Last year I came to the conclusion that at 86 it was time to hand over to one of my other collectors but still keeping our own round. During the years we had collected a considerable amount of money and I was delighted and surprised to be awarded the RNLI's silver statuette of a lifeboatman for our efforts. Mary should really have been the recipient because she did much of the collecting when I was unable to do so and also most of the banking of money.

On 8th February 1989 Mary's mother, Granny Bull, or Granny B, who has been mentioned so many times in this book, died; she was 93 and had come to us for Christmas, as was her wont in recent years, but was taken ill shortly after and was nursed here until the end by a wonderful mixture of volunteers from the village and later on by Marie Curie nurses. Though living in Exmouth she had made quite a mark in Instow, and the Crematorium was filled for the funeral service. Widowed in her mid fifties, life for her had not been easy and yet she was always outward-giving and always looking to see how she could help others. Nothing pleased her more than to have friends for a meal in her house, cooked by her and always delicious, though in the few years before her death we always found several burnt-out saucepans outside the backdoor. She had been a lifeline for us on many occasions. Faithful to her church and leading light in the Devon branch of the Mothers Union there was a huge and moving memorial service for her in Exmouth. The church was packed and, with the combined choirs of the three Exmouth churches, it was an occasion which really did justice to her life. Her ashes were interned in her husband's grave at Littleham Church.

It was on 23rd July 1996 that my world fell in! I had raced my catamaran on the previous Sunday and won; on Monday all was well; on Tuesday morning I cut down a tree in the garden but by lunch time I was in agony. The whole of my body hurt to touch and I couldn't move. Mary sent for the ambulance and I was rushed to the hospital in Barnstaple. There I was taken into intensive cure and given massive doses of anti-biotic. It seemed that I had got a serious infection of MRSA type in my left hip and for which there was no instant cure. I ran a very high temperature and was placed naked on a bed with a battery of fans blowing air on me to try and cool me down. This went on for several days and I believe that a number of people thought that I was not going to recover. Luckily, that thought never entered my head. All the family rallied round and Mary was constantly there. The nursing was wonderful and after a week I began to get on top of the infection. After about three weeks I was able to come home but closely monitored and still on high doses of anti-biotic. Slowly life began to return to normal but on Armistice Sunday, just after I had done my stuff in Church, I felt the pain in my hip returning. Dumping my medals, Mary rushed me to Barnstaple Hospital and I was back in intensive care. This time they knew the answer, which was to remove the offending hip joint altogether. Once more stabilized, I was sent home to wait for an appointment. It was a difficult and lengthy operation and it had to be done in Exeter at the Princess Elizabeth Orthopaedic Hospital by a specialist team. This finally happened just after Christmas and I was operated on by a first class Belgian specialist with a German assistant. The result was excellent but I was left without a hip joint for a number of months and got quite expert at hopping along on crutches with my useless leg dangling. Later in the year I was back there again for a new hip joint to be inserted and to this day all has gone well. But it was goodbye to my catamaran and Mike took the little yacht *Champagne* to Portsmouth. However, we still had the rather pedestrian Drascombe Dabber which would have to suffice and I thought up ways to improve her rig and sailing qualities.

I would hate to give the impression that we did nothing but voluntary works; nothing could be further from the truth. We have always liked entertaining and seldom a week went by without us going somewhere or people coming to us and, looking back in the diaries, I was amused to see that in the 70s and 80s the dress for dinner parties was frequently black tie. Not so today when almost anything seems to go. In the last few years dinner parties have been replaced by lunches and, while in the old days everything happened in a flash, it now takes the best part of two days. However the arrangement that Mary and I made early on still applies: she does the main course and I do the puddings. We have had great fun having our grandchildren here to stay at all ages and with and without their parents. Now they are all grown, some with children of their own, but every summer the house gets filled up. All the children have learnt to sail, with the youngest of the bunch, George – David and Alex's younger child – showing considerable aptitude. We also loved dancing and went monthly in the winter to Scottish Country Dancing but ballroom was best. We have also been lucky to have an active and well-run theatre in Barnstaple, to which we go regularly, and enjoy the variety of concerts, plays, musicals, ballet and, in fact, the lot.

Last year was just about the first since leaving the Navy that we had not been to France either to do our own thing or to visit old friends. For many years in September when the sailing season had eased off we used to drive down to the south of France and spend some time with our great friends of Noisy-sur-Ecole days, the Dérouledes. They had a lovely house tucked away in the hills behind Plain de la Tour. Though there was a large swimming pool, both Généviève and we far preferred the sea and she always seemed to know which private beaches to go to without being turned off! In 1999 we were invited to her 90th birthday party in Paris. It was a great occasion with some sixty family and friends sitting down to an excellent lunch. I was both surprised and delighted to find that I had been placed next to the birthday girl and Mary next to André. Happily my French held up and it was a wonderful occasion. Sadly both died in the next few years but of course we still keep in touch with the family. In more recent years we have also paid several visits by sea to Santander, mainly for the voyage, but it is always a delightful spot and the country round about is terrific.

However the great event in 1999 was our eldest granddaughter Amelia's wedding in September in Instow Church, where she married Nicholas Hassall. They were both working in Hong Kong, she running an art gallery and he as a banker. It was a big affair with a large number of guests and our house bulged at the seams. Quite a large contingent, mostly Chinese, had flown over from Hong Kong and took over the Seagate Hotel in Appledore. Instow Church was packed and in the evening there was dinner and dancing in a marquee in Tapeley Park with a grand firework display as a finale. There have been other family celebrations since. My 80th in 2000, Mary's two years later and on 1st January 2005 we again had a house full for our Diamond Wedding, with the youngest member of the family, Fred, only 3 weeks old! When you have lived in the same place for such a long time it is always difficult to know who to ask so we took the easy way out and had open house for friends round about and in the village from eleven o'clock in the morning until five in the evening and were delighted to welcome over a 140 to the house. Happily the champagne didn't run out and the caterer, whom I had asked to provide for 80, miraculously kept going so that everyone was fed.

Now, in June 2007, as I write this we are still living in Landfall. Michael and Philippa live in Hampshire. Mike, now retired from the Navy and, like me, a Captain, is now Clerk to a London Livery Company and Philippa is at the Chichester

Theatre. Two of our great-grandchildren, Oscar and India, live in Hong Kong with their parents, Nick and Amelia, and our third, Fred, in France with his parents Alexandra and Harry. Their other daughter, Charlotte is returning to University for a MA. David and Alex live in Bristol, David a performance poet and playwright, Alex a much sought after Landscape Architect. Of their two children, Rosie recruits personnel for a world-wide bank and George is a student at University. Mary and I believe that our Guardian Angel has done us proud and that we have a great deal for which to be thankful.

Paralalia
BRISTOL